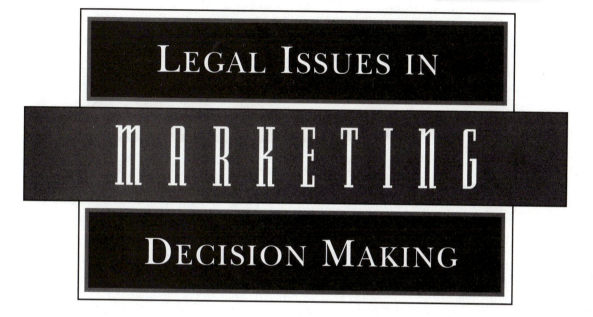

LEGAL ISSUES IN

MARKETING

DECISION MAKING

Dorothy Cohen, Ph.D.

Distinguished Professor of Marketing
& International Business
Hofstra University

SOUTH-WESTERN College Publishing

An International Thomson Publishing Company

Sponsoring Editor: Rob Jared
Production Editor: Holly Terry
Production House: Trejo Production
Internal Design: Joseph M. Devine
Cover Design: Michael H. Stratton
Marketing Manager: Stephen E. Momper

SS64AA
Copyright © 1995
by SOUTH-WESTERN COLLEGE PUBLISHING
Cincinnati, Ohio

I(T)P

International Thomson Publishing
South-Western College Publishing is an ITP Company. The trademark ITP is used under license.

1 2 3 4 5 MA 8 7 6 5 4
Printed in the United States of America

Library of Congress Cataloging-in-Publication Data:

Cohen, Dorothy.
    Legal issues in marketing decision making / Dorothy Cohen.
        p.   cm.
    Includes index.
    ISBN No. 0-538-84537-6
    1. Marketing--Law and legislation--United States. 2. Business law--United States.
    3. Marketing--United States--Decision making--Case studies. I. Title.
    KF1609.C63   1995
    343.73'084--dc20   94-19634
                                                                CIP

DEDICATION

To Richard, Susan, Fred and Marc, and in loving memory of my husband, Morris.

ACKNOWLEDGMENTS

Many people have provided me with the incentive and support to write this book. My husband, Morris Cohen, a dedicated and enthusiastic attorney, aroused my initial interest in law. I would like to thank Philip Kotler, whose suggestion that I author a book on legal issues encouraged me to begin this project. My sincere thanks also go to Harold Kassarjian, whose combined compliments and (constructive) criticisms provided me with the enthusiasm and contributions necessary to complete this project.

At Hofstra University, colleagues Guy Adamo, Benny Barak, Herman Berliner, Barry Berman, Joel Evans, Andrew Forman, Pradeep Gopalakrishna, Joel Greene, Ulric Haynes Jr., William James, Keun Lee, Anil Mathur, William McDonald, Rusty Moore, James Neelankavil, Ehsan Nikbakht, James Parker, Elaine Sherman, Nancy Stern, and Arthur Weinstein created an environment that supported my efforts. I would like to thank my research assistants, Karen Kirshner and Kent Moss, for their contributions to this work.

Special thanks go to those who served as reviewers and who provided insightful comments and valuable suggestions in the planning and writing of this book: Karl A. Boedecker, University of San Francisco; Ward Hansen, Purdue University; Harold Kassarjian, University of California, Los Angeles; Ross Petty, Babson College; Brad Reid, Abilene Christian University; Charles R. B. Stowe, Sam Houston State University; Ray O. Werner, Colorado Springs, Colorado.

In closing I would like to thank the many students I have taught over the years who encouraged me to undertake this project by declaring that they found relevant, interesting, and useful the legal issues I discussed .

I am dedicating this book to my family—Richard, Susan, Fred, and Marc—who gave me continuing love and support during the preparation of the manuscript; and in loving memory of my husband, Morris.

Dorothy Cohen
Hofstra University

Preface

With the expansion of the global economy, the need for a multidisciplinary curriculum in the teaching of business courses is becoming more apparent. This book offers an opportunity to apply that concept by combining marketing and business law in a logical format. It is designed to present as clearly as possible the legal issues that impact on marketing decisions. Most marketers accept the fact that legal aspects represent an important element in appraising the marketing environment. Frequently, however, although marketers may have a general knowledge of marketing laws, they may not be familiar with the legal implications of specific marketing decisions. An understanding of those issues can be useful both in the development of an effective marketing strategy and in the avoidance of potential pitfalls that can be costly in competitive as well as monetary terms.

The focus of this text is on marketing activities. Rather than provide extensive discussions of the laws and the regulatory agencies it attempts to offer legal information that parallels the procedures involved in planning decisions relevant to the major elements of the marketing mix — frequently designated as *product*, *promotion*, *price*, and *channels of distribution*.

A knowledge of the legal issues during their decision-making functions provides significant benefits to marketing managers. An understanding of the marketing issues that face legal challenge is beneficial to students of business law. Marketers may find it useful for such purposes as avoiding potential conflicts with the law and devising strategies for both proactive and reactive responses to emerging problems. While this book can be used as an information source, it also serves as a mechanism for establishing lines of communication between marketing and legal personnel. Such knowledge may serve to alert marketers to the need for legal assistance, indicate ways marketing may aid legal counsel in developing effective responses to legal entanglements, and suggest how marketers can prepare to act on resulting recommendations.

There is no specific intent to present recommendations for changes in the law. There is, however, the hope that providing marketers with knowledge of current law, and how law affects marketing activities, will generate the motivation for more active participation by that group in the evolvement of future marketing law.

The text is organized in relation to the major marketing functions. There are six parts containing fourteen chapters, as follows:

Part One: Understanding the Legal Environment (Chapters 1–2)
Part Two: Legal Issues in Product Decisions (Chapters 3–6)
Part Three: Legal Issues in Promotion Decisions (Chapters 7–9)
Part Four: Legal Issues in Pricing Decisions (Chapters 10–11)
Part Five: Legal Issues in Distribution Decisions (Chapters 12–13)
Part Six: Legal Issues in Merger and Joint Venture Decisions (Chapter 14)

Each part briefly describes marketing functions and discusses the major legal implications of marketing decisions in those areas. Efforts are made to avoid legal pitfalls by recommending proactive strategies, and suggestions are offered for reactive strategies should problems arise.

Cases at the end of Chapters 3–14 feature issues relevant to the chapter and suggest discussion questions based on the chapter's material.

Contents

PART I

Understanding the Legal Environment

Understanding the Legal Environment

Awareness of the extensive rules and regulations affecting marketing activities is a requisite for the student who wishes to become a marketing practitioner, as well as for all business managers involved in the marketing process. Legal problems, regardless of how they arise in competitive business activity, cannot be solved without a general understanding of the laws. Knowledge of one law is not sufficient and is even potentially dangerous because a course of conduct can escape one law only to be caught in another. The laws must be understood as a totality or body of law, although they were not so enacted.

In formulating marketing policies, the practitioner must know the statutes that affect marketing decisions and the legal defenses available under these statutes. Of greater importance are the judicial interpretations of these statutes, for these interpretations establish precedents for acceptable or unacceptable business conduct. Nor is it sufficient to become familiar with the current legal environment. Since markets and marketing will continue to change, public policy and regulatory control will not remain fixed. Good managers must be sensitive to the signs that may signal future redefinition of legal standards.

This book is designed to provide managers with the necessary knowledge and background to understand the implications of the current legal environment. In addition, it should encourage managers to be alert to the emerging legal trends that may affect marketing decision making. Its primary objectives are to provide managers with an explanation of some of the basic considerations of the legal environment and the regulatory framework that drive strategic decision making in the marketing area and to aid in the development of proactive and reactive strategies in response to these issues.

The materials appearing in this publication are for informational purposes only and should neither be considered legal advice nor be used as such. For a specific legal opinion, readers must confer with their own counsel. It is hoped, however, that the information herein will help managers avoid serious legal pitfalls where necessary, encourage them to interact with legal personnel, and enable them to offer input for potential changes in the regulatory environment that will promote their own goals and the public welfare as well.

CHAPTER ONE
Regulatory Background

This chapter provides a general understanding of the legal environment. It presents a brief review of the development and current status of the laws that affect marketing activity. Specific marketing functions that may generate legal problems are discussed in subsequent chapters.

HISTORICAL BACKGROUND

The U.S. economy is a commercial-exchanging economy based on the system of free enterprise (free entry and free competition). A free enterprise system is, by definition, inconsistent with extensive direct regulation by government. In economic theory, in a truly free enterprise system, unrestrained competition would provide the optimal allocation of resources. In actual fact, economies have been subject historically to some government regulation, although the degree has varied greatly from one country to another.

The free enterprise system in the United States has proven deficient in producing a healthy, competitive environment by failing to prevent two major abuses: restraint of trade and deceptive practices. Producers and sellers of goods and services have often sought to increase profits by restraining trade, specifically by limiting the entry of competitors into the market. Moreover, since consumers cannot be informed about all the alternative goods and services available, businesses have at times taken advantage of this consumer ignorance through resort to deceptive practices, to the detriment of both.

Common Law

Early control of business activities in the United States was achieved through English common law. Common law refers to that part of the law that grew up without benefit of legislation and resulted from court decisions; these rulings then became the precedent for subsequent litigation.[1] Legal theory has it that the colonists brought the common law of England with them to America.

The legal regulation of competitive practices under common law served to foster competition indirectly by the provision of a few private remedies for private wrongs. The courts afforded redress to persons injured by unfair methods of competition: the term *unfair competition* was first applied to the passing off or misrepresentation of the goods of one competitor as those of another.[2] Other types of injury to business interests that were afforded the rights of action were misappropriation of trade secrets and malicious interference with business, such as malignancy of a competitor's character or disparagement of a competitor's product.[3]

With the passage of time, the common law doctrines that had developed were no longer sufficiently applicable to conditions in the United States. They could not keep pace with the development of the new so-called unfair and predatory techniques for eliminating competition. The use of fighting brands, tying contracts, and the operation of bogus independents lay entirely outside the scope of common law regulation, since they did not give rise to special injury to one particular competitor. Instead, they were designed to make competition from any quarter difficult.

Under common law regulation, no consideration was given directly to the interests of the public. It was assumed that if business practices were kept free, open, and fair, and a just regard paid to the rights of those directly concerned, the public should be adequately protected. In addition, "the charlatanry of the deceiver, secure in the Latinity of 'caveat emptor' was virtually impregnable at common law." The buyer had to beware, had to prove fraudulent intent, could collect very little to compensate for the time and money expended, and faced social ridicule for the admission of gullibility.

There were procedural, as well as substantive, deficiencies under common law. The courts, which were responsible for the administration of rules, could vindicate rights and redress wrongs. They were not, however, organized for vigilance; nor could they prevent injury.

Development of the Laws of Competition

The power to regulate business inheres in federal, state, and local governments. The federal government's power is found in the so-called commerce clause of the U.S. Constitution. Article I, Section 8, of the Constitution provides that "Congress shall have Power . . . To regulate Commerce with foreign Nations, and among the several States, and with the Indian Tribes." In 1824, Chief Justice Marshall defining the power said, "It is the power to regulate, that is, to prescribe the rules by which commerce is to be governed."[4] However, Justice Marshall also noted that the power to regulate commerce among several states meant the power to regulate interstate commerce, not the power to regulate intrastate commerce.

Although the authority of the federal government was supreme within the sphere of powers expressly or implied delegated to it, all other powers were reserved to the states under the Tenth Amendment of the Bill of Rights, which declares, "The powers not delegated to the United States by the Constitution nor prohibited by it to the States are reserved to the States respectively, or to the people." There have, however, been many cases expanding the commerce clause to encompass intrastate activities that have a substantial effect on interstate commerce.

The rapid expansion of industrial activity in the United States after the Civil War was accompanied by the increasing concentration of business in the hands of a limited number of relatively large firms. The rapid growth of individual firms in the years immediately following the Civil War resulted in particularly severe competition. In part, this was evidence that the newer, large-scale firms were driving smaller, less-efficient rivals out of business.

To avoid the destructive effects of unrestricted price rivalry, competing firms began to form combinations, or mergers. The merger movement was stimulated by the prospect of profits that could be realized through the exercise of monopoly power. As the merger process accelerated, many groups—farmers, producers of raw materials, owners of small businesses, and workers—suffered. Farmers experienced a persistent decline in farm prices; producers of raw materials often found only a single buyer, who manipulated the market to depress prices; and workers crowded into growing cities and faced increasing competition for jobs.

These developments gave rise to widespread discontent and resulted in the development of a strong political movement against monopoly. The granger movement, as it was called, against concentration had its roots in farmer organizations; by 1890, twenty-one states, mostly in the South and Middle West, had passed statutory or constitutional prohibitions of monopoly and agreements in restraint of trade. Regulation by individual states proved inadequate, however, and in 1890, a federal antitrust statute was passed, considered by some a minor measure of appeasement to farmers.

Prior to the merger movement, the basic policy of the federal government toward industry had been one of modified laissez-faire, or nonintervention.

This policy still obtains—in principle; however, it is a principle to which more and more exceptions have been made.

It must be noted that many of the laws that now regulate business have been enacted not in the face of business opposition but at the urgent solicitation of business itself.[5] If the government outlaws unfair methods of competition and curbs discrimination in the prices that are quoted by competing firms, it is because competitors demand protection. If it requires licenses to operate a business, this may be at the behest of business competitors. For example, early radio broadcasters used any frequency they wished and the result was pandemonium. Interference was general, and the usefulness of radio as a communication medium was virtually destroyed. Complaints from broadcasters led to the passage of the Radio Act of 1927, which forbade broadcasting without a license, and ultimately to the establishment of the Federal Communications Commission.

Government controls are also enacted to protect consumers, as, for example, in prohibiting the sale of impure foods and drugs and in conserving the nation's resources.

Historically, laws on trade regulation have been designed to regulate two areas of business conduct: activities relating to competition (most frequently called antitrust legislation) and deceptive acts and practices. Although the major thrust of marketing law has been directed toward maintaining competition, much of current law is concerned with deceptive acts and practices, particularly those related to consumers. These efforts are represented mainly in regulatory policy set forth in four laws: the Sherman Act, the Clayton Act, the Federal Trade Commission Act, and the Robinson-Patman Act. These laws were not enacted as a unit; they came into existence as the need for each was perceived. The growth of this regulatory policy is not as noticeable in new congressional legislation as it is in the expanding judicial and administrative application of the laws to new situations as they arise in business. A brief history of the emergence of these laws is presented here.

Sherman Antitrust Act (1890)

The Sherman Antitrust Act, passed in 1890 in response to the granger movement against monopoly, is short and simple—unlike most acts of Congress. Briefly, it declares to be illegal "every contract, combination in the form of trust or otherwise, or conspiracy in restraint of trade or commerce among the several states, or with foreign nations." In substance, the legislation contained nothing new; its major contribution was to turn restraint of trade and monopolization into federal offenses.

It was soon apparent that the Sherman Act fell short of its purpose. The laws were scarcely enforced during the administrations of Cleveland and McKinley. Powerful new combinations began to be formed in steel, tin cans, farm machinery, and many other industries. During Theodore Roosevelt's administration, monopolistic abuses were disclosed in hearings before congressional committees at which victims of predatory methods (pricing below cost by rich monopolists in order to drive competitors out of the market and entrench their own positions) expressed dissatisfaction and urged that the law should intervene before the methods took their effect.

In 1903, the Bureau of Corporations, as part of the Department of Commerce and Labor, was established in the hope that investigating and publicizing the conduct of large combinations would be sufficiently remedial. This proved to be a vain hope, which was further shattered when in the Standard Oil and American Tobacco[6] cases the Supreme Court announced that combinations that were not "unreasonable" would be allowed to stand.

Two standards were imposed in the development of the Sherman Act: the rule of reason and per se illegality standards.

Rule of Reason. Section 1 of the Sherman Act prohibits "every contract . . . , combination, or conspiracy in restraint of trade." However, in 1898, the Supreme Court determined that the act "must have a reasonable construction, or else there would scarcely be an arrangement or contract among business men that could not be said to have, indirectly or remotely, some bearing on interstate commerce, and possibly to restrain it." The Supreme Court's announcement, in the 1911 Standard Oil and American Tobacco cases, that combinations that were not "unreasonable" would be allowed resulted in the formulation of a "rule of reason," effectively inserting the word *unreasonable* into Section 1 between the words *every* and *contract*." Under this rule, in determining reasonableness, the court must ordinarily consider numerous facts, including the history of the restraint, the evil believed to exist, the intent of the restraint, the nature of its effect, and other relevant factors.

Per Se Illegality. A more simple standard was sought in what came to be known as a per se (i.e., in itself) standard, which related to conduct perceived to be in and of itself unreasonable. According to the court, some violations could be found illegal without any inquiry into the harm caused or the justifications offered. Among the practices found by the court to be per se unreasonable are price fixing, division of markets, group boycotts, and some tying arrangements.

Clayton Act (1914)

In the national campaign of 1912, as a result of the failure of the Sherman Act and the Bureau of Corporations to retard monopolistic practices, monopoly again became an issue. Two streams of thought crystallized in the new movement for legislation: One group desired to repeal the rule of reason and to effect the total disintegration of trusts. The leaders of this group included Louis D. Brandeis, Senator Cummins of Iowa, and Representatives Clayton of Alabama and Stevens of New Hampshire.[7] Brandeis expressed the thesis that big business was less efficient than the smaller enterprise, and if the excessive growth of business were forbidden by government, natural forces could be relied upon to maintain healthy competition. This group advocated the creation of a new commission to make antitrust law enforcement more efficient.

The other group was made up of leaders of the business community who were much more content with the rule of reason, who believed monopoly to be inevitable, and who felt that Congress should set up machinery to regulate it. In the eyes of this group, a new commission was desirable as a body to review, in advance, potentially illegal acts.

In 1911 and 1912 there was a series of extended hearings at which a senate committee listened to some 103 witnesses.[8] Some of the witnesses favored a federal commission that should have power to license interstate corporations and to validate their proposed actions or policies submitted for its examination. President Wilson recommended that the uncertainty concerning the meaning of the Sherman Act be removed and suggested that "item by item we can put in our statutes what constitutes restraint of trade, not leaving it to the courts for generalizations which may fit some cases and not others."[9]

Members of Congress participated in a series of exhaustive debates, but a comprehensive list of items could not be obtained. It was felt that as soon as one set of prohibitions were laid down, new methods or new variations developed by enterprising businesspeople could spring up, and so the attempt was finally abandoned. Eventually, Wilson agreed to endorse a proposal by Congressman Stevens that the various items be covered by a general prohibition of unfair methods of competition. Two bills were finally presented—one dealing with the Federal Trade Commission and its prohibition of unfair methods of competition and the other, named for Chairman Clayton of the House Judiciary Committee, grouping together a host of provisions relating to monopoly and restraint of trade.

The Sherman Antitrust Act is broad and general. The Clayton Act of 1914, on the other hand, is more specific by prohibiting particular business practices. None of these prohibitions is absolute; these practices are forbidden only when their effects "may be to substantially lessen competition or tend to create a monopoly." The specific practices outlawed by the Clayton Act are discrimination in prices, exclusive and tying contracts, corporate stock acquisition, and interlocking directorates.

There are important differences between the Clayton Act and the Sherman Act. For example, the latter is general in terms, and the former is explicit. The older law dealt with monopoly as an accomplished fact and placed emphasis on punishment. The newer law was concerned with methods by which monopoly was obtained and with prevention. Moreover, enactment was generally strengthened by the newer law.

A provision to the Clayton Act was added in 1950 with passage of the Celler-Kefauver Act, an amendment that prohibited the acquisition of stock or assets, "where in any line of commerce, in any section of the country, the effect of such acquisition may be substantially to lessen competition, or to tend to create a monopoly." The law is concerned with effects; there is no need to prove intent.

Federal Trade Commission Act (1914)

The Federal Trade Commission Act, which created the authority most active in controlling deceptive marketing practices, was originally passed in 1914 to strengthen antitrust enforcement measures. The Federal Trade Commission Act supplemented the Sherman Act with additional prohibitions and procedures. The new act established the Federal Trade Commission (FTC)—an independent regulatory agency with enforcement responsibility. Its sole substantive provision provided that "unfair methods of competition in or affecting commerce are hereby declared unlawful." The FTC was given concurrent jurisdiction with the Department of Justice in prohibiting monopolistic practices forbidden by the Clayton Act.

In 1920, the Supreme Court ruled that unfair competition includes (1) individual practices against a competitor, involving misrepresentation, deception, and fraud and (2) methods of competition having a dangerous tendency to unduly hinder competition or create a monopoly.[10] This latter interpretation has been used by the FTC to attack restrictive agreements; concurrent actions on price; predatory price cutting practiced by a single business firm; and restrictive dealer franchise arrangements.

Since 1914, numerous amendments have been made to the FTC Act; additional statutes have also been enacted, expanding the commission's jurisdiction. The 1938 Wheeler Lea Amendment to the FTC Act rewrote Section

5 of the act to read, "unfair methods of competition in commerce and unfair or deceptive acts or practices are hereby declared unlawful." The addition of the phrase "unfair or deceptive acts or practices" made it no longer necessary for the commission to show that competition was impaired; if business practices resulted in injury to the public, the commission was empowered to act. A detailed discussion of the various activities by the Federal Trade Commission in exercising its authority over marketing practices is presented in Chapter 7.

Robinson-Patman Act (1936)

The Clayton Act's price discrimination provision was amended in 1936 by the Robinson-Patman Act, which detailed and extended coverage for a wider range of protection.

Section 2 of the original Clayton Act was designed primarily to prevent large manufacturers from eliminating smaller rivals by temporarily cutting prices in particular markets while prices elsewhere were maintained (i.e., predatory pricing). In the years following World War I, however, independent wholesalers and retailers encountered increasing competition from chain stores and other mass distributors, who could and did charge lower prices, at least in part because of the lower prices they paid. Such competitors' bargaining power enabled them to obtain concessions from suppliers in many forms: broker commissions when no broker was employed, services provided by suppliers in addition to the delivery of goods, promotional costs when chains featured the manufacturer's products in advertising and store displays, and discounts for purchasing in large quantities. Such preferential price treatment was generally valid under exceptions in the Clayton Act. The independents, contending that these concessions were larger than could be justified, demanded that the freedom of suppliers to discriminate in favor of chain stores be limited.

The Robinson-Patman Act was passed in response to their demands. The act makes many changes to the original provisions of the Clayton Act, whose net effect has been to expand government authority in controlling price differentials. The heart of the Clayton Act, as amended by the Robinson-Patman Act, is as follows:

> . . . it shall be unlawful for any person engaged in commerce . . . to discriminate in price between different purchases of commodities of like grade and quality . . . where the effect of such discrimination may be substantially to lessen competition, or tend to create a monopoly in any line of commerce, or to injure, destroy, or prevent competition with any

person who either grants or knowingly receives the benefit of such discrimination, or with customers of either of them.

Specific provisions of the Robinson-Patman Act and their significance in pricing decisions are discussed in Chapter 11.

Additional Federal Statutes

Over the years, a number of federal statutes have been passed whose effect on marketing decisions will be discussed in relevant chapters. These include the Lanham Act (concerned with trademarks and advertising); the Food, Drug, and Cosmetic Act (supplementing the Pure Food and Drug Act, which had established the Food and Drug Administration); the Consumer Product Safety Act (which created the Consumer Product Safety Commission); and various consumer protection acts.

Federal Preemption

The question of federalism has been a perplexing and persistent issue in our constitutional history.[11] United States federalism springs from the problems inherent in a multistate system. The assumption is that without a centralized authority, states may act in destructive intrastate competition to preserve their individual interests at the expense of the national good.[12]

Federal preemption requires that federal law take priority over state law and local law. It is rooted in the supremacy clause and it provides the framework for the balance of powers between the states and the federal government. The supremacy clause provides:[13]

> This constitution, and the Laws of the United States which shall be made in Pursuance thereof; and all Treaties made, under the Authority of the United States shall be the supreme Law of the Land; and the Judges of every State shall be bound thereby, any Thing in the constitution of Law of any State to the Contrary notwithstanding.

Nonetheless, as noted earlier, the Bill of Rights declares "The powers not delegated to the United States by the Constitution . . . are reserved to the States." In a determination of whether federal law supersedes state law, a number of factors must be considered.[14] Primarily, the court must attempt to discern Congress's intent to preempt. There are three kinds of intent tests for preemption.[15] First, Congress can always enact legislation explicitly preempting state antitrust laws, either broadly or in specific areas; however, it has rarely done so.[16] Second, in the absence of an explicit statement of congressional intent, preemption may be implicit if Congress has enacted legislation that "occupies the field" in such a pervasive way that it would be inappropriate for the states to supplement federal law or law enforcement.[17] Third, state law may be preempted if it conflicts with federal law. Conflict obviously arises if it is literally impossible to comply with both state law and federal law. State law may also be invalidated if it "stands as an obstacle to accomplishment of the full purposes and objectives of Congress" in enacting federal law.

Federal trade regulation laws are both preemptive of and concurrent with state regulation.[18] Federal regulation of patents and copyrights, for example, is currently expressly preemptive of state patent and copyright protection. Thus states may not give patent or copyright protection to inventions or writings that are protectable under federal law.

In contrast to patent and copyright law, trademark law and antitrust law are not preempted by federal law, but are designed to supplement and run concurrently with state law.

Concurrent jurisdiction may be exercised by the state and federal governments as in the field of food advertising regulation.[19] There have been recent recommendations that the states and the federal government cooperate in regulatory enforcement procedures. A 1989 report by the American Bar Association on the role of the Federal Trade Commission recommended that "the States' primary mission should be [against] those practices that harm consumers within a single state; the FTC's special mission should be [against] those practices that harm consumers in many states.[20]

Whether or not federal laws have supremacy over state requirements may require adjudication by the courts. For example, as discussed later, a recent Supreme Court decision declared that states are preempted from regulating airline rate advertising under a provision in the federal Airline Deregulation Act.[21]

STATE REGULATION

Much of state law on trade regulation is patterned after, is analogous to, or specifically incorporates federal statutory law or administrative trade regulation rules. This gives federal policy a local application. Although most states had adopted antitrust laws by the early twentieth century, only a few had active enforcement programs until the mid-1960's.[22] In general, the purpose of state antitrust laws is the prohibition of contracts, combinations, or conspiracies in restraint of trade. State laws declare monopolies to be contrary to public policy, and the majority of states have enacted laws containing prohibitions similar to those of the Sherman Act. Some state constitutions embody antitrust policy.

State actions may be based on a number of other grounds. They include the common law of unfair competition, antifraud and deception acts (including little FTC acts), consumer protection health warning statutes, and specific false advertising statutes. Some statutes grant broad rulemaking authority to state agencies. Under that authority, numerous state food labeling and advertising regulations have been issued.

In some respects, however, state statutory law protects trade relations in ways other than common law or federal statutory law.[23] For example, anti-dilution state statutes protect distinctive trademarks from dilution. This provides protection for distinctive trade symbols and prohibits other businesses from using them, even if they create no confusion in the marketplace (which is required under the Lanham Act), but merely dilute the impact of the original symbol. This is discussed in detail in Chapter 8. Many state laws condemn more specific types of conduct such as sales below cost, even though this pricing practice may fall short of a federal antitrust violation.

Current State Enforcement Activities

State antitrust and consumer protection enforcement has increased considerably during the past decade. States do not have the power to enforce the FTC Act. Their only powers now are under their own state statutes. All fifty states and the District of Columbia have enacted one or more consumer protection statutes.[24] These are referred to in different states as UDAP statutes (which broadly prohibit unfair or deceptive acts or practices), little FTC acts, consumer protection acts, deceptive trade practices acts, and consumer fraud acts.

These statutes apply to consumer transactions generally and, unlike the FTC Act, do not apply to a particular practice or industry. Although the FTC Act relates to the public interest only and does not provide for private redress, all states but four authorize private rights of action, which usually include the award of attorney's fees. Many of these provide for treble damages and punitive damages. Many state laws provide for criminal penalties, the civil remedies of administrative penalties, and injunction.

State courts acknowledge FTC decisions as guiding but deny that these federal standards are binding. They have permitted practices under state UDAP laws that violate the FTC Act, and they interpret the UDAP provisions of their laws more broadly than provisions of the FTC Act. Nevertheless, they view uniformity between federal and state consumer protection policies as important and acknowledge both the expertise of the FTC in trade policy matters and the interstate nature of many commercial activities affecting consumers.[25]

The National Association of Attorneys General

In an effort to coordinate their activities and provide some uniformity in regulatory control, the attorneys general of the various states formed the National Association of Attorneys General (NAAG). The NAAG comprises elected and appointed attorneys general from all fifty states and five territories. NAAG has no law enforcement authority but can express the opinions of its membership, adopt policy resolutions, and participate in litigation.

In 1987, the NAAG adopted the Air Travel Industry Enforcement Guidelines. These guidelines contain standards governing the content and format of airline fare advertising designed to be enforced through the states' general consumer protection statutes, which typically permit suits for deceptive advertising.

Despite objections to the guidelines by the Department of Transportation and the FTC on preemption and policy grounds, the attorney general of Texas sent notices of intent to sue so as to enforce the guidelines against the allegedly deceptive fare advertising of several airlines. The airlines then filed suit, claiming state regulation of fare advertising is preempted by federal law. The Supreme Court agreed and declared that the provision of the Airline Deregulation Act that prohibits states from enforcing a law "relating to [air carriers'] rates, routes or services" operated expressly to preempt state regulation in the field of airline rate advertising, including proscribing allegedly deceptive fare advertising.

In 1993, the NAAG adopted a new version of its Horizontal Merger Guidelines designed to "provide a uniform framework for the states to evaluate the facts of a particular horizontal merger and the dynamic conditions of an industry.[26]

For managers it is clear that a knowledge of the laws relevant to the state in which they operate is both desirable and required. For those who operate in many states, the complex and sometimes confusing regulations create problems. The efforts of the NAAG may help create state law uniformity and reduce the confusion.

INTERNATIONAL REGULATION

World trade has been an economic fact for centuries. Along with the development of new technology, as well as improved transportation and communication capabilities, the expansion of international marketing activities has accelerated in recent years. A recurrent theme in the law of international business transactions is the need to balance the protection of local industries from harm by foreign competitors and the desire to encourage trade across national borders. In an effort to secure this balance, countries have cooperated in the formulation of regional economic unions and have established international trade agreements.

Regional Economic Communities

In the past, it was necessary to know the laws of all countries involved in international transactions. Due to the complexity of this situation, as well as the increased number of countries in the world since the end of World War II, countries in common geographical areas have banded together to form economic unions that facilitate trade.[27] The two most significant regional groupings are the European Community (EC), currently made up of twelve Western European nations, and the North American Free Trade Agreement, which comprises the United States, Canada, and Mexico. Other groups in Asia, Africa, Latin America, and the Caribbean are formulating legal foundations for their own free trade areas.

The EC was created by the treaty of Rome in 1957. As of this writing the member states are Belgium, Denmark, France, Germany, Greece, Ireland, Italy, Luxembourg, the Netherlands, Portugal, Spain, and the United Kingdom. Other nations have applied to join the EC. The EC's primary objective is one of harmonization, which involves the need to break down the national boundaries between its member states. A large body of directives and regulations have been issued, which are designed to encourage common standards relating to marketing decisions.

International Trade Agreements

In recent years there has been a shift toward freer international trade because of the diminished restrictions on imported goods. Nonetheless, a number of devices tend to restrict trade, including tariff barriers (such as import and export duties) and nontariff trade barriers (such as import quotas, import licensing procedures, and safety, environmental, and other minimum manufacturing standards).[28]

In a desire to increase global trade and harmonize world trade policies, a number of international agreements have been established. Of particular importance to marketers are the ongoing General Agreement on Tariffs and Trade (GATT) and the recently established North American Free Trade Agreement (NAFTA).

GATT

After World War II, the reconstruction of the world economy and the restoration of world trade, which had virtually stopped during the war, became paramount global concerns. Twenty-three countries were engaged in drafting a charter for the International Trade Organization (ITO), which would have been a United Nations special agency designed to encourage freer trade. A framework for such negotiations had already been staked out in Geneva in 1947 under a document entitled General Agreement on Tariffs and Trade, based on parts of the draft ITO charter. Although it was anticipated that ITO would assume responsibility for GATT, the United States failed to ratify the ITO treaty and the ITO organization failed. However, the United States agreed to sign GATT, which had been negotiated in 1947 and went into effect in 1948.[29]

Currently, GATT is a multilateral treaty, subscribed to by 116 countries. It has evolved into an international organization that sponsors tariff negotiations, settles trade disputes, and generally administers the GATT.

Since its founding, GATT has sponsored eight rounds of trade discussions: the first five rounds; the Kennedy Round (1964–67), which was noted for its achievement of across-the-board tariff reductions; the Tokyo Round (1973–79), which engendered agreements about several areas of nontariff barrier trade restraints; and the Uruguay Round.

The most recent—the Uruguay Round—began in 1986. Negotiations under this round were focused on cutting tariffs on thousands of products; providing greater protection from patent abuse, copyright theft, and counterfeiting; and liberalizing rules governing banking, securities, and other services. While some agreement has been reached, legislation implementing this proposed pact is to be submitted to Congress. Some of the key results of the Uruguay Round, still subject to congressional approval at this writing, include the following:[30]

Tariffs: The United States, Europe, and other major industrial powers agreed to eliminate tariffs altogether on pharmaceuticals, construction equipment, medical equipment, paper, and steel. Tariffs also are to be cut on chemicals, wood, and aluminum.

Dumping: GATT actions to resolve disputes over use of antidumping laws (invoked by the United States and Europe to impose penalties on foreign producers that sell goods abroad below cost) will be quicker and tougher.

Textiles and apparel: A Multi-Fiber Arrangement that limits imports of textiles and apparel to the United States and other developed nations will be phased out over ten years.

Intellectual property: Protection of patents, trademarks, and copyrights is increased, but developing countries are allowed at least ten years to phase in patent protection for pharmaceuticals.

Agreements on agriculture and services remain controversial.

NAFTA

In 1993, NAFTA was passed by Congress. This agreement, which involves the United States, Canada, and Mexico, is based on virtually the same principle as GATT: freer trade. However, whereas NAFTA would over time eventually eliminate virtually all barriers between the United States, Canada, and Mexico, GATT would eliminate some, but hardly all, barriers between most countries.

NAFTA will eventually eliminate all tariffs between the United States, Canada, and Mexico and will provide new markets for many industries. The agreement will reduce or eliminate restrictions on trade and investment, permit delivery of services directly between member countries, ensure protection of intellectual property rights (i.e., patents, copyrights, and trademarks), and ease restrictions on business travel between member countries.

NAFTA is considered the most "environmentally conscious" trade agreement in history.[31] NAFTA addresses environmental concerns both substantively and as a matter of international trade policy. It provides for strict national and international environmental standards, natural resource conservation, environmental investment, and technical transfers, participation in government procurement, protection of intellectual property rights and environmental dispute resolution. NAFTA also authorizes exceptions from the Agreement for environmental purposes and encourages the development of joint environmental standards.

While the potential effects of NAFTA are the subject of significant controversy (e.g., concerns over loss of jobs, environmental and safety issues), it is too early to make accurate judgments at this writing. There are indications that NAFTA has encouraged trade expansion in, for example, the creation of joint ventures between the United States and Mexico in the communications industry and the acquisition of 120 of Canada's Woolco discount stores by Wal-mart Stores, Inc., which noted that the recent passage of NAFTA is facilitating its move to Canada.

It appears, however, that the possibility of increasing legal disputes requiring the assistance of attorneys in specialized areas exists.[32] For example, the environmental accord in the agreement indicates that there will be more vigilant enforcement requiring environmental expertise. Customs expertise may be necessary to determine whether various products qualify for tariff reductions. Products made in North America will be subject to a schedule of such reductions, but since many of their components are shipped from abroad, it is not easy to determine where a product is manufactured.

SUMMARY

Control of marketing practices is set forth mainly in four federal laws—the Sherman Act, the Clayton Act, the Federal Trade Commission Act, and the Robinson-Patman Act. Briefly, the primary focus of the Sherman Act was on activities that result in restraint of trade and monopolization. The Clayton Act was designed to remove uncertainty concerning the meaning of the Sherman Act; it outlawed specific practices, such as price discrimination, that "substantially lessen competition."

The Federal Trade Commission Act supplemented the Sherman Act with additional prohibitions and procedures. It declared "unfair methods of competition" unlawful and established the Federal Trade Commission as an independent regulatory agency with enforcement responsibility.

The Robinson-Patman Act amended the Clayton Act; it provided details for and extended coverage to protection against price discrimination.

Generally, federal law on trade regulation supersedes state and local law. However, the Bill of Rights declares, "the powers not delegated to the United States by the constitution . . . are reserved to the States, meaning there are circumstances when state law supersedes federal law. Much of state law on trade regulation is patterned after, is analogous to, or specifically incorporates federal statutory law or administrative trade regulation rules; nonetheless, trade laws may vary from state to state. In an effort to coordinate their activities and provide some uniformity in regulatory control, the attorneys general of the various states formed the National Association of Attorneys General.

The expansion of international marketing has encouraged efforts to increase global trade and harmonize world trade policies. Regional economic communities have been formulated to facilitate trade. International trade agreements have been established. Recent activities relating to the ongoing General Agreement on Tariffs and Trade and the newly established North American Free Trade Agreement will impact on managerial efforts to expand markets to other countries.

ENDNOTES

1. Dudley F. Pegrum, *Public Regulation of Business* (Homewood, Ill.: Richard D. Irwin, 1959), p. 21.

2. Merle Fainsod, Lincoln Gordon, and Joseph Palamountain Jr., *Government and the American Economy* (New York: W. W. Norton, 1959), p. 487.

3. Myron W. Watkins, "Public Regulation of Competitive Practices, A Report to the Divison of Industrial Economics of the Conference Board" (New York: National Industrial Conference Board, 1940), p. 21.

4. *Gibbons* v. *Ogden*, 22 U.S. (9 Wheat) 1 (1824).

5. Clair Wilcox, *Public Policies toward Business* (Homewood, Ill.: Richard D. Irwin, 1960), p. 9.

6. *Standard Oil Co. of New Jersey* v. *U.S.*, 221 U.S. 1; American Tobacco Co., Ibid. 106 (1911).

7. Merle Fainsod, Lincoln Gordon, and Joseph C. Palamountain Jr., *Government and the American Economy* (New York: W. W. Norton, 1959), p. 487.

8. U.S. Senate, *Hearings before the Committee on Interstate Commerce,* 62 Cong., 1912, pp. 1089 ff.

9. Fainsod, Gordon, and Palamountain, *Government and the American Economy*, p. 493.

10. *Federal Trade Commission* v. *Gratz*, 253 UI.S. 421 (1920).

11. Joseph L. Lieberman, "Modern Federalism: Altered States," *The Urban Lawyer* 20 (Spring 1988), 285–342.

12. "To Form a More Perfect Union? Federalism and Informal Interstate Cooperation," *Harvard Law Review* (February 1989), 842–863.

13. U.S. Const., Art. VI, cl.

14. Marilyn P. Westerfield, "Federal Preemption and the FDA: What Does Congress Want?" *Cincinnati Law Review* 58, 263–283.

15. *California* v. *ARC America Corp.*, 109 S. Ct. 1661, 1665 (1989).

16. Malcolm R. Pfunder, "Constitutional Limitations on State Antitrust Enforcement," *Antitrust Law Journal* 58 (1989), 207–213.

17. *Schneidewind* v. *ANR Pipeline Co.*, 108 S. Ct. 1145, 1150 (1988).

18. Charles R. McManis, *Unfair Trade Practices*, 2d ed. (St. Paul, Minn.: West Publishing Co., 1988), p. 39.

19. Susan Beth Farmer, "Introduction: Dual Enforcement of State and Federal Antitrust Laws," *Antitrust Law Journal* 58 (37th Annual Spring Meeting, Washington, D.C., April 5–7, 1989, 197–200).

20. Report of the American Bar Association Special Committee to Study the Role of the FTC, Trade Reg. Report No. 46 (April 13, 1989).

21. *Dan Morales, Attorney General of Texas* v. *Trans World Airlines, Inc.* et al., CCH #69,828) (S. Ct., No. 90-1604, June 1992).

22. McManis, p. 40.

23. Donald R. Stone, "The Federal State Relationship Concerning USDA Regulated Food Advertising: The FTC, the States, and Others," *Food Drug Cosmetic Law Journal* 44 (1989), 315-323.

24. Lawrence R. Fullerton, William E. Kovacic, Jane E. Larson, Marilyn S. Richmond, Stephen A. Stack Jr., and Mason E. Wiggens Jr., "Reliance on FTC Consumer Protection Law Precedents in Other Legal Forums, Working Paper No. 1," American Bar Association Section of Antitrust Law (July 1, 1988).

25. Fullerton et al. p. 6.

26. National Association of Attorneys General, "1993 Horizontal Merger Guidelines," CCH, TRR, #256 (March 30, 1993).

27. Daniel V. Davidson, Brenda E. Knowles, Lynn M. Forsythe, and Robert R. Jespersen, *Business Law, Principles and Cases*, 4th ed. (Belmont, Calif.: Wadsworth Publishing, 1993), 1177–1182.

28. Ralph H. Folsom, Michael Wallace Gordon, and John A. Spanogle Jr., *International Business Transactions*, 3rd ed. (St. Paul, Minn.: West Publishing, 1988), p. 229.

29. Subhash C. Jain, *International Marketing Management*, 4th ed. (Belmont, Calif.: Wadsworth Publishing Co., 1993).

30. The Uruguay Round's Key Results," *The Wall Street Journal*, December 13, 1993, A6.

31. Nicolas Kublicki, "The Greening of Free Trade: NAFTA Mexican Environmental Law, and Debt Exchange for Mexican Environmental Infrastructure Development," *Columbia Journal of Environmental Law*, 19 (1994), 59–140.

32. Ellen Joan Pollock, "Nafta Creates Work for Certain Lawyers," *The Wall Street Journal,* November 22, 1993, B8.

CHAPTER TWO
Regulatory Enforcement

The federal antitrust and trade regulation laws are enforced primarily by the Department of Justice (Antitrust Division) and the Federal Trade Commission. The federal Constitution is based on the principle of separation of powers: law-making power is assigned to the legislature, law-enforcing power to the executive, and law-deciding power to the judiciary. Theoretically, each branch provides checks and balances on the other two branches.

To provide a mechanism for dealing with the multiple problems of regulating business practices, federal regulatory agencies—a so-called fourth branch of government—were established. These organizations were created as semi-independent agencies operating under general legislative powers. They were to have the advantage of expertness, flexibility, and impartiality. Since the economy and society are constantly changing, the regulatory rules established by these agencies were to be flexible. Thus agencies' policies have changed over time, in terms of both specific requirements and enforcement efforts.

FEDERAL REGULATORY AGENCIES

Federal regulatory agencies usually are created to deal with current crises or to redress serious social problems. The first such agency, the Interstate Commerce Commission, was established in 1887 primarily to relieve the discontent of farmers and small business groups dependent on railroads who were facing what they considered to be excessively high freight rates. Since that time, a number of other agencies have been created. Some were designed for specific industries; examples are the Federal Communications Commission and the Nuclear Regulatory Commission. Others crossed industry lines in an attempt to eliminate unfair practices and enforce certain norms of conduct throughout the economy; these range from the Federal

Trade Commission to the more recently established Environmental Protection Agency and the Equal Employment Opportunity Commission.

Many regulatory agencies are provided with powers that are characteristic of the three branches of government. Some agencies have legislative power to issue rules that control behavior and carry penalties for violation, executive power to investigate violations of rules or statutes and to prosecute offenders, and judicial power to adjudicate disputes concerning failure to comply with standards.

The advantages of administrative regulation lie in the potential for expert knowledge from the experienced commission members, continuous oversight of a specific area, and prompt action. Administrative agencies may also formulate sound and consistent policy, thus providing businesspeople with assurances of uniformity and predictability. Nevertheless there have been criticisms that this fourth branch of government is at odds with traditional democratic policies and that it acts in a bureaucratic manner. There are also complaints that such agencies do not provide sufficient protection for the public interest. According to Louis Kohlmeier, Pulitzer prize–winning reporter for *The Wall Street Journal*, who examined the performance of a number of regulatory agencies:[1] "The agencies have institutionalized industrial protectionism. They are umpires, not of the consumer interests versus business interest, but of competing business interests . . . They are the nemesis of competition as defined by the antitrust laws and the Department of Justice."

It should be noted, however, that administrative agencies are subject to control through judicial review. Courts may invalidate administrative rules and administrative decisions on the substantive ground that they violate the Constitution or the statutes of Congress. Administrative decisions may also be overruled on the procedural ground that they are arbitrary and capricious, because they are not supported by substantial evidence, or on the ground that the firm was not given a fair hearing.

Rather than permit these regulatory agencies to formulate new policy as the times and circumstances require, current congressional action appears to be directed toward formulating more precise standards for regulatory agencies such as the Federal Trade Commission, the Food and Drug Administration, and the Federal Communications Commission.

Enforcement Methods

The Department of Justice has the responsibility for enforcing the Sherman Act, the Clayton Act, and the Robinson-Patman Act through civil or criminal suits, whichever may be authorized. The FTC has the responsibility for enforcing the Federal Trade Commission Act and Sections 2, 3, 7, and 8 of the Clayton Act. The FTC also enforces a number of federal acts dealing with specific products and promotional activities. These include the Wood Products Labeling Act of 1939, the Fur Products Labeling Act of 1951, the Flammable Fabrics Act of 1953, the Textile Fiber Products Identification Act of 1958, the Fair Packaging and Labeling Act of 1966, and the Magnuson-Moss Warranty Act of 1975. In addition, the FTC enforces several statutes governing provision of credit to consumers.

Violations of the federal antitrust laws may come to the attention of the Antitrust Division of the Department of Justice in a number of ways. The division itself may uncover antitrust violations; businesspeople may complain about activities of their competitors, their suppliers, or even their customers; consumers may complain about the prices they pay; and congressional hearings or reports may disclose violations of the law. Government agencies can bring violations to the attention of the division. Private antitrust suits, state antitrust suits, or patent suits may be sources of information.

These methods are also available to the FTC for uncovering violations of the law. Moreover, the FTC reviews advertisements in publications or over radio and television to detect unfair or deceptive practices. For antitrust activities, it reviews trade publications and financial papers. The FTC may also use its investigatory powers under Section 6 of the FTC Act to uncover problems. The FTC has utilized mailed questionnaires to determine possible violations of the law.

A company whose business or property is injured as a result of an antitrust law violation has a number of recourses. It may complain to the Department of Justice or to the FTC. It may also sue to stop the violation; two private remedies of injunctions and triple compensation are available under the antitrust laws. The latter is designed to compensate for injuries already sustained.

Depending upon the law violated and the enforcement agency involved, antitrust and trade regulation law may be enforced by various means. The methods include civil actions for injunctive relief, criminal actions for the imposition of fines or prison terms, cease-and-desist-order proceedings, civil actions for damages, and actions for forfeiture of property. A company may be required to sell assets, a part of its business, or stock holdings in other companies. Compulsory licensing of patents may be required.

Enforcement under RICO

The Racketeer-Influenced and Corrupt Organizations Act (RICO), a federal statute whose impact, at least initially, did not seem designed to affect legitimate businesspeople, has taken on significant dimensions for managerial decisions in recent years.

To aid in eradication of the serious and detrimental influence of racketeering activity wrought by criminals, the RICO Act was passed in 1970. In its origins, RICO was designed to combat organized crime. On the criminal side, it provides for various sentences and has been used to prosecute members of organized crime.[2] In recent years, however, the courts have interpreted RICO to apply to civil cases as well as to criminal cases. RICO permits individuals who sue in civil actions to secure triple damages and attorney's fees from businesspeople when such would not otherwise be awarded.

Private suits may be maintained by persons injured through a "pattern of racketeering." This pattern of activity is not clearly defined; however, it has been interpreted to require only two violations of federal statutes. The violations can relate to mail fraud, wire fraud, or fraud in the sale of securities, as well as other offenses that are not by themselves ordinarily thought of as racketeering activities.

Triple damages and attorney's fees were awarded by a New Jersey District Court in a RICO action alleging breach of contract and fraudulent misrepresentation relating to fees for services. Hirsch, a manufacturer of gold jewelry, employed the Enright Refining Co. to refine the scrap gold collected at the manufacturer's plant. Hirsch alleged that in addition to the disclosed fee charged by the refiner, there also was a fraudulently charged undisclosed fee in the form of retainage (a percentage of gold retained as partial payment for the services rendered).

Hirsch sued Enright, alleging fraud under state common law and also a RICO violation. The court found that Enright had perpetrated a common law fraud and rejected Enright's argument that RICO applied only to actions involving organized crime activities. According to the court, a pattern of racketeering activity, as described in RICO, included mail fraud. And such a pattern was established when Enright mailed a series of fraudulent bills from its New Jersey office to Hirsch's office in New York. Several states have passed state RICO laws that expand the definition of racketeering activity and incorporate more stringent penalties.

Critics of the new applications of RICO contend that these applications go beyond congressional intent. Some courts have attempted to eliminate such RICO claims by holding that RICO does not apply unless the defendant is associated with organized crime. Some judges have criticized the wave of RICO cases, noting "the extraordinary, if not outrageous" use of RICO provisions against "respected and legitimate" companies, thereby labeling them as racketeers in these civil suits. However, the courts have generally indicated that because the RICO statute has been written broadly, they cannot narrow its interpretation. It is up to Congress to revise this legislation.

The controversy over RICO is ongoing; recently, its significance has expanded in both scope and impact. In 1994, the Supreme Court ruled unanimously that the Federal RICO antiracketeering law, designed originally to fight organized crime, can be used against other groups if a criminal conspiracy can be proven. In this case, the National Organization for Women (NOW) and two abortion clinics sued Operation Rescue and related groups for three times their actual costs from nationwide clinic blockades, arson, extortion, and other antiabortion crimes.

A federal appeals court had ruled against NOW, declaring that there had to be an economic motive by the organization conducting the conspiracy and that there was no such motive on the part of abortion protestors.

The case was appealed to the Supreme Court, which ruled 9 to 0 that NOW, representing abortion clinics, *could* file a racketeering suit against groups that targeted abortion providers. In an opinion, Chief Justice William Rehnquist declared Congress had made no mention of economic motive in the racketeering law. The fact that the antiabortion protesters were acting out of conscience and not for personal gain did not protect them from being prosecuted as racketeers, according to the court. The court noted that although NOW is free to pursue its suit, it still must prove that antiabortion violence in the United States is the product of an organized criminal conspiracy.

The final outcome of NOW's suit has not been determined at this writing. However, concerns that RICO is being interpreted in too broad a manner are expressed from numerous sources. There are fears that enlarging RICO's scope may result in the inhibition of free speech and political activity. Moreover, RICO's effect over companies with economic motives may be expanded.

The questions and controversy surrounding current RICO applications suggest that businesspeople should become familiar with what constitutes evidence of a "pattern of racketeering." Since RICO has generally been applied to mail or wire fraud, marketers involved in telemarketing and direct mail advertising are particularly vulnerable. Moreover, the lack of a clear definition of *pattern of racketeering* poses potential problems for other types of business activities as well.

It would be useful for business organizations to become actively involved in encouraging a comprehensive examination of congressional intent so as to determine whether the act was designed to make business and noneconomic violations subject to the same procedures and penalties under RICO as organized crime is. As noted by commentators, the remedy for RICO must come from Congress, rather than the courts. Suggestions include repealing it altogether and amending it so that its reach is less broad and focuses on organized crime.

Sentencing Guidelines

The U.S. Sentencing Commission is a permanent, independent federal agency created as part of the Comprehensive Crime Control Act of 1984. The central purpose of the commission is to establish sentencing policies and practices "by promulgating detailed guidelines prescribing appropriate sentences for offenders convicted of federal crimes." The new guidelines for sentencing organizations (entities other than an individual) convicted of federal offenses became effective on November 1, 1991.[3] Many companies may thus be affected because any company may be held liable for the acts of employees and agents. These guidelines are designed not only to punish and deter but also to encourage organizations to maintain mechanisms for preventing, detecting, and reporting criminal conduct.

Under the new, tougher guidelines, corporate lawbreakers face sanctions and fines that can reach hundreds of millions of dollars. However, also under these guidelines, companies can accrue credits against potential penalties by showing they have established corporate compliance programs. A well-documented compliance program is one of the few mitigating factors available to reduce the size of fines imposed on a convicted company.

MARKETERS' RESPONSE TO REGULATORY ENVIRONMENT

Marketers can engage in a number of proactive and reactive activities designed to offset the negative impact of regulatory control. A useful approach is the litigation audit.[4] Such an audit should include recognition of an evolving legal issue that may affect the firm before it becomes embodied in legislation or judicial decisions, determination of which direction the issue is evolving, and how rapidly and how best to respond. For example, as noted earlier, marketers have been encouraged to urge Congress to reconsider interpretations of RICO as applied to legitimate businesses.

Compliance Programs

"Good ethics is good business" is not just a catchy slogan—it represents a concept of increasing importance to businesspeople. The federal Sentencing Guidelines authorized the imposition of large fines for violating federal criminal law. However, by offering greatly reduced penalties to those corporations that implement effective compliance programs, the guidelines encourage efforts aimed at reducing the potential for criminal corporate conduct.

Corporate compliance programs can be a significant aid in avoiding problems under antitrust and trade regulation laws. An effective ethics program can have a tremendous impact on an organization facing potential fines. Under the Sentencing Guidelines, the existence of an effective program to prevent and detect violations of law can reduce an organization's culpability score by three points and also reduce its criminal fine. Companies implementing such programs can have federal fines reduced by up to 95%; large companies without effective programs may pay up to 400% of an original fine.[5]

Organizations will not be able to mitigate their fines merely by showing they had a compliance program on paper. An effective compliance program serves to inform company personnel how to avoid legal problems, assists them in resolving problems when they do arise, and monitors compliance so that the business as a whole is not placed in jeopardy by the misconduct of any one employee. Even if litigation is not entirely avoided, the existence of an effective compliance program may help limit culpability and reduce the penalties for a violation.

Although not mandated by the guidelines, organizations should establish an Ethics Task Force, composed of senior managers from different functional areas of the company. According to the guidelines, each company should tailor a compliance program to the particular business involved. Several factors that should be addressed when designing any ethics program are (1) the size of the organization, (2) the likelihood of violation occurring due to the nature of the business, and (3) the prior history of the organization.

The guidelines set out seven steps that are essential to any effective compliance program for mitigation:[6]

1. The organization should establish standards and procedures to be followed by its agents and employees that are reasonable capable of reducing the prospect of criminal conduct.

2. A specific, high-level person must be assigned ultimate responsibility to ensure compliance with those standards and procedures.

3. Due care should be taken not to delegate significant discretionary authority to persons whom the organization knows, or should know, have a propensity to engage in illegal activities.

4. Standards and procedures must be effectively communicated to agents and employees.

5. Reasonable steps should be taken to achieve compliance with the standards.

6. The standards must be consistently enforced through appropriate disciplinary mechanisms.

7. After an offense has been detected, the organization must take all reasonable steps to respond appropriately to the offense and to prevent further similar offenses.

Department of Justice Antitrust Division Corporate Leniency Policy

The Antitrust Division of the Department of Justice has changed its Corporate Leniency Policy under which corporations may receive amnesty for antitrust activity. If corporate parties come forward before a Justice Department investigation begins and if they satisfy six criteria, they will receive amnesty.

The six criteria are the following:[7]

1. At the time the corporation comes forward, the division has not received information about the activity from any other source.

2. The corporation, on discovery of the illegal conduct, must take prompt and effective action to terminate its participation therein.

3. The corporation must report the wrongdoing with candor and completeness and provide full, continuing, and complete cooperation throughout the investigation.

4. The confession must truly represent a corporate act as opposed to isolated confessions by individual employees acting on their own.

5. When possible, the corporation must make restitution to injured parties.

6. The corporation must not have coerced another party to participate in the illegal activity and must not have been the leader in, or originator of, the misconduct.

In March 1994, Miles, Inc., the nation's leading manufacturer of steel wool scouring pads, was fined $4.5 million upon pleading guilty to conspiring to fix prices.[8] The firm had agreed to the plea and fine after its chief competitor told the government that the companies discussed pricing. Prices and discount levels had been discussed at meetings and by telephone throughout 1992. According to information filed by the Department of Justice in federal district court in Chicago, the manufacturers agreed to increase prices and issued price announcements in accordance with the agreements reached. The competitor was not prosecuted because it participated in the Antitrust Division's corporate amnesty program.

ALTERNATIVE DISPUTE RESOLUTION

Managers should be aware that there are alternatives to traditional court-oriented dispute resolution. The adversaries process is at the heart of the traditional view of the U.S. legal system. The parties and their attorneys prepare for trial for the ultimate purpose of determining a winner and a loser at trial. Anything short of trial is described as a separate alternative dispute resolution (ADR). ADR, as a formal technique for settling legal disputes and as an accepted business practice, emerged in the 1970s. For managers, ADR may provide a speedier and less expensive resolution in private complaint cases.

Many businesses have taken what is known as the ADR pledge.[9] The pledge is a simple two-paragraph statement committing a company to explore ADR techniques whenever it is involved in a dispute with another company that has also signed the pledge.

The most common forms of ADR are arbitration, mediation, a rent-a-judge program, summary jury trial, and minitrial.[10] An in-depth explanation of these techniques is beyond the scope of this book, but a brief discussion may create an awareness of their existence.

Arbitration is a procedure that most resembles litigation, but is conducted outside the courts. Each of the parties presents its side of the dispute to a mediator (arbitrator) or a panel of mediators, who consider the evidence, apply the law, and render a decision on the claims. Usually the decision is binding. Arbitration as a form of resolution has been adopted by federal agencies such as the Environmental Protection Agency.[11] Under recent decisions of the Supreme Court, provisions in franchise agreements requiring that a dispute be submitted to arbitration are enforced.

Mediation differs from arbitration in that the mediator does not impose a solution, but rather helps parties resolve their own dispute.

The *rent-a-judge-program* involves a retired judge who is chosen by the parties to hear their case. This program uses normal trial court procedures, and the judge's decision has the legal status of a real court judgment.

Summary jury trial is based on the selection by opposing lawyers of a small jury from a regular jury pool. It is designed to give disputants a non-binding indication of how their claims might actually be received by a court.

Minitrial is a completely voluntary procedure initiated by the disputants themselves. It usually involves one high-level executive from each side of the dispute plus one neutral adviser. At a hearing, each side uses an allotted time to present its best case to the neutral observer and the two executives. At the hearing's conclusion, the executives may seek the neutral adviser's opinion about a likely trial outcome before they begin settlement talks, or they may solicit advice only if they cannot settle on their own.

ADR provides many benefits. It may be less costly and less time-consuming than traditional dispute resolution methods. Texaco and Borden, for example, were engaged in a lawsuit involving a $200-million antitrust and breach-of-contract claim. After several years of expensive legal activity and with half a million documents already assembled, both counsels decided to accept a minitrial. Surprisingly, the case was settled in three weeks.[12]

In 1993, ten major food companies, including General Mills Inc., Kellogg Co., and Ralston Purina Co., signed a pact promising to mediate trademark, packaging, and marketing disputes that arise among them. The pledge calls for the companies to try to mediate problems that cannot be resolved in thirty days without a neutral go-between. If the dispute is not settled after the mediator has been involved for at least sixty days, the parties can resort to the courts. The companies' concerns involve not only potentially high litigation costs but also their fear that they will lose consumer goodwill if product packaging and marketing strategies must be altered after lengthy court battles.

A group of food franchisers, including Pepsico Inc.'s Pizza Hut, McDonald's Corp., and Burger King Corp., have signed a similar pledge to mediate disputes with franchisees. Franchisees have not been asked to sign the pledge and can go to court rather than mediate. However, the franchiser must at least offer the option. The food company and food franchise pledges are being sponsored by the Center for Public Resources, a nonprofit organization that promotes litigation alternatives.

ADR procedures usually terminate disputes informally and silently, thus eliminating unwanted publicity. Furthermore, such procedures often provide for more flexibility and creativity in resolving the dispute. ADR procedures create greater client involvement in the disputes. This tends to focus more fully on the merits of the case, rather than on abstract tactical legal exercises.

Recently, the Federal Trade Commission (FTC) announced a proposal to amend its regulations in order to encourage ADR.[13] The commission's proposed policy statement implements the Administration Dispute Resolution Act, which requires federal agencies to develop a policy regarding the use of ADR in their administrative programs. Both the Administrative Dispute Resolution Act and the Negotiated Rulemaking Act authorize and encourage agencies to use arbitration, mediation, negotiated rule making, and other consensual methods of dispute resolution. The FTC noted that the decision whether to use ADR would be determined on a case-by-case basis.

Nevertheless, ADR is subject to potential pitfalls and its use should not be considered a panacea. It works poorly unless executives get involved. It may not have any effect on slowing the so-called litigation explosion, since its potentially lower cost may in fact increase the number of suits. Furthermore, consumers may not be well-informed of their rights under ADR. Traditional dispute resolution mechanisms guide or order society generally and, in particular, affect a large number of citizens who attempt to comply with positive law. This ordering and guidance function of substantive law provides the clear, unambiguous norms and plays a significant role in our society.[14]

SUMMARY

Enforcement of federal antitrust and trade regulation laws primarily is the responsibility of the Department of Justice (Antitrust Division) and the FTC. The federal regulatory agencies that are semi-independent agencies operating under general legislative powers also provide enforcement. Such administrative agencies usually are created to deal with current crises or to redress serious social problems. Some of these agencies are designed for specific industries. Others cross industry lines in an attempt to eliminate unfair practices throughout the economy.

Violations of the federal antitrust laws may be uncovered a number of ways. There may be complaints from competitors, suppliers, or customers or through the agency itself. In recent years, a federal statute (RICO) designed to combat organized crime has been applied to fraudulent business activities. This application permits individuals to sue in civil actions in order to secure triple damages and attorney's fees from businesspeople when these would not otherwise be awarded.

The U.S. Sentencing Commission has established guidelines that are designed not only to punish corporate lawbreakers convicted of federal crimes but also to encourage organizations to maintain mechanisms for preventing, detecting, and reporting criminal conduct.

Marketers may engage in proactive strategies to avoid potential regulatory problems through the use of a litigation audit and the organization of compliance programs. Managers should be aware that in response to private complaint cases, alternatives to traditional court-oriented dispute resolution are available. ADR involves formal techniques for settling legal disputes out of court.

ENDNOTES

1. Louis M. Kohlmeier Jr., *The Regulators—Watchdog Agencies and the Public Interest* (New York: Harper & Row, 1969), pp. 93–94.
2. Dorothy Cohen, "RICO—A Weapon Aimed at an Uncertain Business Target," *Marketing News*, May 10, 1985, 7.
3. 56 Fed. Reg. 22,762, 22,786-97 (1991).
4. David Silverstein, "The Litigation Audit: Preventive Legal Maintenance for Management," *Business Horizons* (November–December 1988), 34–42.
5. Paul E. Fiorelli, "Fine Reductions through Effective Ethics Programs," *Albany Law Review* 56 (1992), 403–439.
6. Details for the requirements under each of these steps appear in Paul E. Fiorelli, "Fine Reductions through Effective Ethics Programs," pp. 413–439.
7. Enforcement Talks Corporate Leniency Policy, CCH, TRR, No. 288, November 9, 1993, p. 9.
8. *U.S.* v. *Miles Inc.*, Case No. 4025, TRR, CCH #45,093 (March 1994).
9. Tamara Lewin, "An Alternative to Litigation," *The New York Times* (March 4, 1986), D2.
10. John R. Allison, "Five Ways to Keep Disputes out of Court," *Harvard Business Review* (January–February 1990), 166–177.
11. Robert O. Raven, "Alternative Dispute Resolution: Expanding Opportunities," *The Arbitration Journal* 43 (June 1988), 44–48.
12. Allison, p. 117.
13. 59 Federal Register 6605, February 11, 1994.
14. Edward Brunet, "Questioning the Quality of Alternative Dispute Resolution," *Tulane Law Review* 62 (November 1987), 1–56.

PART II

Legal Issues in Product Decisions

Part II

Legal Issues in Product Decisions

This chapter examines legal concerns in the development of a product. The next chapter discusses legal issues relevant to the commercialization process (introduction to the marketplace). Chapters 5 and 6 focus on protecting the product idea, the particular form in which the idea is expressed, and its identification or, more specifically, the use of patents, copyrights, and trademarks.

CHAPTER THREE
Product Development

Legal issues may enter all phases of the product decision process, from the generation of the product idea until the product's introduction in the marketplace, sometimes to provide protection for the firm, sometimes to impose obligations on the firm's activities. In fact, during this process it may be necessary to consider the legal aspects of other marketing decisions as well; for example, it is in the early stages that research and development departments can determine which promotional claims will withstand future criticism. Some stages may require the expertise of legal professionals, for example, to secure an appropriate patent for a product. Other stages require the involvement of marketing personnel, such as in the creation of proactive strategies for avoiding potential product liability claims or in the development of reactive strategies for handling major project recalls.

The typical new product planning process provides a format for discussing major legal issues in product decision making. Seven stages are involved: idea generation, product screening, concept testing, business analysis, product development, test marketing, and commercialization.[1]

During the initial stages of the new product planning process, a variety of new product ideas are generated. These ideas are then subject to an initial screening process, which examines the new product's compatibility with the company's resources and objectives. Frequently a survey is conducted in which consumers are given a brief description of the product and asked questions to elicit their reactions to the product concept. If reactions to the concept of the product are favorable, a more detailed business analysis is performed to evaluate the product proposal's attractiveness. Typically this analysis includes estimates of demand, costs, projected sales volume, and profitability.

When the early stages of the new product planning process indicate the feasibility of the potential offering, the product development process is ini-

tiated. Upon completion of this process, a decision is made whether to
engage in market testing. Market testing may be expensive and may reveal
the product characteristics to potential competitors. However, it also may
provide valuable information about potential product problems, consumer
and dealer reactions, market strategy effectiveness, and other relevant marketing information. Once the decision is made to launch the new product, the
commercialization process is put into effect. During all these stages it is important to examine the legal requirements and obligations as well as the protective opportunities that underscore the numerous decisions required.

During the product development stage, attention is focused on the attributes and characteristics to be incorporated in the product. Product quality
is considered a major component of an effective market strategy. It is also a
product decision that requires reference to numerous legal requirements and
restrictions. Significant legal considerations in the product development
process include the use of product warranties as well as information offered
on labels and product packages, all of which are subject to regulatory
control.

USE OF WARRANTIES

To indicate that a product has the quality and characteristics that are
suitable for consumers, the producer may offer product warranties. In the
past, such warranties were confusing and often illusory, and in response,
states adopted a Uniform Commercial Code, which provides for certain warranty requirements and restrictions. Currently, the code is accepted by all
states in the Union. Under the code, warranties are divided into categories of
express and implied.

Express warranty is created by any affirmation of fact or promise or
sample or technical specifications made by the buyer that relates to the
goods. This includes, for example, advertising and handouts. It is not necessary for sellers to use formal words such as *warrant* or *guarantee* or that
sellers have the specific intention to make a warranty. For example, a
statement that a used car was a *good runner* was considered an express warranty.[2]

Implied warranty, as distinct from express warranty, is not dependent
upon the words of the seller, either oral or written. This is considered a warranty of merchantability, which means that the article sold shall be "of the
general kind described and reasonably fit for the general purpose for which
it shall have been sold."[3] There is also an implied warranty of fitness for a
particular purpose when the buyer communicates buyer's specific needs to
the seller and relies on the seller to select appropriate goods. For example, a

casino's complimentary drinks were subject to the implied warranty of merchantability.[4] Such warranties differ in that obligation under an express warranty emerges from an agreement between the seller and buyer and an obligation under an implied warranty emerges from the law.

Despite the existence of the Uniform Commercial Code there was widespread congressional belief that consumer product warranties under state law often were too complex to be understood, too varied to allow meaningful comparisons, and too restricted to provide meaningful warranty protection. In 1976, the Magnuson-Moss Warranty–Federal Trade Commission Improvements Act created a federal private cause of action for consumers damaged by failure of a seller of consumer goods to comply with obligations under a written warranty. To remedy the perceived ills, the act imposes extensive disclosure requirements and minimum content standards on particular types of written and implied warranties and enforces these warranties beyond the gaps in the Uniform Commercial Code. The act also details remedial apparatus that includes informal dispute settlement procedures as well as private and governmental judicial actions.[5]

The Magnuson-Moss Act does not require any manufacturer or seller of consumer products to extend a warranty with its goods. Once a written warranty is offered with a consumer product, however, a manufacturer or seller is subject to the act's regulatory requirements and must provide certain disclosures. The Federal Trade Commission has the authority to provide specific regulations.

Disclosure Requirements

Warrantors must make detailed disclosures of information necessary to enable consumers to understand and enforce written warranties. Disclosure is required when a product actually costing the consumer more than $15 has a written warranty. The following information must be presented in a single document in simple and readily understood language:

1. the identity of the party or parties to whom the written warranty is extended

2. a clear description and identification of products or parts, or characteristics or components, or properties covered by [the warranty]

3. a statement of what the warrantor will do in the event of a defect, malfunction, or failure to conform with the written warranty

4. the point of time or event on which the warranty terms commence

5. a step-by-step explanation of the procedure the consumer should follow in order to obtain performance of any warranty obligation

6. information respecting the availability of any informal dispute settlement mechanism elected by the warrantor

7. any limitations on the duration of implied warranties;

8. any exclusions of or limitations on relief such as incidental or consequential damages

9. a statement in the following language: "This warranty gives you specific legal rights, and you may also have other rights which vary from state to state" (16 C.F.R. Sec. 701. 3[a] [1980]).

Written Warranty

As set forth by the FTC, the term *written warranty* is defined as

(A) Any written affirmation of fact or written promise made in connection with the sale of a consumer product by a supplier to a buyer which relates to the nature of the material or workmanship and affirms or promises that such material or workmanship is defect free or will meet a specified level of performance over a specified period of time, or

(B) Any undertaking in writing in connection with the sale by a supplier of a consumer product to refund, repair, replace or take other remedial action with respect to such product in the event that such product fails to meet the specifications set forth in the undertaking (15 U.S.C.A. Sec. 2301[6](a) and [b]).

For this section to apply, the written affirmation of fact or promise must relate directly to the contract of sale of consumer goods and is exclusive of all other written promises surrounding the offer of sale. Thus brochures, manuals, consumer advertising, and other forms of communication circulated generally to the public are not in fact written warranties as required in the act.[6]

Full and Limited Warranties

When written warranties are offered, they must be conspicuously designated as either full or limited. Under a full warranty, the warrantor must (1) remedy the defects or malfunctions without charge and within a reasonable period of time; (2) make no limitation on the duration of an implied warranty on the product; (3) provide for no exclusion or limitation of consequential damages unless conspicuously stated; and (4) refund or replace the product if, after a reasonable number of repairs, the supplier fails to remedy defects or malfunctions.

If these four standards are not met, the written warranty must be designated as limited. A limited warranty offers less than a full warranty. For example, unlike the second standard of the full warranty, if the warranty is limited, the duration of the implied warranty may be limited to the duration of the limited warranty, but only if the limitation is reasonable in length, conscionable, set forth in clear and precise language, and prominently displayed on the face of the warranty.

For marketers the decision to provide a full or a limited warranty is not an easy one; the former is more costly; however, the latter may be overshadowed by a competitor's full warranty for a competing product. Should the marketer wish the warranty to be limited, this must be so designated; otherwise, the Federal Trade Commission will assume it is a full warranty.

The Magnuson-Moss Act required retailers to make warranties available to consumers before consumers purchase their products. Initially the FTC adopted a rule specifying that the text of warranties must be accessible with the product. The warranty could be attached to the package, be visible on a poster, or be available in a binder. The FTC modified the rule in March 1986, and now allows retailers to comply with the act by making warranties available to consumers upon the consumer's request. In doing so, retailers must post signs that warranties are in fact available upon request.[7] This modification is designed to give retailers greater flexibility in meeting their obligations under the act.

Remedies for Breach of Warranty

Buyers may sue for breach of warranty under the Uniform Commercial Code for repayment price and possible incidental and consequential damages. The Magnuson-Moss Act provides for payment of attorney's fees as an additional remedy; the Uniform Commercial Code does not. It is also possible under the Magnuson-Moss Act to secure recovery of economic losses; however, to do so, the aggrieved buyer must show privity of relationship.

To avoid the potential expenses of court actions, companies may adopt informal mechanisms for settling disputes arising under warranties. Although warrantors are not required to do so, the FTC rules implementing the act allow them to establish such mechanisms. In fact, private parties may not bring a civil action under the Magnuson-Moss Act until they have first resorted to an informal dispute resolution mechanism that has been created by the warrantor.

If an informal mechanism is adopted, it must conform to the FTC's Informal Dispute Mechanism Rules, and disclosures concerning the availability of the mechanism must be made on the face of the warranty. Marketers should consider the adoption of such a mechanism, since it offers a number of advantages:[8]

- Complexities in setting up the mechanism occur only in the initial phase.
- The mechanism allows warrantors to defend themselves in one centralized place, rather than in courts throughout the country.
- A dispute subject to an informal mechanism does not require use of a lawyer (corporations frequently are not allowed to appear in court without attorneys).
- The informal process is less expensive and less time-consuming.
- The warrantor may be able to satisfy the customer in the informal process, thus heading off the possibility of extensive litigation and class-action suits.

LABELING AND PACKAGING

Packaging and labeling decisions are required for many products that enter the marketplace. Considerations in these areas involve both marketing implications and legal concerns. Product packages perform numerous marketing functions, including protection for the contents, communication of information, and supplementary promotion. Similarly, labels identify the product, describe the product, provide instructions for use, and aid in promotion. For both packages and labels, however, there are numerous rules and regulations that must be observed. Occasionally, strategic choices may conflict with legal requirements. Recently, for example, Hanes Co. decided to discontinue its L'Eggs container for hosiery, which has worldwide promotional value. In part, this decision was due to growing environmental concerns and potential green restrictions.

Regulatory Agencies

Various federal and state agencies statutes oversee labeling requirements. The FTC has the responsibility for establishing labeling rules for wool, fur, and textile garments. The FTC also promulgates trade regulation rules for labeling, for example, setting requirements with respect to the labeling of home insulation. The Consumer Product Safety Commission has the power to mandate warnings on dangerous substances. The Food and Drug Administration regulates the labeling of foods, drugs, devices, and cosmetics, as well as hazardous substances. The Department of Agriculture regulates the labeling of meat, poultry, and eggs. The Federal Alcohol Administration controls the labeling of distilled spirits, wine, and malt beverages. The National Marine Fisheries Service sets rules pertaining to fish labeling.

Labeling and packaging regulations are designed to protect consumers in various ways. They provide relevant information, promulgate warning notices, and prevent false and misleading statements.

Informative Labeling and Packaging

The primary purpose of a label is to provide truthful disclosure: to identify merchandise and give directions for its use. The first FTC case involving textile care labeling rules to be litigated occurred in 1993, when a federal district court in New Jersey upheld FTC charges against a defunct New Jersey sweater manufacturer and its president.[9] The manufacturer and its president were fined $10,000 for inserting labels into novelty sweaters that directed the purchaser to dry-clean the garment, without any additional information. Trade association laboratory studies showed that the sweaters could not be cleaned in any type of commercially available dry-cleaning solvent without resulting damage to the garments.

Adequate information on labels is necessary to avoid product liability claims (discussed in detail in Chapter 4). This includes the presentation of instructions and directions. Instructions are affirmative statements of ways to safely operate, maintain, install, or repair a product. Adequate instructions should be written during the initial design stage as this will help identify hazards in the product. Although instructions can be much more detailed than any warning label, they should not be so detailed and involved that it unlikely that the user will read or understand them. In addition, they should be written for the comprehension level of those persons who will be using the product.

Directions are calculated primarily to secure the efficient use of a product. When a departure from directions may create a serious hazard, however, a separate duty to warn arises. A women who immersed her hands for 4½ hours in a mixture of a cleaner and water she was using consequently contracted dermatitis. On a label that said, "It's Kind to Your Hands," were also instructions as to the proper mixture of water and cleaner, which the woman had ignored. The court held the company liable because the instructions were "directory only" and did not reveal any danger from their violation.

A number of federal and state laws have established rules requiring information in the labeling and packaging of goods.

Fair Packaging and Labeling Act of 1966 (Truth-in-Packaging Act)

The basic objective of this law is to provide the consumer with better information to facilitate value comparisons. The law requires that a label provide the identity of the product; the name and location of the distributor or manufacturer of the product; the net quantity of the contents, accurately stated in terms of unit measurements such as fluid ounces, linear foot, yards, or inches; and, when the contents are designated in servings, a clear translation of that into terms of net quantity of each serving.

Except for food, drugs, cosmetics, and devices, which are regulated under the federal Food, Drug and Cosmetic Act, violations of these provisions are specifically designed to be violations of Section 5 of the FTC Act.

1992 Amendments to the Fair Packaging and Labeling Act[10]

Under this legislation, technical amendments will be made to the Fair Packaging and Labeling Act with respect to treatment of the metric system of the International System of Units. Under proposed amendments to FTC regulations implementing these requirements, effective by 1994, labels and packages for many common consumer products will state the contents in both the customary English measurement system and the metric system.

Federal Trade Commission Information Disclosure Requirements

Under its regulatory authority, the FTC has issued a number of rules designed to provide clear information disclosure on the package and label. For instance, the FTC requires that, for consumer products, the ingredients must be listed in order of quantitative importance.

Price Representations. Other rules relate to retail price representations. For example, before the words *Cents-Off* may appear on a label or package, the product must have been sold by the packager in the most recent and regular course of business in the trade area in which the cents-off promotion is made, the product must be sold at a reduction from the ordinary and customary price, and the reduction must be at least equal to the amount of the cents-off representation.

Economy Statements. Rules concerning economy size refer to printed matter on labels or packages containing the words *economy size, economy pack, budget pack, bargain size,* or *value size,* or words of similar import. These terms cannot be imprinted on the label unless the manufacturer at the same time offers the same brand of that commodity in at least one other package size or labeled form.

Slack-filling. Restrictions are placed on slack-filled packages. This refers to packages that are filled to substantially less than their capacity for reasons other than the protection of the contents of the package or the requirement of machines used for enclosing the contents of the package.

The FDA has also issued many information disclosure rules with respect to food, drugs, devices, and cosmetics. For foods, for example, the labels must designate the ingredients in descending order or prominence.

Automobile Information Disclosure Act (P.L. 85-506, 1958)

This act is designed to provide full and fair disclosure of certain information in connection with the distribution of new automobiles. It requires a label to be affixed to the windshield or side window of every new automobile, disclosing information that gives the make, model, identification number, final assembly point, name and location of dealer, and method of transportation used in making delivery. Additional information required about the auto includes (1) the manufacturer's suggested retail price; (2) the manufacturer's suggested retail price for each accessory or item of optional equipment, physically attached to the auto, that is not included within the price; (3) the amount charged, if any, for transportation of the auto to the dealer; and (4) the total of the amounts specified in 1, 2, and 3.

The requirement that the manufacturer's retail price must be specified on the label tends to be in contradiction with the rules concerning suggested retail prices for other products. However, typical sales of automobiles apparently warranted this information, since purchasers could not easily make comparisons of automobile prices without information concerning the prices of the options that varied from auto to auto.

Warnings on Labels and Packages

Several types of potentially dangerous products may require warning labels. The Consumer Product Safety Commission (CPSC), formed in 1973 under the Consumer Product Safety Act, is responsible for developing safety standards that cover the labeling of more than 1,500 consumer products. The CPSC's primary enforcement tool is product recall, whereby the commission orders companies to recall and modify, or discontinue, unsafe products. The Food and Drug Administration (FDA) has authority to prevent the misbranding and adulteration of foods, drugs, and cosmetics. The FDA also has the power to recall mislabeled items.

Cigarette Labeling and Advertising Act (1965)

This act set requirements for warning labels on cigarette packages and authorized the FTC to establish rules. To some extent, the cigarette act has provided a defense against complaints of inadequate warning as to the danger of smoking cigarettes. The act has been interpreted as preempting all states from passing their own restrictions on cigarette marketing. Though the cigarette act did not expressly preempt state common law claims relating to cigarette smoking and health, the courts have concluded that Congress preempted these types of claims.[11]

Numerous suits have been brought against cigarette manufacturers for failure to warn about the product's hazards. However, the courts have generally declared that warning notices were mandated and have appeared on the product's labels. The 1965 federal Cigarette Labeling and Advertising Act (Section 4) provided that the following warning be printed on every package of cigarettes: "Caution: Cigarette Smoking May Be Hazardous to Your Health." Section 5(b) of the act provided, "No statement relating to smoking and health shall be required in the advertising of any cigarettes the packages of which are labeled in conformity with the provisions of this Act."

Subsequently, the Public Health Cigarette Smoking Act of 1969 changed sections 5(b) to provide: "No requirement or prohibition based on smoking and health shall be imposed under State law with respect to the advertising or promotion of any cigarettes the packages of which are labeled in conformity with the provisions of this Act." According to the courts, this provision preempted state courts from requiring additional warnings.

In a state court in New Jersey, Cipollone sued Liggett for damages for failure to warn against the hazards of cigarette smoking. The case ultimately went to the Supreme Court for determination of the extent of product liability.[12] The Supreme Court decision left some confusion about what is and what is not a permissible state tort claim against a cigarette manufacturer.[13] However, Justice Stevens's plurality opinion noted that the revised Section 5(b) of the act indicated that federal law preempted state law after the 1969 act was passed. However, the 1965 version of Section 5(b) did not preempt any state law tort claims. The court reasoned that the act prohibited state rule-making bodies only from mandating statements in advertising that were somehow at variance with the statement set forth in the 1965 act. Thus all tort claims against cigarette manufacturers that arose before the effective date of the 1969 statute are, and will be, cognizable in state court.

As for claims after 1969, Justice Stevens pointed out that the act did not preempt Cipollone's claims insofar as those claims relied "solely on respondent's testing or research practices or other actions unrelated to advertising and promotion."

Interestingly, the Cipollone case was voluntarily dismissed.[14] However, the situation remains that it is possible for cigarette manufacturers to be sued for negligence on the basis of their testing and research practices or other actions not related to advertising or promotion.

Alcoholic Beverage Labeling Act

In 1988, Congress passed an act requiring manufacturers to place warnings on alcoholic beverage containers. The act's warning states:

> Government Warning: (1) According to the Surgeon General, women should not drink alcoholic beverages during pregnancy because of the risk of birth defects. (2) Consumption of alcoholic beverages impairs your ability to drive a car or operate machinery, and may cause health problems. (Alcohol Act #204[a])

The alcohol act also contains a preemption provision; however, whether or not this will be interpreted as preempting state common law actions against alcohol manufacturers for injuries sustained after enactment of the federal law is not quite clear.

Basic Rules on Product Safety Warnings

A number of general rules should be observed in providing warning notices.[15]

When are warnings required? A general rule concerning warnings notes they are "required to prevent a product from being unreasonable dangerous." Generally there is no duty to warn against obvious dangers; nor is there a duty to warn against dangers or uses of the product that are not foreseeable. There is no duty to warn when the danger is very slight, and it may not be necessary to warn when only a very small minority of users might be exposed.

What is a legally adequate warning? Warnings should be placed conspicuously on the product—not in a manual or other literature. Warnings should communicate the level of danger and should contain information that assists the consumer in avoiding the danger. Warnings should include a statement of the consequences of disregarding the warning. Aggressive or sales efforts that might vitiate an otherwise adequate warning should be avoided. When a safety warning is given, representations on the label that the product is safe should be avoided.

Who should be warned? Generally, individuals who use a potentially unsafe product or who might be endangered by such use should be given safety warnings. According to the court, "The adequacy of the warning must be evaluated in connection with the knowledge and expertise of the user of the product."[16]

False and Misleading Labeling

In recent years there has been a significant increase in health and nutritional claims in advertising and labeling, which has been accompanied by the so-called cosmetic wars. In part these activities are due to changing demographics and lifestyles: There is an aging population that wishes to retard the appearance of age and that emphasizes the maintenance of health.[17] Furthermore, there has been an increased focus on environmental concerns, resulting in a multitude of greening claims.

Health and Nutritional Food Labeling

The FDA has jurisdiction over labeling; however, when false and misleading labeling constitutes an unfair business practice, the FTC may regulate it. The two agencies have entered into a liaison arrangement-agreement pursuant to which the FDA exercises primary jurisdiction over food labeling and the FTC assumes primary jurisdiction over food advertising.

The FDA had articulated a policy barring health claims in food labeling as late as 1979. In 1984, Kellogg Co. challenged the FDA's policy by introducing a labeling and advertising campaign that discussed the role of All Bran cereal in the prevention of cancer. Other prominent food manufacturers soon followed with analogous disease prevention claims in reliance on the dietary recommendations of prestigious scientific organizations.

Nutrition Labeling and Education Act (1990)

By 1990 the excessive use of confusing nutritional claims encouraged passage of the federal Nutrition Labeling and Education Act, which seeks to make nutrition information more precise and understandable. This act required the FDA to mandate a uniform nutrition label on most foods. The final rule was published in January 1993.[18] The compliance date for food manufacturers to change their labels was May 8, 1994.

The label will be required on an estimated 257,000 processed food products. Exempt from the nutrition labeling rules are foods produced by small businesses, restaurant food, food served for immediate consumption, ready-to-eat food prepared on-site, food sold in bulk that will not be consumed in bulk, medical foods, and plain coffee, tea, some spices, and other foods that contain no significant amounts of any nutrients. Packages with less than 12 square inches available for labeling will not have to carry nutrition information.

The rule defines serving sizes for 139 FDA-regulated foods so that definitions will be more uniform. It also specifically defines descriptors that appear on the front of a package—such as *light*, *low fat*, and *high fiber*—to abolish false claims about foods. In addition, the FDA defined numerically such nutrient content descriptors as *low fat*, *low sodium*, and *low calorie*, so that the food must meet the definition before a descriptor can be used. For example, *low sodium* means less than 140 mg per serving, and *very low sodium* equals less than 35 mg per serving. The words *little*, *few*, and *low source of* can be substituted for low.

For the first time, the FDA is allowing mention of seven relationships between a food and the risk of a disease to appear on food packages. Health claims may not state the degree of risk reduction but may use only the word *may* or *might* in discussing the food-disease relationship. An acceptable example of a health claim, according to the FDA, might state, "While many factors affect heart disease, diets low in saturated fat and cholesterol may reduce the risk of this disease."

The labeling rules specify that, with few exceptions, all product labels contain a mandatory nutrition panel. Specified nutrients, except for vitamins and minerals, must be listed in metric units and as a percentage of recommended daily intake (RDI) or daily reference value (DRV)—if one of these is defined—with primary emphasis on the percentage of metric.[19]

The FDA also released regulations that will require dietary supplements to live up to the same standards as foods. The FDA stressed that the rules will not require removal of dietary supplements from the shelves; they will require, however, prior approval for health claims on supplement bottles, in catalogs, or implied by a product's catchy name.

The rules do not provide a blanket ban on health claims. Instead such claims would be authorized if qualified experts reach significant scientific agreement about their validity. For example, labels are allowed to claim that folic acid may reduce the risk of certain birth defects and that calcium supplements can combat osteoporosis.

However, the FDA refused to authorize health claims that fiber prevents cancer and heart disease, that antioxidant vitamins prevent cancer, that fatty acids prevent heart disease, and that zinc fights immune deficiency in the elderly.

FTC Guidelines for Health and Nutrition Claims in Food Advertising

On May 13, 1994 the FTC issued its guidelines for health and nutrition claims in food advertising. Essentially the guides inform food marketers to follow the requirements of the new FDA food-labeling regulations, as it regards ad terminology.[20] The FTC requires marketers that use terms such as *light* and *reduced* in ads to satisfy the same definitions as established by the FDA for food labels. For example, a product whose label states fat free contains less than 0.5 grams of fat per serving, and that must also be the case for a product advertised as fat free.

The FTC's rules for advertising health/disease claims are not as rigid as those established by the FDA. The 1990 Nutrition Labeling and Education Act allows only seven health claims in labels. But the FTC will allow other disease claims if well supported. At this writing legislation is pending in both the House and Senate to synchronize food advertising and labeling regulations. However, there are researchers in the area of food labeling who feel that since nutrition information is important to consumers some of the current restrictions may be too rigid.

Cosmetic Labeling

The cosmetic wars have been encouraged by interactions between the pharmaceutical industry and cosmetic companies. Many of the latter are owned by drug houses.[21] Cosmetic manufacturers have problems similar to food companies in the amount of health information that can be offered on their labels. The FDA's definition of a drug states, in part, "articles intended for use in the diagnosis, cure, mitigation, treatment, or prevention of diseases . . . , and articles . . . intended to affect the structure of any function of the body . . ."

Cosmetics are defined as "articles intended to be rubbed, pureed, sprinkled, or sprayed on, introduced into, or otherwise applied to the human body or any part thereof for cleansing, beautifying, promoting attractiveness, or altering the appearance."

In 1988, in a letter to cosmetic skin care companies, the FDA stated, "Claims that a product 'counteracts,' 'retards,' or 'controls' aging or the aging process, as well as claims that a product will 'rejuvenate' or 'renew' the skin, are drug claims because they can be understood as claims that the structure of the body will be affected by the product.[22] However, the FDA noted that it does not object to claims that a product will temporarily improve the appearance of outward signs of aging and that it considers a product that claims to moisturize or soften the skin is a cosmetic.

What constitutes a traditional cosmetic claim may not be clarified for some time and may ultimately depend on a court's perception of what the consumer recognizes as a description of cosmetic change. The marketer must be prepared to defend against regulatory action by the FDA and also must anticipate the possibility of a Lanham Act challenge by a drug company that can make a legitimate drug performance claim for its product.

Moreover, as cosmetic marketers move further away from the traditional puffery of subjective types of claims to more specific product attribute or performance claims, the possibility of running afoul of the Lanham Act increases. Thus cosmetic manufacturers should be certain that they have valid data that will hold up in court when making substantive product performance or comparative claims or drug claims. Moreover, if marketers have doubts about the defensibility of such claims, they should keep them off the product's packaging and labeling.

Environmental Labeling

Nutritional and environmental claims are considered by the FTC as credence claims because they often rely on complicated sciences and most consumers cannot evaluate for themselves. For example, the claim that a particular food product tastes good can easily be assessed; however, the claim that the same food product will confer a health benefit is one that consumers reasonably may not be able to evaluate. The FTC considers it important to examine credence claims and to ensure that they are adequately supported.

Guide for the Use of Environmental Claims in Marketing

The FTC considers the so-called safe harbor as one tool it uses to minimize the risk of violating the law. The safe harbor specifies particular conduct against which the commission will not take enforcement action. The safe-harbor concept underlies much of the guidance the commission has provided in its recently issued *Guide for the Use of Environmental Claims in Marketing*.[23] The guides are designed to provide the basis for voluntary compliance with the law; conduct inconsistent with the positions articulated in the guides may result in corrective action by the FTC.

The guides apply to environmental claims in labeling, advertising, promotional materials, and all other forms of marketing, such as brand-name emblems, logos, and depictions, and they relate to any environmental claims made for a product or packing. Any party making an objective assertion about the environmental attribute of a product or package must, at the time the claim is made, possess and rely upon a reasonable basis for substantiating the claim. For environmental marketing claims, such substantiation often requires competent and reliable scientific evidence.

General Principles

    a. Qualifications and disclosures should be sufficiently clear to prevent deception.

    b. The environmental benefit should be presented so as to indicate that it refers to the product, the packaging, or a portion or component of the product or packaging.

    c. The claim should not overstate the environmental attribute or benefit either expressly or by implication.

    d. Comparative environmental claims should be presented in a manner that makes the basis for the comparison sufficiently clear so as to avoid consumer deception.

Environmental Marketing Claims

    a. *General environmental benefit claims.* It is deceptive to misrepresent either directly or by implication that a product or package offers a general environmental benefit. Such unqualified general claims are difficult to interpret.

    b. *Degradable/biodegradable/photodegradable.* An unqualified claim that a product is degradable, biodegradable, or photodegradable should be substantiated by competent and reliable scientific evidence that the entire product or package will completely break down and return to nature.

    c. *Compostable.* An unqualified claim that a product or package is compostable should be substantiated by reliable and competent scientific evidence that all of the materials in the product or package will break down into or otherwise become part of usable compost.

    d. *Recyclable.* A product or package should not be marketed as recyclable unless it can be collected, separated, or otherwise recovered from the solid waste stream for use in the form of raw materials or in the manufacture or assembly of a new package or product.

    e. *Recyclable content.* A recycled-content claim may be made only for materials that have been recovered or otherwise diverted from the solid waste stream.

    f. *Source reduction.* Source reduction claims should be qualified to the extent necessary so as to avoid consumer deception about the amount of the source reduction.

g. *Refillable.* An unqualified refillable claim should not be asserted unless a system is provided for either the collection and return of the package for refill or the consumer's later refill of the package with product subsequently sold in another package.

h. *Ozone safe and ozone friendly.* It is deceptive to misrepresent either directly or by implication that a product is safe for or friendly to the ozone layer. A claim that a product does not harm the ozone layer is deceptive if the product contains an ozone-depleting substance.

Marketers' Response to Labeling Requirements

It is clear that marketers should be aware of labeling requirements for their specific products and the ways such requirements can be fulfilled. Suggestions relevant to the latter issues are discussed in the next chapter.

However, marketers can make significant contributions by researching the effectiveness of current labeling rules and suggesting measures for improvement. A number of studies already have been conducted, particularly in the area of alcohol warning labels.[24] Studies in consumer behavior have indicated that there are differences among consumers in believability, attitudes, and the effects of behavioral change toward alcohol warning labels. Labels may not influence the behavior of risk drinkers. Experimental studies have shown that label design factors can stand improvement because the labels on current alcohol containers lack noticeability.

Evaluations of warnings are needed to determine what, if any, effects such warnings have and how closely these effects are related to the initial goals of legislation.

SUMMARY

During the product development stage, decisions must be made concerning product quality. Such a determination requires a knowledge of the product standards established by government regulation.

Quality assurances for the product can be provided for consumers through product warranties. States have adopted Uniform Commercial Code to provide for certain warranty requirements and restrictions. Warranties can be express or implied. Express warranties emerge from an agreement between the seller and buyer; implied warranties of merchantability or fitness for use are obligations emerging from the law.

The Magnuson-Moss Warranty–Federal Trade Commission Act provides additional warranty protection for consumers. This act does not require a manufacturer or seller to extend a warranty; however, if a written warranty is offered with a consumer product, it must provide certain disclosures.

Buyers may sue for breach of warranty under both the Uniform Commercial Code and the Magnuson-Moss Act. To avoid the potential expense of court actions, companies may adopt informal mechanisms for settling such disputes. These mechanisms, which offer numerous advantages to marketers, are available under the Magnuson-Moss Act.

A number of federal and state laws establish rules concerning the packaging and labeling of goods. Regulations are also designed to provide the consumer with better information so as to facilitate value comparisons.

Recently, attention has focused on false and misleading labeling, particularly in the area of health and nutritional food, cosmetics, and greening claims. Current activity by the FDA and the FTC suggests that marketers should be alert to emerging requirements and should exercise care in order to avoid making false and misleading claims on labels.

CASES:
Susan J. Reynolds, Thomas L. Markley, Harland v. Olson, et al *v.* S & D Foods, Inc., aka Consolidated Pet Food Inc., CCH #70,174 (U.S. DC. D Kansas, No. 91 1442-PFK, February 8, 1993); Thomas P. Muchisky *v.* Frederic Roofing Co. Inc. CCH #70,036 (Missouri C A, E.D, Division Four No. 60669, August 4, 1992).

FACTS

Reynolds v. *S & D Foods* concerns the illnesses and deaths of sixty-six greyhounds boarded in one of three kennels operated by Reynolds, Olson, and Markley. The remaining plaintiffs were owners of the greyhounds.

Consolidated Pet Food produced the greyhound pet food product, known as 4-D meat, specifically as food for racing greyhounds. Both parties admit that Consolidated made no type of written guarantee concerning its 4-D meat, but the kennel owners contend that Consolidated salespeople made express oral representations and warranties.

The kennel owners fed 4-D meat to the greyhounds. Sixty-six greyhounds fell ill and died or were euthanasic. The cause of the illness was in dispute; however, the kennel owners and greyhound owners alleged the illnesses were attributable to *Salmonella* contained in the 4-D meat product. They filed suit based upon negligence, strict liability, implied warranty of wholesomeness of food, implied warranty of merchantability, implied warranty of fitness for a particular purpose, express warranty, and claims under the Magnuson-Moss Warranty Act.

S & D claims that its product did not cause the death of the dogs and moved for summary judgment with respect to claims relating to greyhounds for which no evidence exists to establish a connection with their illnesses and 4-D meat. S & D requested partial summary judgment for the plaintiffs' claims under the Magnuson-Moss Warranty Act.

ISSUE

Do the facts in this case fit the requirements under the Magnuson-Moss Warranty Act?

HOLDING

No. The Magnuson-Moss Act concerns consumer products. A pet food used in the greyhound industry is not a consumer product, since such a pet food is not for normal personal, family, or household use. The pet food was marketed for kennels and breeders and not for private consumers.

REASONING

The Magnuson-Moss Warranty Act creates a private cause of action that permits a "consumer" to sue a warrantor for violating the substantive provisions of the act. The act defines consumer as a "buyer other than for purposes of resale of any consumer product." Consumer product is defined as "any tangible personal property which is distributed in commerce and which is normally used for personal, family or household purposes."

The important phrase in the statute is *normally used*. The information before the court in this case reveals that the normal use of 4-D meat is for the greyhound industry. It is not marketed for private consumers. It is packaged in 10-pound tubes and is marketed for kennels and breeders of greyhounds.

Summary judgment with respect to the claim under the Magnuson-Moss Act was granted to S & D. However, the court denied S & D's motion for summary judgment under the Kansas Consumer Protection Act.

FACTS

Muchisky v. *Frederic Roofing Co.* concerns a contract to reroof the Muchisky home. After the contractor installed the roof and made two attempts at remedial work, Muchisky filed a petition alleging breach of contract, breach of warranty, and a violation of the Magnuson-Moss Warranty Act. The claims were submitted to a jury, which found in favor of the homeowner on each claim and awarded $10,000 as damages on each claim.

It additionally awarded $11,200 as attorney's fees for violation of the Magnuson-Moss act.

The reroofing contractor appealed, asserting that the contract sued upon was a services contract, not a sales contract, and being a services contract, the provisions of the Magnuson-Moss Act do not apply.

ISSUE

Is the reroofing of a home a consumer product as defined by the Magnuson-Moss Act?

HOLDING

Yes. Congress intended the act to cover some items, which normally become part of real estate.

REASONING

Under the Magnuson-Moss Act, the term consumer product means any tangible personal property that is distributed in commerce and is normally used for personal, family, or household purposes, including any such property intended to be attached to or installed in any real property without regard to whether it is so attached or installed.

The purchase of materials was in connection with a home improvement, repair, or modification. The products were not integrated into the structure at the time of the sale, which occurred when the consumer and the supplier had entered into a binding contract.

DISCUSSION QUESTIONS

Discuss the various claims that may arise in a dispute over warranties. What mechanisms are available to marketers for settlement of such disputes?

What are the basic requirements for instituting an action under the Magnuson-Moss Warranty Act?

ENDNOTES

1. Joel R. Evans and Barry Berman, *Marketing*, 6th ed. (New York: Macmillan 1994), pp. 414–440.
2. *Crothers by Crothers* v. *Cohen*, 384 N.W. 2d 562 (Minn. App., 1986).
3. *Keenan* v. *Cherry & Webb*, 47 R.I. 125 (1925).
4. *Levondsky* v. *Marina Associates*, 731 F. Supp. 1210 (D.N.J. 1990).

5. Alex Devience Jr., "Magnuson-Moss Act: Substitution for UCC Warranty Protection?" *Commercial Law Journal* 95 (Fall 1990), 323–337.

6. *Skelton* v. *General Motors Corporation*, 660 F. 2d 311 (7th Cir. 1981).

7. Modification of the Magnuson-Moss Consumer Product Warranty Act of 1975, CCH Trade Reg. Rep. No. 746, March 10, 1986: "Legal Developments in Marketing," *Journal of Marketing* 51 (January 1987), 111.

8. David C. Hjelmfelt, *Executive's Guide to Marketing, Sales, and Advertising Law* (Englewood Cliffs, N.J.: Prentice-Hall, 1990).

9. *FTC* v. *Bonnie & Co. Fashions, Inc.* (DC N.J., October 1993).

10. 58 Federal Register 43726, August 1993.

11. Carter H. Dukes, "Alcohol Manufacturers and the Duty to Warn: An Analysis of Recent Case Law in Light of the Alcoholic Beverage Labeling Act of 1988," *Emory Law Journal* 38 (Fall 1989), 1189–1222.

12. *Cipollone* v. *Liggett Group, Inc.*, 112 S. Ct. 2608 (1992).

13. Thomas C. Galligan Jr. "Product Liability—Cigarettes and Cipollone: What's Left? What's Gone?" *Louisiana Law Review* 53 (January 1993), 713–752.

14. DC N.J., No. 83-2864, dismissed 11/5/92.

15. Michael Ursic, "Product Safety Warnings: A Legal Review," *Journal of Public Policy and Marketing* 4 (1985), 80–90.

16. *Koonce* v. *Quaker Safety Products & Manufacturing*, 798 F. 2d 700 (5th Cir. 1986).

17. Emale G. Murphy, "Cosmeceuticals—The Regulatory Environment of the Cosmetic Wars and Other Phenomena," *Food Drug Cosmetic Law Journal* 44 (1989), 41–48.

18. "FDA Issues Final Rules on Food Nutrition Labeling," U.S.L.W. 61 LW 2433 (January 26, 1993).

19. Pauline M. Ippolito and Alan D. Mathios, "New Food Labeling Regulations and the Flow of Nutrition Information to Consumers," *Journal of Public Policy and Marketing* 12 (Fall 1993).

20. Steven W. Colford, "FTC's rules for food ads win healthy reaction," *Advertising Age*, May 16, 1994, 2.

21. Murphy, p. 41.

22. Ibid., p. 44.

23. 16 CFR 260, July 28, 1992.

24. See, for example, J. Craig Andrews, Richard G. Netemeyer, and Srinivas Durvasula, "Believability and Attitudes toward Alcohol Warning Label Information: The Role of Persuasive Communication Theory," *Journal of Public Policy and Marketing* 9 (1990), 1–15. Also Michael E. Hilton, "An Overview of Recent Findings on Alcoholic Beverage Warning Labels, 1–9; Janet R. Hankin, Ira J. Firestone, James J. Sloan, Joel W. Ager, Allen C. Goodman, Robert J. Sokol, and Susan S. Martier, "The Impact of Alcohol Warning Label on Drinking during Pregnancy," 10–18; Karen L. Graves, "An Evaluation of the Alcohol Warning Label: A Comparison of the United States and Ontario, Canada in 1990 and 1991, 19–29; Lee Ann Kaskutas, "Changes in Public Attitudes toward Alcohol Control Policies since the Warning Label Mandate of 1988, 30–37; Kenneth R. Lauhghery, Stephen L. Young, Kent P. Vaubel, and John W. Brelsford Jr., "The Noticeability of Warnings on Alcohol Beverage Containers" 38–56; J. Craig Andrews, Richard G. Netemeyer, and Srinivas Durvasula, "The Role of Cognitive Responses as Mediators of Alcohol Warning Label Effects," 57–68; Andrea M. Fenaughty and David P. MacKinnon, "Immediate Effects of the Arizona Alcohol Warning Poster," 69–77; Michael J. Kalsher, Steven W. Clarke, and Michael S. Wogalter, "Communication of Alcohol Facts and Hazards by a Warning Poster," 78–90—all in *Journal of Public Policy and Marketing* 12 (Spring 1993).

CHAPTER FOUR
Product Decisions: Commercialization

Commercialization has been defined as "a stage (usually the last) in the development cycle for a new product. Commonly thought to begin when the product is introduced into the marketplace, but actually starts when management commits to marketing the item."[1]

Prior to a product's introduction to the market, it should be subjected to a careful testing process for both its attributes and functional capabilities. Some products are also test-marketed to estimate the demand potential and to iron out any bugs that may emerge. Although there are no specific regulations concerning test marketing, during this period manufacturers should invoke all of the protective mechanisms discussed earlier. Once the commercialization process is initiated and the product introduced to the marketplace, the potential for product liability exists, as does the possibility for consumer complaints and/or product recalls.

PRODUCT LIABILITY

A significant risk factor in introducing products into the marketplace is the potential for product liability. In addition to regulatory requirements for acceptable product standards, there is a body of law—product liability—that is concerned with injuries caused by products that are defectively manufactured, processed, or distributed. The liability attaches to those who make a profit throughout the channel of distribution—from the extractors of raw materials, to the makers of component parts, to the retailers. The production and distribution of harmful products can result in serious consequences for the institutions involved in this process, as in the cases of asbestos material for making articles fireproof and diethylstilbestrol (DES—a pharmaceutical used as a miscarriage preventative).

Although elements of product liability law existed in the fifteenth century, major evolvement occurred in the twentieth century, generating increasing implications for modern marketing managers. Earlier restrictions in product liability cases related to privity of contract, that is, a suit could not be brought against a party by one who has no contract with that party. For example, a consumer had to purchase directly from the manufacturer to sue that manufacturer. In 1916, in a landmark case, privity of contract as a requirement was eliminated.[2] In part, this movement is in response to the growth of large-scale manufacturers and their direct appeals to consumers through extensive marketing efforts. Along with the elimination of privity there has been an expansion in the doctrines under which product liability claims can be invoked.

Product liability law nowadays is determined by states and local courts. Although many states currently have statutes, no two are alike.[3] This inconsistency poses complex questions for firms who seek to design and market a product regionally or nationwide.

While there is a movement toward the passage of federal law, currently the substantive body of product liability law varies from jurisdiction to jurisdiction. Thus marketers should be familiar with the product liability theories most frequently applied in the various states and in the federal courts.

Product Liability Theories

Product liability actions arise from injuries to persons or property caused by dangerously defective products. The definition of a product in such cases has been expanded by the courts to include not only the product but also its container and package. While the courts have been reluctant to accept the notion of purely service transactions as involving a product, those that are hybrid—that is, involving the sale of a good and the rendition of a service—have been considered as encompassing a product.[4]

Every product liability case involves a definition of defect; however, defining what constitutes a defect creates more problems than defining a product. The defect may have resulted from the manufacturer's decision, it may have occurred during the production process, or it may have happened because of a failure to warn or warn adequately of a possible danger.

The traditional product liability theories of recovery are warranty, negligence, and strict liability.

Warranty

Breach of warranty is related to the law of contracts and has a statutory basis in the Uniform Commercial Code adopted by almost every state in the nation. Under the law of contracts, product liability can emerge from breach of express warranty or breach of implied warranty.

As noted in the previous chapter, if a seller expressly warrants that a product performs in a superior manner and purchasers are injured because they relied on that warranty, then the seller is liable even if there is no defect. Implied warranty, as distinct from express warranty, is not dependent upon words of the seller, either oral or written. In fact "a warranty that goods shall be merchantable is implied in a contract for their sale if the seller is a merchant with respect to goods of that kind." This rule is contained in Section 2-314 of the Uniform Commercial Code and has been accepted by every state of the Union. Neither the homemaker who sells home-baked cookies nor the factory owner who makes a onetime sale of a piece of machinery would come under this rule.

Negligence

Negligence is part of tort litigation. A tort is a wrong other than breach of contract committed against a person or person's property for which the law gives a right to recover damages. A significant case in the development of product liability occurred when Justice Cardozo ruled that consumer actions against negligence may be taken against manufacturers of any product. In *MacPherson* v. *Buick Motor Co.*, it was held that an action in negligence could be maintained against a remote manufacturer of an automobile with a defectively made wheel that broke, causing injury to the plaintiff. This decision has been so widely accepted that the issue of privity is no longer raised in personal injury cases involving negligence.

Negligence may arise when manufacturers or sellers fail to comply with the necessary standards in the design of a product, fail to fully inspect or test a product, or fail to warn or to warn adequately of foreseeable dangers. Liability for negligence may also occur if a seller saw or should have foreseen that a purchaser might be injured by the seller's negligent act or omission.

Strict Liability

Proof of negligence in product cases tended to be difficult because the entire manufacturing process from design to packaging is within a manufacturer's control. Manufacturers could easily produce expert witnesses from among their own employees and consultants to show there was no negligence in the entire process. Nor are warranties considered sufficient to resolve all product liability issues. The courts have indicated that the purpose of liability is to ensure that the costs of injuries resulting from defective products are borne by manufacturers rather than by injured persons who are powerless to protect themselves.[5] Warranties are not sufficient to serve this purpose.

The concept of product liability was significantly expanded with the promulgation of the law of strict liability in tort.

In 1965, the American Law Institute published the Second Restatement of Torts S402A, which has been widely adopted by the courts as the rule of strict tort liability. According to these rules, strict liability requires a sale, does not depend on proof of negligence or fault or the presence or absence of a warranty, and can occur regardless of whether the injured person who is suing was a party to the contract or sale. While strict liability significantly expands the potential or product liability actions, marketers should be aware that it does not mean absolute liability; liability occurs only if the product is defective. For example, a consumer may inadvertently cut off a part of a finger while using a kitchen knife. Even though the product caused the injury, no liability attaches to the seller unless the consumer can prove a *dangerous* defect in design or manufacture that *caused* the injury. Holding the seller liable on the basis of causation alone would amount to absolute liability, meaning, liability for any injury caused by the product regardless of whether the product was defective.

Market Share Liability

Until recently, plaintiffs generally have been required to prove that their injuries were caused by an act of a particular defendant. Under an exception created for DES called market share liability, the causation requirement was eliminated. The case concerned DES, a drug that physicians administered in the late 1940s and early 1950s as a miscarriage preventative. Offspring of women who took the drug exhibit a high incidence of cancer and precancerous conditions.

Sindell alleged that as a result of her mother's ingestion of DES during pregnancy, she developed a malignant bladder tumor. She was unable to identify the manufacturer of the drug claimed to be responsible for her injuries; nonetheless, she brought an action against eleven drug companies.[6]

The theory of market share liability was created in order to help ease the plaintiff's burden in proving that a particular defendant was in some way responsible for the defective product. Under this theory, a plaintiff may bring an action when the specific manufacturer of the drug causing the injury is indeterminable for reasons not the fault of the plaintiff.[7] As long as the plaintiff names enough defendants who were in business at the time of the injury to cover a substantial share of the DES market, the burden shifts to each defendant to exonerate itself. Any defendant who fails to do so is liable for that portion of the total judgment represented by its share of the total market.

To date, market share liability has been applied primarily in DES cases. The theory may broaden to drug manufacturers and other manufacturers who allegedly unleash a dangerous, fungible product.[8] It is suggested that all marketing managers should keep accurate, detailed records of their sales of products for an extended period of time. Such records can be useful in providing evidence that a manufacturer could not have sold the product that caused the injury, which allows a manufacturer to escape liability in a particular lawsuit.

However, in a recent case in New York, a court of appeals ruled companies that made the drug can be liable, even if they prove that they did not manufacture the DES a plaintiff says caused injury. Although New York is the only state that has done so, this approach has been criticized as having a potentially chilling effect on the manufacturers of pharmaceuticals. It seems reasonable that companies that can prove they did not market or produce the DES that injured a plaintiff should be permitted to exculpate themselves.[9]

Marketers' Responses to Product Liability Issues

Marketers should familiarize themselves with the various aspects of product liability so that they can aid in avoiding such lawsuits. Moreover, should product liability claims emerge, marketers can aid in the preparation of defensive strategies. Marketing skills in the area of behavioral science, specifically in relation to nonverbal behavior, communication processes, and survey research, are especially useful in developing appropriate defenses.[10]

Regulatory Approval Unit

Pharmaceutical companies traditionally set up a separate organizational unit to focus on government regulatory approvals; consumer marketers have rarely done so. As marketers diversify into the nutrition, environmental, and cosmetic product markets, however, such units may aid in providing the necessary expertise. In 1990, Procter & Gamble Co. (P&G) created a Regulatory and Clinical Development Group to prepare P&G's submissions to regulatory agencies worldwide and to work with these agencies throughout the approval process.[11]

Product Design

Potential liability for design defects constitutes the most significant basis for product liability.[12] Marketers can contribute to the preparation of a well-documented safety analysis throughout the design process. In their doing so, attention should focus on the standards of the industry, state-of-the-art considerations, and tests used by the courts to determine whether a product design is legally defective.

Although the prevailing standards of the industry are not considered conclusive evidence of due care, considerable weight is given to such evidence. Nevertheless, the testimony of expert witnesses that the standard fails to ensure safety and that precautionary measures are feasible will permit a finding of negligence. To avoid such liability, it is useful, therefore, to examine the scientific and professional literature in the field in order to determine appropriate standards.

In the context of product liability law, *state of the art* refers to that scientific knowledge and technology that were available to a manufacturer at the time that manufacturer introduced its product into the stream of commerce. In negligence cases, a manufacturer could respond to a claim of negligence in designing its product by offering evidence to show that at the time of its introduction onto the market, the product was partaking of the latest technological advances and was therefore as safe as the reasonable manufacturer could make. However, the courts have rejected state-of-the-art defenses in many product liability cases in which an entire industry has failed to incorporate readily available design changes or other improvements it either knew or should have known about.

The Duty to Warn

During the past twenty years, the duty to warn has been significantly emphasized in product liability litigation. Such cases have proliferated for several reasons: Failure-to-warn cases are less technical and less expensive to prosecute than design defect cases, and there is widespread recognition that almost all products capable of causing injuries could be made less hazardous by giving effective warnings to users. Manufacturers may be held liable for their failure to warn of product dangers or for providing inadequate warranties under negligence, strict liability, and breach-of-implied-warranty theories. Thus, satisfaction of these duties is described as a manufacturer's informational obligation.[13]

Negligence. Under negligence principles, manufacturers must warn of product risks when they know or should know that without warnings, the product is likely dangerous for the use for which it is supplied. Manufacturers should know information that is obtainable from reasonable inquiry of experts and from a reasonable search of the scientific literature. The duty to warn turns here on whether the injury was reasonable foreseeable by the manufacturer in one of two ways: Was the product being used in a foreseeable manner? Was the injury itself reasonably foreseeable?

Risk/Utility Balancing. This theory is used in considering the manufacturer's duty to warn under negligence principles. Among the relevant factors to be considered are the likelihood that the product would cause consumers harm and the seriousness of that harm, whether or not these things outweigh the burden on the manufacturer to design a product that would have prevented that harm. Considerations are the technological and practical feasibility of a safer-designed product, the effect of a proposed alternative design, and the additional harms that might result from an alternative design. Such an analysis can benefit from input by the marketing department in combination with the information submitted by various other entities such as the engineering, manufacturing, purchasing, and legal departments.

Strict Liability. The difference between strict liability theories and negligence theories in warning cases is basic: in strict liability cases, manufacturers' knowledge of product dangers is assumed or imputed, whereas in negligence cases, plaintiffs must prove that manufacturers knew or should have known of dangers.

The consumer expectations test is the most prevalent means for determining whether a product is unreasonably dangerous. It is derived from 402A, which defines *unreasonably dangerous* products as those dangerous to an extent beyond that which would be contemplated by the ordinary consumer who purchases it or those in a condition not contemplated by the ultimate customer.

Breach of Implied Warranty. This is the least-utilized theory in duty-to-warn cases, since the seller's obligation is limited to providing a merchantable or fit product at the time of the sale. If a product is not considered unreasonably dangerous at the time it leaves the manufacturer, it cannot later become unreasonably dangerous due to lack of warnings.

Defenses to Duty to Warn.[14] The best defense to alleged failure to warn is for the manufacturer to convey adequate warnings to foreseeable product users. However, there are a number of affirmative defenses available. For example, manufacturers have no duty to warn of hazards that are obvious to ordinary consumers or to knowledgeable or sophisticated users. Sophisticated users are those who, by reason of experience or knowledge, possess greater knowledge of a product's dangers than does the general public. Thus, when a manufacturer markets a product to members of a trade or profession and the product dangers are well-known to such customers, there is no duty to warn.

Consumer Research

Consumer behavior research can be applied to examination of issues relating to the consumer's conduct in establishing product liability. Several research questions such as the following can address this area:[15]

- Did the consumer behave unreasonably in disregarding the obvious defect or in voluntarily exposing himself or herself to an obvious and potentially dangerous situation?
- Could the manufacturer have reached the final consumer to be sure the latter was exposed to a warning?
- Was it foreseeable that a person with the consumer's background would use the product?

Marketers, too, can conduct research in order to aid in determining such foreseeability. To do so it is necessary to identify the product's ultimate customers, customers' needs and reasonable expectations, and the uses and possible misuses of the product. The environment in which the product will operate, existing regulations, and pending legislation must also be considered.

Many of the defenses-to-product-liability complaints relate to the actions of consumers. These defenses include the following.[16]

Contributory or Comparative Negligence. If a supplier can show that customers' own carelessness exposed them to harm, then contributory negligence may bar these customers' recovery. However, under product liability statutes that are designed to protect themselves, contributory negligence may not be a defense. In comparative negligence, the award is simply reduced by the consumer's proportion of the fault involved.

Assumption of Risk. When consumers are injured after voluntarily assuming a known risk, they will be barred from recovery under both strict liability and negligence. For this defense to be successful, the seller must show that consumers had actual knowledge of the risk they were taking.

Misuse, Abuse, or Modification of the Product. In a defense that claims misuse of a product by a consumer, the key issue is foreseeability. If a misuse is foreseeable, the manufacturer must design the product to be safe during this misuse or must specifically warn against the misuse. For example, a screwdriver must be designed so that it can both pry open paint cans and safely turn screws. However, if the harm that can befall a consumer is remote or unforeseeable, liability will not be imposed. A seller may be exonerated from product liability when a product is altered after leaving the seller's hands. Such alteration must be substantial and must be the cause of the injury in order to relieve a seller of liability.

The problem of the unusually susceptible consumer arises most frequently in the area of cosmetics. The general rule is that an idiosyncratic, hypersensitive, or allergic consumer may not recover in a product liability case. However, there may be a duty to warn such individuals.

The sophisticated-user defense provides the manufacturer with an additional defense in failure-to-warn cases, because such users have the sophisticated knowledge to understand any risks associated with the product.

PRODUCT LIABILITY AMONG CHANNEL MEMBERS

Product liability extends to all members of the distributive chain. Such liability increases as channel members become more involved with one another's activities. In trademark franchises, for example, the goods are manufactured by a trademark owner and sold in a distribution franchise, and such manufacturers and all those afterward along the chain of distribution may be jointly, severally, and strictly liable for damages consequently suffered by the consumer. Even when dangerously defective goods are manufactured by a franchisee and sold with the franchisor's trademark clearly associated with them, the trend of recent cases is to hold the franchisee and franchisor equally liable for injuries consequently suffered, regardless of whether or not the owner of the mark exerted any actual control over the manufacturing process. When a dress worn by a woman caught fire at a party, Joseph Bancroft & Sons was held liable for injuries because the dress was made by one of its licensees and carried a hangtag market *BAN-LON*, a Bancroft trademark.

A franchisor can minimize the risks of product liability by carefully preparing the trademark licensing agreement. The agreement must specify minimum quality standards for the manufactured goods and should describe the sanctions to be applied for failure to meet those standards; generally, sanctions should include revocation of the license if the standards are not maintained.[17]

Franchisors might also specify that licensees shall indemnify them for any judgments they are required to pay because of substandard goods the franchisees sold that were not supplied by the trademark owners. If the franchisee is selling goods that are not intended to be identified by the licensed trademark, the franchisor should take steps to alert the public to that fact, for example, by insisting on the posting of appropriate signs or other notices at point of sale.

Wholesalers' Responses

Wholesalers can be held responsible for product-related injuries when a product is said to have been defectively designed, labeled, or tested. Strict liability has been imposed even when the wholesaler had neither control of a defective product's development nor a realistic opportunity to discover its dangerousness.[18] A wholesaler who had never removed a hammer from the box in which it was received but who merely shipped it on to the retailer was found liable for injuries caused by the hammer. A jury verdict of $50,000 was awarded against the manufacturer, the wholesaler, and the retailer when an individual was blinded by a chip of the hammer that flew off as he was using it to strike a piece of metal.

Wholesalers are exposed to liability even when they never had possession of the product that caused the injury. When a jobber ordered a dynamite fuse from a wholesaler, the wholesaler simply passed the order on to the manufacturing company, which shipped the fuse directly to the jobber. The wholesaler never possessed the fuse but did pay the manufacturer's invoice and billed the jobber. The dynamite exploded prematurely, killing nearby workers. Citing S402A, a California court allowed recovery against the wholesaler.

The extension of liability to nonmanufacturing sellers has caused wholesalers to attempt to exercise more influence in a product's manufacture or labeling. Such wholesalers have therefore become even more vulnerable to litigation. To minimize this potential, wholesalers should familiarize themselves with the issues discussed earlier: design, warnings, and foreseeability of use.

Retailers' Responsibilities

Retailers have been considered liable for negligent misrepresentation. A purchaser of an auto was injured when, in spite of the dealer's assurances that no problem existed, the steering gear of his new car finally locked and caused a crash. The court said, "Negligence may be inferred not only from Hackensack's failure or refusal to repair or even examine the reported defect, but also from its representation to Alphonse that the steering deficiency was normal and should cause him no concern."[19]

Retailers are also liable on strict tort grounds or for breach of warranty. In a case involving a car dealer, a court gave policy reasons for imposing strict tort liability upon all types of retailers. "Retailers . . . are an integral part of the overall producing and marketing enterprise that should bear the cost of injuries resulting from defective products. In some cases the retailer may be the only member of that enterprise reasonably available to the injured plaintiff. In other cases the retailer himself may play a substantial part in insuring that the product is safe or may be in a position to exert pressure on the manufacturer to that end; the retailer's strict liability thus serves as an added incentive to safety."

Retailers have recourse through actions against the manufacturer or distributor responsible for the defect. However, retailers should become involved in helping to eliminate defects by careful examination of products for safety defects and by immediately reporting any complaints to manufacturers.

Potential Damages for Product Liability Claims

Efforts to avoid product liability claims are economically sound. The potential for damages is significant, because damages can be recovered for losses, injuries, and, on occasion, emotional distress. In addition, punitive (or exemplary) damages can be awarded for gross carelessness or malice in product liability cases. Such damages are considered desirable so as to punish for prior conduct and to prevent future misconduct. Although punitive damages have not been awarded frequently in the past, they have tended to increase in recent years. Marketing behavior also can lead to punitive damages, including such practices as postsale failure to warn, conscious failure to warn, intentionally misleading advertising, and blatant salesperson lies.[20]

GLOBAL ISSUES

Product liability issues may vary among nations, but it is important to note that a Directive on product liability was adopted by the Council of Ministers of the European Community in 1985. By now, most of the member states have adopted legislation to comply with the provisions of this Directive.[21]

Although product liability legislation is generally associated with consumer protection, the Directive does not focus on that issue alone. In fact, one of its declared objectives is to harmonize the rules and regulations of the twelve member states with regard to product liability. Two basic issues involved in the Directive should be noted: the concept of product liability and the meaning of strict liability.

Essentially, product liability refers to the liability of a producer for personal damage or property damage caused by a defective product during use or consumption of the product. With regard to the Directive, it is of no importance whether or not the defective product is intended for industrial use or for use by consumers.

The liability under the Directive is the so-called strict liability used in the United States. This means that no fault on the part of the producer is required for the liability to come into effect. Although this is common in the United States, it tends to be a more severe product liability requirement than the member states have been used to. However, it should be understood that this does not mean absolute liability when no defenses would be allowed, as there still are certain circumstances in which the liability of the producer can be lifted.

International marketers should explore these requirements in detail and determine how requirements differ in various countries.

HANDLING COMPLAINTS

In recent years, the importance of appropriate complaint handling has increased. A formalized procedure for monitoring consumer problems and complaints and for providing necessary information can help avoid both product recalls and product liability. This procedure requires an effective system both for receiving feedback so as to ensure that products perform adequately and safely in service and for monitoring of complaints. When a complaint or other user feedback is received, steps should be taken to evaluate the cause of the problem and to determine the measures to be taken in order to prevent similar problems in the future.

Marketing personnel should be encouraged to pass along on a regular basis information about potential product difficulties. An internal information system headed by an internal committee is a useful mechanism for collecting and distributing all information related to product difficulties. The committee can authorize additional testing of any product—new or already marketed. The committee should also be responsible for clearing all label and/or instruction wording as well as all promotional and advertising material that implies any type of warranty.[22]

Other proactive strategies include (1) training salespersons not to lessen the impact of warnings and (2) disseminating advertising programs that encourage reasonable product use.

PRODUCT RECALLS

Occasionally manufacturers find it necessary to recall products. Such recalls may be initiated under federal statutes by federal regulatory agencies. The Food and Drug Administration (FDA) can request the court to order recalls of food, drugs, or cosmetics. The Consumer Product Safety Commission can request voluntary recalls and order corrective action. The National Highway Traffic Safety Administration and the Environmental Protection Agency can order recalls.

Recalls frequently occur when a product hazard exists. Automobiles may turn out to be faulty in their performance and subject to recall. Boats and mobile homes are subject to statutory recalls. Products may be recalled as a result of tampering within distribution channels, as in the case of Tylenol. However, safety is not the only basis on which recalls can be required. Companies that infringe on another's trademark or package design may be required to recall their products. The FDA can recall products that are mislabeled; for example, it seized Citrus Hill orange juice when Procter & Gamble did not remove questionable freshness claims.

Preventing Recalls

Recalls not only are costly but also may serve to tarnish the image of a company due to unfavorable publicity. Moreover, recalls create the potential for product liability claims. A good preventive strategy involves a company-wide commitment to quality control and adequate testing. The company's intermediaries should be encouraged to keep careful inventory records so that if a problem arises, the location of goods can be easily tracked.

When a manufacturer becomes aware of a defective product, even though recalls have not been initiated, actions should be taken to avoid potential liability. At a minimum, they should include:

1. Offers to repair the product at no cost to the purchaser
2. Communications concerning the offer of free repairs in time to prevent accidents
3. Warnings of the risks and damages involved in continuing to use the product without repair

Responding to Recalls

Several procedures can be useful in minimizing the impact of recalls. Many firms are expanding their insurance coverage so that they may recover their loss of profits, the advertising expense for repairing a tarnished image, and the expenses of getting the product back on the market after recalls.

A useful strategy is the establishment of a crisis committee, which can develop techniques for handling recall situations. Jackson and Morgan offer

a number of specific measures for implementing a recall process; their recommendations include the following:[23]

1. Determine whether the danger should be downplayed or stated directly.
2. Ensure that the first announcement reaches as many people as
   possible.
3. Tell consumers the consequences of continuing to use the
   product, and give retailers the information to pass along to in-
   quiring consumers. Notify distributors.
4. Review current and planned communication programs to ensure
   they do not encourage consumers to purchase faulty goods.
5. Compensate customers for recalled goods.
6. Put in place a cooperating network including marketing intermediaries for the recall process.

TAMPERED PACKAGES

Despite the care exercised by manufacturers to prevent the distribution of
faulty products, once the commercialization process is begun, the possibility
exists that goods may be adulterated by persons outside the standard channel
of distribution. Widespread awareness of the possibility of product tampering occurred in 1982, when the deaths of seven Chicago area residents
who had taken Extra-Strength Tylenol capsules laced with potassium
cyanide shocked the nation. The incident cost Johnson & Johnson over $100
million as well as damage to its goodwill and reputation.[24]

As a result of the Tylenol tampering and a wave of copycat incidents, in
1983 Congress passed the federal Anti-Tampering Act. The act is designed
to restrain and penalize individuals who may attempt to contaminate goods.
It provides sanctions for tampering with products with intent either to cause
death or injury or to damage the reputation of a business. The act also sets
penalties for making a false claim of a tampering that, if true, would pose a
hazard to human safety. Although the focus of this act is on criminals, marketers who face serious economic consequences from tampering can design
programs to help prevent such occurrences.

Morgan offers a number of recommendations for marketers that can aid
in improving the tamper-resistant capabilities of their packages and help
minimize tampering opportunities.[25]

1. The firm can focus on developing packages that minimize the possibility of unnoticed tampering. This requires careful monitoring of
   packaging regulations and pending legislation, investigating techno-

logical innovations in packaging, and designing programs for developing new package technology that can make tampering obvious.

2. Channel members should be alerted to the possibility of goods tampering, particularly since intermediaries can become codefendants in tampering lawsuits if they allowed the tamperer access to goods.[26] Intermediaries should be encouraged to assist in tamper-proofing efforts by establishing security measures that would minimize the accessibility of goods to potential tamperers.

3. Consumer cooperation should also be secured through consumer education programs such as those conducted by trade associations that communicate tampering-awareness to consumers.

Crisis teams may be of particular use when tampering occurs. In June of 1993, a number of claims were made that syringes and hypodermic needles were found in Pepsi-Cola and Diet Pepsi-Cola. In what has been called a "textbook case of how to come through a PR crisis,"[27] shortly after the report appeared, Pepsi-Cola Co. assembled a crisis team of twelve executives. The following evening, Pepsi-Cola North America President and CEO Craig Weatherup appeared on network newscasts, with video footage showing how Pepsi-Cola products are bottled. The process, in which cans are turned upside down and filled within seconds, leaves no room for foreign objects to be inserted. Pepsi also instituted a discount coupon program. The FDA ultimately helped to resolve the tampering product issue when the head of the agency declared that the FDA could not confirm a single tampering report.

Pepsi-Cola estimates that the June syringe hoax cost the company and its bottlers about $35 million in lost sales and increased expenses. However, Pepsi's July and August sales were up 7% from the prior year, the biggest gain since it started keeping such records in 1989.

SUMMARY

Product liability law involves injuries caused by products that are defectively manufactured, processed, and distributed. Traditional product liability theories of recovery include breach of warranty, negligence, and strict liability.

Marketers can adopt a number of measures in response to product liability issues. To aid in meeting government requirements, a regulatory approval unit can be established. During the design process, marketers can contribute to the preparation of a well-documented safety analysis. Marketing research can offset the potential for product liability claims. Marketers should be aware of the significant potential for damages in product liability cases.

Despite all efforts to eliminate product problems during the product development and test-marketing stages, the potential for consumer complaints exists, as does the possibility of product recalls. Marketers should be involved in the creation of a formalized procedure for monitoring consumer problems and complaints. In addition, a formalized procedure should be established to handle product recalls, and a crisis committee should design appropriate techniques for that process.

CASE
Griggs *v.* Bic Corp. *BNA, 61 USLW 2415 (CA 3, No. 92-7213, 12/31/92).*

FACTS

An infant sustained serious injuries when his three-year-old stepbrother ignited a disposable butane cigarette lighter, causing a fire in his home. The infant's parents sued the lighter manufacturer, alleging that the failure to manufacture a childproof lighter constituted both defective and negligent design. According to a district court, the manufacturer had no duty, under Pennsylvania strict liability law, to manufacture a lighter resistant to child play. The court also found that the manufacturer was not liable on the negligence claim.

The parents appealed.

ISSUES

1. Is the manufacturer strictly liable to unintended users of its products?

2. Is the manufacturer liable in negligence for creating unreasonable risk of foreseeable harm to a broader range of foreseeable users, including children?

HOLDING

1. No. The manufacturer of cigarette lighters that are not designed to be childproof may not be held strictly liable, under Pennsylvania law, to unintended users of its product, such as children.

2. Yes. The manufacturer may be held liable in negligence for creating unreasonable risk of foreseeable harm to a broader range of foreseeable users, including children.

REASONING

The Pennsylvania Supreme Court has adopted Section 402A of the Second Restatement of Torts as the law of strict product liability in Pennsylvania. It has held that Section 402A imposes strict liability in tort for injuries caused by defective manufacture or design of products. The Pennsylvania Supreme Court has stated that strict liability requires only two elements of proof: that the product was defective and that the defect was the proximate cause of the plaintiff's injuries.

The appeals court reviewed the district court's findings on strict liability. The district court had concluded that "a product may not be deemed defective unless it is unreasonably dangerous to *intended users*." Because children are not intended users, the manufacturer is not strictly liable. The parents also alleged that the manufacturer is strictly liable under Section 402A because it designed a lighter unreasonably dangerous to foreseeable users: young children. However, there was no evidence to support the contention that in Pennsylvania a manufacturer has a duty in strict liability law to guard against foreseeable use by unintended users. The appeals court affirmed the district court's holding that the manufacturer was not strictly liable.

In discussing the issue of negligence, the appeals court noted the difference between strict liability and negligence under Pennsylvania law. In strict liability, the focus is on a defect in product, regardless of fault, and defect is determined in relation to a subset of the general population: the intended user who puts the product to its intended use. In negligence, the focus is on the reasonableness of manufacturer's conduct, and this reasonableness is determined in relation to a different subset of the general population—one that is generally broader: anyone who foreseeably may be subject to unreasonable risk of foreseeable harm.

The appeals court noted that the manufacturer had conceded foreseeability for purposes of its summary judgment motion. A finding of duty in negligence would turn on whether the foreseeable risks were unreasonable. The classic model for analyzing this aspect of negligence law is the risk-utility form of analysis, which balances the risk in light of social value threatened and of the probability and extent of the harm to society, against the social utility of sales of lighters without childproof features.

Based on Consumer Product Safety Commission reports, the gravity of the possible harm—in terms of both personal injury and property damage by child-play fires—is appreciable, recurring, and serious. The social value of the safety to be secured is indisputably high. The social utility of sales without childproof features may be minimal; the social consequences of such sales may be catastrophic. Thus, according to the court, the risk of harm with respect to duty may indeed be unreasonable. The court remanded the negligence claim for further proceedings.

DISCUSSION QUESTIONS

Discuss the various product liability theories, with specific emphasis on negligence and strict liability.

What kinds of research can manufacturers conduct to aid in offsetting product liability claims?

CASE
James M. Pree *v.* Brunswick Corporation *(CA-8, No. 91-3042 January 7, 1993), 983 F. 2d 863,* CCH Product Liability Reports, #13,476 *(July 1993).*

FACTS

James Pree was injured in 1985 when he fell from the back of a 1985 Wellcraft Scarab pleasure boat owned by Todd Beckman. Beckman was attempting to dock the boat, which was powered by twin Mercury Marine 330 horsepower motors. It was raining, the water was choppy, and there was some lightning. As Beckman backed the boat into the slip, he asked Pree to "get the back of the boat." Pree was standing on the swim platform on the back of the boat. As he reached out to grab the dock pole, the boat suddenly moved forward, and Pree fell off the boat into the water. Pree was severely injured by the unguarded, rotating propeller blades. He suffered compound fractures, cut tendons, and permanent muscle and nerve damage.

In 1989, Pree filed suit in the Circuit Court of the City of Saint Louis, Missouri, against Brunswick, the parent company of Mercury Marine, the designer and manufacturer of the motors and the drive mechanism, which required a propeller. In September 1991, the case was tried in the district court. Evidence was presented that Pree had been drinking various alcoholic beverages all day and well into the night shortly before the accident. The district court also heard expert testimony from both sides on whether the twin engines had been defectively designed. The district court gave the following contributory-fault instruction to the jury:

> Your verdict must be for [appellee Brunswick] if you believe:
> First, when plaintiff James Pree was standing on the swim platform at the rear of the boat, plaintiff knew of the danger of

coming in contact with the propellers and appreciated the danger. And second, plaintiff James Pree voluntarily and unreasonably exposed himself to such danger. And third, such conduct directly caused or directly contributed to cause any damage plaintiff James Pree may have sustained.

The Jury returned a general verdict in favor of Brunswick. James Pree appealed.

ISSUES

Can James Pree recover under the theory of strict liability for a defective design? Missouri law requires that a plaintiff prove the following elements:

1. [the] defendant sold the product in the course of its business;
2. the product was then in a defective condition [and] unreasonably dangerous when put into a reasonably anticipated use;
3. the product was used in a manner reasonably anticipated;
4. [the] plaintiff was damaged as a direct result of such defective condition as existed when the product was sold.

HOLDING

No. James Pree cannot recover under the theory of defective design.

REASONING

For purposes of imposing liability under Missouri's law of strict liability, a product's design is deemed defective when it is shown that the way the product has been designed renders it "unreasonably dangerous." Missouri courts have left the meaning of *unreasonably dangerous* to the common sense of the fact finder. A product has been considered defectively designed if it "creates an unreasonable risk of danger to the consumer or user when put to normal use."

The court based its decision on the second element for a defective design. Pree argued that the absence of propeller guards was a design defect that caused the engines to be unreasonably dangerous. Pree further contended he had presented evidence showing that the alternative and safer propeller guard design proposed by him was technically feasible and practical in terms of cost and the overall operation of twin motors.

Brunswick argued that Pree's evidence was insufficient to prove that the engines were defectively designed because the propellers met the reasonable expectations of the ordinary consumer as to safety. Brunswick further argued that a safer, practical, alternative design was not available to Brunswick at the time it manufactured the twin motors.

In reference to a consumer expectations test, the court noted that the Missouri Supreme Court has not adopted this into its lexicon in deciding product liability action; nevertheless, it has not rejected it. In fact, in a number of cases, Missouri courts have concluded that "the plaintiff has the burden of proving that the product was unreasonably dangerous to the extent beyond that which would be contemplated by the user with ordinary knowledge common to the community as to its characteristics."

The consumer expectations test focuses attention on the consumer rather than the manufacturer of the twin engines. A consumer expectations test was applied in a factually similar case in which a court determined, as a matter of law, that a pleasure boat's unguarded propellers were not dangerous beyond the expectations of the ordinary consumer (*Elliott* v. *Brunswick Corp.*) 903 F. 2d 1505 (11th Cir. 1990). In reversing a jury verdict for the plaintiff, the court concluded that there are "certain products whose inherent danger is patent and obvious [and that these products] do not, as a matter of law, involve defects of the sort that a jury should resolve." The court reasoned that some products, by their nature, place both users and bystanders in some measure of danger. "A knife or an axe may cut persons, as well as their intended targets. Fishhooks can wound, saws can maim, and revolving propellers can cause fearful damage. Yet . . . we do not hold manufacturers liable simply because the use of their products involves some risks."

The court declared not only that the evidence presented in the foregoing case supported the jury's verdict but also that the evidence was sufficient for the trial court to hold, as a matter of law, that the unguarded propellers were not unreasonably dangerous beyond the expectations of the ordinary consumer, including Pree.

The district court's judgment in favor of Brunswick was affirmed.

DISCUSSION QUESTIONS

What precautions can marketers take to prevent product liability for design defects?

What is meant by the consumer expectations test and what is its purpose?

ENDNOTES

1. Peter D. Bennett, ed., *Dictionary of Marketing Terms* (Chicago: American Marketing Association, 1988).
2. *MacPherson* v. *Buick Motor Co.*, 111 N.E. 1050 (N.Y. 1916).
3. Robert W. Kasten Jr., "Bring the Law out of the Twilight Zone," *American Bar Association Journal* (February 1984), 12–16.

4. Fred W. Morgan, "Strict Liability and the Marketing of Services vs. Goods: A Judicial Review," *Journal of Public Policy and Marketing* (June 1987), 43–57.

5. *Greenman* v. *Yuba Power Products, Inc.*, 377 P. 2d 897 (Cal. 1963).

6. *Sindell* v. *Abbott Laboratories, Inc.*, Cal. 3d 588, 607 P. 2d 924, 163 Cal. Rptr. 132 (1980).

7. Mary Jane Sheffet, "Market Share Liability: A New Doctrine of Causation in Product Liability," *Journal of Marketing* (Winter 1983), p. 41.

8. *Hymowitz* v. *Eli Lilly & Co.*, 73 NYS2d 487, 541 NYS2d 941 (1989), cert. denied, 110 SCt 350 US (1989).

9. William D. Wilson, "Market Share Liability—Did New York Go Too Far? Hymowitz v. Eli Lilly & Co., *St. John's Law Review* 64 (Winter 1990), 363–377.

10. John C. Mowen, "On the Role of Marketing in the Product Liability Trial," *Journal of Public Policy and Marketing*, 2 (1983), 100–121.

11. Laurie Freeman, "P&G Sets Regulatory Approval Unit," *Advertising Age* (October 29, 1990), 16.

12. Kenneth Ross, "The Role of Attorneys in Product Liability Prevention," *Journal of Products Liability* 6 (1983), 2.

13. Douglas R. Richmond, "Products Liability: Corporate Successors and the Duty to Warn," *Baylor Law Review* 45 (1993), 535–584.

14. Ibid., pp. 545–553.

15. Paul L. Price and Mark D. Roth, "Products Liability Defenses," *Federation Insurance and Corporate Counsel Quarterly* (Winter 1989), 201–218.

16. William H. Volz, "Advising the Wholesaler on Product Liability Exposure," *Journal of Products Liability* 6 (1982), 112.

17. John W. Behringer and Monica A. Otte, "Liability and the Trademark Licensor: Advice for the Franchisor of Goods or Services," *American Business Law Journal* 19 (1981), 149–150.

18. William H. Volz, "Advising the Wholesaler on Product Liability Exposure," *Journal of Products Liability* 6 (1983), 112.

19. *Pabon* v. *Hackensack Auto Sales, Inc.*, 164 A.2d 773 (N.J. Super. 1960).

20. Fred W. Morgan, "The Evolution of Punitive Damages in Product Liability Litigation for Unprincipled Marketing Behavior," *Journal of Public Policy and Marketing* 8 (1989), 279–293.

21. Hank A. Ritsema, *Product Liability, Marketing and Preventive Measures* (Groningen, The Netherlands: Faculty of Management and Organization, University of Groningen, 1991), pp. 1–18.

22. Terry Morehead Dworkin and Mary Jane Sheffet, "Product Liability in the '80s," *Journal of Public Policy and Marketing* 4 (1985), 69–79.

23. George G. Jackson and Fred W. Morgan, "Responding to Recall Requests: A Strategy for Managing Goods Withdrawal," *Journal of Public Policy and Marketing* 7 (1988), 152–165.

24. Paul D. Buhl, "Protecting Business Entities under the Federal Anti-Tampering Act," *Journal of Legislation* 11 (1984), 393–402.

25. Fred W. Morgan, "Tampered Goods: Legal Developments and Marketing Guidelines, " *Journal of Marketing* 52 (April 1988), 86–96.

26. *Baughman* v. *General Motors Corp.* (1985), 627 F. Supp. 871 (D. S. C.).

27. Mercy Mergiera, "Pepsi weathers tampering hoaxes," *Advertising Age*, June 21, 1993.

CHAPTER FIVE
Product Decisions: Protecting the Product

During all the stages of the new product planning process, special attention should be paid to protecting the new product ideas from competitive acquisition. In an economy increasingly based on information and technology, most of a company's wealth is often embodied in product ideas. New products can be generated in the form of inventions, literary or artistic works, or other commercially valuable concepts.

Legal areas relative to product protection include patents, copyrights, and trademarks—traditionally considered forms of intellectual property. It should be understood that the property of intellectual property does not have the concrete form of real property (which refers to land and things that are permanently attached to land); in fact, the aforementioned three legal areas constitute a highly abstract concept of property. However, despite the fact that the term *intellectual property* is relatively abstract, it is not unfamiliar.

Technological innovations are being protected in increasing numbers. In 1990, some 174,700 patents were filed in the United States—an increase of 39% over 1985. The proportion of U.S. patents earned by American inventors is inching upward.[1] In 1993, IBM secured the most U.S. patents of any company. The number of copyrights registered has also increased significantly. In its efforts to maintain competition, the U.S. government does not generally favor protecting work from imitation. However, to encourage the advancement of technology and to promote the creative arts, several bodies of law provide varying degrees of protection for these forms of intellectual effort: patents are granted to inventors, and copyrights are offered to artists, composers, and other creative workers. Copyrights and patents are also available for product labels and packaging.

Not only does the government offer protection of a work from imitation, but it also provides a means for preventing the identification of a work from being acquired by others. Thus trademarks are also designated a form of intellectual property.[2]

PATENTS

Federal patent protection is the exclusive method for retaining rights to publicly disclosed inventions in the United States (states cannot confer patent rights). In Article I, Section 8, the U.S. Constitution provides "The Congress shall have Power . . . To promote the Progress of Science and useful Arts, by securing for limited Times to Authors and Inventors the exclusive Right to their respective Writings and Discoveries."

Under congressional enactments, a patent permits a firm to secure a monopoly or the exclusive use of an invention for a period of seventeen years, which is generally not renewable. However, firms often extend this protection by patenting improvements on their original idea. In the United States, within the limits laid down by the courts, owners of patents may refuse to work them, may work them themselves and refuse to license them to others, or may license them on such terms as they may choose.

Although the underlying policy of the antitrust and trade regulation laws in the United States is the prevention and condemnation of monopolies, patent laws openly grant a monopoly to an inventor. The courts have long struggled with these competing policies in an effort to harmonize them. A basic purpose of the patent system is to encourage the development of technology. In addition, since patent applications are public documents containing complete descriptions of new inventions, information about these inventions, when published, is disclosed to everyone and can therefore be used to aid in the creation of new technological developments.

There are two basic justifications for patent protection: (1) the bargain, or contract, theory and (2) the natural rights theory.[3] The bargain theory is based on the premise that people will have an incentive to create new inventions if there is some reward. This is supported in part by the text of the Constitution, which encourages the useful arts by awarding an exclusive right to exploit an invention for a definite length of time. Under the natural rights theory, a product of mental labor is by right the property of the person who created it. The inventor, therefore, has no obligation to disclose anything and has every right to be compensated for the invention. To allow other inventors to build upon the earlier creation, the government requests disclosure but ensures the exclusive right to profit from the earlier invention.

These two theories are partially incomplete and somewhat inconsistent with each other. Under the bargain theory, the inventor must accept the government bargain or have no protection for an invention. Under the natural rights theory, it is not clear how the government can declare the invention public property after the patent expires. However, these explanations seem supported by both common sense and reason. Furthermore, data by commentators seem to support the proposition that the U.S. patent system has been successful in creating the incentive for more and greater inventions. Countries with less developed patent systems appear less successful in encouraging patentable inventions.

Kinds of Patents

There are three kinds of patents. In ascending order, based on the number granted, they are utility patents, design patents, and plant patents. By far the most frequently sought type of patent is the utility patent, which includes machines, industrial processes, compositions of matter, and articles of manufacture. Recently, for the first time, a utility patent was granted for an animal called a transgenic nonhuman mammal—a genetically developed mouse that is sensitive to cancer-causing chemicals.

Design patents protect the appearance or shape, rather than the function, of articles such as soft drink bottles or dining room chairs. If in fact the design is functional rather than ornamental, the patent is invalid.

Plant patents are awarded for the discovery of certain naturally occurring, and previously uncultivated, plants or for the breeding of novel plants that may be asexually propagated.

Securing the Patent

Patent applications are filed with the Patent and Trademark Office (PTO) of the U.S. Department of Commerce, but no rights immediately accrue. Under the patent act, those who wish to obtain a patent must satisfy certain requirements. Patentees must demonstrate that they have developed a new, useful, and nonobvious process or product (35 U.S. C.A. Sec. 101). To do so, a patent application containing specifications that describe how the invention works must be provided. A second part to this application consists of claims that are the actual patentable features of the invention. Such claims must meet the general standards of utility, novelty, and nonobviousness. Utility is present when an invention has a direct benefit to humanity, novelty requires an invention to be different from prior art, and nonobviousness requires that at the time the invention was made, the subject matter as a whole would not have been obvious to a person having ordinary skill in an area to which the subject matter pertains.

Patent Protection

At an early stage, a company's idea for a new invention is probably in too sketchy a form for a patent to be filed. It may be difficult to determine how to put the idea in practice, and it may not be certain the idea can work at all. Nevertheless, it it vital that the idea be kept secret so that it can remain protected information. To maintain secrecy, those involved in discussing the idea must agree to keep the information confidential, and the employees assigned to developing the product must do the same. Any documents that reveal the idea should be treated as confidential. If employees who know about the product leave the company to work for a competitor before the product is launched, those individuals must be warned that the information is confidential and must not be imparted to the new employer.[4]

Once the idea has been developed into a design, it is potentially patentable, and an investigation into the relevant prior art must be made. This research is frequently done by a patent attorney or agent, aided by the company's design engineers who have knowledge of the literature on the subject. If any potentially troublesome patents are found in the search, a patent attorney's opinion is required, both as the effects of those patents on the patentability of the company's planned design and as to whether the company's design might infringe any of those patents.

The best time to consider applying for a patent is when there is an operative prototype, since at this early stage of development there is much less loss of patent rights through nonconfidential disclosures. The nearer the product is to an official launch, the greater the risk of nonauthorized disclosure of the design.

The patent office examines the application and conducts a search of past patents and of relevant technical literature to ascertain whether the new invention is patentable. The examiner frequently denies patentability to some, or perhaps all, of the claims, and the application may then be revised. This process may go back and forth several times until the patentee and the examiner are in agreement.

Patent rights expire seventeen years after issuance. They may expire earlier through judicial invalidation in the course of infringement proceedings. Such invalidations are common because the patent office has limited expertise in the relevant prior art compared to a competitor in the industry who is challenging the patent. However, a 1982 reorganization of the patent courts created a single Court of Appeals. The court streamlined the appeals process by establishing a unified standard that had been lacking.[5]

Protection from Infringement

Securing and maintaining patent protection is a necessary and financially significant process for an organization. For example, if an invention is put up for sale, used publicly, or described in a publication before a patent application is filed, potential protection is instantly lost throughout much of the world. However, the United States permits a one-year grace period.

Kinds of Infringement. Infringement occurs only if someone other than the patent holder exercises one of the patentee's three exclusive rights: making, using, or selling the product. It is only the patent device that can be infringed, not a smaller, unpatented part of it. Anyone who, without permission, makes, uses, or sells a patented invention is a direct infringer of the patent. When someone actively encourages another to make, use, or sell an invention without permission, the individual providing the inducement is liable for indirect infringement. Knowingly selling a nonstaple item for which the only or the predominant use is in connection with a patented invention is contributory infringement.

A direct infringer need have no knowledge of the patent and cannot offer a defense based on good faith or ignorance. However, in order to recover money damages, the patent owner must have marked a product invention with notice of the patent or must have given actual notice to an infringer. A patent owner legitimately can sue for contributory infringement if someone is selling a nonstaple item whose only substantial use is in connection with the patented device.

Remedies for Infringement. Remedies for infringement under the patent act are injunctive relief, damages, attorney's fees in exceptional cases, and costs. The usual standard for preliminary injunctions—"likelihood of success on the merits" (in a suit)—does not apply to patent cases. Instead, to secure an injunction, the patent owner must demonstrate "beyond question that the patent is valid and infringement" has occurred.

Damages are authorized under the patent act "in no event less than a reasonable royalty for the use made of the invention by the infringer together with interest." Attorney's fees may be granted to either the plaintiff or the defendant in exceptional cases. Exceptional fees are granted the plaintiff in a case involving knowing infringement. Such fees may be granted to the defendant "when the plaintiff has acquired [a] patent by fraud or brings an infringement suit with no good faith belief that [the] patent is valid and infringed."[6]

Patents have the attributes of one's personal property (however, they are called intellectual effort), and other persons may be prevented from making, using, or selling the protected subject matter for the duration of the patent.

Should others infringe on a patent, the owner can institute suit to secure an injunction and recovery of up to three times the damages: In 1990, inventor Robert Kearns was awarded a $10-million judgment against Ford for Ford's violation of Kearns's patent on intermittent windshield wipers. In 1991, Intex Plastics was ordered to pay inventor Charles Hall $5 million in damages for violating his patent on the water bed. In 1992, L.A. Gear agreed to pay $1 million and additional licensing fees to settle claims that it had infringed on Reebok International Ltd.'s patent on its Pump shoes. Recently, Kodak agreed to settle a fifteen-year-old suit for infringing on seven Polaroid instant-photography patents in the amount of $925 million.

Infringement Defenses. Patents can be licensed, and the transaction usually amounts to a promise not to sue for infringement, subject to a payment of royalties. The fact that a patent is involved in a licensing agreement does not mean the transaction is immune from federal antitrust and trade regulatory laws. However, the licensing agreement does not mean the transaction is subject to the prohibitions of these laws. In fact, patent law authorize practices that, in nonpatent transactions, might violate federal antitrust and trade regulatory laws. Nevertheless, attention must be paid to antitrust restrictions in licensing agreements. A violation of the Sherman Act, for example, can bar a patentee from suing for infringement of a patent or enforcing a licensing agreement. The courts may require compulsory licensing of a patent when a company violates the law, particularly if the exchange of patents is used to carry out a conspiracy in restraint of trade.

A defense to infringement is patent misuse. This means that the patent owner has done more than legitimately is authorized by the patent monopoly. Misuse assumes infringement but immunizes the infringer. It prevents patentees from securing relief because of their culpable misconduct. The patent-misuse doctrine developed as a judicial response to the perceived anticompetitive practices of patent owners. It was believed that the patent owner might be able to engage in practices that extended to the patent monopoly beyond its lawful scope.[7] Patent misuse is considered an affirmative defense to a suit for patent infringement or for royalties due under a patent licensing agreement. The courts have considered a claim of patent misuse as valid when patent owners have attempted to use their patents to accomplish price-fixing, tie-ins, and territorial restrictions. Although the Patent Misuse

Reform Act of 1988 eliminated the presumption that use of a patent license to create a tie-in is per se misuse, it did not eliminate the patent-misuse defense. Currently, therefore, a patent tie-in is subject to rule-of-reason analysis in a determination of whether there has been misuse.

Alternative Dispute Resolution for Patent Conflicts

ADR, discussed earlier, may be particularly useful in patent disputes, which can take decades to resolve in the courts and can occupy one-third of a patent's life.[8] Accordingly, in creating contracts with licensees, patent owners should make clear the dispute resolution procedures.

Patent disputes often involve specialized, complex issues of law and technology unknown to most trial court judges. Arbitration provides an opportunity to select an arbitrator with expertise in a particular field. Arbitration of patent disputes also helps to preserve relationships and avoid the spotlight of publicity.

Suggested Changes in Patent Law

In 1992, a Commerce Department advisory commission, in an effort to overhaul U.S. patent law, proposed awarding patents to whoever files first. The proposal is designed to make U.S. patent policies more compatible with others worldwide. Currently, unlike practices in other countries, a U.S. patent is given to whoever first devised an invention. There appears to be growing support for reducing the differences between international patent procedures as a way to boost U.S. competitiveness. The proposal also recommends that patent grants be extended from the current seventeen years to twenty years. This is also designed to conform to global practice. At this writing these proposals have not been implemented.

TRADE SECRETS

Federal patent law provides a method for retaining rights to publicly disclosed inventions. However, should an individual not wish to disclose an invention, a body of state law generally known as the law of trade secrets, protects non–publicly disclosed (nonpatented) inventions, ideas, or information. As indicated, patent law requires disclosure of an invention: trade secret law offers protection from disclosure. Unlike patents, which have a constitutionally mandated, limited life, trade secrets have a potentially perpetual duration.

The major disadvantage of trade secret protection is the suddenness with which the protection can be lost. Whether the trade secret is lost through negligence of the owner, through the illegal acts of another, or through legitimate independent development by another, once a trade secret is in the public domain, it is no longer secret and therefore cannot be protected.

Although the states regulate trade secret law, a Uniform Trade Secrets Act (UTSA) was approved for enactment in all the states in 1979, and clarifying amendments were approved in 1985. The UTSA now constitutes the law governing trade secrets. While the fundamentals are fairly uniform, details may vary from state to state.

Definition of Trade Secret

The most often cited definition of a trade secret is that in the original (1939) Restatement of Torts: "A trade secret may consist of any formula, pattern, device, or compilation of information which is used in one's business, and which gives him an opportunity to obtain an advantage over competitors who do not know or use it." More specifically, a trade secret may be any commercially valuable information, whether in the form of an invention (such as a machine or process), or an industrial or commercial idea (such as a new product concept, the formula for Coca-Cola, or an advertising campaign), or a compilation of data (such as a list of customers or sources of supply). Computer software can be protected under trade secret law. Each software-oriented company may have a body of information that is not generally known to its competitors and that gives it a competitive advantage in the marketplace.

Unlike the federal statutes governing patents, trade secret law is a common law doctrine and varies somewhat from state to state. However, each state's doctrine generally includes the following six factors in determining whether information is protectable by common law as a trade secret:[9]

1. the extent to which the information is known outside [the employer's] business

2. the extent to which it is known by employees and others involved in [the employer's] business

3. the extent of measures taken by [the employer] to guard the secrecy of the information

4. the value of the information to [the employer] and [the employer's] competitors

5. the amount of effort or money expended by [the employer] in developing the information

6. the ease or difficulty with which the information could be properly acquired or duplicated by others

Methods for Protecting Trade Secrets

To protect a trade secret, reasonable security protections must be made to guard it from disclosure. A company must decide which trade secrets are worth protecting and then must act aggressively to protect those secrets. Access to trade secrets should be as limited as possible. Companies should also limit access to the portion of their plant where trade secrets are kept.

Absolute secrecy is not required because the trade secret may be disclosed to employees and others, so long as it is understood that such disclosure is confidential. The fact that others may discover the trade secret will not deprive the secret of protection so long as the other parties are not too numerous and also keep the matter secret.

To counteract the possibility of a claim that an outsider submitted the idea for an internally developed concept, marketers should keep careful records as to the time and place of, and the employees involved in, the discovery of trade secrets.

Nondisclosure Agreements

Employees should be screened carefully, and as few employees as possible should have access to trade secrets. One method for guarding trade secrets from disclosure is to require employees who will have access to secret information to sign a nondisclosure agreement—combined with their employment agreement—promising not to reveal the secret either during the term of their employment or afterward. The following guidelines may be incorporated into a nondisclosure agreement:[10]

- Confidential information should be defined broadly and should include product development information and related agreements.

- Employees are not to use or disclose confidential information to others except if necessary to perform their duties.

- Upon termination of the employment relationship, employees should agree to deliver documents and materials relating to any confidential information.

- Employees should agree not to retain either originals or copies of confidential information.

- Employees should agree to assign to their employer all intellectual property rights in their work.

In a recent case, two former engineers at Texas Instruments were charged with the crime of stealing trade secrets.[11] The engineers claimed that Texas Instruments did not take sufficient steps to safeguard the information it wanted to protect. Although this was partially true, Texas Instruments had required all engineers to sign a nondisclosure agreement when they joined the company and had used an array of security provisions at the plant, such as restricted entry to the lab where engineers worked. The convictions of the engineers have been upheld by the courts.

Protecting Customer Lists

Customer lists are a valued asset for a company. Customer specifications, customer ordering habits, and the identity of a customer's purchasing agent are of significant importance to the success of an enterprise. However, the customer list may be one of the most exposed pieces of critical information in a company's possession and is the most likely to be misused. In order to provide protection against its removal by an employee and subsequent use by a competitor, the list must qualify as a trade secret.[12]

To secure trade secret status for a customer list, attention must be paid to the six major factors listed earlier in defining a trade secret. Their application to customer lists may be somewhat difficult. Trade secret status requires that the information not generally be known to others in the industry. Thus if a competitor can easily duplicate the customer list by reference to telephone directories or trade publications, the information does not qualify as a trade secret. A list consisting of customer names is more difficult to protect than a list that also includes the customer's location, individual buying habits, credit rating, and principal contact.

The time, effort, and capital expended by the employer in developing the customer list is also important. Thus a list of prospects derived from trade listings will not fare as well as a list developed through the screening efforts of the employer's sales staff. Also important are the continual and regular updating of the list and the extent to which the company has clerical staff and equipment to maintain it. Evidence of time and expense in developing the list is also likely to aid in achieving trade secret status.

The general methods for protecting trade secrets must also be applied to protecting customer lists. Nor does the mere determination that the customer list qualifies as a trade secret entitle an employer to relief. However, taking steps to protect the customer list is likely both to aid a company in establishing that an employee acquired the protected information in a wrongful manner and to secure injunctive relief if there exists an imminent threat that the employee will use or disclose the information.

Misappropriation of Trade Secrets

Certain methods of acquiring another's trade secret are clearly improper, will subject one to civil liability, and may result in criminal liability as well.

These include industrial espionage carried out by means of electronic surveillance, planting industrial spies, or bribing another's employees. Inducing former employees to breach an express or implied contract not to disclose their former employer's trade secrets after termination of employment is also actionable. In 1991, two scientists were convicted of conspiracy to sell certain trade secrets of Merck & Co. and Schering Plough in what prosecutors called one of the largest industrial espionage cases in the nation. A former microbiologist with the pharmaceutical companies and another individual were convicted of conspiring to sell the formulas for invermectin (an antiparasitic drug) and interferon (a drug that has shown promise in treating cancer, hepatitis, and ailments associated with AIDS).

A difficult question in the law of trade secrets concerns whether a former employee's use of knowledge gained in the course of the former employment constitutes unacceptable appropriation of a trade secret. Courts consider the extent to which the former employee will be handicapped in seeking new employment if not permitted to utilize certain knowledge. They also consider the extent to which the information the former employer is seeking to protect was developed as a result of the employee's own initiative. If the employee was hired specifically to develop the information, it will generally be held to belong to the employer. Otherwise, employees may be able to claim it as a product of their own knowledge and skill.

Remedies for Misappropriation

Misappropriation of trade secrets gives rise to a number of remedies. The first step in protecting against unauthorized use of a trade secret is to seek a preliminary injunction. If an injunction is granted, it can enjoin the defendant from using the alleged trade secret until there has been an adjudication of the facts. The victim of trade secret misappropriation may also receive compensatory and punitive damages. The trade secret owner can elect the method for calculating the damages, such as choosing to recover lost profits or the misappropriation's wrongful profits. In a case in which the Mercer company accused MacLean Associates of selling computer programs wrongfully derived from Mercer's software, MacLean Associates was assessed over $1 million for misappropriating Mercer's trade secrets.[13]

Defenses to Trade Secret Actions

Trade secret law does not protect against fair and honest discovery of products or process. According to the UTSA, the proper means to discover a trade secret are discovery by independent invention, discovery under a license from the owner of the trade secret, observation of the item in public use or on public display, and obtaining the trade secret from published literature.[14] Moreover, the use of trade secret information obtained by independent effort or reverse engineering cannot be forbidden, unless fraud is involved. In fact, many businesses that would prefer to use trade secret protection may in fact use patent protection when reverse engineering or independent discovery is likely.

COPYRIGHTS

A patent provides exclusive rights in an idea; a copyright covers only the particular form in which the idea is expressed. Thus, although you may have an excellent idea, unless it is set down in a tangible form, it cannot be protected. A copyright also confers a legal monopoly, but the rights of exclusivity are less than those provided by a patent. Moreover, as distinct from trade secrets, the subject matter that is copyrighted need not be kept secret.

The essence of copyright is originality of expression, which implies that the copyright owner originated the work. By contrast to a patent, the work of originality need not be novel; originality implies only that copyright owners created the work themselves and did not copy from someone else. Nor is the aesthetic of the work relevant to its right to be protected.

What Can Be Copyrighted

Copyright protection is available to seven specific classes of protectible works of authorship:

- Literary works: books, periodicals, pamphlets, lectures, addresses, scripts, advertising material (catalogs, directories, product labels), computer programs, and databases
- Musical works
- Dramatic works, including accompanying music
- Pantomimes and choreographic works
- Pictorial, graphic, and sculptural works
- Motion picture and other audiovisual works
- Sound recordings

What Cannot Be Copyrighted

Generally, the following categories of material are not eligible for copyright protection:[15]

- Works that have not been fixed in a tangible medium: These include choreographic works that have not been notated or recorded and unrehearsed speeches that have not been written or recorded.

- Titles, names, short phrases, and slogans; a mere listing of ingredients or contents; familiar symbols or designs; mere variations of typographic ornamentation, lettering, or coloring

- Ideas, procedures, methods, systems, processes, concepts, principles, discoveries, or devices

- Works consisting entirely of information that is common property and containing no original authorship: These include standard calendars, schedules of sporting events, and lists or tables taken from public documents.

Protecting a Copyright

Congress passed the first U.S. Copyright Act in 1790. The most recent revision of this act was passed in 1976 and became effective in 1978. Although, theoretically, states possess concurrent power with the federal government over the subject of copyright, states' power in this area is subject to the supremacy clause of the Constitution, which requires that states' power be preempted when federal law applies. Such preemption occurred to an overwhelming extent under the most recent copyright act.[16]

Under the earlier act, in order to preserve and enforce one's rights in a work, certain formalities had to be observed whenever a work was published. The 1978 act eliminated the traditional notion that protection was triggered by publication of a work. According to Section 102(a) of the act: "Copyright protection subsists in original works of authorship fixed in any tangible medium of expression, now known or later developed, from which they can be perceived, reproduced, or otherwise communicated, either directly or with the aid of a machine or device." Thus copyright protection for a work is now obtained simply by fixing an original work of authorship in a tangible medium of expression. Copyright notice is no longer required, but is encouraged by the act.

Registration is not a requirement for copyright protection. However, to enforce these rights (through suits for infringement), the work should be registered and deposited with the Copyright Office of the Library of Congress, Washington, DC 20559. Registration is still a prerequisite for the recovery of statutory damages and attorney's fees. Generally the owner of copyrightable work will do the following to secure registration for a copyright:

- Deposit with the Copyright Office two complete copies of a published work (one copy of an unpublished work).
- Complete the prescribed form.
- Pay the required fee, which, for most purposes, is $20.

Under the earlier, 1906 copyright act, the copyright term was twenty-eight years, with a right to renew for another twenty-eight years. Under the 1978 act, however, the copyright term is the life of the author plus fifty years. For anonymous or pseudonymous works or works made for hire, the term is seventy-five years from the date of publication or one hundred years from creation, whichever expires first.

Limits to Copyright Protection

As noted earlier, copyright protection is *not* available for any idea, procedure, process, system, method of operation, concept, principle, or discovery. Furthermore, for those works that can be copyrighted, protection does not extend to every aspect of a work but only to those aspects that are original with the work's creator.

Although copyright protection extends an exclusive right to the owner to prevent others from copying the protected work, there are some exceptions. Unlike patent rights, copyright does not include the right to exclude others from making or selling a substantially similar work that was created without reference to the protected work. The other work need only be original to avoid infringement.

The boundaries of copyright protection are not defined by a listed category of works. Case law has defined the boundaries by creating distinctions between functional and nonfunctional objects, as well as distinctions between an idea and the expression of an idea. The courts are unwilling to grant copyright protection to functional works because patent protection is reserved for such works of utility. Thus to the extent that copyright is sought in the end product itself such as a dress by drawing a picture of a dress, copyright has been denied.[17]

Copyright protection is also not available to ideas, but it is available to the expression of those ideas. Intangible expressions are not copyrightable. A speech or lecture that is not reduced to tangible form is outside the act. Authors should therefore reduce a presentation to writing or to any tangible form so as to ensure protection.

The Supreme Court has defined a writing as any physical rendering of the fruits of creative intellectual or aesthetic labor. Trademarks, however, cannot be protected under these laws, since the expenditure of intellectual labor in the creation of a trademark was considered too trivial to merit copyright protection.

Fair Use. Another exception to copyright protection is the fair use doctrine contained in Section 107 of the 1976 act, which states that use of a copyrighted work for purposes such as criticism, comment, news reporting, teaching, scholarship, or research is not an infringement of copyright. Fair use under this section specifically allows for multiple copying of copyrighted works when done for classroom use under certain conditions. The exact scope of this permissible copying is not defined in the statute. An agreement between a group of publishers, authors, and educational institutions entitled Agreement on Guidelines for Classroom Copying in Not-for-Profit Educational Institutions was published by Congress when it revised the copyright law. Although the agreement does not have the status of law, it is an indication of legislative intent. The agreement allows limited copying of portions of a work when used for scholarly purposes. This copying must be characterized by brevity and spontaneity, implying that wholesale copying of entire works is not desirable and that multiple copies are to be made only if an alternative is not possible due to time limitations. The guidelines emphasize that fair use should not be a substitute for the purchase of other materials.

Directory Lists of Names and Addresses. The alphabetical listing of names and addresses in the white pages of a phone directory is not protected by federal copyright law according to a 1991 unanimous Supreme Court ruling. Justice Sandra Day O'Conner said that "copyright rewards originality, not effort." and that "in no event may copyright extend to the facts themselves." According to Justice O'Conner, the alphabetical listings of names and addresses "do not satisfy the minimum constitutional standards for copyright protection" because they are "devoid of even the slightest trace of creativity."[18]

The full effect of that decision is yet to be determined; however, it appears that it will now be more difficult to obtain copyright protection for compilations of factual material. According to Justice O'Connor, a "vast majority of compilations" would still be entitled to copyright protection as being based on some kind of "original selection or arrangement." However, the protection is "limited to the particular selection or arrangement" and not to the facts that were being arranged.

In a subsequent decision, a federal appeals court ruled that listings from yellow page phone directories can be copied by competitors as long as changes are made in the way the material is organized.[19] While this decision applied only to the Second U.S. Circuit Court of Appeals (covering New

York, Connecticut, and Vermont), it may be particularly influential, since there tends to be a concentration of such cases before that court.

A compiler of public domain materials—listings, facts, court cases, titles, dates—is entitled to copyright protection for the compilation. Nevertheless, a subsequent compiler may take the factual data contained in public domain material, rearrange the data in a different fashion, and not infringe the first compilation. Even though it is substantially similar, if the rearrangement is original, no infringement has taken place. Subsequent compilers may claim copyright protection for the originality of their arrangements.

The decision clearly raises questions concerning copyright protection for databases, since with such compilations it is easier to develop a different arrangement of the same listings. Therefore those who prepare compilations of essentially factual information should incorporate some original or creative efforts into the selection or arrangement of such information. Consideration should also be given to the investment of time and effort required for a compilation that may not be subject to copyright protection.

Computer Program Protection

New technologies have caused problems for lawmakers and copyright owners. Videotaping for home use, according to a Supreme Court 5–4 decision in 1984, is not a copyright infringement and those who use such equipment are not in violation of the law. There have, however, been decisions that declare computer software can be copyrighted.

Copyrightability of computer software was permitted in the 1980 Computer Software Copyright Act, which amended the 1976 Act. Nevertheless, some programs may be ineligible for copyright because they either lack minimal originality or constitute the only way of accomplishing a particular result so that the program can be characterized as embodying an idea.

For those that can be copyrighted, registration of computer programs extends protection both to the literal elements of a program and to the screen displays it generates. The literal components include the source code (understandable by the programmer), the microcode (the instruction set built into a microprocessor), which gives it a vocabulary.[20]

The nonliteral components that may be protected include the sequence, structure, and organization of the program, as well as the screen output or user interface, sometimes called the program's look and feel. However, protection of these components is based on the idea-expression dichotomy and whether these components "are protected depends on whether, on the particular facts of each case, the component in question qualifies as an expression of an idea, or an idea itself."[21] One useful approach for copyright purposes is to keep in mind that a computer program and its user interface are fundamentally different.[22] To highlight this distinction, the single registration of the computer program should be conceptualized as a dual registration that includes registration of the program itself plus registration of the screen displays or user interface.

Copyright and trade secret protection of computer software are not mutually exclusive.[23] In fact, a prudent course of action is to combine the two intellectual property vehicles to best protect one's computer software. Copyright regulations have explicit provisions for retaining trade secrets (which, unlike copyrights, can last forever) within copyrighted software programs.

Copyright protection decisions on computers are complicated because the courts have a difficult time grappling with the unfamiliar concepts. Recent court decisions have been giving more copyright protection to computer codes. However, a federal appeals court recently declared that a video game company that used a reverse-engineering process to make its games compatible with its rival's popular video game did not violate the competitor's copyright by translating its computer code.[24] In fact, it appears that the rules on copyright protection of computer software must be continually updated to meet the rapidly changing technological environment.

Penalties for Infringement

Legal remedies against copyright infringement include an injunction against copying and against distribution. Penalties for infringement of copyrighted works can be severe. Willful infringement can cost up to $50,000 in damages, plus costs and attorney's fees. Statutory damages of up to $10,000 can be awarded in lieu of actual damages. Under the criminal provisions of the law, a first-time offender can be fined up to $25,000 and sentenced to two years in prison.

In the trade secret case discussed in the previous section (*MacLean* v. *Mercer*), in which MacLean was assessed over $1 million for misappropriating trade secrets, the jury also awarded Mercer damages in excess of $955,000 on Mercer's copyright infringement claim.

INTERNATIONAL CONSIDERATIONS

A comprehensive discussion of the international aspects involved in the protection of U.S. intellectual property rights is beyond the scope of this book. Nonetheless, the growth in international firms and global marketing requires attention to the protection of these proprietary rights.

The International Convention for the Protection of Industrial Property (held in 1883 and known as the Paris Union) agreed to procedures that may be used against patent infringers and counterfeiters in international trade. The Paris Union, does not, however, require signatory nations to apply specific standards but requires only that they grant the same protection to nationals of the signatory governments as they do their own citizens. Under this agreement, therefore, protection for product proprietary rights is only as effective as individual national laws. Inasmuch as systems of laws vary, international traders may find they have no legal standing, for they are not held to be in business in the country where they seek a remedy.[25] Thus problems exist for any firm attempting to protect these rights for its international operations.

There are also a number of international conventions for the protection of copyrights, including, for example, the Berne Convention for the Protection of Literary and Artistic Works (Paris Act 1971). Although Congress had declined to join on previous occasions, in 1988, the United States adopted the Berne Convention Implementation Act for the protection of literature and art.[26] A significant increase in copyright piracy made international protection provided by the Berne Convention attractive. One expert estimated that the lost revenue from pirated works sold in foreign countries was $500 million annually. This reciprocal copyright treaty protects the works of authors internationally by allowing the copyrights of individuals in one member country to be recognized by all member countries.

Many countries belong to these international organizations and will make considerable efforts to enforce the provisions of the agreement. Moreover, some countries are revising their laws to strengthen the protection of foreign patents and copyrights. Taiwan, notorious for its imitations, has passed revisions in its law that give explicit legal protection to a wide range of products and impose heavier penalties for copyright piracy.

Several suggestions are offered to firms for protecting intellectual property abroad:[27]

- Register all copyrights and trademarks in countries in which business is conducted.

- Investigate whether the foreign country protects intellectual property, and determine whether its enforcement of its laws is often lax or inconsistent.

- Explore entering into licensing contracts in countries where competition is likely and intellectual property laws are weak.

- Consider distributing only older material overseas (e.g., older software), especially in countries where the state of technology is less advanced.

- Hire private investigators to gather evidence of piracy. A number of U.S. software companies have initiated raids of companies where they suspect pirated software is being used.

- Establish relations with foreign countries' local customs officials. In Japan, Singapore, and Hong Kong, provided they are given reasonable evidence of piracy, officials will conduct raids on the pirates and destroy the infringing.

Foreign Use of U.S. Patents

Under U.S. patent law, a patent owner has a seventeen-year domestic monopoly enforceable against "whoever without authority makes, uses, or sells any patented intention within the United States." Patent and tariff laws provide remedies against domestic and foreign firms that infringe U.S. patents within the United States. In a recent patent infringement suit, Honeywell, a Minneapolis-based high-technology firm, won $96 million from Japan's Minolta.[28]

However, the statutory monopoly inherent in a U.S. patent exists only within the borders of the United States. Thus a foreign company using a U.S. patent violates no U.S. laws as long as the company uses the patent elsewhere.

An inventor who has a patent in the foreign country in which the patented invention is used can invoke that country's laws to enforce the patent monopoly. However, seeking parallel patents in other countries is not always feasible. Foreign patent applications are expensive, legal proceedings in foreign countries are inconvenient, and some countries grant few if any patents.

Patent owners can use U.S. patents and tariff laws for protection against infringing imports. If the infringing items are covered by a U.S. patent, the patent owner can use the U.S. laws to exclude the items regardless of whether or not they were made using an invention patented in the United States. If the imported items are not themselves patented but are the downstream products of an invention patented in the United States, the patent's owner's rights depend on the nature of the product.[29]

Downstream products of a patent are products manufactured by methods that employ the patent. In the consideration of protection for downstream products, patents can be divided into two categories: process patents, which protect "a 'mode of treatment' of materials to 'produce a given result,'" and product patents, which protect "the finished result itself or any devices used to produce the result." The owners of process patents can exclude downstream products of their patent, whereas the owners of other kinds of patents cannot. Product patent owners can control downstream imports only if the imports themselves are either covered by or contain a product covered by a valid U.S. patent.

Currently, no U.S. law protects a patentee against unpatented downstream imports manufactured in a foreign country using methods that employ U.S. nonprocess patents. There are bills before Congress that are designed to repair this particular defect in patent law.

The U.S. International Trade Commission

One source for resolution of patent infringement by foreign competitors is the U.S. International Trade Commission (ITC). The commission is an independent, quasi-judicial agency with broad powers to investigate all factors relating to the effect of U.S. foreign trade on domestic production, employment, and consumption.

The ITC enforces Section 337 of the Trade Act of 1974, which involves unfair methods of competition for imported products and services. Unfair acts that have been brought before the ITC fall into three major categories: infringement of protected property, acts of misrepresentation, and deceptive communication.[30] The majority of cases brought before the ITC in recent years relate to patent infringement.

A review of ITC cases over a fourteen-year period indicate that a substantial portion are settled through agreements.[31] Such a review also suggests that alleged infringers from "newly industrialized countries" were more likely to be found in violation than those from more developed countries. The data also indicate that U.S. firms in high-technology industries receive patent challenges from firms in more developed countries.

The ITC appears to be an effective forum for resolving international patent conflicts. Marketing managers should continually monitor ITC decisions and activities in the area of patent infringement and concerning other unfair practices by foreign firms as international competition increases.

SUMMARY

Federal patent protection is the exclusive method for maintaining rights to publicly disclosed inventions in the United States. While adequate patent protection may frequently require an attorney's expertise, marketers should be aware of the necessity to halt patent infringements, as well as limitations on patent licensing.

Protection of non–publicly disclosed inventions, ideas, or information (trade secrets) is available through state law. Marketers should take the appropriate steps to guard their trade secrets from disclosure. Furthermore, they should be aware of the legal restrictions on acquiring another's trade secrets.

Copyrights do not provide protection for an idea: they cover only the particular form in which an idea is expressed. Currently, copyright protection for a work is obtained simply by fixing an original work of authorship in a tangible medium of expression.

There are a number of exceptions to copyright protection. The fair use doctrine allows the use of a copyrighted work for purposes such as criticism, comment, news reporting, teaching, scholarship, or research.

Copyrightability of computer programs is allowed. There is some confusion as to the extent of this protection, however, and the rules on computer copyright protection are likely to be continually updated so as to meet the changing technological environment.

Patent and tariff laws provide remedies against domestic and foreign firms that infringe on U.S. patents within the United States. A significant source for the resolution of patent infringement by foreign competitors in the United States is the U.S. International Trade Commission.

CASE
L.A. Gear Inc. *v.* Thom McAn Shoe Co., *CA Fed (N.Y.) 988 F. 2d 1117 (1993).*

FACTS

L.A. Gear makes and sells Hot Shots athletic shoes, which feature a unique combination of athletic shoe elements, including a polyvinyl chloride mesh as a trim, piping as a border to the mesh, a two-tone logo on the delta wing, and a color-coded mustache. L.A. Gear obtained a design patent (No. 299,081) for the Hot Shots shoe, which was sold primarily in department, sporting goods, and athletic shoe stores. The shoes were priced from $35 to $60 and were a commercial success.

Melville Corp. sells shoes in discount stores through its divisions Thom McAn and Meldisco, and Pagoda Trading Co. arranges for the manufacture of the shoes in the Far East and their importation into the United States.

L.A. Gear sued these organizations (collectively Melville) for patent infringement, and a district court found design patent infringement. Melville appealed.

ISSUE

Is the patent invalid because the design is functional and obvious, or is it a valid design patent?

HOLDING

The patent is a valid design patent, and Melville infringed on that patent.

REASONING

A design patent must be ornamental, not functional, and nonobvious. Melville argued that each element composing the shoe design had a functional purpose. According to Melville, the delta wing provides support for the foot and reinforces the shoelace eyelets; the mesh on the side also provides support; the mustache at the back of the shoe provides cushioning for the Achilles tendon and reinforcement for the rear of the shoe; and the position of each of these elements relates to its function.

The court declared, however, that the relevant inquiry for a design patent concerns not the utility of each element, but the overall appearance of the article. The relevant inquiry for obviousness in a design patent concerns whether the ornamental quality of the combination of elements was suggested in the prior art. However, the court noted that although all the elements of the design were known, they had not previously been combined in a single shoe design, and therefore the design was nonobvious. Absent some evidence that this particular design was suggested in the prior art, a reconstruction of known elements does not invalidate a design patent, and there was no such evidence here. The commercial success of the patented design and Melville's copies were also relevant to a finding of nonobviousness.

Although the district court concluded that Melville's patent infringement was not willful, accepting Melville's claim that it had a good faith belief that the patent was invalid and unenforceable based on the opinion of counsel, the federal court noted that Melville had introduced no evidence supporting its receipt of such an opinion.

Melville admitted copying and offered as justification the suggestion that such practice is prevalent in the fashion industry. The court stressed that the law imposes an affirmative duty of due care to avoid infringement of the known patent rights of another.

Because of Melville's deliberate copying and willful infringement, without any exculpatory evidence, the appellate court reversed the ruling that the infringement was not willful, and it indicated that enhanced damages may be warranted.

DISCUSSION QUESTIONS

Discuss the basic types of patents that are offered and the standards necessary relevant to the claims of patentable features.

Discuss the court's analysis of the patentable features of a design patent in the foregoing case.

CASE
Atari Games Corp. and Tengen, Inc., *v.* Nintendo of America, Inc. and Nintendo Co. Ltd., *CA Fed (Cal.) 975 F. 2d 832 (1992).*

FACTS

Nintendo sells the Nintendo Entertainment System (NES). Two of Nintendo's competitors—Atari Games Corporation and its subsidiary Tengen, Inc.—sued Nintendo for, among other things, unfair competition, Sherman Act violations, and patent infringement. Nintendo sued Atari for, among other things, unfair competition, patent infringement, copyright infringement, and trade secret violations. The two cases were consolidated by a district court in California and the court preliminarily enjoined Atari from exploiting Nintendo's copyrighted computer program. Atari appealed, claiming, among other things, copyright misuse by Nintendo.

ISSUE

Has Nintendo shown a likelihood of success on its copyright infringement claims sufficient to support the preliminary enjoinment?

HOLDING

Yes. Because Nintendo has shown a likelihood of success on its copyright infringement claims, the appeals court confirmed the preliminary enjoinment.

REASONING

Nintendo's home video game system—NES—includes a monitor, console, and controls. The console is a base unit into which a user inserts game cartridges that contain game programs. The user responds to video display by manipulating the console controls. Nintendo designed the program—the IONES—to prevent the NES from accepting unauthorized game cartridges. When a user inserts an authorized cartridge into a console, a slave chip, or key, unlocks the console. When a user inserts an unauthorized cartridge, the console detects no unlocking message and refuses to operate the cartridge.

Atari first attempted to analyze and replicate the NES security system in 1986 and could not do so. In 1987, Atari became a Nintendo licensee and paid Nintendo to gain access to Nintendo's technology. Under the license, Nintendo would take Atari's games, place them in cartridges containing the IONES program, and resell them to Atari. Atari could then market the games to Nintendo owners.

In early 1988, Atari's attorney applied to the Copyright Office for a reproduction of the IONES program, stating that Atari was a defendant in an infringement action and needed a copy of the program for the litigation. Atari falsely alleged that it was a defendant in the case and assured the Library of Congress that the requested copy would be used only in connection with the specified litigation. However, no such suit existed at that time.

The Copyright Office copy facilitated Atari's replication of Nintendo's IONES object code. After deciphering the program, Atari developed its own program—the Rabbit program—to unlock the NES. Although the Rabbit uses a different microprocessor and is programmed in a different language, as the district court found, the Rabbit program generates signals functionally indistinguishable from the IONES program. The Rabbit gave Atari access to NES owners without Nintendo's strict license conditions.

Nintendo asked the district court to enjoin Atari's alleged infringement of its IONES copyright. Atari asked the court to enjoin Nintendo's alleged antitrust violations, specifying Nintendo's misuse of its copyright.

Copyright Infringement

To prevail in its copyright infringement claim, Nintendo must show both ownership of the IONES program copyright and copying by Atari of protectable expression from the IONES program. Ownership was not in dispute, and therefore Nintendo need prove only that Atari had copied protectable expression from the IONES program.

In its review of copyright law, the court noted that literary works are protected and that these include computer databases and computer programs to the extent that they incorporate authorship by way of the programmer's expression of original ideas, as distinguished from the ideas themselves. Literary works copyright protection extends to computer programs and to instructions encoded on silicon chips.

Protectible Expression

According to the court, copyright protection does not extend to any procedure, process, system, or method of operation. However, under the standards of patent law, protection is provided for the process or method performed by a computer in accordance with a program. Thus patent and copyright laws protect distinct aspects of a computer program.

The court's initial task therefore was to separate protectible expression in the IONES program from its unprotectible elements. In considering copyright protection, the court noted that Nintendo's IONES program contains more than an idea or expression necessarily incident to an idea. Nintendo has incorporated within the IONES program creative organization and sequencing unnecessary to the lock-and-key function (a process or method of operation). Nintendo chose arbitrary programming instructions and arranged them in a unique sequence to create a purely arbitrary data stream that serves as a key to unlock NES. This unique arrangement of computer program expression, which generates the data stream, is a creative element of the IONES, and Nintendo may protect it under copyright. According to the court, the IONES program contains unprotectible expression, and Nintendo may protect under copyright the unique and creative arrangement of instructions in the IONES program.

Next, the court had to show that Atari either literally copied the IONES or had access to the IONES and produced a substantially similar copy. A single copy is sufficient to support a claim of copyright infringement. Atari had no reason to expect litigation from Nintendo when it requested a copy of the IONES program from the Copyright Office; therefore the court reasoned that Nintendo is likely to show successfully that Atari infringed the IONES copyright by obtaining and copying the source code from the Copyright Office.

Fair Use

Fair use of a copyrighted work for purposes such as criticism, comment, news reporting, teaching, scholarship, or research is not infringement. To obtain a fair use exception, an individual must possess an authorized copy of a literary work. Because Atari was not in authorized possession of the Copyright Office copy of IONES, any copying of IONES source code from the Copyright Office does not qualify as fair use.

Reverse Engineering

Atari made copies of Nintendo programs in an attempt to reverse-engineer. Reverse engineering, untainted by the purloined copy of the IONES program and necessary to understand IONES, qualifies as fair use. The Semiconductor Chip Protection Act of 1984 permits, in some limited circumstances, reverse engineering to reproduce a mask work. However, that act does not apply to this case. Atari did not reproduce or copy Nintendo's chip or mask work. In fact, Atari used an entirely different chip. Atari instead allegedly copied the program on Nintendo's chip.

Copyright Misuse

As a defense to copyright infringement, Atari asserted Nintendo has misused its copyright of its lockout program. Atari alleged Nintendo has conditioned the license of its copyright lockout program on the acceptance of contract provisions that give it control over the games developed by independent, third-party software developers. Although several circuit courts have entertained defenses of copyright misuse, only one circuit has sustained this defense. In this case, the court noted that under the appropriate factual setting, copyright misuse may be a viable defense against a claim of copyright infringement. However, any party seeking equitable relief (such as that under copyright misuse) must come to the court with clean hands. Thus, even if an equitable copyright misuse defense were permitted, Atari appears ineligible to invoke the defense.

The appeals court concluded the district court had not erred by granting Nintendo's request for an injunction. Nintendo is likely to prove that the IONES program contains protected expression, that Atari made unauthorized copies of the IONES program, that Atari's Rabbit program is substantially similar to the IONES program, and that Atari infringed the IONES copyright by obtaining and copying the source code from the Copyright Office. Nintendo is also likely to overcome Atari's assertion of copyright misuse as a defense.

DISCUSSION QUESTIONS

Describe the different methods whereby a firm may legally protect its products.

Discuss the defenses available to an organization involved in a dispute over ownership of intellectual property.

What issues may be significant in a court's considerations?

ENDNOTES

1. "The Global Patent Race Picks Up Speed," *Business Week*, August 9, 1993, 57–61.
2. Thomas G. Field Jr., "Brief Survey of Intellectual Property," *Idea—The Journal of Law and Technology* 31 (1990).
3. Arthur R. Miller and Michael H. David, *Intellectual Property Patents Trademarks and Copyright* (St. Paul, Minn.: West Publishing, 1990).

4. Hilary Pearson, "Putting Intellectual Property Law into Use," *Texas Bar Journal* (July 1990), 701–711.

5. Thomas G. Field Jr., "Brief Survey of Intellectual Property," *Idea—The Journal of Law and Technology* 31 (1990), 95.

6. *Arbrook, Inc.* v. *American Hospital Supply Corp.*, 645 F. 2d 273 (5th Cir. 1981).

7. Jere M. Webb and Lawrence A. Locke, "Intellectual Property Misuse: Developments in the Misuse Doctrine," *Harvard Journal of Law and Technology* 4 (Spring 1991), 251–267.

8. Tom Arnold, Michael G. Fletcher, and Robert J. McAughan Jr., "Managing Patent Disputes through Arbitration," *Arbitration Journal* (September 1991) 5–11.

9. Robert C. Scheinfeld and Gary M. Butter, "Using Trade Secret Law to Protect Computer Software," *Rutgers Computer & Technology Law Journal* 17 (1991), 381–419.

10. Scheinfeld and Butter, pp. 398–419.

11. James Lyons, "Ask Before You Pack," *Forbes* (March 16, 1992), 106.

12. Joel S. Feldman and G. Todd Jackson, "Protecting Customer Lists," *Employee Relations Law Journal* 16 (Spring 1991), 507–516.

13. *MacLean Associates, Inc.*, v. *William M. Mercer-Meidinger-Hansen, Inc.*, 18 U.S.P.Q., 2d (BNA) 1807 (E.D. Pa. 1991).

14. Richard J. Cippola Jr., "A Practitioner's Guide to Oklahoma Trade Secrets Law, Past, Present, and Future: The Uniform Trade Secrets Act," *Tulsa Law Journal* 27 (Winter 1991), 137–178.

15. William E. François, *Mass Media Law and Regulation*, 4th ed. (New York: John Wiley & Sons, 1986), p. 611.

16. Francis M. Nevins Jr., "Copyright: An Introduction for the Estate Lawyer," *Probate & Property* 5 (July/August 1991), 23–28.

17. *Goldstein* v. *California*, 93 S.Ct. 2303, 37 L. Ed. 2d 163 (1973).

18. *Feist Publications* v. *Rural Telephone Service*, U.S. Kan. 111 S. Ct., 1282 (1991).

19. *Key Publications* v. *Chinatown Today*, CA-2, (N.Y.) 945 F. 2d 509 (1991).

20. *Apple Computer, Inc.*, v. *Franklin Computer Corp.*, 714 F. 2d 1240 (3rd Cir. 1983).

21. *Johnson Controls, Inc.*, v. *Phoenix Controls Systems, Inc.*, CA 9 (Ariz.) 886 F. 2d 1173 (1989).

22. Thomas K. Pratt, "A Legal Test for the Copyrightability of a Computer Program's User Interface," *Kansas Law Review* 39 (1991), 1045–1069.

23. Scheinfeld and Butter, p. 407.

24. *Sega Enterprises Ltd.* v. *Accolade Inc.* (CA 9, San Francisco, No. 92-15655, September 1992).

25. Michael Litka, *Cases in International Business Law* (Boston: PWS-Kent Publishing, 1991), p. 73.

26. Stephen M. Stewart, assisted by Hamish Sandison, *International Copyright and Neighboring Rights*, 2nd ed. (London: Butterworths, 1989). Provides the text of the various conventions as well as the countries adhering to them, as of January 1, 1989.

27. Timothy M. Casey, "The Visual Artists Rights Act," *Hastings Communication/Entertainment Journal* 14 (1991), 85–105.

28. *Honeywell, Inc.*, v. *Minolta Camera Co. Ltd.* Civ. A. 87-4847 (D.N.J., February 7, 1992).

29. Nelson Johnson, "The Foreign Use of U.S. Patents: Damming the Flow of Downstream Products," *Columbia Journal of Transnational Law* 30 (1992), 145–178.

30. Robert J. Thomas, "Patent Infringement of Innovations by Foreign Competitors: The Role of the U.S. International Trade Commission," *Journal of Marketing* 53 (October 1989), 63–75.

31. Ibid., p. 75.

CHAPTER SIX
Product Decisions: Protecting the Trademark[1]

A trademark similar to a patent or copyright is a form of intellectual property and can be extremely valuable to its owner. For example, it has been suggested that if all the plants and inventories of the Coca-Cola Company were to go up in smoke overnight, the company could acquire funds to rebuild by using the inherent goodwill in the marks alone as security.

Trademarks do not protect a product; they do protect product identification. A successful trademark can help a company build a strong brand franchise that can be licensed, sold, or used in brand extensions. Many consumer product manufacturers, faced with increasing financial risk in entering new markets, are using established brand names to facilitate such entrance.[2]

HISTORICAL BACKGROUND

In passing the 1946 trademark law, commonly called the Lanham Act, Congress expressly recognized the fundamental basis of trademark protection as a measure "To protect the public from deceit, foster fair competition, and . . . to secure to the business community the advantages of reputation and good will.[3]

For the act's first thirty years, there was only one minor substantive change made in the law. In 1986, a two-year study of trademark activities was conducted under the auspices of the U.S. Trademark Association through its Trademark Review Commission. Throughout the process, input from diverse public and private interests was gathered. The commission concluded that although the Lanham Act had worked well for many years, it needed updating and fine-tuning to reflect changes in other laws and business practices. These changes were incorporated in the 1988 Trademark Law Revision Act (Table 1).

According to the Revision Act, business protection apparently is becoming the major justification for trademark law. The act is designed to "bring the trademark law up-to-date with present day business practices, to increase the value of the federal registration system for U.S. companies, to remove the current preference for foreign companies applying to register trademarks in the United States and to improve the law's protection of the public from counterfeiting, confusion, and deception."[4] These changes, together with several recent court decisions, have a significant impact on marketing decision making.

TRADEMARK DEFINITIONS

A trademark by definition must meet three fundamental requirements: (1) It must consist of a device, symbol, name, work, "or any combination thereof" that the Patent and Trademark Office or the courts have found to be a valid mark. (2) It must be adopted and used by a manufacturer or merchant. (3) It must identify and distinguish goods sold or manufactured by one individual from those of another.[5]

TABLE 6-1

MAJOR PROVISIONS OF THE
1988 TRADEMARK LAW REVISION ACT

- Introduces intent-to-use system: This permits application for federal registration of a trademark prior to its use in commerce.
- Eliminates token use: In an attempt to remove some of the disparity between foreign company and U.S. company trademark registration rights, token use has been replaced by intent to use.
- Facilitates the removal of deadwood—unused and abandoned marks—that currently clog the federal trademark register.
- Introduces the term *generic name* to replace the Lanham Act's previously used term *common descriptive name*, and declares that no incontestable right can be acquired in a generic name.
- Revises Section 43(a), which permits suit against false representation in the promotion of trademarked goods. This had been interpreted to relate to a firm's misrepresentation of its own goods, not those of a competitor. The revision now states legal action may be brought when "commercial advertising or promotion misrepresents . . . another person's goods."
- Specifies that all remedies available for trademark infringement are available as remedies for false advertising, including injunctive relief, monetary damages, and attorney's fees.

Trade dress is a term used to refer to the appearance and image of a product: its packaging and labeling, including the shape, color, design, and style of lettering. When packaging merely accompanies goods, is merely a component of the sales process, and does not serve primarily to distinguish and identify goods, it cannot be registered. However, trade dress legitimately can serve as a trademark if it actually identifies and distinguishes the service or goods with which it is used. Duplication of the trade dress of another's goods is actionable under both common law and the Lanham Act.

In a recent case, a federal judge issued a preliminary order blocking Johnson & Johnson Co. from selling Tylenol PM in its current packaging, saying the packaging intentionally copies the trade dress of Bristol-Myers Squibb Co.'s Excedrin PM. Under the order, Johnson & Johnson must stop advertising and shipments to stores of Tylenol PM, which, like Excedrin PM, is in a dark and light blue package. The judge's decision was based on an analysis of the logotype, graphic devices, and color configuration of both packages.

In 1992, the Supreme Court found that a distinctive Mexican style for its theme used by a restaurant was trade dress protected by Section 43(a) of the Lanham Act.[6]

Adopting a Mark

Under common law, in order to obtain rights to a trademark, a firm merely adopts it and uses it as a trademark. The first one who adopts the trademark becomes the owner of these rights. The 1946 Lanham Act supplemented common law by offering federal protection through federal registration. Registration is not mandatory but is encouraged by providing trademark owners with benefits. For example, registration confers nationwide protection for marks that, under common law, would be only locally protected in those markets in which they are actually being used or into which expansion is probable.

Under both common law and the Lanham Act, the prime requirement for adopting a trademark was its use in commerce. The maxim "no trade, no trademark" has been a staple of U.S. trademark law.[7] Under the prior use requirement, after selecting a mark and making a sizable investment in packaging, advertising, and distribution prior to its use in commerce, a firm may learn that the mark infringes on the rights of another, who acquired it while the firm was preparing its product for launching. The firm may then face not only the loss of trademark rights but also payment of damages.

The 1988 Trademark Law Revision Act simplifies the adoption process and, for the first time, permits businesses to reserve a trademark in the early stages of the new product planning process. The revision does not change availability of common law rights. It does, however, establish a dual system of registration. The old system of registration requiring use in commerce is still available. Under this system and under common law, when two or more parties are using the same or confusingly similar marks, the law recognizes that the first user in commerce, and thus the first who accrued the goodwill connected with the mark, has the right to exclusive use of the mark, or what is called the right of priority.

Under the new system, a federal trademark application for registration may be filed even before a mark has been used in interstate commerce. The firm need have only a bona fide intention to use the mark in commerce. Although actual use must occur before registration has been granted, once a mark is registered, the applicant is given credit for constructive use, which means trademark rights will date back to the filing date of the application.

To illustrate, under the new intent-to-use system, company A files a trademark application before using the mark in interstate commerce (say, in January 1995). Actual use in commerce may begin in April 1995, at which time registration will occur. However, the applicant will have a priority use of the trademark as of January 1995, when the period of constructive use began. The significance of this is that company A now has priority rights to the trademark over any other company that may have begun using that trademark during the period between January 1995 and the date company A actually used the mark in commerce: April 1995.

It should be noted that there must be actual and continuing intent to use the mark. This intent must be bona fide (i.e., not just to reserve the mark) and must exist throughout the federal application process until actual use occurs. However, although the initial period allowed is three months, extensions are permitted and an application can be kept pending for several years.

There are a number of benefits in the new intent-to-use system. It eases the process whereby a business may acquire priority rights in new trademarks before going to the considerable expense of making first use of the mark in commerce. Without the constructive use provisions, a pirate could scan the *Official Gazette* for desirable marks or marks applied for by successful corporations, could begin to use such marks in commerce prior to the successful corporation's first use, and then could secure a profit by selling the mark to the applicant.

The system may also reduce geographical fragmentation of trademark rights. Marks secured through initial use but not registered typically provide protection only in local markets. An intent-to-use applicant has nationwide constructive priority. This means that not only those who wish to register the mark and use it in commerce during the constructive use period but also sub-sequent users who attempt to claim common law right priorities in their own territories are prevented from doing so.[8]

The new system requires the removal of unused and abandoned marks (called deadwood) that currently clog the register, and thus the reliability of trademark registration will increase. Moreover, trademark registrations and renewal periods are now valid for only ten years, rather than twenty years, thus restoring many more unused marks sooner to the available trademark pool.[9]

Since federal rights now can be established prior to actual use of a mark in commerce, it is increasingly important for firms to consider turning to federal trademark protection. The Patent and Trademark Office will likely be inundated with intent-to-use trademarks, and thus it is clear that an intensive search is still required for new trademarks. Preliminary checks can be made through the *Trademark Register*, the *Trade Names Directory*, or the *Thomas Register* to determine if a proposed mark is available for adoption. On-line screening devices are now widely available and relatively inexpensive. For example, using TRADEMARKSCAN and TRADEMARKSCAN STATE databases can provide a record of a proposed trademark virtually in seconds.[10] Prudent trademark owners should delay a firm commitment to the mark until follow-up searches are made, so as to guard against the possibility that a prior application might have been filed that was not revealed by the original search. However, once a firm has selected a mark and verified the mark's availability, the company can immediately proceed with a federal ap-plication to reserve the mark as its own.

Approximately 128,000 trademark applications were filed in fiscal year (FY) 1990; the number dropped to about 120,000 in FY '91, and filings in FY '92 appear to be roughly at the same level as FY '91. In FY '90, about 44% of the filings were intent-to-use applications; this rose to 47% in '91 and 48% in '92. According to the Patent and Trademark Office, in spite of the many changes that have taken place, the problem areas are few in number and relatively minor in impact. A useful discussion of relevant information concerning the PTO's experience in examining intent-to-use applications is provided by the Administrator for Trademark Policy and Procedure, U.S. Patent and Trademark Office, who offers a number of tips to help practi-tioners avoid problems.[11]

Although marketers can avail themselves of the benefits of the new trademark adoption process, the system also provides an incentive for in-creased trademark applications by others and limitations on the registration and renewal periods. Accordingly, trademark owners must be prepared to develop proactive and reactive strategies for adequate protection of their marks.

When preventive activities fail to resolve potential conflicts, trademark owners should be prepared to take legal action. Marketing managers must familiarize themselves with the relevant issues in trademark protection and provide appropriate aid and interaction with legal counsel.

TRADEMARK CONTROL

A program of aggressive policing of a trademark is necessary to ensure its efficient usage in marketing activities. Such a program should include efforts to reduce trademark counterfeiting, to prevent the trademark from becoming generic, and to institute suits for infringement of the trademark.

Trademark Counterfeiting

Although commercial counterfeiting has existed since the nineteenth century, in recent years it has taken on more significant proportions. This is manifest in the increased sophistication and organization of commercial counterfeiters, the increased internationalization of their efforts, and the huge increase in the size, scope, diversity, and success of their efforts.[12]

The Lanham Act defines a counterfeit as "a spurious mark which is indistinguishable from . . . a registered mark. . . ." The act provides, however, for only civil penalties for counterfeiting, which are frequently considered by the counterfeiter as a cost of doing business. Furthermore, under the act, only the victims of commercial counterfeiters have the obligation of tracking them down, building a case against them, and establishing that case in court. While other federal and some state statutes occasionally have been applied to combat commercial counterfeiting, these have had limited success in minimizing the activity.

Commercial counterfeiting is now a major problem, not only for luxury goods, such as watches and cameras, but also for a wide range of health and safety-related items, such as drugs, fertilizers, chemicals, glasses, computer components, and automobile and aircraft parts. Examples include brakes that have caused auto accidents, low-quality polio vaccines distributed to unsuspecting patients, and drugs believed to have been responsible for a number of deaths.[13] Many nations are even more vulnerable to the evils of commercial counterfeiting. For example, Kenya's annual coffee crop, a mainstay of the economy, was virtually destroyed through the application of counterfeit (and defective) agricultural chemicals bearing the counterfeit label of a respected U.S. manufacturer (Chevron), which then suffered much of the blame.

The ability to prevent trademark counterfeiting is limited. Whereas a product itself may be protected as a trade secret and therefore is not apt to be copied precisely, a trademark is widely susceptible to imitation. There are, however, steps that can be taken by firms to penalized counterfeiters and possibly limit their activities.

Injunctions and Seizure Orders

One of the difficulties involved in past attempts to halt counterfeiters' activities was that such efforts usually required notice to the counterfeiters, who then would try to conceal their activities. In 1979, a court held that a temporary restraining order can be issued without notice.[14] Subsequently the courts permitted the issuance of without-notice seizure orders whereby a U.S. marshal or a private investigator, employed by a trademark owner, can enter a counterfeiter's premises and seize (1) all counterfeit goods, (2) all records relating to the distribution, and (3) all materials and apparatuses used in its manufacture.[15] Such seizure orders have been valuable in the war against counterfeiters.

Registration with the U.S. Customs Service

A trademark owner may record a registered mark with the U.S. Customs Service, which will then prohibit entry of goods bearing infringing marks. The Customs Service has a two-tiered classification scheme for counterfeit trademarks: (1) colorable imitation is "any mark which so resembles a registered mark as to be likely to cause confusion, or mistake or deceive," and (2) counterfeit trademark is a "spurious trademark which is identical with, or substantially indistinguishable from, a registered trademark."

The significance of these distinctions emerges from the consequences that are attached to the two categories. Colorable imitations are considered as merely infringing articles, and they may be imported, provided that the "objectionable mark is removed or obliterated prior to importation." Counterfeits, however, are treated harshly, and unless the trademark holder consents to their importation, they may be seized and forfeited. Rolex recently contended that a shipment of gold bracelets bearing a crownlike design and detained by a customs import specialist contained counterfeit marks. Rolex demanded the shipment be forfeited, and a court of appeals upheld the contention.[16]

Federal Anticounterfeiting Law

As early as 1899, legal scholars noted that among major commercial nations offering trademark protection, only the United States had no national law providing penal sanctions for trademark counterfeiting.[17] In 1984, a federal anticounterfeiting statute was passed as part of the Continuing Appropriations, Comprehensive Crime Control Act (P.L. 98-473). The new law provides for up to five years' imprisonment and a $250,000 fine for first-time traffickers of counterfeit goods with registered trademarks. Corporate offenders may be fined up to $1 million for the first offense, and the federal courts are authorized to issue orders without notice to seize bogus goods with counterfeit marks.

Preventing Genericness

Although generic terms cannot be protected, the 1946 Lanham Act does not use the word generic; rather it refers to "a mark which is any common descriptive word of any article." The basic formulation frequently cited in determining whether or not a mark is a "common descriptive work" occurred when Kellogg lost the right to the exclusive use of *Shredded Wheat.* Under what has been designated the public perception approach, a firm "must show that the primary significance of the term in the mind of the consumer is not the product but the producer," that is, whether consumers perceive the name as indicating the source of the product.[18]

In a case concerning the Monopoly trademark of Parker Brothers—a division of General Mills—a different standard for determining genericness was established. In deciding whether another firm could call its board game Anti-Monopoly, rather than consider consumer perception, the court examined purchaser motivation for buying trademarked goods. A lower court ruled the trademark was generic based on the opponent's marketing survey that showed most consumers were motivated to buy Monopoly because they liked the game, *not* because it was a Parker Brothers product.[19] In 1983, the Supreme Court let this decision stand. The motivation test, however, was criticized by legal commentators as threatening to undermine the clarity and stability of federal trademark law. In 1984, Congress passed the Trademark Clarification Act, which reiterates the traditional trademark protection legal test of consumer perception of the origin of the product.

The 1988 Revision Act clearly includes the word *generic* and declares that no incontestable right can be acquired in a mark that is "the generic name for the goods or services . . . for which it is registered." The revision also specified, "A mark shall be 'abandoned' . . . when any course of conduct of the owners . . . causes the mark to become the generic name for the goods or services on or in connection with which it is used. . . . Purchaser motivation shall *not* be a test for determining abandonment under this paragraph." This last statement is designed to reinforce the major provision of the

Trademark Clarification Act, which declares that consumer perception, not consumer motivation, is the test for determining whether a mark is generic.

Whether the 1984 Trademark Clarification Act has made a significant difference in the development of trademark law is problematic; in fact, the term *generic* remains an elusive concept.[20] Nonetheless, since a generic designation for its product names may cause a firm to lose the benefits and goodwill associated with these names, efforts should be made to prevent this occurrence. Until such time as further clarification is provided, the formulation of a common descriptive name still applies; that is, a generic name is commonly understood to be a product name that all are free to use—necessarily implying that it is only rarely understood to be a trademark.[21] Public perception is the standard by which this determination is to be made.

Preventive Techniques

Most of the law concerning trademarked generic words has been developed through private litigation. An injured party may sue for damages or other relief, charging unfair competition. Most of the governing procedures have resulted from actions initiated by competitors. Competitors may challenge an initial federal trademark registration as generic before the Trademark Trial and Appeal Board, or they may petition the board to cancel existing registrations because the mark has become generic. Competitors may simply infringe, await suit, and defend on the ground that the trademarked word is generic. There appears to be no case on record in which a consumer or consumer group has sought legal relief from an improperly trademarked generic word.

A number of factors may account for the linguistic deterioration of trademarks into generic words: misuse of the mark by its holder in advertising and labeling, insufficient policing, improper use of the trademarked word, or the absence of a short and simple alternative name for the product. Most significant is the propensity of trademark owners to encourage the public to adopt their marks as generic household words.[22] Case law has been inconsistent in specifying the conditions under which a word is to be classified as generic, and adequate guidelines have not been established to indicate what constitutes evidence of genericness. Nevertheless, a firm may follow certain procedures that will prevent "genericide."

To do this, a trademark owner should reinforce the source designation of a trademark by including the term *brand* between the trademark and the generic name (e.g., Jell-O-brand gelatin dessert and Sanka-brand decaffeinated coffee). Furthermore, a company name can be used with a product mark, but these should be separated. For example, ads should read, "Ritz crackers by Nabisco" rather than "Nabisco Ritz crackers." Marks denoting a product line are not likely to be considered generic, such as Del Monte, or General Foods Birds Eye.[23]

Passage of congressional bill (S. 2926) has made it easier for generic drug producers to secure clearance for their less expensive drug equivalents of branded or trademarked drugs. Manufacturers of trademarked drugs are making efforts to protect their trademarked products by designing distinctive tablets or capsules in the hope that when their patents expire, consumers will be skeptical of switching to a generic product that does not feature the familiar symbol or trademark. For example, Hoffman–La Roche carved a distinctive *V* shape in the product Valium to protect its franchise when the patent expired.

Policing the Use of Trademarks. A firm should institute a media-monitoring program, with follow-up letters reminding editors, publishers, broadcasters, and other business and public figures who have misused the trademark that the mark is protected. Positive advertising may also reinforce the trademark. Thus, a series of ads by Xerox notified readers that Xerox was a protected trademark and should not be used as a noun ("I used a xerox") or a verb ("I xeroxed some papers") but as an adjective ("I used a Xerox copying machine").

Defensive Techniques

When a claim is made that a word is generic, the decision is based on the proof presented. The kind of proof offered may differ based on whether one is instituting a case to have a term declared generic (opponent) or whether one is defending (proponent). The opponent can present evidence of initial genericness, generic usage in trade, improper usage by the opponent, or failure to police the mark adequately. Either side may use a lexicographer. Although survey evidence is also valuable in generic cases, the type of survey selected depends on whether the evidence is being secured by the opponent or the proponent.

- *Opponent survey:* The opponent's affirmative task is to prove that the term in question is the name of something (a product, not a producer). One approach was successfully used by the opponent in declaring *thermos* to be generic.[24] Respondents were first asked about their general familiarity with containers to keep liquids hot or cold and then were asked a variety of questions, including, "If you were going to buy one, what would you ask for?" The survey results indicated that about 75% of the familiar respondents would have called such a container a thermos.

The same approach was relied on heavily by opponents in *Anti-Monopoly.*[25] When asked, "If you were going to buy this kind of game . . . what would you tell the sales clerk you wanted?" about 80% of the respondents said "Monopoly."

- *Proponent survey:* For the proponent, the thermos approach is inherently unsuitable because the only affirmative responses it can generate indicate genericness. The approach for the proponent is the one endorsed in the Teflon case, in which respondents were asked directly whether the term is generic or a trademark, with some prefatory explanation of what the difference is. Respondents were told the differences between the brand name and a common name, using *Chevrolet* and *automobile* as examples. They were then asked whether various terms, including *Teflon*, were brand names or common names. The results were as follows:

	Brand Name	*Common Name*
STP	90%	5%
Thermos	51	46
margarine	9	91
Teflon	68	31
Jell-O	75	25
refrigerator	6	94
aspirin	13	86
Coke	76	24

The court characterized this as the "only survey which really gets down to the critical elements of the case" and also noted that "the responses of the survey reveal that the public is quite good at sorting out brand names from common names."[26]

While the proponents in the *Anti-Monopoly* case introduced a Teflon-type survey, there was a flaw in the instructions. Respondents were told a brand name means a name like Chevrolet that is made by one company, and a common name means an "automobile which is made by different companies." The results were dismissed as having "no relevance," the court noting that under the definition given the respondents, Monopoly "would have to be a 'brand name' because it is made by only one company."

To avoid this problem, the following suggestions are offered.[27] The instructions should make it clear that there can be more than one generic or common name for a product, such as *car* and *automobile*. Mention should be made that even if only one company makes a product, that does not necessarily mean that product is trademarked. The list of terms should be chosen carefully and fairly and should include ones that are clearly generic or clearly trademarked, as well as ones that are marginal.

Protection from Infringement

According to the Lanham Act, infringement of a registered trademark will be found if its use by another "is likely to cause confusion, or cause mistake, or to deceive" (Sec. 32[1] 1982). This statement has been neither changed nor further clarified under the Revision Act.

Preventive Activities

The right to sue for infringement is an important right for the trademark owner. However, certain steps should be taken to protect that right in order to enforce it. Trademark registration offers significant protection. It provides notification of who owns the mark. It allows the Customs Bureau to exclude the importation of infringing goods shipped from abroad. In court, registration is also considered prima facie evidence of a trademark's validity, which means that the opponent will be obligated to provide evidence of invalidity.

A mark should usually be displayed with the symbol *TM* while the registration procedure is pending and with the letter *R* enclosed in a circle after the mark is registered. The trademark must continue to be used and carefully policed in order to determine whether a competitor is using the mark.

Defensive Techniques

When there is evidence of potential infringement and the infringer refuses to cease, steps should be quickly taken to stop this activity.

In a suit for infringement, evidence must be presented that a competitor is employing a mark similar to your own, which is "likely to cause confusion, or cause mistake, or to deceive" the public as to the source of the goods. A specific test for the likelihood of confusion has not been established by the Supreme Court. However, with few exceptions, all circuit courts recognize the following seven factors should be considered when determining whether a likelihood of confusion exists:[28]

1. The similarity of the trademarks, which is generally determined by comparing the overall impression conveyed by the sight, sound, and meaning of the two trademarks.

2. The stronger or more distinctive the senior trademark, the greater the likelihood of confusion from the junior mark.

3. The degree of similarity between the goods of the trademark owner and those of the alleged infringer.

4. The extent to which similar marketing and advertising channels are used for competing goods.

5. The care exercised by consumers: the greater the care consumers exercise in purchasing goods, the less likelihood of confusion.

6. Evidence of actual confusion, which is considered persuasive proof that future confusion is likely.

7. Although the junior user's intent in adopting a mark is relevant to determination of the likelihood of confusion, such wrongful intent will not be deemed sufficient to demonstrate likelihood for confusion if other factors demonstrate there is no such likelihood.

Of the three principal methods of proving likelihood of confusion— "survey evidence; evidence of actual confusion; and/or argument based on a clear inference arising from a comparison of the conflicting marks and the context of their use"—survey evidence is perhaps the best.[29] In fact, in the Southern District of New York, which decides many infringement cases, a judge declared that an adverse inference was to be drawn from the failure of a financially well-endowed litigant to present survey evidence.[30]

The primary purpose of a trademark survey is to establish that a significant number of relevant persons confuse one trademark with another trademark. Several types of marketing research techniques have been used by firms to prove likelihood of confusion. These include telephone surveys, shopping mall studies, experiments conducted in the marketplace, and probability surveys on a national or regional basis. Not all of these marketing research techniques are equally effective in trademark litigation.[31]

Mall Intercept. A mall intercept involves a research technique wherein consumers are intercepted at a mall and asked to be respondents in a survey. The large number of people who can be contacted at such a location, plus the ease with which they can be approached, has resulted in widespread use of this technique for survey purposes. Although the data cannot be projected to a universe, such research is routinely accepted by marketers in making marketing decisions. Thus, in the court's discretion, it is acceptable as evidence having some weight.[32] The researcher, however, must be certain the selected mall caters to people with ascertainable socioeconomic characteristics and a standard of living similar to that of the actual universe.

Experiments. Experiments can provide evidence of *actual* confusion and thus can be a more meaningful technique than those offering proof of *likelihood* of confusion. Confusion may be related to (1) product (e.g., "Raffles are Ruffles"); (2) source (e.g., "Raffles are put out by the makers of Ruffles"); and (3) sponsorship (e.g., "Raffles are approved and endorsed by the makers of Ruffles").[33]

The best opportunity to secure proof through experiment occurs in the case of product confusion. The following hypothetical example of such an experiment involves a determination of whether Vita-Slims would be confused with Vita-Thins diet multivitamins.[34] In one or more retail pharmacies, two products can be either arranged on a side-by-side basis, placed one above the other, or separated and rotated so as to eliminate possible positional bias. Consumers entering the store can be given a discount coupon offering $1 off on each $3 purchase and stating that the discount is available "on one purchase of Vita-Thins this day only." If the purchaser mistakenly selects Vita-Slims from the shelf and presents the coupon when paying for this "wrong" product, that is evidence of confusion.

Although the results of such an experiment are not projectable, the test does constitute actual evidence of what may occur in the marketplace. Such an experiment, which indicated a 20% level of confusion, has been held to be reliable evidence of the likelihood of confusion.[35]

Surveys. Although surveys are widely used as evidence, there are no clear guidelines to the kinds of surveys that are acceptable. The courts have judged similar tests in different manners.[36]

Whether or not to introduce a survey is an initial issue that must be resolved. There are indications that the failure of a trademark owner to conduct a survey to support a claim of likelihood of confusion gives rise to the inference that the results may be unfavorable.[37] Moreover, in determining likelihood of confusion, even a survey that is apparently free from fault can be at most only partial evidence and never conclusive. Too, any survey taken can be faulted to some degree by a resourceful attorney.

One solution is to submit questions and methodology to the court for approval prior to making a survey. However, this requires that the opponent be involved, and such a prescreening by the court does not indicate the weight the court may ultimately give the survey.[38] Another solution is to ensure that the survey conforms to the process traditionally used by the courts in determining likelihood of confusion. While there are no widespread precedents, some cases have suggested guidelines, such as the following.

- Who should design the survey? Qualified experts, such as marketing researchers, should be used to design, supervise, and present a survey to a court or jury. An attorney may work with the expert in defining the "precise scope of the issues in [the] litigation."[39] If an attorney is involved in designing the questions to be asked, however, a survey may ultimately be accorded little or no weight. Nor should a survey be conducted by or supervised by an attorney. Ideally, the surveyor should not even know that the survey will be used in litigation.

- The universe and sample: A fundamental precept is that answers given by survey respondents who constitute the sample reflect the view of the universe, which consists of people whose views the court determines are proof of the issues submitted for determination.

The universe may be considered the target, including a bull's-eye. If the researcher misses the target in defining the universe, the survey data are rendered meaningless. If the researcher hits the edge of the target, the views of that universe may have little weight, depending on proximity to the bull's-eye. If the researcher hits the bull's-eye, the data are meaningful, assuming all other quality control factors exist.[40] The court decides on the bull's-eye, the bull's-eye's width, and the accuracy of the researcher's shot.

An appropriate universe should be broad enough to include all possible potential purchasers. It is useful to include one or more subuniverses under the umbrella of the broad universe so that the relevant data from each can be collated and compared to those from the broader area. This approach was successfully used in a probability survey in a case concerning lack of authorization of jerseys sold with the National Football League emblem.[41]

A broad universe was designed, with subuniverses of prior purchasers, fans, and fans plus (fans who were shown a replica survey for a favorite team). Although minor variations in the data for each universe were noted, the general consistency of the data established the validity of testing the perceptions of the umbrella universe, given the celebrity of the marks of the National Football League clubs among the population at large. The perceptions of the umbrella universe and the comparative data for the subuniverses were found by the court to be persuasive.

- Tests for confusion of source: Confusion ("Raffles are put out by the makers of Ruffles") may be shown through a survey; however, surveys can determine only the likelihood of confusion and have been subject to considerable rejection by the courts due to the possibility of bias.[42]

For the claimant, confusing surveys that are mere word association tests are not acceptable. Thus, although some respondents to a survey confused the source of Holiday Out campgrounds with that of Holiday Inn motels and hotels, the survey was considered defective by the court because it failed to consider the effect that the word *Holiday* alone had on the responses.[43] Furthermore, lack of word association can provide negative evidence of confusion and could be used to defeat a claim of infringement.

Questions may be added to such word association tests to improve their acceptability. The maker of Eveready batteries, flashlights, and miniature bulbs was successful in a suit for infringement based on confusion of source against Ever-Ready, a name used by another company for lamps and bulbs.[44]

The pertinent part of the survey utilized in this case was as follows (showing a picture of Ever-Ready): "Who do you think puts out the lamps shown here? What makes you think so? Please name any other products put out by the same concern which puts out the lamp shown here."

The criticism of this method is that it tends to lead the respondent's mind in directions and channels that one does not necessarily take in the marketplace when making purchasing decisions. One possible method to correct this deficiency is to use controls; that is, make comparisons among other, similar products so that the level of confusion between the marks at issue can be compared to that of the marketplace in general.

- Tests for confusion of sponsorship: The National Football League (NFL) has demonstrated convincing evidence of this type of confusion in three court cases. In *National Football League* v. *Wichita Falls* (1982), concerning the lack of authorization on jerseys sold with the National Football League emblem, respondents who had seen the official jersey (those containing an emblem licensed by the NFL) were asked whether they thought the company that made the jersey had to "get authorization or permission to make it." If the interviewee responded yes, the person was then asked from whom the authorization was obtained. The same test was repeated using identical copies of the defendant's jersey, and the court accepted the results of these tests as establishing the likelihood of confusion.

- Additional guidelines: Morgan offers several guidelines to marketers and researchers for the development of survey evidence:[45]

    — Be prepared to argue that the survey related strongly to the issue in question and is superior to alternative forms of evidence.

    — Remember that interested persons (judge and jury) with little background in survey research methods will be trying to understand the results. (As more survey evidence is provided in litigated cases, this situation may change.)

    — Eliminate methodological flaws that could appear to affect results.

    — If possible, utilize surveys conducted prior to litigation.

    — Be prepared for an all-out adversary evaluation of the survey.

    — Be prepared to offer a concise interpretation of survey results.

Morgan also provides an extensive review of federal case law covering judicial standards for survey evidence.[46] A specific suggestion to marketers gathering survey evidence for trademark cases is to use field experiments that demonstrate actual in-store confusion, when possible.[47]

Protection from Dilution

Dilution of a trademark differs from traditional infringement. Infringement laws are designed to protect consumers; in contrast, dilution statutes protect owners. The 1946 Lanham Act did not contain an antidilution provision. Such a provision was initially proposed for the 1988 Revision Act, but was ultimately rejected.

Protection against trademark dilution is, however, available from state law. Currently, twenty-five states have antidilution laws, but court decisions in this area have been inconsistent.[48] Nonetheless, managers should be alert to relevant issues, particularly because some states have recently adopted trademark dilution laws. Moreover, recent court decisions in this area have been providing more precise guidelines for trademark owners.

A dilution claim is not based on infringement or deception. It is based on the values of a trademark to its owner; these values have been termed the mark's commercial magnetism.[49] The weakening of a mark's commercial magnetism is known as trademark dilution. Harms through dilution can occur through blurring or whittling away. When a car dealership used the slogan *THE GREATEST USED CAR SHOW ON EARTH*, a state court held in favor of a dilution cause of action by Ringling Bros.–Barnum & Bailey Combined Shows, Inc. According to the court, the car dealer's slogan "would blur the strong association the public now has between Ringling Bros.' mark and its circus and thus inflict irreparable harm."[50]

Tarnishment is subsumed under the term *dilution*. Trademark tarnishment not only blurs a mark's distinctiveness but also mars a mark's positive associational value. Campbell Soup Co., producers of Godiva Chocolate, sued a firm that marketed a dog biscuit under the name *DOGIVA* and in trade dress similar to Godiva's gold foil. The court granted relief under California's antidilution law because "of the association which the public makes between DOGIVA—treats for animals and GODIVA—premium quality food products which are intended for human consumption."[51]

Guidelines for a dilution claim were presented when Toyota sought to establish use of the mark *Lexus* for a new line of automobiles. Mead filed a complaint, alleging trademark dilution, under the new York General Business Law, of its *LEXIS* mark for computer-assisted legal research.

A U.S. Circuit Court held that Toyota's use of *Lexus* did not dilute Mead's mark, noting the legislation was intended to prevent such "hypothetical anomalies as DuPont Shoes, Buick Aspirin tablets, Schlitz varnish, Kodak pianos, Bulova gowns," and so forth.[52] The court refused to find blurring unless there was a mental association between the two marks; since the

LEXIS mark circulates only in a limited market and has no distinctive quality for the general public, there can be no blurring here.

The court listed the following criteria that must exist for a dilution to be considered present:

- The senior mark must be distinctive.

- The marks should be similar; differences in pronunciation, context, and physical appearance tend to reduce such similarity.

- The products covered by the marks should be similar.

- Does the junior product target unsophisticated customers? (The more sophisticated the consumers, the less likelihood of blurring.)

- Was there predatory intent? That is, did the firm that adopted the mark hope to benefit commercially?

- The more well-known the senior mark is, the more it warrants protection.

- The greater the prospect that the junior mark will become famous, the more protection should be applied to the senior mark.

There is a reluctance on the part of many courts to use the dilution theory even when it has been enacted into law by a state legislature. Judges seem to view it with distaste because they believe the dilution theory may ask too much legal protection for a trademark.[53] Thus, a useful strategy for marketers who are concerned about dilution is to combine a dilution claim with an infringement claim when a state statute is available.

GLOBAL ISSUES

Virtually all countries offer some legal protection to trademarks; however, obtaining international trademark protection requires separate registration under the law of each nation. And the scope of trademark protection may differ substantially from country to country. Generally, a valid trademark will be protected against infringing use. However, a trademark can be valid in one country (ASPIRIN-brand tablet in Canada) but invalid in another country because it is considered generic (BAYER-brand aspirin in the United States).[54]

Several treaties provide international recognition of trademarks. The Paris Convention, the 1957 Arrangement of Nice concerning the International Classification of Goods and Services, is now administered by the UN's World Intellectual Property Organ (WIPO).

The 1973 Vienna Trademark Registration Treaty (to which the United States is a signatory) is designing an international filing and examination scheme, which has not yet been fully implemented.

Twenty-nine European and other Mediterranean countries are parties to the Madrid Agreement for International Registration of Marks (1891, as amended). International filings to obtain national trademark rights are permitted under this agreement.

European Community (EC) countries are moving in the direction of creating a Community Trade Mark—a single registration valid throughout the EC. Toward that end they have promulgated a Trademark Harmonization Directive requiring all member states to change their national laws in order to create a more uniform system.[55] This does not require the member states to have identical laws, nor are they likely to.

A primary purpose of the Trademark Law Revision Act was to remove the current preference for foreign companies applying to register trademarks in the United States. The United States was the only developed country that required use of a mark before application for registration. Foreign companies, however, could register their marks in the United States under Section 44 of the Lanham Act, which allowed a foreign organization to base its registration on an application in a foreign country within the previous six months. Earlier, it had been thought necessary for such foreign-based applicants to at least allege use of the mark somewhere, though not necessarily in the United States. However, in the 1984 *Crocker* decision by the Trademark Trial and Appeal Board, it was held that a Section 44 applicant was not required to allege prior use of a trademark anywhere in order to obtain priority registration.

Prior to revision of the Lanham Act, token use was considered an opportunity for U.S. firms to be placed on an equal footing with foreign companies in securing trademark registration. Under token use, a single (or very limited) sale of a product bearing the mark was sufficient to satisfy the use-in-commerce requirement. However, token use was criticized as delaying the filing of trademark application, perpetuating clogging of the trademark register, placing significant risks on the introduction of new products and services, and giving preference to certain industries over others.[56]

The new definition of a trademark eliminates token use and presents intent to use as an attempt to remove the disparity between foreign company and U.S. company registration rights. The revision does not provide complete parity, because U.S. registration can still be secured by a foreign firm without an actual use in commerce, whereas intent to use by a U.S. firm still requires proof of actual use prior to registration. However, foreign as well as

U.S. applicants must now be prepared to show bona fide intent to use the mark in the United States.

SUMMARY

Under the Lanham Act, a trademark is a device, symbol, or name, adopted and used by a manufacturer, that identifies and distinguishes the goods sold or manufactured by one company from those of another. A trademark protects a product's identification.

After adopting a trademark, a firm must police the mark to retain control. Such activities include continuing efforts to reduce trademark counterfeiting, efforts to prevent the trademark from becoming generic, and instituting suits for infringement of the trademark. Specifically, firms should establish monitoring techniques, and use market research efforts as aids in both defensive and offensive positions in trademark litigation.

The basic criterion for determining infringement under the Lanham Act is whether the similar trademark is "likely to cause confusion or to cause mistake or to deceive" the public as to the source of goods. There are, however, state laws that provide additional protection; twenty-five states have laws that protect trademarks from dilution, that is, from weakening a trademark's commercial magnetism.

Managers should become familiar with the requirements for trademark protection in international markets.

CASE
Major League Baseball Properties, Inc., *v.* Sed Non Olet Denarius *DC SNY No. 90 CIV 2170 (CBM) 4/6/93, BNA PTCJ, 1993, Vol. 46, 4/6/93, pp. 34–35.*

FACTS

Major League Baseball Properties, Inc. (Properties), is the official trademark licensing arm of the twenty-six Major League Baseball clubs, including Los Angeles Dodgers, Inc. Formerly known as the Brooklyn Dodgers, the organization changed its name in 1958, when it moved the site of its home games from Brooklyn, New York, to Los Angeles. Departure of the team from Brooklyn was accompanied by hard feelings of abandonment.

In 1987, Senatore, Picardi, and Boyle opened a restaurant in Brooklyn with a nostalgic setting and considered the name *Ebbets Field* after the baseball park where the Brooklyn Dodgers had once played. They learned of the use of this name by a restaurant in New York and so decided to search the name Brooklyn Dodger. There were no registrations of that mark, so the group, incorporated as SNOD, began doing business in 1988 as the Brooklyn Dodger Sports Bar and Restaurant and applied to register *The Brooklyn Dodger* as a service mark.

Upon discovering SNOD's use of the mark, Properties asked SNOD to cease and desist; it ultimately filed suit against SNOD, claiming infringement of the Brooklyn Dodgers mark. Los Angeles applied to register its Brooklyn Dodgers marks after the suit had begun.

ISSUE

Was SNOD infringing on Major League Baseball Properties' Brooklyn Dodgers trademark?

HOLDING

No. Los Angeles failed to prove a likelihood of confusion, having abandoned use of its Brooklyn Dodgers mark from 1958 to 1981.

REASONING

Likelihood of Confusion

The court acknowledged that (1) Los Angeles's Brooklyn Dodgers mark is strong to the extent that the public identifies it with the Brooklyn-based baseball team and (2) SNOD's mark is similar. However, the two parties' services share no common feature, are not competitive, and are not inherently comparable. Nor has Los Angeles ever bridged the gap by opening a sports bar in its hundred years of existence.

Abandonment

While minor changes in a trademark do not constitute abandonment, the change from Brooklyn Dodgers to Los Angeles Dodgers was not minor and involved an essential element, thus affecting the public's perception of the mark and the team, according to the court.

Resumption of Use

Los Angeles abandoned its Brooklyn Dodgers mark in 1958 and after a twenty-three-year hiatus, resumed its use in 1981—and then only on novelty items, clothing, and jewelry. According to the court, abandonment is not cured by resumption of use. If Los Angeles had any interest in a Brooklyn Dodgers that interest arose in 1981. Los Angeles could have protected its trademark at that point by filing an application to register it;

however, such an application was not filed until 1989, a year after SNOD applied to register the mark. The court also noted that although Properties resumed use of this mark, it did not invest the mark with goodwill, since the Los Angeles goodwill nexus to the Borough of Brooklyn "was irretrievably shattered" by the team's departure.

According to the court, SNOD acted in good faith in electing, adopting, and using its mark and in conducting a trademark search. At no time did SNOD try to trade on the reputation of Los Angeles. As Judge Motley observed, given the notoriety of Los Angeles's departure from Brooklyn, trading upon Los Angeles's "goodwill" in Brooklyn would have been fatal to SNOD.

At this writing, Major Baseball Properties has appealed the district court's decision.

DISCUSSION QUESTIONS

What are some of the significant factors managers should be aware of in adopting and protecting their trademarks?

What situations may lead to a loss of trademark rights?

CASE
Fruit of the Loom, Inc., v. Girouard, CA 9, No. 91-56338, BNA PTCJ, Vol. 46 (5/18/93) pp. 97–98.

FACTS

Fruit of the Loom, Inc. (FOL), owns various Fruit of the Loom registered trademarks applied to a wide array of children's, women's, and men's clothing. Some of the marks include pictures of apples and grapes.

Girouard's company, Two Left Feet (TLF), began producing thongs and women's bustiers adorned with plastic fruit, calling them Fruit Flops and Fruit Cups. TLF's products sell for $35 to $45 at boutiques and other upscale stores. FOL filed suit for trademark infringement, violations of Section 43(a) of the Lanham Act, and trademark dilution under the California Business and Professional Code.

The district court found for TLF, declaring that confusion was not likely as to source, sponsorship, or approval and that no kind of mental association existed in reasonable buyers' minds between FOL's Fruit of the Loom and TLF's Fruit Flops and Fruit Cups.

FOL appealed this decision.

ISSUES

Has TLF engaged in trademark infringement and do its actions cause trademark dilution?

HOLDING

The appeals court affirmed the district court's findings and held that there had been no trademark infringement or dilution to Fruit of the Loom trademarks.

REASONING

As the district court noted, several of the confusion criteria used by the courts in such cases sided with TLF. The marks are dissimilar in sound, sight, and meaning; there was no present proximity of goods or marketing channels; TLF's goods are purchased with care; and there was no evidence of either actual confusion or intent to deceive on the part of TLF.

On the issue of dilution, FOL argued that TLF could tarnish FOL's goodwill and reputation with TLF's marks because TLF does no product testing for safety or quality. The court of appeals declared that evidence of TLF's quality controls was not relevant because there is no association of TLF products with FOL, and it noted that the parties' marks are not at all similar.

The court also noted that according to McCarthy (in *McCarthy on Trademarks and Unfair Competition*, a noteworthy source), to be protected against dilution, a mark must be not only distinctive but famous. Tiffany, Polaroid, Rolls Royce, and Kodak are examples of protectable marks. The courts have protected trademarks such as Century 21, the national brokerage network, and the Oscar of the motion picture academy against dilution.

The appeals court acknowledged that *Fruit of the Loom* is a strong mark; however *Fruit* alone is not strong enough to deserve protection under California Law. If *Fruit* by itself fell within the protected domain, then under the antidilution statutes, the "humble, humdrum" word *fruit* would be barred from use by the Fruit Basket, Fruit Gallery, and Fruit King, which are currently in business in San Francisco.

The appeals court declared the purpose of the antidilution law is directed against the whittling away of a trademark. Whittling away will not occur unless there is at least some subliminal connection in a buyer's mind between the two parties' uses of their mark. Such a connection is not the same as required for proof of likelihood of confusion, but it does require a threshold showing some mental association between the protected mark and the alleged diluter. According to the appeals court, the district court had rightfully found that there was no such a threshold association between FOL's *Fruit* and TLF's whimsical gewgaws.

DISCUSSION QUESTIONS

Explain the legal differences involved between a trademark owner's complaint of likelihood of confusion and a complaint of trademark dilution.

Discuss the factors that should be considered in a determination that likelihood of confusion exists, and explain their significance.

Discuss the considerations in a determination of the existence of trademark dilution.

ENDNOTES

1. Dorothy Cohen, "Trademark Strategy," *Journal of Marketing* 50 (January 1986), 61–74 and "Trademark Strategy Revisited," *Journal of Marketing* 55 (July 1991), 46–59 (Chicago, Ill.: American Marketing Association). Permission granted.

2. David A. Aaker and Kevin Lane Keller, "Consumer Evaluation of Brand Extensions," *Journal of Marketing* 54 (January 1990), 27–41.

3. Senate Report 1946.

4. Senate Report 1988.

5. Patricia Kimball Fletcher, "Joint Registration of Trademarks and Economic Value of a Trademark System," *University of Miami Law Review* 36 (1982), 297–335.

6. *Two Pesos, Inc.*, v. *Taco Cabana, Inc.*, 112 S. Ct. 2753 (1992).

7. Willis Raymond Davis Jr., "Intent-to-Use Applications for Trademark Registration," *Wayne Law Review* 35 (Spring 1989), 1135–1155.

8. Maureen Casey, "Intent-to-Use Legislation under the Trademark Law Revision Act of 1988: Modernization of the Trademark Registration Process," *Seton Hall Legislative Journal* 13 (1989–90), 200–212.

9. Barbara E. Johnson, "Trademarks: Evolving Law, Practice and the Lollipop Lady," *Journal of the Patent and Trademark Office Society* 71 (September 1989), 759–761.

10. Thomas Q. Henry, "New Law Will Significantly Change Selection, Adoption of Trademarks," *Res Gestae* 33 (November 1989), 211–213.

11. James T. Walsh, "Tips from the United States Patent and Trademark Office," *Trademark Reporter* 82 (1992), 452–466.

12. Jed S. Rakoff and Ira B. Wolff, "Commercial Counterfeiting: The Inadequacy of Existing Remedies," *Trademark Reporter* 73 (September-October 1983), 498.

13. Rakoff and Wolff, pp. 501–502.

14. *Vuitton et Fils. S.A.* v. *Crown Handbags* (1979), 492 F. Supp., 206 USPQ 907 (S.D.N.Y. 1979), *aff'd.*, 622 F. 2d 577 (CA-2, 1980).

15. Joseph Bainton, "Seizure Orders: An Innovative Judicial Response to Trademark Counterfeiting," *Trademark Reporter* 73 (September–October 1983), 459–475.

16. *Montrose Rolex, S.A.* v. *Dennis Snyder, Regional Commissioner*, U.S. Customs Service and G.S. Customs Service (1983), (CA-2, September).

17. Rakoff and Wolff, p. 494.

18. *Kellogg Co.* v. *National Biscuit Co.* (1938), 305 US 111, 118, 39 USPQ 296, 299.

19. *Anti-Monopoly Inc.* v. *General Mills Fun Group* (1979), 611 F. 2d 296, 301 (9th Cir.).
20. Vincent N. Palladino, "Trademarks and Competition: The *Ives* Case," *John Marshall Law Review* 15 (1982), 319–356.
21. Palladino, p. 678.
22. Ralph H. Folsom and Larry L. Teply, "Trademarked Generic Words," *Trademark Reporter* 70 (1980), 206–242.
23. Sidney A. Diamond, "Properly Used, Trademarks Are Forever," *American Bar Association Journal* 68 (December 1982), 1578.
24. *American Thermos Products Co.* v. *Aladdin Industries, Inc.* (1962), 207 F. Supp. 9, 20, 134 USPQ 98 D. CT.
25. *Anti-Monopoly Inc.* v. *General Mills Fun Group* (1979), 611 F. 2d 296, 301 (9th Cir.).
26. *E. I. duPont de Nemours & Co., Inc.*, v. *Yoshida International, Inc.* (1975), 393 F. Supp. 502, 527, 185 USPQ 597 (E.D.N.Y.).
27. Allan W. Leiser and Carl R. Schwartz, "Techniques for Ascertaining Whether a Term Is Generic," *Trademark Reporter* 73 (July–August 1983), 386.
28. Michael H. Bierman and Jeffrey D. Wexler, "Toward a Reformulation of the Test for Determining Trademark Infringement," *Trademark Reporter* 80 (1990), 1–35.
29. J. Thomas McCarthy, *Trademarks and Unfair Competition*, 2nd ed. (Rochester, New York: Lawyers Co-operative Publishing, 1984).
30. *Mushroom Makers, Inc.*, v. *R. G. Barry Corp.* (1979), 200 USPQ 832.
31. John Paul Reiner, "The Universe and Sample: How Good Is Good Enough?" *Trademark Reporter* 73 (July–August 1983), 366–375.
32. Reiner, p. 373.
33. Bradlee R. Boal, "Techniques for Ascertaining Likelihood of Confusion and the Meaning of Advertising Communications," *Trademark Reporter* 73 (July-August 1983), 405–435.
34. Ibid., pp. 407–408.
35. *RJR Foods, Inc.*, v. *White Rock Corp.* (1979), 201 USPQ 578 (S.D.N.Y. 1978), *aff'd.*, 603 F. 2d 1058, 203 USPQ 401 (CA-2, 1979).
36. Boal, p. 425.
37. Albert Robin and Howard B. Barnaby, "Trademark Surveys—Heads You Lose, Tails We Win," *Trademark Reporter* 73 (July–August 1983), 436–445.
38. Ibid., p. 441.
39. *American Luggage Works, Inc.*, v. *United States Trunk Co.* 1957, 158 F. Supp. 50, 54, 116 USPQ 188 (D. MA).
40. Reiner, p. 370.
41. *National Football League Properties, Inc.*, v. *Wichita Falls Sportswear, Inc.* (1982), 532 F. Supp. 651, 215 USPQ 175 (W.D. WA).
42. Boal, p. 413.
43. *Holiday Inns Inc.* v. *Holiday Out of America* (1973), 481 F. 2d 445, 178 USPQ 257 (CA-5).
44. *Union Carbide Corp.* v. *Ever-Ready Inc.* (1976), 531 F. 2d 366, 381-382, 188 USPQ 623 (CA-7).
45. Fred Morgan, "The Admissibility of Consumer Surveys in Courts," *Journal of Marketing* 43 (Fall 1979), 33–40.
46. Fred W. Morgan, "Judicial Standards for Survey Evidence: An Update and Guidelines," *Journal of Marketing* 54 (January 1990), 59–70.
47. Peter Weiss, "The Use of Survey Evidence in Trademark Litigation: Science, Art or Confidence Game?" *Trademark Reporter* 80 (January–February 1990), 71–86.
48. Mark Borgman, "Give a Hoot, Don't Dilute: The Case for a Federal Dilution Statute," *Review of Litigation* 8 (1989), 347–379.
49. Frank I. Schechter, "The Rational Basis of Trademark Protection," *Harvard Law Review* 40 (1927), 813.
50. *Ringling Bros.–Barnum & Bailey Combined Shows, Inc.*, v. *Celozzi-Ettleson Chevrolet, Inc.* (1988), 855 USPQ2d 1072.
51. *Cynthia Grey* v. *Campbell Soup Co.* (1986), 231 USPQ 562.

52. *Mead Data Central Co.* v. *Toyota Motor Sales, U.S.A., Inc.* (1989), 10 USPQ2d 1961.
53. Felix Kent, "Reversal of Trademark-Dilution Decision," *New York Law Journal* (June 23, 1989), 2–3.
54. Ralph H. Folsom, Michael Wallace Gordon, and John A. Spanogle Jr., *International Business Transactions* (St. Paul, Minn.: West Publishing, 1988, pp. 335–339.
55. W. R. Cornish, "The International Relations of Intellectual Property," *Cambridge Law Journal*, 52 (March 1993), 46–43.
56. Senate Report 1988.

PART III

Legal Issues in Promotion Decisions

Legal Issues in Promotion Decisions

This chapter examines the Federal Trade Commission's efforts to eliminate advertising abuse. Chapter 8 examines the impact of the First Amendment and the Lanham Act on advertising, and the restraints placed on the promotional aspects of direct marketing. Chapter 9 discusses the legal restrictions on personal selling and sales promotion activities.

CHAPTER SEVEN
Advertising and the Federal Trade Commission

A sale is a measure of commercial marketing success. It is a basic element in the network of marketing activities that precedes, accompanies, and follows the exchange of goods and services for money. Although there is no best method for achieving sales, there are a variety of selling activities available to a firm. These techniques can be encompassed in what is known as a promotional mix, and they include advertising, personal selling, publicity, and sales promotion. In recent years, the technique called direct marketing has become a major component of this mix. All of these promotional activities may be subject to legal concerns. This chapter focuses on advertising, which is the promotional area in which most legal issues may arise and in which the law is fairly well developed.

GOVERNMENT REGULATION OF ADVERTISING

Government control over advertising emanates from various federal, state, and local agencies through laws, judicial precedents, rules, and guides. By far the greatest force is exerted by the federal government, and several federal laws impact on advertising decisions.

The Federal Trade Commission (FTC) Act of 1914, which created the federal authority most active in controlling advertising abuse, was originally passed to implement the antitrust concept, one of a series of laws that attempted to restrain monopolistic practices and unfair methods of competition. It contained no statement about advertising.

The Wheeler Lea Amendments, passed in 1938, seemed to broaden the commission's power over advertising when the important Section 5 of the FTC Act was rewritten to read: "Unfair methods of competition and unfair or deceptive acts or practices are hereby declared to be unlawful." The addition of the phrase *unfair or deceptive acts or practices* was designed to indicate that if there were injury to the public as well as to competitors, the commission was empowered to act.

The amendment also specified that false advertising of foods, drugs, cosmetics, and devices was an unfair or deceptive act or practice. This did not add much, as all false advertising was held to be deceptive, but Section 15(a) was helpful in defining the term *false advertising*:

> False advertising means an advertisement other than labeling, which is misleading in a material respect, and in determining whether the advertisement is misleading, there shall be taken into account (among other things) not only the representations made or suggested by statement, word, design, device, sound, or any combination thereof, but also the extent to which the advertisement fails to reveal facts material in the light of such representations.

In subsequent years, a number of acts were passed relating to advertising, and their enforcement was placed under the FTC. For example, the Public Health Smoking Act of 1970 banned cigarette advertising on radio and television, and the Comprehensive Smokeless Tobacco Health Education Act of 1986 placed a similar ban on the broadcast advertising of smokeless tobacco products. The FTC is required to report annually to Congress on the effects of cigarette advertising and promotion and has designed warning notices to appear in print advertisement for smokeless tobacco.

The Magnuson-Moss Warranty–Federal Trade Commission Improvements Act (1975) considerably expanded the commission's authority. The Magnuson-Moss warranty section of the act was designed to enable consumers to make "valid and informed comparisons of warranties for similar products" and as noted in Chapter 3, gave the FTC the power to promulgate rules for any product warranted in writing with an actual cost to the consumer exceeding $15.

The FTC improvements section of the act broadened the scope of the FTC's activities to cover practices that affected commerce rather than only those designated as in commerce, and it permitted the commission to order restitution to consumers. Most important, it empowered the FTC to promulgate trade regulation rules that specify unfair or deceptive acts or practices and authorized penalties for violations of these rules.

Acting under its new explicit authority, the FTC undertook eighteen consumer protection rule-making proceedings within several years. However, some of these raised up protests from affected interested groups and business interests generally.[1] After the commission proposed the Children's Television Advertising Rule of 1978, which would have placed limits on television advertisements directed at children, a serious backlash erupted against it, and in May 1980, Congress simply allowed the agency's funding to run out.

In the 1980 Federal Trade Commission Amendment Act, Congress reaffirmed the FTC's basic role but imposed a number of restrictions on it. The act provided for a two-house legislative veto, under which an FTC rule could be overturned by congressional action within ninety days of a rule's promulgation. This provision later was held unconstitutional. The act also prohibited the FTC from using unfairness in trade regulation rules directed toward children's television advertising. The FTC's unfairness authority was to be clarified in its reauthorization bill scheduled for 1983. However, the FTC has not been reauthorized by Congress since 1980. It has been operating under continuing resolutions, which are temporary approvals by Congress that allow the FTC to function in the same capacity as in 1980. House and Senate conferees are scheduled to iron out differences in the reauthorization bills. In the interim, however, the FTC has redefined its mission so that its mandate to enforce consumer protection statutes is now predicated on an underlying belief in the free-market economy.[2] In keeping with its new policies, the commission proposed a major revision in its mandate over advertising.

FTC ENFORCEMENT ACTIVITIES

In enforcing its advertising requirements, the FTC has the authority to issue administrative complaints charging firms with unfair or deceptive acts or practices, which, if not settled with a consent order, are tried before an administrative law judge. Appeals from the administrative law judge's findings may be taken to the FTC and then to the federal appellate courts. When the courts uphold the findings of a violation, the FTC may enter a cease-and-desist order prohibiting the offending conduct. The cease-and-desist order may then be enforced through civil penalty action.

The FTC has the authority to promulgate trade regulation rules, subject to court review, which carry the force of law and may be enforced by civil penalties. The FTC also has a number of other mechanisms such as interpretive guidelines, enforcement policy statements, and advisory opinions. These are not binding. Advisory opinions provide guidance in relatively specific factual situations in response to inquiries, whereas guidelines and policy statements are broader, applying either to entire industries or to broad subject areas.

FTC Regulatory Standards

Pursuant to the FTC Act and in accordance with decisions by the courts, the commission's actions against advertisers are predicated upon several prerequisites, namely, that:

- the advertisements must have been deceptive or unfair.
- the deception or unfairness must concern a fact material to the addressees of the advertisements.
- the public interest must require action.

Deception Standard. Although no strict guidelines had been established, the standard for deception most frequently applied by the FTC in its enforcement actions was "the tendency or capacity to deceive." In late 1983, the commission issued a controversial policy statement declaring the FTC will find deception if there has been "a misrepresentation, omission, or practice that misleads the consumer, acting reasonably in the circumstances, to the consumer's detriment."

This standard imposes a greater burden of proof on the FTC to show a violation of Section 5. First, the FTC must show probable, not possible, deception, and second, the FTC must show potential deception of "consumers acting reasonably in the circumstances," not just any consumers.[3]

Unfairness Standard. The commission made relatively little use of its unfairness authority in protecting consumers from advertising abuse until recently. In 1972, the Supreme Court noted that the consumer, as well as the merchant and manufacturer, must be protected from unfair trade practices.[4] The court had clearly recognized the commission's authority to act "like a court of equity" and to consider "public values." Although the FTC continued to make only limited use of unfairness in its case-by-case approach, it applied the concept in a number of trade regulation rules that were either issued or proposed in subsequent years. Many of these rules did not deal specifically with advertising.

In response to the free-market antiregulatory posture of the Reagan Administration and to criticisms from business and Congress that the FTC's unfairness authority was both used excessively and potentially unbounded, the commission issued an Unfairness Policy Statement in 1980. Its articulated guidelines defined unfair acts or practices as those that are likely to (1) cause substantial injury to consumers, (2) not be reasonably avoidable by consumers themselves, and (3) not be outweighed by countervailing benefits to consumers or competition. The immoral, unethical, oppressive, or unscrupulous criteria were considered unnecessary.

Marketers should be aware that these policy statements on deception and unfairness are not binding and may be changed by future commissioners.[5] However, some guidance is available through court decisions as discussed in the next section.

Public Interest. As enacted, Section 5(b) of the FTC Act limited the commission's jurisdiction to cases in which "it shall appear to the commission that a proceeding . . . would be to the interest of the public."

Many federal administrative agencies are required to function in the public interest; all too often, however, the Supreme Court cites public interest in a manner that is vague and undefined. Nevertheless, it was not until the present decade that the FTC revised its definitions of unfairness and deception so as to characterize the public to be protected as "the consumer acting reasonably."

Legal Guidelines for Advertising

A number of areas must be addressed in determining how to avoid FTC complaints of deceptive advertising.

Who Is the Target of the Ad?

The target groups in whose interest advertising is regulated have been referred to as the public, the purchasing public, the consuming public, the consumer, the average consumer, the customer, the buyer, the individual, and the average individual. Moreover, the mind and intelligence of these individuals are subject to close scrutiny. According to the courts, the public may include both the "trusting as well as the suspicious" and "that vast multitude which includes the ignorant, the unthinking, and the credulous."[6] The commission, however, has noted that it would not hold an advertiser liable for misconceptions "among the foolish or feebleminded."[7]

The current FTC, which added the phrase "consumers acting reasonably" to a finding of deception, has declared the consumer to be the average individual, except in cases when ads target the elderly, children, or the terminally ill. In those cases, the commission will consider a reasonable member of that group.

Developing the Advertising Message

Although the terms *deception* and *unfairness* have not been defined precisely, they have acquired meaning through FTC decisions and judicial interpretations. This is particularly true of *deception*, because there are years of precedent that have helped establish criteria for the commission's actions in protecting consumers from deceptive practices. In legal terminology, deception is "having the capacity or tendency to deceive." Under the current administration, a new definition has emerged, with the FTC declaring that a finding of deception will occur when there is "a representation, omission, or practice that is likely to mislead the consumer acting reasonably in the circumstances to the consumer's detriment." FTC activities and court decisions indicate the kinds of questions to be raised by advertisers in determining whether their ads will be considered deceptive.

Is the Representation (Claim) True?

Attempts are made to determine the truth of an advertisement by examining the claim (also called the representation, the promise, and the benefit). The claim may occur in any part of an advertisement or in accompanying promotional material. It may be presented pictorially, in the copy, or by affixing trade names and trademarks.

Objective Claims. In determining the falsehood of an objective claim, the FTC will generally consider a statement deceptive when a standard exists for determining the truth of the representation and when there is sufficient knowledge to establish its falsity. Of course, the difficulty arises in deciding which standards to use as yardsticks against which representations are measured. The commission may use dictionary definitions, government definitions or specifications, general usage, and expert opinion as its authoritative standard and in recent years has used consumer surveys.

Proof of the falsity of an objective claim may be accomplished with relative simplicity as, for example, in an ad that claimed that the user of the denture adhesive Poligrip could eat problem foods such as apples and corn on the cob without embarrassment or discomfort. In fact, dentures are usually constructed with front teeth that are virtually useless for biting, with or without Poligrip, and that serve only cosmetic purposes.[8] Claims that are clearly and objectively false have appeared relatively infrequently in the commission's recent caseload.

Subjective Claims. Subjective or opinion claims are difficult to prove false, especially because trade puffery is generally considered beyond the scope of the commission. A puff has been defined as a statement that "probably would not be taken too seriously by the ordinary reader."[9] Such claims are often considered as incapable of proof or disproof, not because of inadequate knowledge, but because the applicable criterion is so personal and individual that it defies objective measurement. Thus, statements that a toothpaste "will beautify your smile" and a sewing machine "is almost human" are considered by the courts as puffing.

Nevertheless, when superlatives are used that can be objectively disproved, they may be considered deceptive. For example, the FTC has ordered companies to stop advertising safety helmets as "finest, safest, or best"[10] and batteries as "trouble free for five years."[11]

Implied Claims. The courts have ruled that in assessing the meaning of a communication, the FTC must look at the impression that is likely to be created. Deception by innuendo, for example, may occur through the use of certain words or phrases. The FTC issued a cease-and-desist order to a debt collection agency, noting that the use of the word *Letegram* in its mailing to various people misrepresented the immediacy of any action the agency might take against a debtor.[12]

Uniqueness Claim. When a company indicates that its product is the only one to possess a particular attribute, it is using a uniqueness claim. If such a claim is made for a product characteristic that indeed exists in competitive products, the uniqueness claim may be considered misleading and deceptive. An ad for Cope stated, "Cope looks different, is different. Besides a powerful pain reliever, Cope gives you a gentle relaxer. The others don't. . . . A unique formula for really effective relief of nervous tension headache. And you get it only in Cope." The FTC declared that the ads that portrayed Cope as unique were false and misleading.[13]

The Claim with False Proof. This situation emerged from the particular characteristics of television as an advertising medium. One of television's major advantages as a medium is its ability to demonstrate the product or service advertised. To perform this demonstration effectively in a television commercial message, advertisers and their advertising agencies have in a number of cases resorted to mock-ups—devices made to simulate real objects and prepared specifically for a particular purpose relevant to a commercial message.

The mock-up may be used for purely background purposes—as, for example, in the use of shaving cream to represent whipped cream because the latter melts rapidly under the hot lights—or it may be used for technical ease in an attempt to prove some superiority or desirable quality of a product. In the initial sandpaper shaving case originating in 1961, the Court of Appeals set aside the FTC's orders against the use of mock-ups on the grounds that they were too broad; ultimately, clarification was requested of the Supreme Court.

In the sandpaper shaving case, a television commercial used a mock-up of sand and Plexiglas instead of sandpaper to represent the claim that even sandpaper could be shaved after the application of shaving cream; this was declared deceptive. Suggestions made to control the questionable use of mock-ups include:

1. Prohibiting the use of all mock-ups.

2. Prohibiting the use of all mock-ups that attempt to prove a claim.

3. Prohibiting the use of all mock-ups that attempt to prove a claim that is not valid.

The FTC held that the prohibition extend to suggestion number 2, declaring that there is prejudice in attempting to prove something by spurious means, valid or not. The advertising world was willing to accept the requirement that mock-ups attempting to prove nontruthful claims should be prohibited.

The Supreme Court accepted the FTC's suggestion, with modifications, and prohibited the undisclosed use of a mock-up that attempts to prove a claim. The court upheld the commission's order and declared that the respondents were to cease and desist from: . . . unfairly or deceptively advertising any . . . product by presenting a test, experiment or demonstration that 1) is represented to the public as actual proof of a claim made for the product which is material to inducing its sale, and 2) is not in fact a genuine . . . demonstration being conducted as represented and does not in fact prove the claim because of the undisclosed use and substitution of a mock-up or prop instead of the product. . . .[14]

In interpreting the order, the court cited an example of a commercial that extolled the goodness of ice cream while giving viewers a picture of a scoop of mashed potatoes. If the mashed potatoes prop is not used for additional proof of a product claim, no problem exists; if, however, the viewer is invited to see the ice cream's rich texture, deception would be present.

The FTC ruled that a television commercial in which clear marbles were put in the bottom of soup misled viewers because the marbles kept the soup's solid ingredients at the top, thus implying a thicker consistency that in fact existed.[15]

Case: In Re Volvo North America Corp., et Al.

In a recent case, the FTC indicated that firms and their advertising agencies who misrepresent that any advertised demonstration, picture, experiment, or test either proves any material feature of a product or proves its superiority to another product may be both subject to FTC orders prohibiting such feature misrepresentations and required to make disgorgement payments.[16]

In a Bear Foot ad campaign for Volvo cars, a monster truck was depicted running over a row of cars and crushing all but a Volvo 240 station wagon. The FTC charged both Volvo and Scali, its ad agency, with falsely depicting the comparative performance of cars. The FTC alleged that some of the Volvos used in the demonstration had been structurally reinforced and subjected to less severe monster-truck treatment than competing cars and that the structural supports in some of the competing cars had been severed.

A consent order agreement to settle these charges prohibits future misrepresentations of either the strength, structural integrity, or crashworthiness of any automobile or the safety of a vehicle occupant in a collision. In addition, both Volvo and Scali are required to pay $150,000 each to the U.S. Treasury as disgorgement (the surrender of something illicitly obtained).

The order specifies four examples of advertising techniques that are prohibited if they misrepresent that a demonstration proves a material feature of a product: (1) the undisclosed use or substitution of a material mock-up or prop; (2) the undisclosed material alteration of the advertised product, any product to which it is being compared, or any material prop or device shown in the ad; (3) the use of a visual perspective or camera, film, audio, or video technique to which it is being compared, or any other material aspect of the demonstration; and (4) the undisclosed differential treatment to which advertised product and any product to which it is compared are subjected.

Volvo had previously agreed to settle similar charges leveled by the Texas attorney general. That settlement does not include Scali.

The Claim with Two Meanings

An advertisement that is capable of two meanings, one of which is false, is misleading. The commission issued a cease-and-desist order prohibiting the National Commission on Egg Nutrition (NCEN) from advertising the statement "There is no scientific evidence that eating eggs increases the risk of . . . heart disease." NCEN appealed the order on the grounds that the statement is true. The topic is controversial: some medical experts believe existing evidence indicates that increased consumption of dietary cholesterol, including that in eggs, may increase the risk of heart disease; others, however, do not believe in this relationship. A court of appeals upheld the commission order declaring that when an advertisement conveys more than one meaning, one of which is false, the advertiser is liable for the misleading variation.[17]

Is the Claim Adequately Substantiated?

Much of the FTC's recent activity relates to claims that are not adequately substantiated. According to the FTC, it is illegal to advertise an affirmative claim for a product without having a reasonable basis. The requirement to substantiate advertising claims relates to those made regarding a product's safety, performance, efficacy, quality, or comparative price.

The substantiation requirements emerged from a program introduced by the commission in the 1970s and were crystallized in an FTC decision in which the commission stated that it was unfair to advertise a claim without having a reasonable basis to support it, even if the claim were true and the product ultimately performed as advertised. Advertised claims that had been considered to be inadequately substantiated ranged from a beauty product that claimed it removed wrinkles to automobile tires that were designated as safe.[18]

The substantiation concept was broadened considerably in 1972 in a complaint issued against Pfizer, a drug manufacturer, charging the company with unfair and deceptive advertising for its new product Unburn.[19] Although charges against Pfizer were ultimately dismissed, the opinion expressed by the commission has been used as the basis for most of its subsequent complaints relevant to adequate substantiation.

Commissioner Kirkpatrick explained the obligation of advertisers to substantiate advertising claims before they are made. In the opinion of the commission, it is unfair and illegal to advertise an affirmative claim for a product without having a reasonable basis for making such a claim. Such unfairness may exist even if the claim is true or if the product performs as advertised. According to the commission, the fundamental unfairness results from imposing on the consumer the unavoidable economic risk that the product may not perform as advertised, if neither the consumer nor the manufacturer has a reasonable basis for belief in the product claim.

Adequate Substantiation: What Is It? It is clearly in the interest of advertisers to have some listing of the kinds of data that would be considered adequate substantiation. Unfortunately, according to an FTC staff member, "'adequacy of substantiation' . . . cannot be considered in the abstract."[20] The requirements vary in accordance with several relevant factors. Two important considerations relate to the kind of product for which the claim is made and the particular representation, express or implied, in the ad.

The Scope of Responsibility for Substantiation. The advertising substantiation program has a clear impact on many manufacturers' advertising decision; moreover responsibility for substantiation of a claim has been expanded beyond the producer of the advertised product. The FTC's position, expressed in a number of recent complaints and orders, indicates that in addition to the manufacturer of the product, the advertising agency who prepared the ads,[21] the retailer who disseminates the ads,[22] and even the celebrity who endorses the ads[23] may be responsible for the reasonable basis requirement. The FTC has indicated that the advertising agency may rely on substantiation furnished by its client, but it must evaluate such substantiation as to its reasonable basis.

Designing a Control System. In the design of a management information system relevant to the advertising substantiation program, information should be disseminated to anyone having potential involvement in advertising decisions. As an example, this can include:

- The kinds of claims that require a reasonable basis prior to dissemination, e.g., the product's safety, performance, efficacy, quality, or comparative price.

- The FTC's enforcement policies relevant to substantiation requirements.

- The kinds of documentation that may be required as a reasonable basis for a claim.

- Questions that are to be answered relevant to specific advertisements, including:

   — Is there an implied claim consumers may perceive, which is not adequately substantiated?

   — Is a claim that is adequately substantiated presented in a manner that may be considered a misrepresentation?

In addition to developing an information system, companies and their advertising agencies can conduct consumer research that may be mutually beneficial to the company and the FTC. As noted, a dispute often centers on the meaning of an ad, and the FTC may find that companies do not have substantiation for certain implied meanings. One way to avoid this, according to the FTC, is to pretest an ad to determine what meanings or impressions flow from it. Research revealing a campaign has no significant implied claims for which the company does not have documentation could have a major effect on the FTC's decision not to pursue an investigation.

Has Material Information Been Omitted?

Not only what is said but what is not said may constitute a deceptive act.[24] According to the current commission, a material representation is one that is likely to affect a consumer's conduct regarding the choice of a product. Where a material representation is omitted, it is an indication that an injury to the consumer is likely to exist (i.e., consumer detriment will occur). Certain categories of information are considered material, including expressed claims and information that the seller knew or should have known an ordinary consumer would need in order to evaluate a product or service. Information concerning health, safety, and the central characteristics of a product is generally considered to be material.

If an ad makes claims and omits material facts that may relate to those claims, it may trigger affirmative disclosure requirements in future ads. For example, Fresh Horizons bread was highly touted for its fiber content. According to the FTC, the presence of wood in the bread was a material fact and in a consent order agreement required the ads to state, "The source of this fiber is wood" or "Contains fiber derived from the pulp of trees."[25] In an Aspercreme case, the FTC required the company to disclose in all advertising and labeling that Aspercreme did not contain aspirin.

Unfair Advertising

The precedents for a finding of unfairness are much less developed than those concerning deception. In 1972, the Supreme Court encouraged the commission to apply unfairness in protecting consumers.[26] Nevertheless, in most of its case-by-case adjudications, the commission continued to use unfairness only in conjunction with deception.

The FTC has complained of advertising to children in several cases, expressing its concern about ads that may have the tendency or capacity to influence children to engage in unsafe behavior. Hudson Pharmaceutical agreed not to use a hero figure such as Spiderman in its vitamin advertising because such advertising could induce children to take excessive amounts of vitamins.[27] General Foods agreed not to depict Euell Gibbons picking and eating certain wild plants because some plants may be harmful if eaten.[28] Mego agreed to discontinue an ad for its Cher doll showing a little girl seated next to a sink full of water and using an electric hair dryer to dry the doll's hair.[29]

The 1980 FTC Act prohibited the FTC from promulgating trade regulation rules on the basis of unfairness in advertising and indicated that this prohibition would be reevaluated when the next FTC appropriations bill was passed. It did not prevent the FTC from proceeding against unfair advertising on a case-by-case basis; however, there has been relatively little activity in this area. The FTC has issued a policy statement providing a more detailed sense of the definition and limits of unfairness. The basic criterion is that the unfairness must cause substantial consumer injury, outweighed by any countervailing benefits, and the injury must be one the consumer cannot reasonably avoid.

A court of appeals ruled that a practice may be shown to be unfair even without a showing of intent to deceive.[30] Orkin Exterminating Corp., a termite and pest control company, had raised its annual reinspection fee for customers whose contract permitted them to renew their "lifetime" guarantees for treated structures for a fixed annual fee. The FTC found that Orkin had violated Section 5 by unilaterally breaching more than 200,000 contracts, and it issued an order requiring Orkin to cease and desist from conduct the commission found to constitute unfair acts or practices.

The company appealed, arguing that "a mere breach of contract" that does not involve some sort of deception or fraudulent behavior is outside the ambit of Section 5. The Court of Appeals declared that the U.S. Supreme Court has put its stamp of approval on the FTC's evolving use of a consumer unfairness doctrine not traditionally moored in anticompetitiveness or deception.[31] Moreover, the FTC is charged, by statute, with the duty of prescribing "interpretive rules and general statements of policy with respect to unfair or deceptive acts or practices."

The commission's unfairness standard, enunciated in its Policy Statement, focuses on unjustified consumer injury. For an act or practice to be unfair:

1. The injury must be substantial. Although the actual injury to individual consumers may be small on an annual basis, this does not mean that such injury is not substantial. According to the FTC, Orkin's breach of contract generated more than $7 million in revenues from renewal fees to which the company was not entitled.

2. The injury must not be outweighed by any countervailing benefits to consumers or competition. According to the commission, the increase in the fee was not accompanied by any increase in the level of service. Requiring Orkin to roll back its fees would have no adverse effects on its competitors.

3. Consumers could not reasonably avoid the injury. Such was the situation in this case.

The appeals court declared that the FTC's conduct in this case "fully and clearly comports with the standard set forth in its Policy Statement on unfairness," and it enforced the cease-and-desist order.

Remedies for Unfair and Deceptive Advertising

The FTC was not established to resolve private disputes, but to end illegal practices. Its objective was to restrain future violators, not to punish violators for past misconduct. In fact, initially, the FTC was not empowered to require penalties for unfair and deceptive practices. Its basic remedy was to issue a cease-and-desist order; penalties were imposed only if a firm continued to commit the prohibited acts in violation of that order. Nevertheless, the scope and impact of these remedies have increased in recent years.

Advertising Agency Liability

The commission has, on occasion, found advertising agencies, as well as their clients, liable for their involvement in the creation of allegedly deceptive ads. Most recently, in the Volvo monster truck ads, the commission charged that the ad agency had falsely represented that the monster truck ads used unaltered cars.

In deciding which entities to charge, the commission considers the extent to which an ad agency actually participated in the deception. It investigates whether the agency participated in producing the ad and whether it knew or had reason to know that the ad was deceptive or unsubstantiated. Such issues are likely to arise in produce demonstrations. According to FTC Commissioner Owen's view, the degree of technical control that an advertising agency exercises over product demonstration may sustain charges that the agency knew or had reason to know of the deception.[32]

An alleged violation may come to the attention of the commission in a number of ways: through a complaint about a competitor's ad, by way of a consumer complaint, from government agencies upon referral by the courts, or through the commission itself.

Cease-and-Desist Order

The earliest remedy available to the FTC for ending false advertising is the cease-and-desist order, which is issued after the commission investigates an alleged violation, serves a formal complaint, and receives no reply. If a reply is made, a formal hearing is held before a trial examiner, who issues an initial decision. Unless this decision is appealed by either side or unless the commission places it on its own docket for review, the initial decision becomes the final decision of the commission. This decision may incorporate an order to cease and desist from the practice that was the subject of the complaint.

Consent Order

At any stage in the proceedings before the hearing, a settlement may be negotiated between the FTC and the advertiser. When both sides agree, a consent order is prepared. The order contains a statement that the signing is for settlement purposes only and does not constitute an admission by a firm that it has violated the law. However, the firm agrees not to engage in the activities that were the subject of the complaint.

In the largest false advertising settlement in FTC history, the commission required General Nutrition Inc., the largest retailer of nutritional supplements in the United States, to pay $2.4 million to settle charges that the company made unsubstantiated claims for its products.[33] General Nutrition was charged with violating the terms of two previous FTC orders by failing to substantiate disease-treatment, weight-loss, muscle-building, and endurance claims for over forty products. The company signed a consent decree that would also prohibit them from making unsubstantiated claims for hair-loss products not covered under the 1970 and 1989 orders, which were allegedly violated.

Signing a consent agreement with the commission is not an admission that any law was violated, but the company felt it desirable since they thought they were vulnerable on the issues.

Penalties

Until 1973, the maximum penalty for a single violation of an FTC cease-and-desist order was $5,000; in 1973, it was raised to $10,000. Moreover, such penalties can take on significant proportions.

Reader's Digest agreed to a consent order in 1972 that required that publisher, which regularly uses a sweepstakes in its promotional efforts, to cease and desist from engaging in various practices in connection with such sweepstakes. Among the practices proscribed were using or distributing simulated checks and currency and using or distributing any confusingly simulated items of "value." In 1978, an FTC motion for partial summary judgment was granted on the basis that *Reader's Digest* had violated the order by mailing approximately 14 million simulated travel checks and over 4 million simulated bonds in connection with its promotional efforts.

In 1979, the FTC requested the court to impose civil penalties of $1.75 million. *Reader's Digest* declared that since there were only six series of promotional mailings of such "checks" and "bonds" in 1973 and 1974, there were only six violations. Five of the mailings had occurred in 1973, when the penalty was $5,000, and the last in 1974, when the penalty was $10,000. According to *Reader's Digest*, the maximum penalty allowable in this case was therefore $35,000.

The FTC, on the other hand, contended that *Reader's Digest* had distributed a total of almost 18 million individual mailings containing checks or bonds and was therefore guilty of approximately 18 million separate violations. Although the total maximum penalty for these items could have amounted to more than $89 billion, the FTC was requesting a fine of only $1.75 million.

Reader's Digest ultimately appealed to the Supreme Court, declaring that the ruling set a precedent for imposing a fine on each item mailed and could have a chilling effect on publishers and advertisers. The Supreme Court, however, refused to set aside the fine of $1.75 million, declaring that a civil penalty should represent more than a mere license fee amount or an acceptable cost of violation of an order and should provide a meaningful deterrence.[34]

Affirmative Disclosure

Affirmative disclosure requires that a company disclose in its advertising the deficiencies or limitations of a product or service so that a consumer may be aware of the negative, as well as the positive, attributes of an item. As noted earlier, omission of a material fact in an ad can trigger an affirmative disclosure requirement. Usually the facts to be disclosed involve health or safety considerations. The most widespread use of affirmative disclosure is represented by the cautionary statements in cigarette advertising.

Corrective Advertising

Corrective advertising is designed to overcome the continuing effects of inaccurate information in prior deceptive advertising. Whereas it is similar to affirmative disclosure, its objectives are somewhat broader and include (1) dispelling the residual effects of prior deceptive advertising, (2) restoring to the stage the level of competition that prevailed before the unfair practice, and (3) depriving firms of falsely obtained gains to which deceptive advertising may have contributed. In addition, corrective advertising specifically addresses the misinformation previously offered; affirmative disclosure adds information that was not previously offered.

The marbles-in-the-soup case was the first in which such a remedy was suggested: While shooting an ad, Campbell Soup Company was alleged to have placed marbles in a soup bowl in order to force the solid ingredients to the surface, thus creating the false impression that there was more stock than actually existed. A group of law students, designating themselves SOUP (Stamp Out Unfair Practices) recommended that the commission require Campbell to use corrective advertisements; however, the FTC accepted a consent agreement from Campbell in which Campbell agreed to change its advertising in the future. Although the commission did not consider the corrective order appropriate in this case, it did use it in a number of subsequent cases.

In the first litigated order (the firm appealed to the courts) involving corrective advertising, the FTC declared that since 1921, Listerine advertisements had fostered the belief that Listerine was effective in the treatment and prevention of colds and sore throats. Accordingly, the FTC required Warner-Lambert to spend an amount equal to the average Listerine annual advertising budget—which has been estimated at $10 million—on a corrective advertising campaign. The commission ordered Warner-Lambert to place the corrective statement "Listerine will not help prevent colds or sore throats or lessen their severity" in its ads. The Supreme Court upheld this order and Warner-Lambert conducted the campaign.

The effectiveness of corrective advertising as a remedy has been questioned by researchers. Proposals to increase the efficiency of this remedy include suggestions that the FTC stress consumer responses during a campaign and provide advertisers with incentives to seek effective corrective communication.[35]

Redress of Consumer Injury

The Magnuson-Moss Act authorizes the commission to bring civil actions to redress consumer injury. This may include rescission of contracts, refund of money, return of property, and payment of damages. The courts may not, however, award exemplary or punitive damages.

The commission can bring such actions only if there has been a violation of a trade regulation rule, if there has been a violation of a cease-and-desist order, and when a reasonable person would have known under the circumstances that the act was dishonest or fraudulent. In 1981, Horizon Corporation, one of the largest sellers of undeveloped real estate in the Southwest, was ordered to pay $14.5 million to purchasers who had bought land because of the company's false and misleading claims.

The FTC has also engaged in activities designed to notify consumers of redress capabilities. In 1981, Ford Motor Company ran the first repair-information advertising ordered by the FTC. The commission had charged that Ford was repairing cars powered by four-cylinder engines that were inadequately lubricated; by quietly fixing a widespread problem only for those who complained, Ford was providing a secret warranty. Ford was ordered to run black-and-white, one-page ads in magazines such as *Newsweek, Reader's Digest, Sports Illustrated, Time* and *U.S. News & World Report.* The headline stated, "Ford Motor Co. introduces the customer information system. It makes greater after-sales service even better."[36]

Injunctions

Until fairly recently, the FTC's enforcement authority has been implemented primarily through its own administrative process. A striking development in recent years concerns a proviso, in the 1973 Alaska Pipeline bill, that specifies that "in proper cases the commission may seek, and after proper proof, the court may issue, an permanent injunction."[37] Although this proviso was used on only one occasion, in the late 1970s, since 1980 it has been used with increasing frequency in cases involving unfair or deceptive acts or practices. Currently, the commission's Bureau of Consumer Protection has more enforcement cases in progress before federal judges in federal court than it has before administrative law judges.

In a 1989 Report of the American Bar Association Special Committee to Study the Role of the FTC, the committee declared that though the FTC's unfairness authority has generated controversy, if unfairness is so egregious that it borders on fraud, the FTC should challenge it using its Section 13(b) authority.[38]

Under the permanent injunction proviso to Section 13(b), the FTC may seek from a federal district court permanent, not just preliminary, relief, thereby obviating the need for an administrative proceeding. Relief in a suit for permanent injunction is not limited to the prohibition of the unlawful practices; rather, the FTC may seek, and courts have not hesitated to grant, (1) restitution and rescission to defrauded consumers, (2) asset freezes, and (3) receiverships. The FTC has used this remedial arsenal to challenge unfair or deceptive practices in connection with the offering and sale of rare coins, works of art, diamonds and gemstones, oil and gas partnerships, travel services, franchises, prefabricated housing, time-share condominiums, second-trust loans, and photocopy supplies.

According to a district court in a recent case, the penalties can become increasingly severe if firms continue to violate injunctions against misleading sales-and-marketing practices. A firm that repeatedly violates a prior injunction prohibiting its owner and its agents from making misrepresentations in the marketing and sales of its goods and services may be subject to a subsequent injunction under which it is permanently banned from engaging in any marketing or sales of such goods and services. Furthermore, any violation of the new injunction would result in holding the owner in custody for civil contempt and possible criminal contempt proceedings.[39]

SUMMARY

The 1914 Federal Trade Commission Act created the federal agency most active in controlling advertising abuse. The 1938 Wheeler Lea Amendments tended to broaden the power of the Federal Trade Commission by rewriting Section 5 of the act to include the statement "Unfair . . . or deceptive acts or practices are hereby declared to be unlawful." This statement was designed to indicate that if there were injury to the public as well as to competitors, the commission was empowered to act. It also defined the term *false advertising*. The 1975 Magnuson-Moss Warranty–FTC Improvements Act gave the FTC the power to promulgate trade regulation rules that specify unfair or deceptive acts or practices and authorized penalties for violations of these rules. The 1980 FTC Amendment Act prohibited the FTC from using unfairness in trade regulation rules directed toward children's television advertising.

In the FTC's enforcement proceedings against advertising, no strict guidelines for defining *deception* and *unfairness* were established until the 1980s. Currently, the FTC's policy is that it will find deception if there has been "a misrepresentation, omission, or practice that misleads the consumer, acting reasonably in the circumstances, to the consumer's detriment." To determine the truth of an advertisement, the FTC examines the kinds of claims being made and the extent to which there is a reasonable basis on which the claims can be substantiated.

In an Unfairness Policy Statement issued in 1980, the FTC declared that unfair acts or practices are those that are likely to: (1) cause substantial injury to consumers, (2) not be reasonably avoidable by consumers themselves, and (3) not be outweighed by countervailing benefits to consumers or competitors.

A number of remedies for unfair and deceptive advertising have been established by the commission. These include cease-and-desist orders, consent orders, monetary penalties, affirmative disclosure, corrective advertising, redress for consumers, and injunctions.

CASE
Kraft, Inc. *v.* Federal Trade Commission, *CCH # 69,911 (CA 7, July 31, 1992).*

FACTS

The FTC determined that Kraft's advertisements claiming its Kraft Singles cheese food product slices contained the same amount of calcium as five ounces of milk and more calcium than most imitation cheese slices were deceptive. The FTC ordered Kraft to cease and desist from making these representations and Kraft filed a petition for review.

ISSUES

Are Kraft Singles cheese slices ads deceptive?

Is the FTC required to use extrinsic evidence in its determination that an advertisement is deceptive?

HOLDING

The appeals court held that Kraft's ads claiming that its cheese food slices contained the same amount of calcium as five ounces of milk and more calcium than most imitation cheese slices were deceptive.

As a matter of law and FTC policy, a determination by the Federal Trade Commission that advertising claims are deceptive does not require extrinsic evidence of consumer deception, according to the U.S. Court of Appeals for the Seventh Circuit. The FTC practice of viewing advertisements first and, if unable to determine with confidence what claims are conveyed, turning to extrinsic evidence was proper. However, the court recommended that reliance on extrinsic evidence should be a rule rather than an exception in FTC decisions and that the commission "adopt a consistent position on consumer survey methodology—so that any uncertainty is reduced to an absolute minimum."

In November 1992, Kraft submitted to the Supreme Court a request that the court review the FTC's findings that ads for Kraft's single cheese food products were deceptive. Among other questions, Kraft asked whether the commission can rely solely on its own reading of an advertisement that is true on its face in determining whether the ad conveys an implied misrepresentation or whether the commission must base its determination on extrinsic evidence of the public's understanding of the ad.

Kraft's request for Supreme Court review was denied.

REASONING

Under the FTC Act, according to the court, an advertisement is deceptive if it is likely to mislead consumers, acting reasonably under the circumstances, in a material respect. In implementing that standard, the commission examines the overall net impression of an ad and engages in a three-part inquiry: (1) What claims are conveyed in the ad? (2) Are those claims false or misleading? and (3) Are those claims material to prospective customers?

What Claims Are Conveyed in the Ad?

Claims in an ad may be express or implied. Express claims directly represent the facts at issue, while implied claims do so in an oblique or indirect way. The court presented the following illustration:

Suppose a certain automobile gets poor gas mileage, say, ten miles per gallon. One of its ads boasts that it gets thirty miles per gallon, while another identifies the car as the "Miser," depicts it rolling through the countryside past one gas station after another, and claims the car is inexpensive to operate. Both ads make deceptive claims; the first does so expressly, the second does so impliedly.

Extrinsic evidence. In determining what claims are conveyed by a challenged advertisement, the commission relies on two sources of information: its own viewing of the ad and extrinsic evidence. If, after viewing the ad, the FTC is unable on its own to determine with confidence what claims are conveyed in the ad, it turns to extrinsic evidence. The most convincing extrinsic evidence is a survey "of what consumers thought upon reading the advertisement in question." However, the FTC also relies on other forms of extrinsic evidence including consumer testimony, expert opinion, and copy tests of the ads.

Kraft declares this approach acceptable in determining whether an ad conveys express claims, but it contends the FTC should be required, as a matter of law, to rely on extrinsic evidence rather than on its own subjective analysis in all cases involving implied claims.

The court declared that while Kraft's arguments may have some force as a matter of policy, they are unavailing as a matter of law. Kraft's arguments rest on the faulty premise that implied claims are inescapably subjective and unpredictable. In fact, implied claims fall on a continuum ranging from the obvious to the barely discernible. The commission does not have license to go on a fishing expedition in order to pin liability on advertisers for barely imaginable claims falling at the end of that spectrum. Nonetheless, in a confrontation with claims that are implied, yet conspicuous, extrinsic evidence is unnecessary because common sense and administrative expertise provide the commission with adequate tools to make its finding. Since the implied claims that Kraft made are reasonably clear from the face of the advertisements, according to the court the commission was not required to use consumer surveys in reaching its decisions.

Are Those Claims False or Misleading?

Kraft asserts that claims in some of its challenged ads are literally true, because its cheese slices are made from five ounces of milk and they do have a high concentration of calcium. However, the court noted that even literally true statements can still have a misleading implication. Average consumers are not likely to know that much of the calcium was lost in the processing, which leaves them with a misleading impression about calcium content.

First Amendment considerations. Kraft introduced a First Amendment defense, declaring that by relying on its own subjective judgment—that an ad while literally true implies a false message—the FTC chills nonmisleading protected commercial speech because advertisers are unable to predict whether the FTC will find a particular ad misleading. The net result will be an excess of feel-good ads, offering no consumer information but designed to avoid unpredictable FTC decisions.

According to the court, Kraft's First Amendment challenge is doomed by the Supreme Court decision in *Zauderer*, which established that no First Amendment concerns were raised when facially apparent implied claims are found without resort to extrinsic evidence. In addition, commercial speech is generally considered less susceptible to the chilling effect of regulation than other, more traditionally recognized forms of speech, such as political discourse.

Are Those Claims Material to Prospective Customers?

A claim is considered material if it "involves information that is important to consumers and, hence, likely to affect their choice of or conduct regarding a product." Kraft asserted that its claims that Kraft Singles contain the same amount of calcium as five ounces of milk, even if made, are not material to consumers. According to the court, the commission is entitled to apply, within reason, a presumption of materiality and it does so with three types of claims: express claims, implied claims with evidence that the seller intended to make the claim, and claims that significantly involve health, safety, or other areas with which reasonable consumers would be concerned.

The FTC found solid evidence that consumers placed great importance on calcium consumption and rationally concluded that a 30% exaggeration of calcium content was a nutritionally significant claim that would affect consumer purchasing decisions. The court pointed to the manufacturer's own surveys—which showed consumer calcium deficiency concerns—and the fact that the manufacturer had designed the ads with the intent to capitalize on those concerns. A presumption of materiality with regard to the superiority claims was based on evidence, including internal company documents and increased sales and market share, that the manufacturer intended to convey such a message.

Scope of the Order

Kraft objected to the FTC's cease-and-desist order that prohibits Kraft both from running the challenged ads and from advertising any calcium or nutritional claims not supported by reliable scientific evidence. The order extends not only to Kraft Singles but to all Kraft cheeses and cheese-related products. Kraft contends that the order is too broad, bans constitutionally protected commercial speech, and is not rationally related to Kraft's violation of the act. The court ruled that the specific prohibitions imposed on

Kraft in the orders are not broader than reasonably necessary to prevent deception and hence are not violative of the First Amendment.

In an opinion that concurred with the order, Judge Manion expressed concern with the FTC's ability to avoid extrinsic evidence by simply concluding that a deceptive, implied claim is facially apparent. According to the judge,

> Unfortunately, judicial groping for a distinction between cases where extrinsic evidence is necessary and those where it is not, is leaving both advertisers and the FTC uncertain . . . Rather than leaving judges to hew the new contours of this issue the FTC would be well-advised to take this court's suggestion—apply its expertise and develop a consumer survey methodology that advertisers can use to ascertain whether their ads contain implied, deceptive messages.

DISCUSSION QUESTION

What considerations should an advertiser evaluate in an effort to avoid ads from being declared deceptive or misleading?

CASE
In re Campbell Soup Company, FTC Dkt. 9233, CCH #22,967 (April 8, 1991).

FACTS

In 1989, the FTC issued a complaint charging Campbell Soup Company, which controls about two-thirds of the over $2-billion retail soup market in the United States, with making deceptive and unsubstantiated claims for its soups. Campbell's ads, which were part of its Soup Is Good Food campaign, linked the low fat and low cholesterol content of its soups with a reduced risk of heart disease.

ISSUES

Did Campbell fail to disclose material information in its Soup Is Good Food ads?

Did Campbell have a reasonable basis for its claim that its soup contributes to a diet that reduces the risk of heart disease?

HOLDING

Campbell failed to disclose material information.
Campbell did not have any data to substantiate its claim.

REASONING

Campbell's ads—Soup Is Good Food—failed to disclose that Campbell's soups are high in sodium and that diets high in sodium may increase the risk of heart disease. The ads also represented that Campbell's soups contribute to a diet that reduces the risk of heart disease, but they failed to substantiate the claim.

Advertisers who make deceptive and unsubstantiated health claims in their food ads can be required in future advertising to make affirmative disclosure concerning their food's content. In a consent agreement reached in April 1991, Campbell agreed that, for any soup containing more than 500 mg of sodium in an eight-ounce serving, it will disclose the sodium content in any ad that directly or by implication mentions heart disease in connection with the soup. In addition, the company has agreed that it will not imply there is a connection between soup and a reduction in the risk of heart disease.

In a dissenting statement, Commissioner Strenio said that the consent agreement neither cures the alleged deception nor prevents its recurrence. Strenio declared that consumers would have to interpret the content disclosure as meaning that Campbell's soups are high in sodium and would also have to understand the relationship between high sodium consumption and heart disease in order for the consent order to solve the problem.

DISCUSSION QUESTIONS

What are the criteria used by the FTC to determine if an ad is false and deceptive and what remedies may be imposed?

Do you agree with Commissioner Strenio's dissent? Explain.

ENDNOTES

1. William J. Baer, "At the Turning Point: The Commission in 1978," *Journal of Public Policy and Marketing* 7 (1988), 11–20.
2. Neil W. Averitt and Terry Clavani, "The Role of the FTC in American Society," *Oklahoma Law Review* 39 (Spring 1986), 39–50.
3. *Southwest Sunsites, Inc. et al.* v. *FTC*, TRR, CCH, #67,021 (1986).
4. *FTC* v. *Sperry & Hutchinson Co.*, 405 US 233 (1972).

5. Ross D. Petty, "FTC Advertising Regulation: Survivor or Casualty of the Reagan Revolution?" *American Business Law Journal* 30 (1992), 1–34.

6. *P. Lorillard* v. *FTC*, 186 F. 2d 52 (1950).

7. In re Heinz v. Kirschner, TRR, CCH # 16,664 (1963).

8. In re Block Drug Co., Inc., 3 Trade Reg. Rep. #21,360 (1977).

9. Necchi Sewing Machine Sales Corp., 53 FTC 1040 (1957).

10. In re Lew Siegler, Inc., 3 Trade Reg. Rep. #20,412 (1973).

11. National Dynamics Corp., 82 FTC 488 (1973).

12. In re Capax, Inc., et al., 3 Trade Reg. Rep. #21,427 (1978).

13. In re Sterling Drug, Inc., Dancer-Fitzgerald-Sample, Inc., and Lois Holland Callaway, Inc., FTC Docket No. 8919, Trade Regulation Reports No. 604 (July 19, 1983).

14. *FTC* v. *Colgate-Palmolive Co.*, 5 Trade Reg. Rep. #71,409 (62 Supreme Court, April, 1965).

15. In re Campbell Soup Company, 3 Trade Reg. Rep. #18,706 (March 1969).

16. In re Volvo North America Corp. et al. and Scali, McCabe, Solves, Inc., CCH #23,041 (August 1991).

17. *National Commission on Egg Nutrition et al.* v. *FTC.*, 570 F. 2d 157, 162 (7th Cir. 1977).

18. Dorothy Cohen, "The FTC's Advertising Substantiation Program," *Journal of Marketing* 44 (Winter 1980), 26–35.

19. In re Pfizer Inc., 3 Trade Reg. Rep. #20,056 (July 1972).

20. *Trade Regulation Reporter* (1978f, 1979b).

21. *Trade Regulation Reporter* (1977b).

22. *Trade Regulation Reporter* (1978c, 1979c).

23. *Trade Regulation Reporter* (1979b).

24. Dorothy Cohen, "The Concept of Unfairness as It Relates to Advertising Legislation," *Journal of Marketing* 38 (July 1974), 8–13.

25. In re ITT Continental Baking Co., Inc., 3 Trade Reg. Rep. #21,546 (1979).

26. *FTC* v. *Sperry & Hutchinson Co.*, 405 U.S. 233 (1972).

27. In re Hudson Pharmaceutical Corp., 3 Trade Reg. Rep. #21,191 (1976).

28. In re General Foods Corp., 3 Trade Reg. Rep. #20,928 (1975).

29. In re Mego Int'l., Inc., 3 Trade Reg. Rep. #21,399 (July 1978).

30. *Orkin Exterminating Corp., Inc.*, v. *Federal Trade Commission*, CCH #67,969 (CA-11, July 1988).

31. *FTC* v. *Sperry & Hutchinson Co.*, 92 S. Ct. 898 (1972).

32. "FTC Deceptive Advertising Enforcement—Commissioner's Views," TRR, CCH #50,089 (September 9, 1992).

33. In re General Nutrition, Inc. FTC, CCH #23,600 (May 1994).

34. *United States* v. *Reader's Digest Association*, 5 Trade Reg. Rep. #64,431 (1980); "Legal Developments in Marketing" *Journal of Marketing* 45 (Winter 1981), 142.

35. William L. Wilkie, Dennis McNeill, and Michael B. Mazis, "Marketing's Scarlet Letter: The Theory and Practice of Corrective Advertising," *Journal of Marketing* 48 (Spring 1984), p. 28.

36. "Ford to Run FTC-Ordered Ads in 1981," *Advertising Age* (October 27, 1980), 28.

37. 15 U.S.C. 453(b).

38. "In re Report on the Role of the FTC," Trade Reg. Rep. No. 46 (April 13, 1989); "Legal Developments in Marketing," *Journal of Marketing* 54 (January 1990), 118.

39. *Federal Trade Commission* v. *David L. du Pont*, CCH #69,898 (DC ED Pa., July 15, 1992).

CHAPTER EIGHT

First Amendment, Lanham Act, and Direct Marketing Activities

Advertising control emanates from various federal laws and court decisions, as well as Federal Trade Commission (FTC) enforcement discussed in the previous chapter. This chapter first examines two areas of current significance in advertising decision making: the Supreme Court's decisions on advertising and freedom of speech and the Trademark Law Revision Act. The rest of this chapter is devoted to a discussion of the legal issues in direct marketing with specific reference to promotion decisions.

ADVERTISING AND THE FIRST AMENDMENT

The First Amendment to the U.S. Constitution declares: "Congress shall make no law . . . abridging the freedom of speech or of the press." Traditionally, speech has been protected in order to allow the generation of information and discussion in order to facilitate self-expression, self-realization, and needed social change. Information and opinion disseminated in a commercial context such as advertising were considered mercantile in origin and not subject to the same First Amendment protection as other forms of expression.

The doctrine that commercial advertising did not enjoy the same First Amendment protection as other forms of speech emerged in a 1942 Supreme Court case testing the constitutionality of an antilittering ordinance. The Supreme Court referred to many earlier cases, which held that the streets are proper places for the communication of information and opinion. However, the court concluded that "the Constitution imposes no such restraint on government as respects purely commercial advertising."[1]

This doctrine, which was to serve as a standard for the next thirty-four years, did not suggest that advertising could be subject to any and all restraints. It did affect advertising regulation to the extent that whenever the defense of freedom of speech was raised against a commercial advertising restraint, this defense would most likely be rejected by a citing of the fact that commercial advertising did not have the protection of the First Amendment.

In 1976, this doctrine was revised when the Supreme Court declared that an advertisement that does no more than propose "a commercial transaction: is entitled to protection under the First Amendment.[2] The case questioned the constitutionality of a Virginia statute that declared it unprofessional conduct for a licensed pharmacist to advertise the prices of prescription drugs. The court's opinion rested fundamentally on the value of audience access to information guiding private economic choices, declaring, "People will perceive their own best interest if only they are well enough informed, and that the best means to that end is to open the channels of communication to them rather than close them."

Although noncommercial speech has been clearly defined as political discourse and expressions about philosophical, religious, artistic, literary, or ethical matters, commercial speech has not been precisely characterized. Nor is commercial speech accorded the same level of First Amendment protection as noncommercial speech. Regulation is not considered valid on the mere basis that an advertisement proposes a commercial transaction. However, areas where potentially valid regulation of commercial speech may occur include advertisements that are false, deceptive, or misleading; advertisements that concern illegal transactions; and advertisements that may require additional information, disclaimers, or warnings. In addition, restrictions may be placed on the time, manner, or place of advertising.

The Supreme Court has vacillated in the past few years in applying First Amendment protection to advertising. The court considers restrictions placed on the content of an advertisement as more invidious than content-neutral restrictions (e.g., restrictions on time, manner, or place of advertising). Thus, regulation of speech based on the content of the advertising is placed on a higher tract (subject to greater protection). In the *Central Hudson* case in 1980, the Supreme Court enunciated a four-part test for scrutinizing regulation of speech based on the content of advertising:[3]

1. Is the activity unlawful and/or the speech misleading or fraudulent?

2. Is the government interest in restricting speech substantial?

3. Do the challenged restrictions of commercial speech directly advance the government's interest?

4. Are the restrictions on commercial speech no more extensive than necessary to serve the government's interest?

However, the distinction between content-based and content-neutral restrictions was blurred in the *Posadas* case, when the court's First Amendment analysis was guided by its classification of gambling as a harmful product. In *Posadas*, the restriction was content-based—prohibiting casino advertising to residents of Puerto Rico based on the fear that the content of the messages would encourage residents to gamble.[4] Although the court was required to apply the *Central Hudson* standard, it applied this test loosely, especially the fourth prong, which requires a state to demonstrate affirmatively that a more limited regulation would not achieve the asserted legitimate governmental interest.

The *Posadas* opinion has been characterized as both ad hoc and aberrational and as the most important development in commercial speech to date. As so eloquently phrased by Justice Stevens, the court's holding in *Posadas* has rendered future applications of the commercial speech doctrine "as unpredictable and haphazard as the roll of dice in a casino."

In 1989, the Supreme Court moved further away from the *Virginia State Board* paradigm, which makes clear that truthful, nondeceptive, noncoercive information concerning the availability, price, and quantity of products and services is worth protecting.

The SUNY campus at Cortland had a regulation prohibiting commercial transactions on campus. When students invited an American Future Systems saleswoman to their dormitory to sell Tupperware-like kitchen utensils, the state tried to prosecute American Future Systems. Todd Fox, together with several other students who had arranged and attended the demonstration, sued on the basis that such action violated the First Amendment.[5]

The students challenged the university's regulation, arguing that the commercial and noncommercial aspects of speech were "inextricably intertwined" and therefore, speech as a whole should be categorized as noncommercial. However, the court determined that the whole of the speech at issue should be considered as if it were solely commercial and that it should be provided with the limited protections accorded commercial speech.

Although the Supreme Court did not rule on the ban, it focused on the fourth prong of *Hudson*, declaring that, instead of a least-restrictive burden, the government must show that its proposed restriction is a reasonable and narrowly tailored fit between the legislature's ends and the means chosen to accomplish those ends. However, the court explained that regulation can go "only marginally beyond" what previously had been referred to as the least-restrictive means. The *Fox* court remanded the case to the district court to determine whether or not the regulation was more restrictive than necessary based on the reasonable-fit standard.

First Amendment protection of commercial speech did receive additional support in a 1993 Supreme Court decision. In the *City of Cincinnati* v. *Discovery Networks*, the Supreme Court ruled that Cincinnati's selective and categorical ban on the distribution, via newsrack, of commercial handbills is not consistent with the dictates of the First Amendment and that it had violated the reasonable-fit standard established in *Fox*.[6]

Cincinnati authorized Discovery Network to place sixty-two freestanding dispensing devices on public property for the purpose of distributing free magazines that consist primarily of advertisements for Discovery's services. In 1990, due to its interest in the safety and attractive appearance of its streets, the city notified Discovery that its permit to use dispensing devices on public property was revoked. The notices explained that Discovery's publication was a commercial handbill under the municipal code, and therefore the code prohibited its distribution on public property.

The case was ultimately heard by the Supreme Court, which declared that the city has not met its burden of establishing a reasonable fit between its legitimate interests in safety and aesthetics and the means it chose to serve those interests. The city had not "carefully calculated the costs and benefits" associated with the burden on speech imposed by its prohibition. The benefit to be derived from the removal of sixty-two newsracks out of a total of 1,500 to 2,000 on public property was small. Because commercial and noncommercial publications are equally responsible for the safety concerns and the visual blight that motivated the ban, the city failed to justify its differential treatment of the two types of newsracks.

In addition to declaring that there was no reasonable fit, Justice Stevens, who delivered the court's opinion, declared that since the city's regulation of newsracks is predicated on the difference in content between ordinary newspapers and commercial speech, it is not content neutral and cannot therefore qualify as a valid time, place, or manner restriction on protected speech.

In another recent case (*Edenfield* v. *Fane*),[7] the lack of this fit also led to the downfall of the State of Florida's attempt to prohibit "direct, in-person, uninvited solicitation," by accountants.[8] The Supreme Court failed to find that the regulation "directly advance(d) the state interest involved; the regulation may not be sustained if it provides only ineffective or remote support for the government's purpose." This decision seemed to support First Amendment protection of commercial speech.

However, the Supreme Court seemed to turn toward the *Posadas* decision in another 1993 case (*United States* and *FCC* v. *Edge Broadcasting*

Company), in which the Court considered "whether federal statutes that prohibit the broadcast of lottery advertising by a broadcaster licensed in a state that does not allow lotteries, while allowing such broadcasting by a broadcaster licensed in a state that sponsors a lottery."[9]

The statute in question prohibited Edge Broadcasting, licensed in North Carolina (which has no state-sponsored lottery), but over 92 percent of its audience was situated in Virginia (which does), from carrying advertising for the Virginia lottery. In this case the Court held that although Edge broadcasts accounted for 11 percent of the radio listening time of residents of North Carolina counties served by Edge, "the restriction, even as applied only to Edge, directly advances the governmental interest within the meaning of *Central Hudson*."

In two free speech rulings in 1994, the Supreme Court struck down a Florida law forbidding lawyers from advertising that they were also certified public accountants, and a Ladue, Missouri ordinance banning signs in residential areas.

According to Mandel, litigation under the *Central Hudson* test has resulted mainly in unpredictability, depriving marketing professionals and others reasonable guidance that good law should provide in a free society.[10]

Controlling Obscenity

The power to exclude obscene material from advertising was accepted rather early in the history of the federal regulatory agencies. In 1904, Congress established that the U.S. Post Office could deny the use of the mails to material regarded as offensive, and obscene material was considered to be such matter. A number of states have laws regulating obscenity.

In a 1973 Supreme Court decision, Justice Warren Burger declared, "This much has been categorically settled by the court, that obscene material is unprotected by the First Amendment" and noted, "We acknowledge, however, the inherent dangers of undertaking to regulate any form of expression."[11]

Some states may choose not to control obscenity. However, in order to place limits on state statutes designed to regulate obscene material, Justice Burger confined "the permissible scope of such regulation to works which depict or describe sexual conduct" and provided the following standards:

The basic guidelines for the trier of fact must be:
  a) whether "the average person, applying contemporary community standards" would find that the work, taken as a whole, appeals to the prurient interest,

    b) whether the work depicts or describes, in a patently obvious way, sexual conduct specifically defined by the applicable state law, and

    c) whether the work, taken as a whole, lacks serious literary, artistic, political, or scientific value.

Justice Burger thus disregarded the previous utterly-without-redeeming-social-value test.

There are currently a number of state laws on obscenity. Generally, prosecutors have chosen not to actively enforce obscenity laws. There are, however, concerns relative to child pornography. The Supreme Court has let states outlaw the sale and distribution of material depicting children in sexual performances or poses, even if such did not meet the legal definition of obscene. The issue of the sale and distribution of child pornography may be clarified in a child pornography case the Supreme Court has agreed to review at this writing.

Another issue that may require further resolution by the courts is the question of conflicts between protecting trademark rights and First Amendment protection of freedom of speech. Except in rare cases, the courts have consistently rejected the First Amendment defense in trademark cases where the issue was considered. Nevertheless, a First Amendment defense to a trademark claim was approved in a case involving a prurient parody of L. L. Bean's mail order catalog. Drake Publishing, in a two-page article entitled "L. L. Bean's Back-to-School Sex Catalog," displayed a copy of Bean's trademark and showed nude models in sexually explicit poses using products described with crude humor. A trial court granted Bean summary judgment based on a claim of dilution of its trademark. However, the circuit court held that sexually explicit but nonobscene material was entitled to First Amendment protection, and it reversed the decision.[12]

A recent Supreme Court decision failed to provide sufficient clarification concerning the use of parodies. Jerry Falwell sued *Hustler* magazine for its publication of an advertisement parody consisting of a fictional testimonial from Falwell that described his first sexual experience. In its decision, the Supreme Court declared that such parodies are protected by the First Amendment.[13] The Supreme Court's decision was not exact in defining *Hustler*'s scope and detailing which types of speech were included. Hence lower courts lack clear guidelines by which to measure the boundaries of the Supreme Court's holdings.

Additional decisions may be forthcoming concerning recent efforts by the Federal Communications Commission (FCC) to reduce the presentation of indecent (as distinguished from obscene) material on broadcasts. Such material, according to the FCC, need not be of a sexual nature to be deemed unacceptable for broadcast. This issue is currently before the courts.

Obscenity issues tend to vary with changes in the social, political, and economic climate. Moreover, the courts have declared controls are subject to "contemporary community standards." It is important for marketers to keep aware of the changes that may occur in this area and to note the potential effects on the target audience.

First Amendment jurisprudence incorporates a continuing struggle to balance conflicting interests. Marketers should carefully follow emerging First Amendment doctrines not only to avoid potential advertising restrictions but also to help support continuing efforts toward a strong commitment to free speech, which is worth preserving despite the difficult compromises that may be required.

ADVERTISING AND THE LANHAM ACT

Although no private right to sue for false advertising exists under the Federal Trade Commission Act, such rights are available under Section 43(a) of the federal Trademark Act of 1946, commonly known as the Lanham Act, discussed in Chapter 6. Section 43(a) of the act provides that a civil suit may be brought against "any person who believes that he is or is likely to be damaged by the use" of false descriptions or representations.

Prior to passage of the Trademark Law Revision Act, the courts generally ruled that complaints of advertising misrepresentation applied only when a company misrepresented its own trademarked goods and services.[14]

The distinction between misrepresentations about one's own goods and misrepresentations about another's goods was criticized by commentators as being artificial. To resolve the issue, the Revision Act amended Section 43(a).[15] The Lanham Act now clearly specifies that misrepresentations about another's goods or services are actionable only if they occur in commercial advertising or promotion. The revision seems to eliminate political speech and editorial content, but it will be up to the courts to decide this point. Nonetheless, the amendment to 43(a) closes a loophole that had been present in the Lanham Act since its inception and eliminates the legal gap that occurs when an advertiser makes a false statement about a competitor's product without mentioning its own.

The Revision Act has also significantly increased the potential for monetary relief in such cases. As there were no specific provisions setting forth remedies available for violation of Section 43(a), the courts in most cases issued injunctions. The Trademark Law Revision Act now specifies that all remedies available for trademark infringement are likewise available as remedies for false advertising. Thus, in addition to injunctive relief, monetary relief and even attorney's fees may now be available to victorious plaintiffs. Though the Revision Act does not specifically take note of such remedies, recall and corrective advertising should still be available, as they are now, in appropriate cases. Punitive damages, however, are not available under Section 43(a) of the Lanham Act.

Implications for Marketers

The full consequences for promotional decision making resulting from the changes in trademark law are yet to be determined. Several false advertising suits have been instituted since the Revision Act went into effect in November 1989, but there have been too few decisions to provide precise guidelines for marketers. Though certain aspects of the actual operation and interpretation of the act are uncertain, present case law is likely to be adapted to the new system.

Accordingly, marketers should become cognizant of trademark case precedents relevant to false advertising. A suggested strategic approach is to institute a coordinated effort between the marketing and legal departments in the creation of an informative program for personnel involved in the preparation of promotional campaigns. Such a program can present legal decisions about the types of claims identified by the courts as violating the Lanham Act. It can review legal guidelines whereby advertising claims will be less vulnerable to challenge and indicate the type of evidence required for support of those claims. This program should be ongoing, and cover emerging legal decisions. Some relevant issues are discussed here.

Marketers may be familiar with Federal Trade Commission advertising guidelines; requirements for a finding of false advertising under Section 43(a) of the Lanham Act have some similarities to those set by the FTC. Both bar ads that are explicitly false and those that, though literally true, have a tendency to mislead; the claims must be material; and a likelihood of injury must be present. Neither considers puffery actionable.

There are important differences, however. The Lanham Act gives firms a private right of action not available under the FTC Act, which required action in the public interest. The Lanham Act, unlike the FTC, does not require substantiation of claims. The advertiser is under no obligation to prove the claim is true, and the competitor must prove it is false. The FTC considers that omission of a material fact in advertising renders it false; such is not the case under the Lanham Act. Though the proposed Trademark Revision Act contained a provision that made material omissions actionable, the final version as passed does not provide for such actions. The FTC does not exercise jurisdiction over labeling and packaging; such jurisdiction is left to the Food and Drug Administration. False claims on labels and packages are covered under Section 43(a) of the Lanham Act.

Criteria for False Advertising under the Lanham Act

To determine the falsity of an ad in Lanham Act cases, the court examines the claims made. Claims may be explicitly or implicitly false. An express claim in an advertisement that is literally or explicitly false may be found "false on its face," and relief can be granted by the court's own findings without proof of consumer reaction. Coca-Cola claimed irreparable harm to its Minute Maid brand from Tropicana's ad for Tropicana Premium Pack orange juice. A commercial showed Bruce Jenner squeezing an orange while saying, "It's pure pasteurized orange juice as it comes from the orange." He then poured the juice into Tropicana's orange juice carton. An appeals court ruled this was "false on its face," because pasteurized juice does not come from an orange and freshly squeezed orange juice generally is not poured directly into the carton.[16]

A claim that is implicitly false—that is, literally true but having a tendency to mislead, deceive, or confuse consumers—will be enjoined if there is evidence of public deception. In a comprehensive analysis, Preston examined the types of implicit claims that have been identified by the courts as violative of the Lanham Act. Among them are claims that (1) falsely imply a test or survey proves the claim to a degree acceptable to appropriate experts; (2) contain inconspicuous or otherwise ineffective qualifications; (3) contain a truthful contrast to a competitor, but imply an additional and more significant false contrast; and (4) are broadly stated with no explicit qualification, thus implying falsely that no qualification exists.[17]

Evidence of public deception arising from implicit claims need not be in the form of consumer surveys. Communication specialists or several misled consumers may provide adequate evidence. Consumer surveys, however, are looked upon favorably by the courts because they offer a broad-based reading of consumer perception. Oscar Mayer sued Bryan Foods for false advertising in Bryan's sales of hot dog, bologna, and of bacon products sold under the Bryan trademark. In a preliminary action for change of venue, Oscar Mayer declared that its sales representatives could testify to actual confusion over the advertisements in question. The court stated, however, that such testimony is of little significance in a false advertising case. In such cases, confusion must be proved by relevant market research and consumer surveys.[18]

Consumer surveys must be carefully designed so as to provide an accurate reading of consumer perception. In Lanham Act cases, a survey is considered properly conducted if (1) it was fairly and scientifically done by qualified experts and impartial interviewers, (2) responses were drawn from a sample of a relevant portion of potential customers, (3) the questions did not appear to be misleading or biased, and (4) the responses were recorded in a completely unbiased manner.[19]

In a recent Lanham Act case, a pharmaceutical firm's television advertising claim that its antacid was the strongest was not literally false, according to the court's appraisal. Because the claim was not literally false, Lanham Act false advertising violation could not be established without proof that a significant number of consumers were mistakenly convinced that the product provides superior relief.

However, the court ruled that consumer surveys on the effect of the advertisements were unconvincing because repetitive and leading questions were asked without a mechanism for filtering respondents to the first series of questions. The questions suggestively flagged the allegedly objectionable claims in the advertisements. Responses to nonleading questions indicated that consumers thought that the main idea communicated by the commercials was that the antacid worked well, but not that it worked better than other antacids.[20]

Deceptive Comparison Advertising

Though the Lanham Act gives an injured competitor a private right of action for deceptive advertising, in the past this fact was largely ignored with respect to deceptive comparison advertising.[21] Recently, several firms have instituted private Lanham Act suits for alleged deceptive comparative ads.

Buchanan and Goldman surveyed the federal court record relevant to comparison advertising and provide several principles whereby a firm's comparative ads can be less vulnerable to a challenge under the Revision Act.[22] They note that virtually all comparative ad injunctions issued in trademark cases were obtained because it was shown either that (1) the words and pictures in the ad did not fully and accurately reflect the supporting data or other known facts or (2) the ad, though literally true, misled consumers into believing something false about the product. They conclude that comparative ad injunctions are issued most commonly after the plaintiff has shown an infidelity or falsity in the way a competitor's advertising communicates the data.

Firms facing a false advertising complaint under the Lanham Act may introduce a counterclaim as an offensive tactic. Such an action, however, may provide only temporary relief. Both American Home Products, maker of Anacin and Advil, and Johnson & Johnson, maker of Tylenol, have instituted and won countersuits in connection with advertising claims for analgesics. However, the ongoing aspirin wars continue between the companies; a half dozen of their Lanham suits already have been tried, but several more remain in the wings.[23]

A more effective tactic is to stop the alleged false advertising. ALPO Petfoods recently challenged Ralston Purina's claim that Ralston Puppy Chow products reduce hip joint laxity and therefore lessen the severity of canine hip disease.[24] By counterclaim, Ralston challenged ALPO's claim that veterinarians prefer the "formula" in ALPO Puppy Food "2 over 1" over the leading puppy food.

The court declared it was particularly disturbed to find that the two leading manufacturers of dog food in the United States had engaged in deceptive advertising practices, and it enjoined both parties from engaging in such practices in the future. The court ordered Ralston to pay ALPO $10.4 million and did not award such damages to Ralston because it felt the magnitude of the wrongdoing by Ralston in comparison was so much greater. Ralston withheld vital information about its research from the public, government agencies, and the court. In addition, Ralston persisted in claiming that its inadequate and distorted research permits it to claim its dog food can ameliorate dog hip problems. The appropriate response, according to the court, was made by ALPO, which acknowledged its misconduct and ceased its offending advertising program.

Ralston appealed, and the appeals court declared that in a false advertising suit under Section 43(a) of the Lanham Act, an award based on defendant's profits requires proof that the defendant acted willfully or in bad faith. Vacating the $10.4-million damages award, the court observed that willfulness requires "a connection between a defendant's awareness of its competitors and its actions at those competitors' expense." The court also rejected the notion that a defendant's profits may be awarded as damages solely because that may act as a deterrent.[25] However, the finding that Ralston had violated Section 43(a) was upheld, and the appellate court remanded the case for a redetermination of ALPO's actual damages.

In a subsequent decision, the Court of Appeals ruled that the district court had properly awarded ALPO damages for the cost of its advertising in response to Ralston's false advertising claims, since recovery is not limited to advertisements that specifically address Ralston's false statements.[26] According to the appeals court, ALPO, at the outset of its responsive campaign, had no way of knowing initially whether Ralston's claim was false and may not have been able to specifically address that claim. It would be unfair to require a party injured by false advertising to prove that such advertisements were the sole reason for its responsive campaign.

It is becoming increasingly important for marketers to become aware of the potential impact of Section 43(a) of the Lanham Act. There has been a significant rise in the number of private suits against false advertising. Recent decisions have involved advertisements for motor oil, puppy food, pharmaceuticals, health care, and real estate services. Business firms have successfully attacked the advertising of competitors as allegedly false or misleading by invoking Section 43(a) of the Lanham Act. Marketers should take note of the criteria used by the courts in establishing a violation.

DIRECT MARKETING

Direct marketing traditionally has been considered a method of product distribution wherein the exchange process is conducted through non-store channels of distribution, such as vending machines and door-to-door selling. Interrelated activities designed by other terms have emerged, including direct mail advertising, mail order selling, and direct response advertising.

Direct mail advertising refers to all forms of promotional messages sent through the post office and through private delivery firms to a specific individual and organization. Since delivery is made through a mass medium—the post office—direct mail is categorized as an advertising medium. Mail order selling is not an advertising medium but a method of distributing products that uses the post office. Promotion used for mail order selling can occur in all media, including direct mail. Direct response advertising is advertising that seeks an immediate action or response and that allows the consumer to respond directly to the advertiser.

In recent years, direct marketing activities have increased significantly, and now direct marketing is considered to embrace all these interrelated concepts. Currently, direct marketing is defined as:

> The total activities by which the seller, in effecting the exchange of goods and services with the buyer, directs efforts to a target audience using one or more media (direct selling, direct mail, telemarketing, direct-action advertising, catalogue selling, cable selling, etc.) for the purpose of soliciting a response by phone, mail or personal visit from a prospect or customer.[27]

Direct Marketing by Mail

Restraints have been placed on a number of practices involved in marketing by mail, including mailing of unordered merchandise, requirements for delivery of mail orders, and negative-option mail order plans.

Unordered Merchandise

Mailing of unordered merchandise is an unfair trade practice under the Federal Trade Commission Act, according to the federal Unordered Merchandise Statute.[28] Exceptions to this statute include free samples—clearly and conspicuously marked as such—and merchandise mailed by charitable organizations soliciting contributions. Unordered merchandise is defined as "merchandise mailed without the prior expressed request or consent of the recipient." The FTC has declared that all unordered merchandise is included in this ban, whether shipped by the post office, United Parcel Service, or any private delivery service. Similar laws have been passed by many states.

If unordered merchandise is mailed, it may be treated as a gift by the recipient, who may retain, use, discard, or dispose of it in any manner without any obligation to the sender. It should be clear to those who mail unordered merchandise that no attempt should be made to bill consumers or dun them for payment. Penalties may be up to $10,000 per violation.

Mail Order Delivery Requirements

In 1976, the FTC promulgated a Mail Order Rule.[29] Essentially this rule is designed to encourage prompt shipment of merchandise that is ordered by mail. Frequently called the thirty-day rule, it prohibits a seller from soliciting an order through the mails unless there is a reasonable basis to believe the order can be filled within the time specified or, if no time is specified, within thirty days. If the merchandise is not shipped within thirty days, the seller may cancel the agreement, and give the buyer a refund of any payments made or may attempt to preserve the sale. A postage-paid-return notice to the buyer must clearly and conspicuously offer the buyer the choice of either canceling the order and receiving a full refund or extending the time for shipment to a specified revised shipping date. Silence by the buyer is considered acceptance of the delay.

In October 1992, a New York-based mail order company agreed to pay $310,000 to settle FTC charges that it failed to refund to consumers the appropriate shipping and handling fees for unshipped merchandise.[30]

Negative-Option Plans

Negative option is used by most book clubs, record clubs, and other continuity programs. It is a merchandising method whereby a seller periodically sends an announcement describing merchandise that will be delivered to subscribers to the plan unless they instruct the seller by a specified date not to send the merchandise.

In response to complaints by consumers that they were being mailed merchandise they did not want, the Trade Regulation Rule for Negative Option Plans by Sellers in Commerce was issued by the FTC in 1973. The rule requires sellers to provide mandatory disclosure of the plan rights of cancellation and details of all items that make up billing charges. Members of the plan must be given at least ten days to notify the seller if they do not want the selected item. If members receive notification less than ten days prior to shipment, the seller must credit them with returns and any postage incurred. Members must also have the right to withdraw from the club at any time without penalty, provided they comply with all other provisions of the contract.

In 1986, the FTC conducted a review of its negative-option rule in order to analyze whether the rule has had an adverse effect on a substantial number of small firms.[31] The FTC found no basis for concluding that the rule has had a significant economic impact on small businesses and concluded the rule serves the interest of both consumers and the industry.

Direct Marketing by Telephone

The term *telemarketing* has been applied to various types of marketing by various types of communication media. Its rapid expansion has led to complaints against the use of junk calls. In response, the Federal Communications Commission (FCC) has adopted a number of rules to carry out the Telephone Consumer Protection Act of 1991, which placed restrictions on marketing by telephone. The rules curb some of the undesirable aspects of automatic dialers, prerecorded messages, and facsimile machines. The FCC took a hard line on telemarketing calls that could pose a health or safety hazard. It barred automatic dialer calls as well as recorded messages to emergency phones, health care facilities, and numbers for which the call recipient may be charged.

Under the rules, telemarketing companies are required to maintain an in-house list of residential telephone subscribers who do not want to be called. The rules have banned telemarketing calls to homes before 8 a.m. and after 8 p.m. They have also barred telemarketers from placing calls to homes by using artificial or recorded voice messages, unless the call is for an emergency or the resident had earlier consented to receive such calls. The law does not apply to nonprofit and public organizations or political fund-raisers. The rules prohibiting recorded-message calls to homes exempt calls from market research organizations, political pollsters, and debt collectors. The rules also ban unsolicited junk fax advertisements and require that fax transmissions clearly indicate the sender's name and fax number.

Recently, the FTC issued complaints against a number of companies for engaging in unfair and deceptive practices in the provision of 900-number telephone services. The Telephone Disclosure and Dispute Resolution Act, enacted in October 1992, granted the FTC rule-making authority in regard to interstate pay-per-call 900-number telephone service.[32] The FTC is ordered to prescribe rules that, among other things, require that service providers disclose in their advertising of a pay-for-call service any costs of the use of the telephone number; disclose the odds of winning any advertised prize or awards; refrain from directing advertising at children under the age of 12; tell individuals under 18 years of age they must have parental or guardian's consent to make the call; disclose the cost per minute of the call; and refrain from advertising toll-free 800 numbers from which callers are connected to an access number for a pay-per-call service.

The significance of such a rule can be seen from a district court decision that has upheld the FTC's orders against a company that advertised its automobile auction information service on both radio and television.[33] The ads encouraged consumers to call a 900 number (900-Hot-Cars) for information regarding government auctions of automobiles. The TV commercials showed pictures of late-model expensive cars while various other aspects of the commercial stressed the prices could be "AS LOW AS" $100. Callers to the advertised 900 number were charged $2 per minute for a 12-minute call at the end of which they were given an 800 number. Those who called the 800 number were solicited to purchase lifetime memberships in U.S. Sales' service for $99.95, which entitled them to receive information concerning additional automobile auctions. The information involved sales at which cars in poor condition were sold at relatively low prices and cars in good condition were sold somewhere in the neighborhood of fair market value.

The FTC declared these and other practices by the company unfair and deceptive and requested injunctive relief and consumer redress from the district court. The court rejected the company's defenses, including the argument that fine-print disclaimers—stating the cars shown were for illustration purposes only—at the bottom of the screen in the final seconds of the TV commercial are sufficient to qualify the express representations of the commercial. The court declared that disclaimers or qualifications in any particular ad are not adequate to avoid liability unless they are sufficiently prominent and unambiguous to change the apparent meaning of the claims and to leave an accurate impression. The court ordered the company to pay consumer redress in an amount of over $9 million and issued a permanent injunction requiring the defendants to obtain a performance bond for any future sales.

Mail or Telephone Order Merchandise Trade Regulation Rule[34]

The FTC amended its Mail Order Merchandise Trade Regulation Rule to include merchandise ordered by telephone. Mail or telephone order sales are defined as sales in which the buyer has ordered merchandise from the seller by mail or telephone regardless of the method of payment or the method used to solicit the order. Telephone refers to any direct use of the telephone to order merchandise regardless of whether the telephone is activated by a human being or a machine.

The rule, effective, March 1, 1994, requires merchants to have a reasonable basis for any express shipment representation in soliciting the sale of telephone-ordered merchandise. If no time is represented, the shipment must be made within thirty days of receipt of the consumer's properly completed order. When the seller is unable to ship merchandise on time, the rule requires the consumer be notified about the delay and offered the option of agreeing to the delay or obtaining a prompt refund.

Telemarketing by Television

Although the term *telemarketing* initially was applied to marketing via telephone, the significant increase in home-shopping TV channels, thirty-minute commercials (called infomercials), and other promotional efforts on cable TV and broadcasting has led to the application of the term to television marketing.

Telemarketers face severe penalties for engaging in deceptive acts and practices. The FTC has the authority, under Section 13(b) of the FTC Act, to request an injunction and require ancillary relief. Potential penalties include court-ordered injunctions against violations, as well as FTC-ordered relief, including asset freezes, rescission of contracts, and restitution to consumers. Furthermore, should telemarketers violate these orders, they may face prison terms.

Amy Travel was found to have engaged in telemarketing fraud in the sale of vacation passports and vouchers.[35] In a suit filed by the FTC, the magistrate found that the wording of the telemarketing scripts through which the products were sold created the misleading impression that the cost of a vacation passport equaled the price of the entire vacation package. In fact, the actual price of the vacation package far exceeded the cost of the passport itself. At the FTC's request, the district court issued a permanent injunction against deceptive acts and practices conducted by the affiliated travel agencies and two related individuals, and it ordered relief in the form of an asset freeze, rescission of contracts, and restitution to consumers.

Infomercials

Program-length commercials first appeared in 1984, when the Justice Department required the National Association of Broadcasters to eliminate restrictions on the duration of television advertising time.[36] Initially, most of these thirty-minute ads appeared on independent TV stations and cable television between midnight and daybreak. They have since been broadcast during daytime hours.

The FTC has sent a signal in several cases that deceptively formatted programming will not be tolerated. The commission has charged a television company; marketers of bee-pollen products promoted for their therapeutic benefits; and a company that used a talk-show format to sell materials telling people how to get government grants, with falsely representing that their program-length commercials are something other than paid commercial advertising.[37] The companies have also been charged with making false and unsubstantiated claims for their products and services.

According to the FTC, should these firms wish to continue using infomercials of periods of fifteen minutes or longer, they must display a notice informing consumers that the program is a paid advertisement. The disclosure must be made within the first thirty seconds of the commercial and also must be made immediately before the instructions for ordering the product or service are given each time such instructions are provided. In addition, the companies are prohibited from making false and unsubstantiated claims.

Other Issues

In general, direct marketers are subject to the same legal controls as other marketers, particularly in regard to unfair, deceptive, or fraudulent acts or practices. Recent Supreme Court decisions are having significant impact on direct marketers. As noted in Chapter 5, a 1991 Supreme Court decision has limited the copyright protection for databases, which tend to be one of the most important resources for direct marketers. A more positive decision for direct marketers occurred in 1992, when the Supreme Court upheld a ban on sales taxes sought by states on purchases by their residents from out-of-state mail order companies. Nonetheless, direct marketing efforts have expanded significantly and encompass some nontypical activities. The legal issues surrounding them are still evolving, and direct marketers should closely monitor their implications.

SUMMARY

First Amendment protection was originally awarded to commercial speech in 1976. However, commercial speech is not accorded the same level of First Amendment protection as noncommercial speech. Deceptive advertising is not protected. Moreover, restrictions may be placed on the time, place, or manner of advertising. However, regulation of speech based on the content of advertising is subject to greater protection and is typically scrutinized under a four-part test enunciated in the 1987 *Central Hudson* case. In recent years, the Supreme Court has vacillated in applying First Amendment protection to advertising, but seems to be permitting additional restrictions.

Private suits for false advertising can be brought under Section 43(a) of the Lanham Act. No private right against false advertising exists under the FTC Act. Prior to passage of the Trademark Law Revision Act, the courts generally ruled that Lanham Act complaints of advertising misrepresentations applied only when a company misrepresented its own trademarked goods or services. The Revision Act amended Section 43(a) and now specifies that misrepresentations about another's goods and services are actionable. The Revision Act also significantly increased the potential for monetary relief in such cases.

There are both similarities and differences between the Federal Trade Commission guidelines for deceptive advertising and the requirements for a finding of false advertising under Section 43(a) of the Lanham Act. Complaints under the Lanham Act generally involve comparison advertising. Marketers should familiarize themselves with the manner in which the court examines the claims in such ads and the kinds of proof that are required.

Direct marketing activities have increased significantly in recent years and are considered to embrace a number of interrelated concepts. A number of restraints have been placed on direct marketing through the mail, including such activities as mailing of unordered merchandise, requirements for delivery of mail orders, and negative-option mail order plans.

Direct marketing by telephone has also been faced with restrictions through passage of the Telephone Consumer Protection Act of 1991, which curbs some of the undesirable aspects of telemarketing calls, and the Telephone Disclosure and Dispute Resolution Act of 1992, which places restrictions on the use of pay-per-call 900-number telephone services.

Television telemarketers face severe penalties for engaging in deceptive acts and practices. Restrictions are placed on infomercials that falsely represent that their program-length commercials are something other than paid commercial advertising and that make false and unsubstantiated claims for their products or services.

CASE
Board of Trustees of the State University of New York et al. *v.* Todd Fox et al. *492 U.S. 409 (1989).*

FACTS

Resolution 66-156 of the State University of New York (SUNY) prohibited private commercial enterprises from operating within SUNY facilities. In 1982, a saleswoman from American Future Systems (AFS), a company that sells housewares, conducted a "Tupperware-like party demonstrating the company's products in a student dormitory at SUNY's Cortland campus. When campus police asked her to leave, she refused; they then arrested her and charged her with trespass and soliciting without a permit.

Todd Fox and several fellow students at SUNY sued for declaratory judgment on the basis that, in prohibiting their hosting and attending AFS demonstrations, the resolution violated the First Amendment. A district court granted a preliminary injunction, but after a trial in 1986, the court found for the university on the ground that its restrictions on speech were reasonable in light of the dormitories' purpose.

The Court of Appeals for the Second Circuit viewed the resolution as an alleged restriction on commercial speech and applied the *Central Hudson* test, which requires four elements for analysis:

1. Is the activity unlawful, or is the speech misleading or fraudulent?

2. Is the government interest in restricting such speech substantial?

3. Do the challenged restrictions on commercial speech directly advance government interest?

4. Are the restrictions on commercial speech no more extensive than necessary to serve the government's interest?

The Appeals Court agreed that the speech here proposes a lawful transaction, is not misleading, and therefore is entitled to First Amendment protection. However, the government interests in support of the resolution are substantial, since it promotes safety and security, prevents commercial exploitation of students, and preserves residential tranquillity. Nonetheless, the Appeals Court did not decide whether the resolution directly advances these interests or whether the regulation it imposes is more extensive than is necessary for that purpose. In 1988, the Court of Appeals remanded the case to the district court for further factual findings. The Supreme Court agreed to review the case.

ISSUES

Did SUNY Resolution 66-156 prohibiting private commercial enterprises from operating in SUNY facilities directly advance the state's asserted interests, and if it did, was it the least restrictive means to that end?

Was the Court of Appeals correct in remanding the case?

HOLDINGS

The Supreme Court did not rule on the ban.

The Supreme Court declared that the remand was correct because further factual findings had to be made. The Supreme Court agreed with the Court of Appeals on the findings of the first three prongs of *Central Hudson*.

However, the Supreme Court objected to the terms of the remand, specifically those pertaining to the last element of the *Central Hudson* analysis. The Supreme Court reversed the judgment of the Court of Appeals and set a more permissive standard for passing First Amendment muster by declaring that, under the fourth prong, the restrictions on commercial speech need not be the least restrictive means of achieving government interest; rather there need be only a fit between the legislative ends and the means chosen to accomplish those ends "that is not necessarily perfect but reasonable."

REASONING

The initial question the court addressed was whether the principal type of expression at issue is commercial speech. The test for identifying commercial speech is, Does it "propose a commercial transaction?" and Tupperware parties fit that description. The students contended that the presentations touch on other subject such as how to be financially responsible, and thus pure speech and commercial speech were inextricably intertwined, and the entirety must therefore be classified as noncommercial. However, the Supreme Court declared that communications can constitute commercial speech notwithstanding the fact that they contain discussions of important public issues, and it examined the ban on the Tupperware-like party as a restriction of commercial speech.

The Supreme Court agreed with the Court of Appeals on the findings of the first three prongs of *Central Hudson* and declared that the remand was correct, since further factual findings had to be made. However, in reference to the fourth prong, the Supreme Court concluded that the Court of Appeals had erred in requiring the district court to apply a least-restrictive means test to SUNY's resolution as it related to commercial speech. Although some cases have supported a strict interpretation of *than is necessary* as the least-restrictive means, the word *necessary* is sometimes used more loosely. Moreover, in applying time, place, and manner restrictions upon protected speech, the court has held that this does not require least-restrictive means.

For passing First Amendment muster there need be only a fit between legislative ends and the means chosen to accomplish those ends. Moreover, the means need not be perfect but narrowly tailored and reasonable. The court rejected the contention that this test for restrictions on commercial speech is overly permissive. Moreover, since the state bears the burden of justifying its restrictions, it must affirmatively establish the reasonable fit that is required.

The court addressed the students' objection that the resolution may be invalidated as overbroad, since it prohibits as well fully protected noncommercial speech. The court agreed that, although the Tupperware-like party was clearly commercial speech, the resolution does reach some noncommercial speech, since it would prohibit for-profit job counseling, tutoring, legal advice, and medical consultation provided for a fee in students' dormitory rooms. While these examples consist of speech for a profit, they do not consist of speech that proposes a commercial transaction, which is what defines commercial speech. Some of our most valued forms of fully protected speech are uttered for a profit.

The majority of the Supreme Court reversed the judgment of the Court of Appeals. The case was remanded for further proceedings consistent with this opinion and to determine whether the resolution was overbroad because it could also restrain noncommercial speech.

Justices Blackman, Brennan, and Marshall dissented, declaring that since the resolution makes no effort to distinguish between commercial and noncommercial speech, it should have been unconstitutional on its face now, in order to avoid chilling protected speech during the pendency of proceedings on remand.

DISCUSSION QUESTIONS

To what extent is commercial speech protected by the First Amendment? Do you agree with the Supreme Court's decision, which appears to have increased the potential for government restraints on advertising and other forms of commercial communication? Explain.

CASE
Castrol Inc. *v.* Pennzoil Co., *BNA ATTR, Vol. 64 (CA 3 No. 92-5353, February 4, 1993).*

FACTS

Motor oils minimize metal-to-metal contact in an engine by providing an optimum protective film between moving parts. Viscosity is a measure of a motor oil's resistance to film and is the basis on which motor oils are classified and marketed. Viscosity breakdown causes both a physical thinning of the lubricant and the formation of sludge and deposits on the engine.

Castrol Inc., a major oil manufacturer and distributor, alleged that its rival Pennzoil Co. had violated Section 43(a) of the Lanham Act when it claimed that its product "outperforms any leading motor oil against viscosity breakdown." The complaint also challenged a secondary claim by Pennzoil—that its motor oil provides "longer engine life and better protection."

A district court held that the advertisements for Pennzoil motor oil contained claims of superiority that were literally false. An injunction was issued including provisions barring Pennzoil from:

c) . . . disseminating . . . any advertisement that claims, directly or by clear implication, that:

i) Pennzoil motor oil outperforms any leading motor oil against viscosity breakdown;

ii) Pennzoil motor oil gives more protection against viscosity breakdown than any leading motor oil;

iii) Pennzoil motor oil provides better protection against engine failure than any leading motor oil;

iiii) Pennzoil motor oil provides better protection against engine wear than any leading motor oil; or

iiiii) Pennzoil motor oil provides longer engine life or greater engine durability than any other leading motor oil.

Pennzoil appealed to a court of appeals.

ISSUES

1. Do Pennzoil's motor oil advertisements contain literally false claims in violation of Section 43(a) of the Lanham Act?

2. Does the injunction by the district court infringe on Pennzoil's right to free speech as protected by the First Amendment?

HOLDINGS

1. Yes. Pennzoil's claims are literally false.
2. No. Claims that are false are not protected by the First Amendment.

REASONING

According to the Court of Appeals in this Lanham Act action, the record was "replete with Castrol's affirmative evidence proving the literal falsity of Pennzoil's claims." Pennzoil relied on a test that was not the industry standard and did not measure viscosity breakdown but rather measured percentage of viscosity loss. In a test accepted by the industry, Castrol's motor oil was shown to be superior in some respects. In another test accepted by the industry, both oils satisfied the test requirements. Thus, according to the only two industry-accepted tests for measuring viscosity breakdown, Pennzoil's claims of superiority were literally false. Moreover, Pennzoil's own president conceded that users of Castrol oil "do not run an enhanced risk of engine failure." Under the Lanham Act, since the claims were literally false, proof of consumer confusion was not necessary.

The Court of Appeals rejected Pennzoil's contention that the injunction constitutes a prior restraint on speech in contravention of the First Amendment. According to the court, the claims that are enjoined "are false at this moment, and thus not protected by the First Amendment."

DISCUSSION QUESTIONS

What are the differences between a case of false advertising under the Federal Trade Commission Act and a case under the Lanham Act?

What kinds of actions can a firm take to avoid and/or defend against a Lanham Act complaint?

ENDNOTES

1. *Valentine* v. *Chrestensen*, 315 U.S. 52, 62, S. Ct. 301, L. Ed. 486 (1942).
2. *Virginia State Board of Pharmacy* v. *Virginia Citizens Consumer Council, Inc.*, U.S. 96 S. Ct. 1817 (1976).
3. *Central Hudson Gas & Electric Corp.* v. *Public Service Commission of New York*, 447 U.S. 557 (1980).
4. *Posadas de Puerto Rico Association* v. *Tourism Company of Puerto Rico*, 106, S. Ct. 2968 (1986).
5. *Board of Trustees* v. *Fox*, 492 U.S. 409 (1989).

 6. *City of Cincinnati, Petitioner*, v. *Discovery Network, Inc., et al.*, U.S.L.W. No. 91-1200 (March 24, 1993).
 7. *Edenfield* v. *Fane* (1993) 61 USLW 4431.
 8. Robert P. Mandel, "Regulation of Commercial Speech: Did 1993 Supreme Court Decisions Clarify the Scope of First Amendment Protection?", *Journal of Public Policy and Marketing*, 13 (Spring 1994), 159–163.
 9. *United States* and *Federal Communications Commission* v. *Edge Broadcasting Company* (1993), 61 USLW 4759.
10. Mandel, p. 163.
11. *Miller* v. *California*, 413 U.S. 15, 93 S. Ct. 2607 (1973).
12. *L. L. Bean* v. *Drake Publishing* (1987).
13. *Hustler Magazine Inc.* v. *Falwell*, 108 S. Ct. 876 (1988).
14. *Barnard Food Industries* v. *Dietene Co.*, 163 USPQ 264 (1969).
15. "a) any person who, on or in connection with any goods or services, or any container for goods, uses in commerce any word, name, symbol or device, . . . or any false designation of origin, . . . or false or misleading representation of fact, which—
       (1) is likely to cause confusion, or to cause mistake, or deceive, . . .
       (2) in commercial advertising or promotion misrepresents his or her or another person's goods, services, or commercial activities, shall be liable in a civil action by any person who believes that he or she is or is likely to be damaged by such act."
16. *Coca-Cola* v. *Tropicana Co.* (CA-2, September 1983).
17. Ivan L. Preston, "False or Deceptive Advertising under the Lanham Act: Analysis of Factual Findings and Types of Evidence," *Trademark Reporter* 79 (July–August 1989), 508–553.
18. *Oscar Mayer Foods Corp.* v. *Bryan Foods, Inc.*, 13 USPQ2d 1079 (1989).
19. *Ortho Pharmaceutical Corp.* SD N.Y., CCH #70,473, 70,475 (SD N.Y., January 1994).
20. *Johnson & Johnson–Merck Consumer Pharmaceuticals Co.* CCH #70,495 (ED Pa., February 1994).
21. Caryn L. Beck-Dudley and Terrell G. Williams, "Legal and Public Policy Implications for the Future of Comparative Advertising: A Look at *U-Haul* v. *Jartran*," *Journal of Public Policy and Marketing* 8 (1989), 124–142.
22. Bruce Buchanan and Donna Goldman, "Us v. Them: The Minefield of Comparative Ads," *Harvard Business Review* 67 (May–June 1989), 39–50.
23. Charles C. Mann and Mark L. Plummer, "The Big Headache," *The Atlantic* (October 1988), 39–57.
24. *ALPO Petfoods Inc.* v. *Ralston Purina Co.*, 12 USPQ2d 1178 (1989).
25. *ALPO Petfoods Inc.* v. *Ralston Purina Co.* (CA-DC, 1990).
26. *ALPO Petfoods, Inc.* v. *Ralston Purina Co.*, 27 USPQ2d 1455 (1993).
27. Peter D. Bennett, ed., *Directory of Marketing Terms* (American Marketing Association, 1988), p. 58.
28. 39 U.S.C. 309.
29. 16 C.F.R. 435.
30. In re Lillian Vernon Corp., CCH 23,270 (October 1992).
31. In re Regulatory Flexibility Act Review of the FTC Trade Regulation Rule for Use of Negative Option Plans by Sellers in Commerce, "Legal Developments in Marketing," *Journal of Marketing* 51 (October 1987), 121.
32. P.L. 102–556.
33. *FTC* v. *US Sales Corp.*, CCH #69,702 (DC ND Ill., January 31, 1992).
34. 58 Federal Register 49096, September 21, 1993.
35. *FTC* v. *Amy Travel Service, Inc.*, CCH #68,549 (CA-7, April 1989).
36. In re Wayne Phillips et al., CCH #22,797 (Feb. 1990); "Legal Developments in Marketing," *Journal of Marketing* 54 (October 1990), 118.
37. In re Twin Star Productions, Inc. et al., CCH #22,821 (Apr. 1990); "Legal Developments in Marketing," *Journal of Marketing* 55 (January 1991), 87.

CHAPTER NINE
Personal Selling and Sales Promotion

Legal issues in promotion decisions encompass areas of significance to marketers in addition to those related to advertising activities, discussed in previous chapters. This chapter examines legal restrictions on other widely used promotional activities: personal selling and sales promotion.

PERSONAL SELLING

Personal selling is a form of promotion that involves face-to-face interaction with the customer. When salespeople serve as a company's personal link to the customer, then accordingly significant planning is required in designing and managing the firm's sales force. The design aspects include setting objectives as well as designing the strategy, structure, size, and compensation of the sales force. Effective management involves recruiting and selecting sales representatives as well as training, directing, motivating, and evaluating them.

The legal issues in personal selling are not as well developed as those relating to advertising. Most selling activities are governed by state law concerning unfair competition, and such law has evolved through numerous cases over the years. Nevertheless, legal questions can arise during the activities involved in personal selling, particularly those that relate to acts and practices by the sales force and its managers.

From a federal perspective, the Federal Trade Commission's (FTC's) jurisdiction over unfair or deceptive acts and practices provides the commission with authority over unlawful selling activities. Sales force misrepresentations are unlawful. In addition, business practices other than those usually thought of as deceptive may be considered unfair because of their tendency to undermine the bargaining or competitive process. As noted in Chapter 1, many states have enacted versions of the Uniform Deceptive

Trade Practices Act, modeled after the FTC Act, which control unlawful personal selling practices.

Unfair Selling Practices

Various types of selling practices, designated as unfair and subject to prohibitions, are discussed below.

Commercial Bribery

According to the FTC, the term *commercial bribery* relates to the practice whereby sellers secretly pay money or make gifts to employees or agents of potential customers to induce them to promote purchases by their own employers from the sellers offering the secret inducement. The FTC has declared that a price, reward, gift, or favor bestowed or promised by a seller for the purpose of influencing the action of public purchasing officials, or its own customers, or its competitors' customers is unlawful.[1]

Push Money

Manufacturers or distributors of a good may find it profitable to encourage sales at the retail level by financially rewarding the individual salespeople of the buyer of their merchandise. The financial reward to employees for pushing a particular manufacturer's product, rather than a competitor's, is known as push money and is also called premium money, PM, and spiff. Originally the FTC considered this an unfair practice and prohibited such an arrangement whether the salesperson's employer had consented to it or not. However, a court decision held that the practice was not illegal if it were done with the consent of the employer.[2] PMs, in existence for a long time, are periodically evaluated to determine their legality and desirability. Currently, the practice is not illegal if the manufacturer notifies the retail outlet and the retailer agrees to permit its salespeople to secure this special compensation.

Bait and Switch

Problems in eliminating bait-and-switch tactics include the difficulty in distinguishing between the unlawful practice of bait and switch and the acceptable selling practice of trading up. The latter may occur when a customer who intended to buy an item advertised at a lower price is encouraged to purchase a higher-priced item. Such a practice becomes bait and switch when the lower-priced item did not represent a bona fide offer, but was merely a lure to secure prospects, who are then induced to buy the higher-priced models by a salesperson's disparagement of the less-expensive product.

The FTC has issued guides against the use of bait advertising designed to lead to switch activities by salespersons. According to FTC guides, several acts or practices by salespersons will be considered in determining if an ad is a bona fide offer or a bait scheme. These include:[3]

- The refusal to show, demonstrate, or sell the product offered.

- The disparagement of the advertised product, its guarantee, or the availability of services, repairs, or parts for the product.

- The showing of a product that is defective, unusable, or impractical for the purpose represented in the ad.

- The use of a sales plan or method of compensating salespeople, or penalizing salespeople, designed to prevent or discourage them from selling the advertised product.

In an effort to distinguish between bait and switch and trading up, the FTC has on occasion examined both the dollar sales volume of a particular product that has been advertised at an exceptionally low price and the dollar expenditures on advertising for this same item. Where the advertising expenditures clearly exceed the total sales revenue of the firm, the commission has reason to believe that the product was used primarily as bait.

The Household Sewing Machine Co. advertised in newspapers that "partially paid for" used sewing machines "left in layaway" were available at a reduced price (the bait). The machines, which were represented to be comparatively new, were "very old and rusty looking" and almost always rejected by customers. The salesman who called at the home in response to the leads would announce, after the rejection, that he just happened to have a new (and much more expensive) machine in his car (the switch).

The commission declared these activities to be deceptive, since the company had spent funds—in advertising used machines—in excess of the total sales volume accounted for by used machine sales. Furthermore, the salespeople's commission plan contained incentives in the form of high commissions for the sale of new machines and little or no commissions for the sale of used machines.[4]

Pyramid Schemes

Multilevel marketing is a legitimate method of retailing in which consumer products are not sold in stores by salesclerks, but are sold by independent business persons called distributors. Such distributors sell consumer products supplied by an established company. The distributors can also build and manage their own sales force and secure both a percentage of the sales of the entire sales group and earnings on the sales to retail customers.

Pyramid schemes are illegal scams involving levels of marketing in which large numbers of people at the bottom of the pyramid pay money to a few people at the top. Each new participant pays for the chance to advance to the top and then profits from the payments of others who might join later.[5]

Pyramid schemes seek to make money from participants; multilevel marketing companies seek to help individuals build a business. To distinguish between them, several questions should be asked.

1. How much money are you required to pay to become a distributor? Start-up fees for multilevel opportunities are generally small; pyramid schemes typically have high start-up costs because they make nearly all their profit on signing up recruits.

2. Will the organization buy back your inventory? Legitimate companies that require inventory purchases will usually buy back unsold products if you decide to quit the business. Some state laws require buy backs for at least 90% of the original costs.

3. Are sales made to consumers? Multilevel marketing depends on selling to consumers and establishing a market. Pyramid schemes are not concerned with sales to end users of the product. Thus, if no sales or not many sales are made to consumers, the scheme is likely to be illegitimate.

Once the Magnuson-Moss FTC Improvements Act of 1975 provided the FTC with the authority to require consumer redress as a remedy for unfair or deceptive practices, the FTC filed its first redress action against Koscot Interplanetary, Inc. At that time, the FTC found that Glenn Turner, who ran the company, had defrauded people out of millions of dollars through the use of fraudulent pyramid marketing schemes for selling toiletries and cosmetics.[6] Koscot appealed, declaring that the FTC could not seek redress for deceptive acts or practices that were committed before a cease-and-desist order had been entered against pyramid sellers. The court stated the FTC had this right, declaring the FTC had given sufficient notice in its complaint that it might seek restitution, and that the FTC had the power to seek such redress.

However, in a review of the multilevel marketing activities of Amway, Inc., the Federal Trade Commission held that the firm does not sell distributorships and is not a pyramid scheme based on the following findings:[7] Amway does not have a head-hunting fee; it makes product sales a precondition to receiving a performance bonus; it requires that its products be sold to consumers; it buys back excessive inventory; and its training program emphasizes sales training, not the recruiting of distributorships.

Coercive Sales Efforts

Coercive efforts by salespersons are unacceptable. Coercion or intimidation of prospective customers, recipients of unsolicited goods or services, competitors, or suppliers is unfair. Several dance studios were charged with unfair and deceptive sales practices in the sale of courses of dancing instruction. According to the FTC, the operators misrepresented that their club offered various types of social activities, but unless the member paid between $450 and $5,000 there were no such activities available. In addition, to sell courses of dance instruction, the studios used unfair practices such as coercive sales effort, relay salesmanship, and intense emotional and unrelenting sales pressure during several hours to persuade people to sign a contract for a substantial number of dancing lessons at a substantial cost.[8]

Wrongfully Forced Deals

Damaging the property of prospective customers in order to force them to buy is unlawful. A furnace manufacturer encouraged its salespeople to dismantle furnaces without permission of the owners and then misrepresent the condition of the dismantled furnaces. They then refused to reassemble the furnaces they had dismantled.[9] Scare tactics to frighten people into buying furnaces have been prohibited by the FTC.

Door-to-Door Sales

In an effort to combat practices such as high-pressure sales tactics and to give customers an opportunity to change their mind after the salesperson leaves, the FTC has promulgated a Trade Regulation Rule for a Cooling-Off Period for Door-to-Door Sales.[10]

A door-to-door sale is defined as the sale of goods or services with a purchase price of $25 or more in which the seller personally solicits the sale and the buyer's agreement to purchase is made at a place other than the place of the sellers. The practices curtailed by the rule include misrepresentations of the nature and price of a product, false savings claims, and the nuisance created by the uninvited salesperson who refuses to leave the home until a sale was made.

The rule, which has also been adopted by a number of states, requires the salesperson to provide the buyer with a copy of any contract pertaining to the sale at the time of its execution. The contract must be in the same language as that used in the oral sales presentation (e.g., Spanish); must contain the name and the address of the seller; and, in boldface type of at least 10 points, must state, "You, the buyer, may cancel this transaction at any time prior to midnight of the third business date of this transaction." Failure to furnish such a contract constitutes an unfair and deceptive act or practice.

The FTC ordered Encyclopedia Britannica to cease and desist from certain customary door-to-door sales practices considered unlawful.[11] The order included a requirement that encyclopedia salespersons identify themselves by presenting to the consumer a 3″ by 5″ card bearing the company's name and its logo and stating, "The purpose of this representative's call is to solicit the sale of encyclopedias."

Britannica petitioned for changes, arguing that the original order contained provisions that were more than necessary to ensure disclosure of its representative's sale purpose and that it placed Britannica at a competitive disadvantage. The commission modified the order by allowing Britannica salespersons to present consumers with a business card instead of the larger-size card.[12] The business card must bear the company's name and logo, the name, address, and phone number of the person presenting the card; and the person's designation as "sales representative." It need not contain the sale-purpose disclosure, but the consumer must be given an adequate opportunity to read the card before the salesperson engages in sales solicitation. According to the FTC, such clear and conspicuous disclosure is required in order to prevent future deception by Britannica. A similar requirement had been placed against Grolier, a principal competitor of Britannica.

Salespersons' Misrepresentations

Salespersons' statements to customers can generate problems for their firm. The FTC is empowered to issue cease-and-desist orders to organizations that engage in unfair or deceptive practices through misrepresentations by their salespeople. In addition, the FTC may hold business concerns responsible for salespersons' statements even when such statements have not been specifically authorized.[13] Private lawsuits for personal defamation may be brought when one's statement disparages the quality of another person's product and implies that the person is dishonest, fraudulent, incompetent, or financially unstable—thus affecting the individual's personal reputation.[14]

Permissible defenses for salespeople's representations include the fact that the representations were mere exaggerations or permissible puffing. For example, sales talk of a fanciful nature would not be taken seriously, such as a statement that a sewing machine was "almost human." According to the FTC, *"puffing*, as we understand it, is a term frequently used to denote the exaggeration reasonably to be expected of a seller as to the degree of quality of his product, the truth or falsity of which cannot be precisely determined.[15] However, the defense of permissible puffing does not include representations assigning to products virtues they do not possess, and representations designed to frighten prospective purchasers into buying, such as statements by salespeople of stainless steel cooking utensils that the use of aluminum cooking utensils would cause illness.[16]

Misrepresentations about Own Offerings

Several types of selling practices may lead to liability problems as follows.[17] Warranties for products may inadvertently be created by salespersons through careless or inflated statements, improper use of promotional materials, showing samples, or silence in the knowledge. Puffery in the form of overstatement is not acceptable when the seller has more knowledge, experience or sophistication about the information in the transaction. Thus, statements by a used car salesperson that a car was "in A-1 shape" and "mechanically perfect" was found by a court to provide an express warranty.[18] This opinion has been endorsed in hundreds of automobile-related cases.

In a recent case that indicates the potential damage caused by salespersons' misrepresentations, Metropolitan Life Insurance Co. was charged with misleading sales practices. Met Life's sales force marketed to nurses and other professionals whole-life insurance in the form of retirement policies. Complaints were made by a number of the insured, who had believed they were purchasing a retirement plan. A multistate probe was instituted by a number of the nation's insurance commissioners to investigate the practice and determine the penalties.

In March 1994, Met Life agreed to pay a precedent-setting $20-million settlement with more than forty states.[19] In addition to that fine, Met Life must also pay as much as $76 million in refunds to the 60,000 allegedly defrauded policyholders. Met Life is responsible for contacting the policyholders and explaining the refund program.

A salesperson's vigorous personal selling efforts in support of a product may dilute a marketer's warning so that a court will find failure to provide adequate warning and thus result in liability exposure. A firm that markets a product that is likely to be dangerous in use, and that knows or has reason to know the intended users may not realize the dangers, has a duty to provide reasonable warning.[20]

Misrepresentations about Competitor's Offerings

A salesperson's negative statement about a competitor's product may lead to liability for disparagement, also referred to as trade libel or injurious falsehood. Although there is some suggestion that comparisons generally unfavorable to a competitor's product are within the privileges of competition and permissible exaggeration, modern courts appear to be losing patience with such defenses. Thus, a sales representative who either intentionally or recklessly makes a statement about a competitor's product or business may be taking a significant step toward creating legal liability for disparagement.[21]

Penalties

While liability generally inheres to an organization, penalties for salespersons' unfair or deceptive acts or practices can be invoked against both the firm and the salesperson. Penalties include injunctions, redress and fines, and the possibility of jail terms.

The FTC sought and received a permanent injunction prohibiting the officers and salespeople of Kimberly International Gem Corp. from misrepresenting the characteristics, quality, and retail value of gemstones and other investments. Kimberly agreed to pay up to $280,000 in redress to settle FTC charges that it misrepresented the value of the stones. The company allegedly had represented its stones were being sold at wholesale prices, when, in fact, they were priced many times greater than the prices retailers charge.[22]

The FTC issued a cease-and-desist order requiring one of the largest sellers of undeveloped real estate to refund $14.5 million to purchasers.[23] Horizon sold undeveloped land in the southwest area of the United States. In marketing its properties, Horizon relied on both national advertising dinner parties held for potential purchasers and in-home sales solicitations. The FTC described a number of circumstances in such sales that will lead to a finding of deception:

- A false verbal representation by a land seller constitutes deception even if such representations are omitted from a written contract.

- The failure to disclose a significant risk that the purchaser of a product cannot reasonably be expected to anticipate constitutes a material omission of fact and is therefore a deceptive practice.

- Failure to apprise purchasers of land that the undeveloped land is not a short-term investment constitutes deceptive omission of a material fact.

Jail terms are rare; however, such potential penalties are possible for violators of FTC cease-and-desist orders. The longest prison term for contempt of an FTC order was imposed by a district court against an individual charged with deceptive marketing pages in connection with selling time-shares in Texas vacation resorts.[24] An injunction prohibited Weiswasser and his agents from misrepresenting the accommodations, facilities, and exchange privileges available to time-share buyers. Nevertheless, Weiswasser encouraged his agents to promote the Texas projects, indicating that they could readily be exchanged, that substantial income was available from these time-shares, and that they were risk free. The commission found these representations were false. After Weiswasser pleaded guilty to violating the injunction, the district court judge sentenced him to three years' imprisonment, one year of which was suspended.

In addition to the jail term, Weiswasser is required to make $250,000 consumer redress payments, is banned permanently from the time-share industry, and is prohibited from misrepresenting other real estate and vacation-recreation programs in the future. If Weiswasser becomes involved in the sale or lease of any other goods, property, or services to consumers who pay in advance, he must post a performance bond to protect consumers from any resulting financial losses.[25]

Compliance Suggestions

Boedecker, Morgan, and Stoltman declare that firms do not include sufficient legal materials in their training of salespeople. They recommend that sales management programs should be designed to direct salespeople to comply with legal guidelines. Specifically, they recommend:[26]

1. Detailed modules on legal guidelines in training schools for beginning salespersons.
2. Provision of updated information on relevant judicial and statutory developments.
3. Development of incentive compensation to reward salespersons for avoiding litigious situations.
4. Review of salesperson performance to identify those whose practices might lead to legal problems.
5. Management by example, that is, following legal guidelines.

Global Considerations

Improper sales tactics in foreign markets are subject to federal control through the Foreign Corrupt Practices Act (FCPA) of 1977.[27] Most of the

FTC's recent proceedings against bribery relate to activities in foreign markets. The FTC has utilized both the FTC Act and the Robinson-Patman Act as the bases for challenging the payment of bribes in U.S. foreign trade when the alleged effect was to exclude other U.S. firms from the foreign market. In contrast to the Foreign Corrupt Practices Act of 1977, which prohibits bribery of foreign government officials, the FTC Act and Robinson-Patman Act apply to private commercial parties as well and provide for civil liability as well as criminal sanctions. In an FTC order, payments by three major aerospace firms to officers and employees of foreign governments as well as to officials of foreign airlines was barred. The maximum monetary penalty for corporations under the federal anti-bribery statute was $1 million. Under FTC orders, the companies could be liable for penalties of up to $3.6 million a year per violation.[28]

Bribery

The bribery provision of the FCPA applies to virtually all U.S. companies filing with the Securities and Exchange Commission. The act prohibits firms from authorizing payments, offers, promises, or gifts for the purpose of corruptly influencing action by governments or government officials in order to retain business for the company. Possible recipients include foreign officials, foreign political parties or party officials, and candidates for foreign political office.[29] Congress's objective in passing the FCPA was to bolster the moral image of U.S. international firms abroad. It was designed to codify and clarify U.S. ethical and financial reporting standards and prescribe specific penalties for wrongdoing in these areas.

The FCPA had two provisions—a bribery provision and an accounting provision; however, the requirements under those provisions were not quite clear.[30] Confusion about inadvertent violation of FCPA prompted passage of the Omnibus Trade Act of 1988, which clarified some of the issues. The Trade Act specifies the types of payments that are acceptable and who may receive them. Transaction bribes, also called grease payments, made to accelerate the performance of a routine function (such as processing papers) by an official, are considered acceptable under the 1988 Trade Act. Variance bribes are considered illegal, since these are payments made to an official to secure the suspension of a legal norm. The original concern of the FCPA Act—outright bribery—is unacceptable. According to the FCPA, all bribes are illegal when performed in the United States or any other country where they are expressly prohibited.

Under the FCPA, U.S. corporations could be held criminally liable if they "know or have reason to know" that a bribery payment was made. Under the

Omnibus Trade Act, when third parties perform transactions in foreign countries, the U.S. firm can be held criminally liable only if it can be shown the firm had actual knowledge that an illegal payment was made to an official of a foreign government.

Since the enactment of the FCPA, America's ability to compete in international markets under such standards has been a major concern of both legislators and businesses. In fact, many European companies do not have such laws. While it is impossible to measure how much business has or has not been lost due to passage of act, some studies have shown that the FCPA may have had very little real impact on America's ability to do business abroad.

Nonetheless, firms must exercise caution in decisions to use bribery tactics in international markets. In a recent Supreme Court case concerning an American builder who had obtained construction contracts with the Nigerian government by bribing Nigerian government officials, the court indicated that a U.S. marketer who uses bribes or other illegal methods to secure a contract with a foreign government can be required by U.S. courts to pay for damages caused to other bidders injured by the acts.[31] This is true even if such judicial inquiry may embarrass the foreign government in a way that perhaps affects foreign relations.

SALES PROMOTION

The American Marketing Association defines *sales promotion* as marketing activities—other than personal selling, advertising, and publicity—that stimulate consumer purchasing and dealer effectiveness. These stimulants are used to encourage the trade to accept stock, and sell the merchandise; to encourage the sales force to increase its solicitations and push the product; and to encourage the consumer to purchase and repurchase the product. The specific activities included can be divided into dealer and distributor stimulants (methods to increase purchasing action on the part of marketing intermediaries) and direct consumer stimulants (techniques for generating consumer purchases).

Although sales promotion is not media advertising, in some cases the two are interrelated; there are advertisements that offer premium or cents-off coupons and those that promote sweepstakes and contests. Furthermore, sales contests and demonstrations—both of which are sales promotional devices—do make use of salespeople.

A number of characteristics distinguish sales promotion as a marketing tool. First, its activities are rarely conducted independently of other promotional efforts; they are intended to be supplementary. Second, sales promotion has an element of immediacy to it: a cents-off coupon is designed to encourage a purchase, and a point-of-purchase display motivates impulse buying.

A third characteristic of sales promotion is that its rates are not fixed, and neither are media commissions available for its performance. Because of the lack of standardization of sales promotion efforts, their intermittent use, and their varying rates, manufacturers often conduct such activities within their own organizational structure rather than use an advertising agency. When an agency is used, it frequently charges the advertiser a fee for planning and producing sales promotion devices. In recent years, a number of agencies specializing in sales promotion have been formed to provide expertise in this area.

Trade Stimulants

Trade stimulants take the form of trade deals, cooperative advertising allowances, and sales force incentives. Trade deals—usually in the form of temporary price reductions when new products are introduced—and advertising allowances are subject to the price discrimination provisions of the Robinson-Patman Act discussed in Chapter 11.

Direct stimulation of channel member's sales force may occur through the use of push money (discussed earlier) or sales force contests. Contests may be used to encourage an outlet's sales force to sell more of a specific manufacturer's merchandise. To be effective and lawful, such channel-of-distribution contests must provide a chance of winning for everyone eligible to enter.

Direct Consumer Stimulants

Sales promotion devices distributed to customers are designed to pull items through marketing channels. These stimulants to encourage consumer purchases include offering potential customers free samples, other items with purchase (premiums), price reductions (coupons or rebates), and gifts (contests, sweepstakes, or trading stamps).

Most consumer stimulants are disseminated by manufacturers who want to (1) motivate consumers to ask for and purchase their products and (2) encourage retailers and wholesalers to stock their merchandise in anticipation of such requests. Although the basic objective of all these sales promotion devices is to increase sales, their primary impacts may differ. For example, contests and sweepstakes increase brand awareness, samples attract new customers, and coupons most often increase sales to current customers.

No federal regulations specifically outlaw these devices, but a number of states have adopted various antipremium statutes, which basically outlaw the use of free goods, premiums, or trading stamps as promotional devices. Moreover, the FTC prohibits the use of these devices in an unfair or deceptive manner.

Samples

In sales promotion, the term *sampling* designates a method of offering a customer a free trial of a product. Samples, unlike other consumer stimulants, are actually based on the merits of the merchandise. For effective sampling, the item should be an accurate representation of a product, and the product itself should be one that is frequently used, is low cost, and offers repeat sales.

While there are no specific legal restrictions on sampling, care must be exercised in sampling distributions. When Lever Bros. introduced Sunlight dishwashing liquid in a mail sampling campaign, some eighty people, apparently believing they had received a sample of lemon juice, ingested the produce and became ill; none seriously, fortunately.

Premiums

A premium is an incentive designed to produce an immediate and obvious increase in sales. It is usually an item of merchandise that may be offered free or at a relatively low cost as a bonus to purchasers. A free premium, by law, must be offered at no extra cost, and the price of the product it accompanies cannot be raised. In states that have statutes prohibiting sales below cost, some courts have held that premiums should be considered in determining whether the sale is below cost.

Coupons

Of all consumer stimulants, coupons are most widely used. In 1991, manufacturers distributed in the United States an estimated 292 billion coupons—or 3,150 per household—with a total potential savings of nearly $132 billion. However, less than 3% of the coupons were redeemed. Manufacturers use coupons for various purposes: to encourage consumers to try new products, to generate repeat purchases after an initial trial, and to increase the use of established products.

In an early statement on enforcement policy concerning the advertising and use of coupons, the FTC noted that distributors of coupons should not place an unreasonably short expiration date on the coupons so that they may have already expired when the product is purchased by the consumer.[32]

Coupons enclosed in consumer products must contain an expiration date and allow purchasers of the product at least six months for redemption. Manufacturers who state in their labels or their advertising that a coupon is enclosed in the consumer product must clearly and conspicuously disclose the limitations of the coupon—for example, that it is valuable only on the next purchase of the same item.

Although coupons rarely generate consumer complaints, a serious problem for distributors of coupons is the high rate of fraudulent redemptions of coupons. In an effort to decrease misredemptions, various controls have been instituted, including coupon investigations, supervision of newspapers that print coupon inserts, and coupon fraud investigations by the Post Office. Even sting operations are used, the most successful of which was launched when coupon ads for a fake detergent called "Breen" were placed in several New York and New Jersey newspapers. Over 200 storekeepers and operators who misredeemed these coupons were convicted of fraud.

Rebates

In recent years, refunds in the form of rebates have been offered for the purchase of expensive products such as automobiles and appliances. Rebates are considered temporary reductions that do not affect prices, unlike discounts, which suggest items are less expensive and which create difficulties in instituting subsequent price increases. Rebates generate from manufacturers, but frequently require the cooperation of dealers, who must absorb the cost of refunds.

Rebates are generally not considered to constitute price-fixing. However, manufacturers should be careful not to require retailers to charge any particular price. To avoid action by state consumer protection bureaus or the FTC, manufacturers must process rebate payment requests correctly and promptly.

Contests, Sweepstakes, Games of Chance, and Lotteries

Contests, sweepstakes, and games of chance are designated as strong sales promotion devices designed to create a high level of consumer involvement in the advertising of products while at the same time encouraging action at the retail level.

Sweepstakes are sales promotion devices in which prize winners are selected by chance, generally by some type of random drawing. Sweepstakes require participants merely to submit their name to be included.

Games are sweepstakes with more involved entry systems. For example, entrants may be required to save up game cards that match each other or that can be put together to complete a game diagram.

In contests, prize winners are selected on the basis of skills. Contests may be of many types: limerick contests, sentence completion, jingle completion, letter writing, or naming products or trade characters. Moreover, contests may require entrants to purchase products.

As a result of criticism directed against the aforementioned games of chance, in 1970 the FTC promulgated a rule prohibiting the misrepresentation of participants' chances of winning. The requirements of the trade regulation rule on Games of Chance in the Food Retailing and Gasoline Industries (16 CFR 419, as amended in 1981) should be heeded by all organizations wishing to engage in such activities. The rule prohibits misrepresenting participants' chances of winning prizes. It requires clear and conspicuous disclosure of the number of prizes in each category and the odds of winning each prize. This must be revised each week a game extends beyond thirty days so as to reflect the existing odds of winning unredeemed prizes. The geographic area covered by the game, the total number of retail outlets participating, and the scheduled termination date of the game must be disclosed.

Game pieces must be mixed randomly, winning game prizes are not to be predetermined, and each retail outlet that uses the game should be posted. No new game may be promoted without a break in time equal to the length of the previous game, or thirty days, whichever is less. The game cannot be terminated prior to the scheduled termination date, and additional winning game pieces cannot be added during the course of the game.

In addition to facing legal restrictions, games of chance can cause unanticipated problems that may result in consumer dissatisfaction and/or that may increase the cost of the promotion. In 1990, Coca-Cola suffered a mishap with its MagiCan promotion, wherein cash or prize vouchers were placed in cans. Sometimes the cans would jam, some people resented the fact that they were unable to quench their thirst, and it is possible that some people sipped the chlorinated water that replaced the soda. Kraft and Anheuser-Busch printed too many winning entries for their contests and had to provide more prizes than they had anticipated.

Lotteries

Although games of chance are generally acceptable, lotteries are prohibited by criminal statutes in many states. This prohibition has little to do with protection of trade relations; rather it is designed to discourage gambling. Generally, a lottery is composed of three elements: consideration, chance, and prize. Consideration usually consists of more than payment of money; it may involve, say, being present at a certain location to win a prize or being required to make a purchase. Chance indicates that winning the prize is not based on skill or judgment. While the statutory rules vary from state to state, an indication that a purchase is required might lead a court to find a consideration.

Trading Stamps

The first documented use of trading stamps in the United States was in the 1890s when Schuster's Department Store of Milwaukee instituted a plan called the Blue Trading Stamp System. Later, the Sperry and Hutchinson Company (S & H) started the first independent-issuer stamp plan, in 1896. Over the years, the trading stamp industry has flourished and foundered and flourished again. A saturation level was reached in 1962, and since then, the share of market held by stamp-giving stores has decreased.

There are few restrictions on the use of trading stamps. Courts in states that prohibit sales-below-cost have held that trading stamps are not to be considered in calculating the cost of an item.

SUMMARY

Legal issues in the area of personal selling are governed by state law on unfair competition. The FTC's jurisdiction over unfair or deceptive acts and practices also provides it with authority over unlawful selling activities. Unfair selling practices include commercial bribery, the use of push money, bait-and-switch activities, pyramid schemes, coercive selling efforts, wrongfully forced deals, and high-pressure practices in door-to-door sales.

Misrepresentations about their own offerings by salespersons to customers can generate problems for their firm. The types of selling practices that may lead to liability problems include product warranties that may inadvertently be created by salespersons through careless statements, improper use of promotional materials, showing samples, or silence in the knowledge of potential problems. A salesperson's misrepresentations about a competitor's offerings may be considered trade libel or injurious falsehood; the penalties for such practices include injunctions, redress and fines, and the possibility of jail terms. To avoid these problems, sales management programs should be designed to direct salespeople to comply with legal guidelines.

Improper sales tactics in foreign markets are subject to federal control through the Foreign Corrupt Practices Act, which prohibits bribery of foreign officials.

Sales promotion refers to marketing activities that stimulate consumer purchasing and dealer effectiveness. Trade stimulants that take the form of trade deals and cooperative advertising allowances are subject to the price discrimination provisions of the Robinson-Patman Act.

Consumer stimulants include free samples, premiums, coupons, rebates, contests, sweepstakes, and trading stamps. No federal regulations specifically outlaw these devices. However, a number of states have adopted various antipremium statutes, which basically outlaw the use of free goods, premiums, and trading stamps as promotional devices. Moreover, the FTC prohibits the use of these devices in an unfair or deceptive manner.

CASE
FTC v. Lloyd Sharp et al. *CCH #69,579 (DC NEV, September 10, 1991).*

FACTS

The FTC sought summary judgment against a number of defendants involved in the sale of ore purchase contracts on three mines. Under the contracts, the sellers purported to convey ore from their mines, to process the ore, and to recover the ore's gold and silver for delivery to purchasers of the contract. The sellers promoted ore purchase contracts through a telemarketing approach that combined oral representations and printed material, and they also solicited investors through print and cable TV.

According to the FTC, the sellers violated Section 5(a) of the FTC Act, which prohibits "[m]isrepresentations of material facts made to induce the purchase of goods or services." The sellers misrepresented the amount and value of the ore in the mines, the timetable for delivery, the portion of the purchasers' payments to be held in interest-bearing trust accounts, and the risk involved. For example, each ton of ore from one project was said to contain $400 worth of gold and silver. However, the FTC's expert concluded that each ton of this ore contained only $2 worth of gold and even less of silver.

ISSUES

1. Have the sellers engaged in unfair or deceptive practices?
2. Can the sellers be held individually liable for these acts?

HOLDING

1. Yes. The sellers made misrepresentations in selling their ore purchase contracts.

2. Yes. Individual salespersons can be held jointly and severally liable for redressing consumer injuries caused by FTC Act violations. In a relatively rare opinion, a district court in Nevada ruled that such liability against salespersons exists where there is evidence that they had been recklessly indifferent to the truth of their representations to purchasers, regardless of their actual knowledge of deception.

REASONING

The court issued an injunction restraining the sellers from future false representations in investment offerings. In the promotion and sale of ore purchase contracts, the following disclosures are required: (1) that ore purchase contracts are high-risk investments; (2) that the past earnings and past performance of this type of investment do not necessarily reflect future earnings; and (3) that mining activities are regulated by a number of state and federal agencies and there may be a delay of several years in obtaining the permits such activities require before mining may begin.

According to the court, an individual defendant can be held jointly and severally liable for consumer injuries caused by violations of the FTCA if (1) the individual defendant made the misrepresentation or had the authority to control the person who made the misrepresentation; (2) the misrepresentation was the kind usually relied on by reasonably prudent consumers and was widely disseminated, and consumers actually purchased the product; (3) the individual defendant possessed the required scienter ("had or should have had knowledge or awareness of the misrepresentations").

Some of the defendants did not deny that the first two elements necessary to hold them personally liable were satisfied, but they claimed they cannot be held liable because they did not know their representations were false. However, the court declared that the knowledge requirement may be fulfilled by showing that the individual had "actual knowledge of material misrepresentations, reckless indifference to the truth or falsity of such misrepresentations, or an awareness of a high probability of fraud along with an intentional avoidance of the truth." In addition, the degree of participation in business affairs may provide proof of knowledge.

The court also decreed that a number of individuals and companies involved in these activities are liable for equitable monetary relief for the injury resulting from their violations of the FTCA. The amount of each defendant's liability will be set by the court on further application by the FTC.

DISCUSSION QUESTIONS

Discuss the kinds of claims made to induce the purchase of goods and services, which claims may be considered unfair or deceptive.

Under what circumstances may the salesperson who made such claims be considered individually liable for redressing consumer injuries caused by such actions?

CASE
In re Pioneer Enterprises, Inc., dba Vita Tek Marketing, Pro Life Marketing, 21st Century II and Sunshine Promotions et al., CCH #23,292, File No. X92 0055 (December 2, 1992).

FACTS

Beginning in 1988, several firms that were engaged in promotional activities made unsolicited calls and mailed notifications to consumers, stating that the consumers had won valuable awards such as a luxury car, cash, jewelry, or a Hawaiian vacation. When consumers responded to the notifications, the firms allegedly made numerous false and misleading statements to induce the consumers to purchase vitamins, water purifiers, or other merchandise at prices ranging from hundreds to thousands of dollars.

ISSUE

Did these organizations run deceptive prize promotions?

HOLDING

Yes.

REASONING

The prices consumers paid for the merchandise far exceeded the value of the prizes typically awarded. The firms also provided other telemarketers and direct marketers with fulfillment services to help them sell their products, including mailing solicitations, providing telephone sales scripts, and offering or providing incentive prizes or awards.

The FTC has issued a series of stringent requirements against six companies and two individuals who allegedly ran a deceptive prize-promotion telemarketing scheme that used false and misleading statements to induce consumers to buy a variety of merchandise at exorbitant prices. In addition to a requirement to pay $1.5 million in consumer redress, the FTC consent judgment places a number of restrictions (as follows) on the future activities of the firms and provides a means whereby the FTC can determine compliance with the settlement.

- There is a general prohibition on the firms' making of any false or misleading claims on any product, service, or product or service features.

- Various disclosure requirements concerning any promotion and the prizes being offered would be required, and the merchandise would have to be shipped within thirty days of receipt of a properly completed order.

- Employees would have to be monitored to ensure they are not violating the provisions, and any person who the defendants know or should know has violated the settlement provisions three times within an eighteen-month period would have to be fired.

- The firms would be required to do research on potential telemarketing or direct mail clients to determine whether such clients' business practices would violate the order; secure a signed, written contract requiring the clients to follow the prohibitions; monitor their clients' business practices; and terminate their relationship with any clients who fail to terminate employees who violate the order three times within an eighteen-month period.

- Finally, the proposed consent judgment would require the defendants to seed any customer lists they sell to other marketers with names provided by the FTC. Thus the FTC-named persons would receive copies of solicitations sent out by the firms' future clients, and through these named sources, the FTC could determine compliance with the settlement.

DISCUSSION QUESTIONS

What kinds of sales promotion activities may be considered unfair or deceptive?

What kinds of penalties do firms that engage in such activities face?

ENDNOTES

1. TRR, CCH #7903.
2. *Kinney-Rome Co.* v. *FTC.*, 275 Fed. 665 (1921).

3. TRR, CCH #39,011.

4. In re Household Sewing Machine Co., Inc., et al., CCH #18,882 (August 1969); "Legal Developments in Marketing," *Journal of Marketing* 34 (April 1970), 84.

5. *Pyramid Schemes: Not What They Seem* (Washington, D.C.: Direct Selling Education Foundation, 1991).

6. In re Glenn W. Turner Enterprises, Inc., CCH #61,942 (D.C. Fla., April 1978); "Legal Developments in Marketing," *Journal of Marketing* 42 (October 1978), 91.

7. In re Amway Corp., Inc., et al., 93 FTC 618 (1979).

8. In re Arthur Murray Studio of Washington, Inc., et al., CCH #18,733 (April 1969).

9. *Holland Furnace Co.* v. *FTC* (CA-7) (1961).

10. 16 CFR 429, 1974, amended 1988.

11. *Encyclopedia Britannica, Inc., and Britannica Home Library Services, Inc.,* v. *FTC.*, CCH #62,793 (CA-7, August 1979); "Legal Developments in Marketing," *Journal of Marketing* 44 (Spring 1980), 100.

12. In re Encyclopedia et al., CCH #21,773 (November 1980); "Legal Developments in Marketing," *Journal of Marketing* 45 (Summer 1981), 188.

13. (CCH #10,823).

14. Steven M. Sack, "Watch the Words," *Sales & Marketing Management* (July 1, 1985), 56, 58.

15. *Better Living, Inc., et al.*, 54 F.T.C. 648 (1957).

16. Karl A. Boedecker, Fred W. Morgan, and Jeffrey J. Stoltman, "Legal Dimensions of Salespersons' Statements: A Review and Managerial Suggestions," *Journal of Marketing* 55 (January 1991), 770–80.

17. Ibid., 71–75.

18. *Wat Henry Pontiac Co.* v. *Bradley* (1949), 202 Ok. 82, 210 P. 2d 348.

19. Greg Steinmetz, "Met Life Will Pay $20 Million to States to Settle Charges Tied to Sales Practices," *The New York Times*, March 8, 1994, A5.

20. Restatement 1979, Torts, p. 388.

21. Sack, p. 56.

22. In re Kimberly International Gem Corp. et al., CCH #22,282 (August 1985); "Legal Developments in Marketing," *Journal of Marketing* 50 (July 1986), 116.

23. In re Horizon Corp., CCH #21,826 (May 1981); "Legal Developments in Marketing," *Journal of Marketing* 46 (Winter 1982), 114.

24. In re Theodore Weiswasser, CCH #22,253 (May 1985); "Legal Developments in Marketing," *Journal of Marketing* 50 (July 1986), 116.

25. In re Paradise Palms Vacation Clubs et al., CCH #22,402 (July 1986); "Legal Developments in Marketing," *Journal of Marketing* 51 (July 1987), 121.

26. Boedecker, Morgan, and Stoltman, p. 76.

27. 15 U.S. C.A. 478.

28. CCH #7903.08.

29. Jack G. Kaitati and Wayne A. Label, "American Bribery Legislation: An Obstacle to International Marketing," *Journal of Marketing* 44 (Fall 1980) 38–43.

30. Glenn A. Pitman, James P. Sanford, and Deborah A. Schlicker, "The Foreign Corrupt Practices Act Revisited: Laws to Improve Global Marketing Practice," in *Developments in Marketing Science*, vol. XV, ed. Victoria Corttenden (San Diego Conference, 1992).

31. *W. S. Kirkpatrick & Co., Inc., et al.* v. *Environmental Tectonics Corp., Int'l.*, CCH #68,894 (S. Ct., January 1990); "Legal Developments in Marketing," *Journal of Marketing* 54 (October 1990), 108.

32. Consumer Products Coupons, CCH #50,265 (January 1970); "Legal Developments in Marketing," *Journal of Marketing* 34 (July 1970), 79.

PART IV

Legal Issues in Pricing Decisions

Legal Issues in Pricing Decisions

This chapter discusses the legal issues involved in pricing decisions; particularly those relating to price fixing. Chapter 11 examines the significance of regulatory control of price discrimination.

CHAPTER TEN
Price-Fixing

For many firms, pricing is an informal process; decisions in this area may be based on executive judgment, historical data, a review of competitors' prices, and so on. The well-organized firm develops a more formalized pricing strategy, encompassing a series of steps that consist of the setting of objectives, development of broad-based price policies, selection of techniques for price determination, and determination of methods for implementing and adjusting actual prices.

Pricing practices, however—perhaps more than any other business activity—raise numerous regulatory problems. Practices that are regulated are divided basically into two groups: individual pricing practices of a business concern and concerted pricing practices by more than one business concern; activities in the latter area are more likely to be considered per se illegal.

To minimize the potential for pricing problems, a firm can develop a comprehensive compliance program in order to make its employees sensitive to pricing laws. A compliance committee can be established consisting both of counsel and marketing executives. The committee can discuss emerging legal developments in pricing. Such a program can help to inform company personnel about ways to avoid pricing problems, resolve questions, and monitor compliance, so that the company is not placed in jeopardy. An effective antitrust compliance program not only may prevent the imposition of serious penalties to the firm but may also be useful in the defense of such prosecutions by the government.

PRICING OBJECTIVES AND POLICIES

Pricing objectives may be sales based so as to maximize sales volume and/or increase market share. They may be designed to maximize profit in the long run, to secure a specified return on investment, or to recoup investment costs rapidly. Status quo pricing objectives may be used by a firm interested in stability or seeking favorable business conditions.[1] Such pricing objectives are mostly lawful. In some cases, however, their implementation may raise legal questions.

Some firms set broad pricing policies designed to coordinate their pricing decisions with their objectives. Such pricing policies, which may relate to either new products or products with competitive offerings in the marketplace, may also involve legal issues.

New Product Pricing Policies

Two frequently instituted policies for pricing new products are termed skimming pricing and penetration pricing. Skimming pricing tends to be a useful policy when competition is likely to be limited, at least initially. It is designed to meet the objective of recouping investment costs rapidly and maximizing revenue in the short run. Penetration pricing utilizes low prices in an effort to capture a significant market share and make it difficult for competitors to enter the market. Since these are new products, absent government pricing controls, there is little likelihood that their prices will be subject to legal constraints.

Competition-based Pricing Policies

When competitors are used as pricing guideposts, a firm may institute a policy of pricing above the market price established by competitors, below that market price, or at the market price.

Pricing above the Market

Some firms set the price for their merchandise at a high level relative to the market. Such a policy may be designed to give an illusion of prestige to the product; for example, Piaget advertises itself as the World's Most Expensive Watch. The high-price level may also indicate a desire to offer additional services such as warranties and repairs.

Until President Nixon's imposition of wage and price controls in the summer of 1971, there had been relatively few efforts to limit the amount marketing managers could charge for their merchandise. These temporary price controls were designed primarily to curtail inflation and are no longer in effect. However, some states may set limits on prices considered as too high. Recently, New York State established a trigger price for milk under an antigouging state law. Retailers who charge more than the trigger price will be told to either lower their prices or justify the higher prices by showing their costs have gone up.[2] Currently, however, there are few legal limitations on marketers' ability to set a price for their merchandise that is relatively higher than the general market price.

Pricing below the Market

For some firms, the best strategy is to price below the market. This may reflect an attempt to secure a low-cost image or to acquire increased market share. Only when prices are cut for the sole purpose of injuring or destroying another business is there an action at common law. When the purpose is to eliminate competition, as noted in Chapter 1, such conduct may violate the Sherman Act. In addition, Section 3 of the Robinson-Patman Act makes it a criminal offense to discriminate geographically or to sell at unreasonably low prices when the purpose of either action is to destroy competition or eliminate a competitor. The maximum penalty is either $5,000, one year in prison, or both.

State Unfair Trade Laws. Marketers should be aware that sales below cost are also prohibited by state statutes. These unfair trade practice laws vary widely from state to state, but most frequently they forbid sales below cost when the intent is to destroy competition or to injure a competitor. In general, state unfair trade laws forbid dealers from making a sale for less than their invoice or replacement cost, whichever is lower, plus a markup designed to cover their operating costs. Exemptions to these unfair trade laws are made for seasonal and perishable commodities, for damaged or deteriorated goods, and for liquidation sales. Sales to meet the lawful price of a competitor are also exempted. Enforcement of sales-below-cost statutes is accomplished by means of criminal penalties and civil actions for damages or injunctions. Currently, twenty states have such unfair trade laws, but the strictness of their enforcement varies from state to state.

Pricing at the Market

Firms may establish a policy of setting prices at the market level. This may be seen as a simple and fair method of setting prices. Such activities may occur through price leadership—a generally accepted practice.

Price Leadership. In concentrated industries, firms may follow the pricing decisions of an industry leader by moving prices up when the leader raises them and by lowering them when the leader lowers them. In such cases, firms may abandon independent pricing decisions either because they fear the outset of warfare if they undercut prices, because they hope to obtain larger profits under this price umbrella, or merely because they find it convenient to follow the leader. Unless there is clear evidence of coercion or collusion, price leadership has not been considered an illegal practice.

PRICE-FIXING

Price-fixing may be horizontal—occurring among competitors at the same level in the channel of distribution (e.g., among manufacturers or among retailers)—or vertical—in which case prices are set among marketers at different levels in the channel (e.g., between manufacturers and their retailers). Current legal interpretations condemn horizontal price restraints between competitors because the preservation of interbrand competition is considered a high priority. In contrast, while vertical price fixing is still considered per se illegal, the Supreme Court has made it progressively more difficult to prove.

Horizontal Price-Fixing

When competing firms act together to set prices, they are in per se violation of Section 1 of the Sherman Antitrust Act of 1890, which declares: "Every contract, combination in the form of trust or otherwise, or conspiracy, in restraint of trade or commerce among the several States, or with foreign nations, is hereby declared to be illegal."

It has been acknowledged in earlier cases and is now well established that explicit agreements by competing or independent firms to fix prices are a primary concern of this section. Such actions are also considered to violate Section 5 of The Federal Trade Commission Act, which reads "unfair methods of competition in commerce are hereby declared to be illegal." In addition, many states have statutes that outlaw price-fixing.

As currently interpreted, practically all price fixing on a horizontal level is in restraint of trade and per se illegal. There are no redeeming characteristics; no evidence as to economic impact is necessary; and nor can there be any defense based on reasonableness. Generally, the method by which prices are fixed is immaterial, and the fixing of either selling prices or buying prices is condemned under the law.

Kinds of Horizontal Price-Fixing Practices

Horizontal price-fixing practices that have been condemned can take various forms.

Agreements. A small number of sellers adopt an agreement to charge a given price, including discounts and credit terms, in the marketplace in which they are in competition.

Bid Rigging. Collusive bidding may occur when contracts are secured on a sealed-bid basis. Firms wishing to avoid price competition may all submit the same bid, so that the supplier may have to choose on some basis other than price. Such bid rigging has been held unlawful in the construction, livestock, and motion picture industries, as well as in procurement of supplies by the government.

In 1991, the U.S. Justice Department investigation of bid rigging on school milk contracts included at least sixteen states and some well-known dairies. At this writing, sixteen people have been sentenced to jail, and fines and damages sought by the Justice Department total $21 million.

Other bidding practices that have been prohibited in judgments in Sherman Act actions include agreements to allocate bids for the purchase of products; the use or adoption of bid forms; coercing or awarding any authority not to seek lower prices after bids are received; submitting bids through a common agent; and submitting sham, fictitious, fraudulent, dummy, or unreasonable bids.

Parallel Pricing. Price-fixing may also occur when there is no specific agreement, as in the case of parallel pricing. Such action may be found in industries that contain few sellers in which the products are highly standardized. Sellers may be charging the same price to "meet the competition." The existence of conscious parallelism alone is not enough to indicate price-fixing. However, when it is accompanied by an exchange of pricing information on a reciprocal basis, it may be considered evidence of a conspiracy.

Price Signaling. Even when executives do not have specific agreements there may be evidence of price signaling. Such signals can occur when competitors talk with one another about price changes in advance of implementation. While this may not be illegal, if there is proof of an ongoing understanding among the competitors regarding how they will react to such announcements, illegality may attach.[3] Signals may also occur in the form of publicly talking at conference or trade association meetings about the need for price increases.

New information technologies can provide signals of pricing strategies. Such technologies can make it easier for competitors to monitor and police one another, thus facilitating collusive behavior.[4] Several U.S. airlines were charged with using their computer network reservation system to fix prices in the late 1980s. None of the airlines admitted wrongdoing, but they set aside $408 million in travel coupons for fliers. Anyone who bought a domestic ticket between January 1, 1988 and June 30, 1992, on American, Continental, Delta, Midway, Northwest, Pan Am, TWA, United, or USAir can file a claim.

Price Reporting. A similar, sensitive area is that of price reporting. Trade associations often perform legitimate services for their industry. When industry members openly gather and disseminate information regarding costs and prices in *past* transactions without attempting to reach any agreement to fix prices, they are not engaged in activity that violates the law. However, when their association serves as a clearinghouse for the compilation and dissemination of future prices, members face the danger of a finding of conspiracy to fix prices.

Current Control of Horizontal Price-Fixing

Despite the fact that businesspeople engaged in price-fixing are subject to heavy fines and criminal penalties, over the past three decades, price-fixing cases have accounted for more than half the antitrust suits filed each year by the Antitrust Division of the Department of Justice. In recent years, the Department of Justice has been treating horizontal agreements as serious felony crimes.[5] It filed 160 criminal antitrust cases in 1989 and 1990 and collected almost $70 million in criminal fines and related civil damages. Many nationally known companies and the soft drink, dairy products, waste hauling, and industrial manufacturing industries were charged with price-fixing or bid rigging.

Price-fixing is the single most common cause of prison terms under the antitrust laws. In 1990, as part of a Crime Control Act, Congress increased the maximum statutory fine for antitrust crimes. For corporations the fine was increased from $1 million to $10 million per Sherman Act count and for individuals from $250,000 to $350,000.[6] In addition, the promulgation and adoption of the U.S. Sentencing Commission's Sentencing Guidelines have encouraged stricter penalties and the realistic threat of some prison term.

Marketers' Response to Price-Fixing Issues

The unquestionably clear message to marketers is that they should not attempt to fix prices. Nor is it permissable in most instances for independent firms either to enter into agreements whose effect on price is indirect. For example, agreements to establish standard charges for check cashing or credit servicing, to change prices at the same time, or not to advertise are per se illegal. Moreover, it is important for businesspeople to avoid discussing prices with competitors in any way.

Any price-reporting arrangement should be carefully monitored. Only the prices charged in past transactions should be reported. Trade associations should not provide information on price forecasts and should not identify individual sellers. It has been said that if the subject of prices should arise at a trade association meeting, an astute member will overturn a water glass and quietly leave the room. Sellers should not have any agreement as to prices to be charged in the future, as to how prices will be quoted in the future, or about any other terms of sale.

The development of new information technologies may create both legal and societal problems. Bloom et al. have provided a checklist of questions that can help managers assess the likelihood of being faced with legal challenges.[7] Prudent marketers should also keep informed about the ways legal precedents and statutes are changing.

Vertical Price-Fixing

In establishing pricing policies, manufacturers must consider not only the price at which they sell their goods to a particular buyer but also the price at which their products are sold as they proceed through the channel of distribution to the final consumer. When manufacturers sell directly to consumers or through their own outlets, setting and maintaining a price is no problem. Any attempt by manufacturers to set the price at which independent middlemen sell their merchandise may be regarded as vertical price-fixing—frequently designated as resale price maintenance.

Historical Background

The Sherman Act does not expressly prohibit resale price maintenance. However, as early as 1911, the Supreme Court found that an agreement between a manufacturer and its distributors to fix retail prices constituted illegal restraint of trade.[8] The court did slightly weaken this rule when it held, in a historic ruling, that a manufacturer's practice of dealing only with sellers who would maintain its indicated prices was not illegal.[9] In what has been termed the Colgate Doctrine, the court declared: "In absence of any purpose to create or maintain a monopoly, the [Sherman Act] does not restrict the long-recognized right of a trader or manufacturer engaged in an entirely private business, freely to exercise his own independent discretion as to the parties with whom he will deal. And, of course, he may announce in advance the circumstances under which he will refuse to sell." In adopting the Colgate doctrine, the court held that a manufacturer could impose on its distributors any price conditions it wanted as long as its conduct was unilateral. Thus a vertical price restraint was lawful if it was imposed from the top down.[10]

Before the 1930s, resale price maintenance had been repeatedly condemned by the courts because it was considered both a violation of the Sherman Act and an unfair method of competition under the FTC Act. The impact of the Great Depression, particularly during the years from 1930 to 1933, and the growth of chain and cut-rate stores offering limited services and lower retail prices, however, crystallized the efforts of retailers and wholesalers for legalization of resale price maintenance. Proponents of the practice designated it fair trade; it has also been called, less euphemistically, vertical price control.

The first fair trade act was passed by the California legislature in 1931 and amended in 1933. The 1933 amendment added a highly significant provision known as the nonsigner clause, stating that a single agreement between a manufacturer and a distributor to fix the resale price of a trademarked product is applicable to all other distributors in the state, even though they do not sign the price maintenance contract. At the request of local trade groups who saw this method as bringing about horizontal price-fixing at the retail level, an additional forty-four states soon adopted these fair trade laws.

As state statutes, fair trade laws apply only to intrastate commerce. Moreover, it appeared that they might contradict federal laws prohibiting price-fixing. In response to the demands of local trade associations to legalize price maintenance contracts in interstate commerce, Congress enacted the Miller-Tydings Act in 1937. This is an enabling act exempting resale price maintenance contracts from the Sherman and FTC acts in states where such contracts were lawful. As a result, existing state statutes were reinforced, and forty-five states authorized resale price maintenance. Many retailers resented the dictation of resale price, and the Supreme Court subsequently interpreted the Miller-Tydings Act to apply only to retailers who voluntarily agreed to keep a manufacturer's prices. Although this decision seemed to dictate the defeat of resale price maintenance, in fact price wars soon broke out in many cities and appeared to make the need for a federal statute more pressing.

New demands on Congress to rescue resale price maintenance resulted in passage of the McGuire Act of 1952, which stated that exemption from federal antitrust laws extended to nonsigners in states having such clauses in their contracts. In other words, the nonsigner clause was added to the federal statutes.

Criticisms of fair trade laws continued, and in 1975 their demise was accelerated by passage of the Consumer Goods Pricing Act. This statute repealed the federal legislation that permitted state fair trade laws to apply to interstate commerce. With the repeal of the Miller-Tydings and McGuire acts, the methods used by manufacturers to maintain resale prices became questionable. This does not indicate that all attempts to maintain resale prices were not necessarily illegal. However, limitations were applied to such practices in court decisions. For example, in 1960, the court ruled that although a marketer's policy of simple refusal to deal with wholesalers not observing a sales price schedule was not illegal, the marketer may not use the threat of refusal to deal as a lever to induce wholesalers not to do business with retailers who would not abide by stipulated prices.[11]

Current Control of Vertical Price-Fixing

In recent years, the Supreme Court changed the interpretation of the per se vertical price-fixing rule in several significant cases. The Supreme Court adopted an antitrust policy founded on a theory originally formulated by the Chicago School of Economics, which to a great extent violated the effectiveness of the per se prohibition against vertical price-fixing.[12]

Under traditional antitrust interpretation, courts often asked the question, Is a competitor harmed? The Chicago School influenced courts to ask instead, Is competition harmed? Is consumer welfare reduced?[13] In the 1980s, two Supreme Court cases reformulated interpretation of unlawful vertical price-fixing.

Monsanto Co. v. *Spray-Rite Service Corp., 1984.*[14] In *Monsanto*, the court increased the evidentiary requirements for a finding of vertical price-fixing. In sum, the court declared that the mere evidence of distributor complaints is not enough to establish a conspiracy to fix prices. Moreover, termination of a price-cutting dealer following complaints by competing dealers without evidence of a conspiracy is not sufficient to declare this practice price-fixing.

Monsanto, a large chemicals producer, had numerous authorized distributors, including Spray-Rite. In 1967, Monsanto announced that it would appoint distributors for one-year terms and that it would renew distributorships according to several new criteria. In 1968, Monsanto declined to renew Spray-Rite's distributorship. Spray-Rite sued, alleging that Monsanto and some of its distributors had conspired to fix the resale prices of Monsanto herbicides. It further alleged that Monsanto had encouraged distributors to boycott Spray-Rite in furtherance of its conspiracy.

In its decision, the Supreme Court declared:

> Permitting an agreement to be inferred merely from the existence of complaints . . . could deter or penalize perfectly legitimate conduct. . . .

Moreover, distributors are an important source of information for manufacturers. . . . To bar a manufacturer from acting solely because the information upon which it acts originated as a price complaint would
create an irrational dislocation of the market.

In fact, to prevail on an action for illegal price-fixing, the complainant
must not only prove a conspiracy to fix prices but also disprove the possible
existence of potential business reasons that might justify the termination of
a distributor by a manufacturer. Thus *Monsanto* dramatically altered the
burden of proof in price-fixing actions.[15]

However, in this case, the court found sufficient evidence, in the record
of other activities by Monsanto, from which a conspiracy could be inferred.
The court upheld the lower court's award of $10.5 million to Spray-Rite.

Business Electronics Corp. v. *Sharp Electronics Corp., 1988.* In *Sharp*, the
Supreme Court became more explicit in its ruling relevant to resale price
fixing and made a far more sweeping break with the past. The court nar-
rowed the scope of the per se illegality of vertical price-fixing under
the Sherman Act to encompass only those agreements that explicitly fix
prices.[16]

Business Electronics and another retailer, named Hartwell, were authorized by Sharp to sell its electronic calculators in the Houston area. When
Hartwell complained about Business Electronics' prices, Sharp terminated
the latter's dealership.

In the resulting litigation, the Supreme Court declared there is a presumption of the rule-of-reason standard in such cases. Business Electronics'
termination was redefined as a not-naked price restraint because Business
Electronics did not disprove that "a quite plausible purpose of the restriction
[was] to enable Hartwell to provide better services under the sales franchise
agreement."[17]

The court affirmed a lower court's decision and held that if manufacturers
find that price-cutting is undermining a competitor's incentive to promote
their product, the manufacturers may illegally terminate the price-cutter. In
order for a manufacturer's termination of a price-cutting dealer to be per se
illegal, the manufacturer and the competitor must expressly agree to set a
price or price level.

In effect, the Supreme Court overruled its 1911 *Dr. Miles* decision, which
stated the rule that agreements between manufacturers and retailers that have
the effect of fixing a brand's prices are illegal per se. The *Sharp* decision nar-
rowed the scope of the per se illegality to encompass only those agreements
that explicitly fix prices.

Marketers' Responses to Resale Price Maintenance Issues

Terminated dealers should take note of a dissenting opinion in the *Business Electronics* case, which indicated the burdens such a dealer will have to overcome to sue a manufacturer successfully.[18]

1. The dealer "must introduce evidence that tends to exclude the possibility that the manufacturer and nonterminated dealers were acting independently."

2. The dealer "must prove that the agreement was based on purpose to terminate it because of its price cutting."

3. The manufacturer may offer "evidence that it entered the agreement for legitimate, nonprice-related reasons."

Thus, as the dissent suggests, under the current circumstances it will be a rare antitrust case that the terminated dealer will win.

Marketers, in general, should be aware that currently, a vertical price restraint is not per se illegal unless it includes some agreement on price. Nevertheless, the possibility exists that these standards of reasonableness in vertical price-fixing cases may revert to per se illegality.

In 1991, the FTC brought its first cases in nearly a decade, charging manufacturers with retail price-fixing. Both of these cases—*Kreepy Krauly*[19] and *Nintendo*[20]—were settled by consent orders. Nintendo represents the first vertical price-fixing case that was settled through the coordinated efforts of the NAAG and the Federal Trade Commission. The FTC and the state attorneys general were involved in negotiated separate settlements with Nintendo. However, the various parties of interest were able to coordinate their settlements so that the injunctive terms of the judgments were identical.

Nintendo, the giant of the home video game industry, was charged with telling stores that they may not charge less than $99.99 for its home video game. Although Nintendo denied allegations of price-fixing, it agreed to a consent order that bars it from (1) fixing the prices at which a dealer advertises or sells any Nintendo products to consumers, (2) coercing dealers, (3) attempting to obtain commitments from dealers to sell at specified prices, (4) reducing the supply of Nintendo products to dealers, (5) imposing differing credit terms on dealers, (6) terminating dealers (for a five-year period) for failure to adhere to minimum suggested prices, or (7) asking dealers to police other dealers' prices.

Although the order does not bar the suggestion of resale prices to dealers, it would require Nintendo to inform dealers, in any promotional materials which Nintendo suggests a resale price, that dealers are free to set their own retail prices for Nintendo products. In addition, the firm must notify all its dealers that they can advertise and sell Nintendo products at any price without adverse action by the company.

In the multistate settlement, involving thirty-nine states and the District of Columbia, the consent order also requires Nintendo to provide Nintendo Entertainment System buyers with discount coupons good for $5 off the price of Nintendo game cartridges. The firm must redeem a minimum of $5 million and a maximum of $25 million in coupons. Nintendo must also pay New York and Maryland a total of $1.75 million to cover the administrative costs of the coupon program and up to $3 million to all the settling states for public uses approved by the court.

More recently, under the terms of a consent decree, Keds, an athletic and casual shoe manufacturer, settled resale price fixing charges brought by all 50 states and the District of Columbia.[21] The manufacturer was charged with establishing a minimum resale pricing policy for six of its most popular products and then monitoring the prices at which retailers advertised and sold their products. Keds was required to pay a total of $7.2 million and to refrain for five years from entering any resale price fixing agreement. Charitable organizations will receive shares of the settlement funds.

Marketers who wish to avoid the possibility of future legal entanglements may adopt earlier court standards whereby it was possible for a manufacturer to maintain a minimum retail price for merchandise, using the following guidelines:[22]

1. Establish a policy of not dealing with discounters (as per the Colgate Doctrine).
2. Use only the manufacturer's own personnel to determine if retailers are discounting merchandise.
3. Do not attempt to persuade the discounting retailers to change their policy.
4. Simply stop dealing with those retailers (there are, however, restrictions on terminating certain types of dealers).

Of particular importance is the issue of persuasion. In some cases, the courts have been willing to infer a resale price maintenance agreement based on such evidence as threats of termination, threats to impose sanctions, threats of penalizing dealers that do not comply, or monitoring a dealer's price in a coercive manner. Thus any action taken by a supplier that could be designed to elicit dealer acquiescence to the supplier's pricing policy may warrant antitrust scrutiny.

Fixing Maximum Prices

Most resale price maintenance cases relate to the fixing of minimum resale prices. However, occasionally, firms may find it desirable to fix the maximum prices at which its products are resold. Atlantic Richfield Oil Company (ARCO) was alleged to have fixed the maximum prices that its own brand-name retail gasoline dealers could charge, so as to match the prices of independents. USA Petroleum, an independent retailer of gasoline, sued ARCO for conspiring with its dealers to fix maximum retail prices at levels that were below market price in order to drive independents out of business. The Supreme Court reversed a lower court ruling of antitrust injury to the independents. According to the court, low prices benefit consumers regardless of how low these prices are set, and so long as they are above predatory levels.[23]

The court declared that although fixing maximum retail prices may be illegal, federal law does not give competitors an automatic right to sue. A company may sue for damages only if it can show that it lost business because a manufacturer set retail prices at predatory levels designed to drive competitors out of business.

Although the court made it more difficult for competitors to successfully sue, this does not prevent individual dealers and consumers from challenging maximum resale prices. Dealers may sue on the grounds that they were unable to offer services to consumers because they could not charge a high enough retail price to cover their cost. Consumers may sue, declaring that all of the retailers charged the maximum price set by the manufacturer, thus eliminating competition.

Reactions to the Changing Rules

Recent decisions in the enforcement of vertical price fixing or resale price maintenance have generated controversy. There are complaints that whereas previously, a vertical price restraint was considered lawful only if it were imposed from the top down, currently such restraints are effectively lawful even if they are imposed from the bottom up—as a result of the pressure from the distributors. The problem with this change in policy is that the Supreme Court has not cited any empirical evidence that will support it; nor has the court advanced any new theory.

In response to criticisms in 1990, a proposal to amend the Sherman Antitrust Act to codify a per se rule of illegality for vertical price-fixing was approved by the Senate Judiciary Committee.[24] Similarly, the Price-Fixing Prevention Act of 1991, codifying the per se rule and describing the evidence sufficient to reach a jury on the issue of termination or refusal to deal by competitors, was passed by a House Judiciary Committee.[25] Currently, however, the legislation is opposed by the Department of Justice. Opponents to it argue that it confuses and obscures the distinction between illegal vertical price-fixing conspiracies and lawful business decisions. However, marketers should be aware that dissent on this issue exists among the lawmakers.

Global Issues

FTC Commissioner Owens has noted that firms should be cautious in setting up price restraints, since antitrust laws can be enforced by a variety of plaintiffs and what may be legal in one country may be illegal in another.[26] Businesspeople must be careful in establishing pricing policies if they are to avoid running afoul of these laws. Whether a policy is illegal or not may critically depend on decisions made early in the formation of the policy and on the ways the policy is continuously implemented. Although the FTC may focus on areas where there is the greatest likelihood of consumer harm in the long run, this may not be the policy in other countries.

European Community (EC) competition law, for example, must be understood in the context of the need to break down the national boundaries between member states of the EC.[27] Pure agreements to fix resale prices are nowadays, for the most part, just as illegal in the EC as they are in the United States, under Article 85(1) of the Treaty in Rome, which prohibits price-fixing. But there is much stricter treatment of vertical agreements under Article 85(1) compared to U.S. antitrust law.

The EC's principal concern in the area of vertical restraints is the continued division of the Common Market along national lines. Unlike current attitude in the United States, EC is deeply concerned about resale price maintenance. This greater concern exists because of the impact of resale price maintenance on the process of community integration as well as the community's differing views of the competitive effect of vertical restraints generally.

SUMMARY

Pricing practices that are regulated may be divided into two groups: individual pricing practices of a business concern and concerted pricing practices by more than one business concern; activities in the latter area are more likely to be considered per se illegal.

For the individual firm, competitive-based pricing below the market level may raise federal complaints, particularly when the purpose is to eliminate competition. Several states statutes prohibit sales below costs. Pricing at the market level may occur through price leadership, a generally accepted practice.

Price-fixing among organizations is very likely to be subject to regulatory control. Horizontal price-fixing (price-fixing occurring among competitors at the same level, e.g., among manufacturers or among retailers) is considered a per se violation of Section 1 of the Sherman Act. Businesspeople engaged in these actions are subject to heavy fines and criminal penalties. Horizontal price-fixing activities include agreements, bid rigging, parallel pricing, price signaling, and price reporting.

Price-fixing at the vertical level (also called resale price maintenance, e.g., between manufacturers and their retailers) is not expressly forbidden in the Sherman Act. However, in 1911, the Supreme Court found that an agreement between a manufacturer and its distributors to fix retail prices constituted an illegal restraint of trade.

Federal legislation passed in 1937 permitted states to pass fair trade laws, which exempted resale price maintenance contracts from the Sherman and FTC acts. The Consumer Goods Pricing Act of 1975 repealed the federal legislation that permitted state fair trade laws to apply to interstate commerce.

In recent years, the Supreme Court adopted an antitrust policy that minimized the effectiveness of a per se prohibition against vertical price-fixing. The court declared that the mere evidence of distributor complaints is not enough to establish a conspiracy to fix prices. In subsequent decision, the court overruled its 1911 decision, which stated that agreements between manufacturers and retailers that have the effect of fixing a brand's prices are illegal per se. Thus, vertical price restraints may be subject to the rule of reason and are not per se illegal unless they include some specific agreement on prices.

Resale price maintenance contracts usually involve minimum prices; however, some firms may find it desirable to fix maximum prices at which their products are sold. According to a recent Supreme Court decision, although fixing maximum retail prices may be illegal, a company may sue for damages only if it can show that it lost business because a manufacturer set retail prices at predatory levels designed to drive competitors out of business.

CASE
Brown University, *Case No. 3798, CCH #50,731, ED Pa. CCH (May 22, 1991);* **Brown University,** *TRR CCH 69,942 (ED Pa., September 1992);* **MIT,** *TRR CCH 70,391 (CA Phil. 1993).*

FACTS

A recent Justice Department investigation suggests that some colleges have used their financial aid programs in violation of antitrust laws by removing price competition from the marketplace for education. The eight Ivy League colleges and universities (Brown University, Columbia University, Cornell University, Dartmouth College, Harvard University, Princeton University, the University of Pennsylvania, Yale University, and the Massachusetts Institute of Technology were accused of violating the Sherman Act in a complaint filed by the Department of Justice in May 1991. In announcing the government's charges, Attorney General Thornburgh observed that "[t]he revered stature of these institutions of higher learning in our society does not insulate them from the requirements of the antitrust laws."

According to the charges, the schools belonged to a group of financial aid administrators known as the Overlap group. The Overlap group schools held a series of meetings each year and allegedly agreed (1) not to offer financial aid based on student merit and (2) to eliminate significant differences between the schools in the amounts that families with similar income and assets would have to pay toward tuition and other school costs.

ISSUE

Did these major educational institutions engage in a conspiracy to fix prices?

HOLDINGS

The eight Ivy League schools agreed to settle the charges through a consent decree agreement. Although MIT chose to proceed to trial, it ultimately acknowledged that it was obligated to act in accordance with the consent decree binding the other colleges facing price-fixing charges when it was dealing with them. Consent decrees are used to facilitate civil proceedings. Under a consent order, no violation is admitted, but the parties agree to abide by the terms of the decree. An advantage to the schools is that because they have not been found guilty of an antitrust violation, the consent decree cannot be used as prima facie evidence against them in a private, treble-damage suit. According to the agreement, the schools would be barred from conspiring on financial aid, from agreeing on or discussing future tuition or faculty salary increases, and from discussing whether to offer merit scholarships.

REASONING

A federal district court in Philadelphia found the agreement between these schools was inherently suspect and declared that elaborate industry analysis was not required to demonstrate anticompetitive character. Students, needy or not, had been deprived of the opportunity to receive competitive tuition reductions and had been denied the ability to compare prices when choosing between member colleges.

According to the court, "the member institutions formed the Ivy Overlap Groups for the very purpose of eliminating economic competition for students. . . . the Agreements themselves . . . directly proclaimed the intent to neutralize the effect of financial aid so that a student may choose among Ivy Group institutions for reasons other than cost. . . . A market which is unresponsive to consumer preferences infringes upon the most fundamental principle of antitrust law."

The court declared, "The issue before the court is narrow, straightforward and unvarnished. It is whether, under the Rule of Reason, the elimination of competition itself can be justified by non-economic designs. The Supreme Court has unambiguously and conclusively held that it may not."

In partial response to this situation, the Higher Education Amendments of 1992 were signed by President Bush and became effective October 1992. Under these amendments to the Higher Education Act of 1965, institutions of higher education may voluntarily agree among themselves to award some financial aid to attending students only on the basis of demonstrated financial need without implicating the antitrust laws. Further, the institutions can discuss and voluntarily adopt defined principles of professional judgment for determining student financial need for aid not awarded pursuant to the federal Higher Education Act.

However, the institutions will not be allowed to discuss or agree on prospective financial aid for specific, common applicants for financial aid. The exemption specifically does not affect any pending antitrust litigation and expires September 30, 1994.

DISCUSSION QUESTIONS

Why is horizontal price-fixing considered per se illegal?

Do you believe there are any mitigating circumstances for price-fixing activities among educational institutions?

CASE
Atlantic Richfield Co. *v.* USA Petroleum Co., *495 US 382 (1990).*

FACTS

Atlantic Richfield Co. (ARCO), an integrated oil company, increased its retail gasoline sales and market share by encouraging its dealers to match the prices of such independents as USA Petroleum Co., which competes directly with ARCO's dealers at the retail level. USA's sales dropped, and it sued ARCO in a district court, charging that the vertical, maximum-price-fixing scheme constituted a conspiracy in restraint of trade in violation of Section 1 of the Sherman Act.

The court granted summary judgment to ARCO, holding that USA could not satisfy the antitrust injury requirement because it was unable to show that ARCO's prices were predatory. USA appealed, and the Court of Appeals reversed, holding that injuries resulting from vertical, non-predatory, maximum-price-fixing agreements could constitute antitrust injury. The Court of Appeals concluded that USA had shown that is losses had resulted from a disruption in the market caused by ARCO's price-fixing.

ARCO appealed to the U.S. Supreme Court.

ISSUE

Does a firm incur an injury within the meaning of the antitrust laws when it loses sales to a competitor charging nonpredatory prices pursuant to a vertical, maximum-price-fixing scheme?

HOLDING

According to the Supreme Court, such a firm does not suffer an antitrust injury and it therefore cannot bring suit under Section 4 of the Clayton Act.

REASONING

A private plaintiff may not recover damages under Section 4 of the Clayton Act merely by showing "injury causally linked to an illegal presence in the market." The court distinguished between antitrust violation and antitrust injury. It noted that in private damage actions under Section 4 of the Clayton Act, antitrust injury must be shown even when per se violations are involved. The per se rule is a presumption of unreasonableness based on business certainty and litigation efficiency; an antitrust injury requirement ensures that the harm claimed by a plaintiff corresponds to the rationale for finding a violation of the antitrust laws. As a competitor, USA has not suffered antitrust injury, since its losses do not flow from the harmful effects on dealers and consumers.

Conduct in violation of the antitrust laws may have three effects, often interwoven: in some respects the conduct may reduce competition, in other respects it may increase competition, and in still other respects effects may be neutral as to competition.

Procompetitive or efficiency-enhancing aspects of practices that nominally violate the antitrust laws may cause serious harm to individuals, but this kind of harm is the essence of competition and should play a role in the definition of antitrust damages.

Although all antitrust violations, under either the per se rule and the rule-of-reason analysis, distort the market, not every loss stemming from a violation counts as antitrust injury. According to the court, although a vertical, maximum-price-fixing agreement is unlawful under Section 1 of the Sherman Act, it does not cause a competitor antitrust injury unless it results in predatory pricing. Antitrust injury does not arise for the purposes of Section 4 of the Clayton Act until a private party is adversely affected by an anticompetitive aspect of the defendant's conduct. In the context of pricing practices, only predatory pricing has the requisite anticompetitive effect.

Low prices benefit consumers regardless of how those prices are set, and so long as they are above the predatory level, they do not threaten competition. Hence, they cannot give rise to antitrust injury.

DISSENT

In a dissenting opinion, Justice Stevens, joined by Justice White, rejected the argument that although a vertical, maximum-price-fixing agreement is unlawful under Section 1 of the Sherman Act, it does not cause a competitor antitrust injury unless it results in predatory pricing. The court accepts that, as alleged, the vertical price-fixing scheme by ARCO is per se illegal under Section 1. Nevertheless, it denies USA's standing to challenge the arrangement, because it is neither a consumer nor a dealer in the vertical arrangement, but only a competitor of ARCO.

According to the dissent, the proposition that states that the "antitrust laws were enacted for the protection of competition, not competitors"— which is often used as a test of whether a violation of law has occurred— cannot be read to deny all remedial actions by competitors.

Differences between vertical and horizontal agreements may support an argument that the former are more reasonable, and therefore more likely to be upheld as lawful, than are the latter. But such differences provide no support for the court's contradictory reasoning that the direct and intended consequences of one form of conspiracy do not constitute antitrust injury, while precisely the same consequences of the other form do.

According to Justice Stevens,

> The court, in its haste to excuse illegal behavior in the name of efficiency, has cast aside a century of understanding that our antitrust laws are designed . . . [to] . . . safeguard more than efficiency and consumer welfare, and that private actions not only compensate the injured, but also deter the wrongdoers. . . . The conspiracy alleged in this complaint poses the kind of threat to individual liberty and the free market that the Sherman Act was en-

acted to prevent. In holding such a conspiracy immune from challenge by its intended victim, the court is unfaithful to its history of respect for this "charter of freedom."

DISCUSSION QUESTIONS

What distinctions do the courts make in reference to horizontal versus vertical price-fixing?

What criteria do the courts use in evaluating vertical price-fixing?

ENDNOTES

1. Joel R. Evans and Barry Berman, *Marketing*, 6th ed. (New York: Macmillan Publishing, 1994), pp. 697–700.
2. T. J. Collins, "Survey Says Milk Prices Too High," *Newsday*, July 20, 1991.
3. Richard M. Steuer, *A Guide to Marketing Law, What Every Seller Should Know* (New York: Law & Business, Harcourt Brace Jovanovich, 1986), p. 92.
4. Paul N. Bloom, George R. Milne, and Robert Adler, "Avoiding Misuse of New Information Technologies: Legal and Societal Considerations," *Journal of Marketing* 58 (January 1994), 98–110.
5. *Department of Justice Report: Antitrust Accomplishments—1989–1990, CCH #50,049, TRR* (January 29, 1991).
6. Comprehensive Crime Control Act of 1990 (S. 3266).
7. Bloom, et al., pp. 105–107.
8. *Dr. Miles Medical Company* v. *John D. Parke & Sons*, 220 U.S. 373 (1911).
9. *U.S.* v. *Colgate & Co.*, 250 U.S. 300 (1919).
10. John B. McArthur and Thomas W. Paterson, "The Effects of *Monsanto, Matsushita* and *Sharp* on the Plaintiff's Incentive to Sue," *Connecticut Law Review* 23 (1991), 333–353.
11. *U.S.* v. *Parke, Davis & Co.*, 326 U.S. 29 (1960).
12. Christopher J. Pettit, "In *Sharp* Contrast to the Past: The Demise of the Per Se Rule against Vertical Price-Fixing," *St. Mary's Law Journal* 22 (1991), 1075–1109.
13. Susan S. Samuelson and Thomas A. Balmer, "Antitrust Revisited—Implications for Competitive Strategy," *Sloan Management Review* (Fall 1988), 79–87.
14. *Monsanto Co.* v. *Spray-Rite Service Corp.*, 465 U.S. 752 (1984).
15. Pettit, p. 1098.
16. Pettit, p. 1099.
17. *Business Electronics Corp.* v. *Sharp Electronics Corp.*, 100 L. Ed 2d 92 (1988).
18. Brad Reid, "Legal Developments in Marketing," *Journal of Marketing* 53 (January 1989), 99.
19. *Kreepy Krauly, USA, Inc.*, No. 901-0089 (final order issued by the FTC December 20, 1991).
20. *Nintendo of America, Inc.*, No. 901-0028 (final order issued by the FTC, November 14, 1991).
21. *Keds Corp.*, TRR CCH #70,549 (SD N.Y., April 1994).
22. *Garret's Inc.* v. *Farrah Manufacturing Co., Inc.*, 5 Trade Reg Rep. #60,833 (Chicago, Commerce Clearing House, 1976).
23. *Atlantic Richfield Co.* v. *USA Petroleum Co.* (U.S. Sup. Ct. 1990) 1990-1 Trade Cases #69,019.
24. Congress Hearings, TRR, No. 147 (February 27, 1991).
25. Congress, Resale Price Fixing, TRR, No. 164 (June 25, 1991).
26. Vertical Price Restraints—FTC Member Views," TRR, CCH #50,078, March ?, 1992.
27. Spencer Weber Waller, "Understanding and Appreciating EC Competition Law," *Antitrust Law Journal* 61 (1992), 55–77.

CHAPTER ELEVEN
Price Discrimination

Once a firm has set its pricing objectives and determines its actual prices, it frequently finds it desirable to offer similar merchandise to different customers at different prices. Such price differences may reflect economic efficiencies; that is, one buyer may purchase in larger quantities than another or may perform more services than another as a reseller. In such cases, price variations are usually designated as price differentials. Price differences, however, may also result from greater bargaining power; that is, some buyers may require a discount in excess of actual savings incurred from quantity, or some buyers may demand excessive promotional allowances not offered to smaller competitors. Such price adjustments may be considered unlawful price discrimination. Not all forms of price discrimination are unlawful, however.

While federal antitrust and trade regulatory laws do not mandate the prices to be charged, they do place prohibitions against sellers charging different prices to different customers (price discrimination). The purpose of these laws is to prevent injury to competitive sellers, competing customers, and competition between persons purchasing from customers of the seller. Furthermore, a firm may be guilty of monopolization if it prices its products below cost and thereby drives its rivals out of business. Section 2 of the original Clayton Act was designed primarily to prevent local price-cutting by monopolistic suppliers seeking to exclude competition from their markets.

In 1936, the Clayton Act was amended by the Robinson-Patman Act, which sought to limit the purchasing power of large buyers—particularly food chain stores. The amendment tried to specify the particular marketing practices involving price differentials that were to be prohibited.

Over the years there has been continuing controversy over the effectiveness of the Robinson-Patman Act in maintaining competition. In the

1970s, an evaluation of the effects of this act was undertaken by the Small Business Committee of the House of Representatives.[1] According to the committee's report, the evidence discredits allegations that enforcement of the Robinson-Patman Act is anticompetitive and promotes rigidity of pricing by prohibiting flexibility of pricing that would rise if sellers were permitted to offer different prices to different customers. The report concluded that the act should not be repealed, amended, or tampered with in any way.

Nevertheless, the government seemed to abandon its enforcement of price discrimination laws. Between 1937 and 1971, the Federal Trade Commission (FTC) brought an average of forty price discrimination cases each year; in the 1980s, there was an average of one or two each year. Furthermore, numerous commentators have declared that the Robinson-Patman Act is antithetical to consumer welfare and that its purpose is not the protection of the competitive process, but the protection of competitors.[2]

Nonetheless, despite the controversy this act has generated, it continues to resist attempts at repeal and is still enforced. This complex and sometimes confusing federal law affects many decisions made by firms in adjusting their prices. It is therefore important for marketers to become familiar with the circumstances under which their pricing decisions may be considered discriminatory.

Enforcement of and litigation over the price discrimination law occurred primarily in private law suits seeking treble damages (or other relief) and in FTC proceedings; on occasion, court action has been initiated by the Department of Justice. In recent years, the Justice Department has been relatively inactive in Robinson-Patman enforcement; the FTC, however, has shown increased interest in this area.

According to the director of the FTC Bureau of Competition, the FTC's approach to enforcement of this act is "best characterized as cautious commitment," with attempts to induce firms to comply with the law voluntarily.[3] The director notes the commission is aware that the Robinson-Patman Act is difficult and full of pitfalls, yet it is also aware of specific circumstances under which price discrimination can be harmful to consumers. The bureau's current activities include responding to questions, monitoring markets, and litigating when appropriate. To facilitate compliance, the FTC is attempting to clarify the law by answering questions and providing information.

Price Discrimination Defined

The Robinson-Patman Act declares: "it shall be unlawful for any person engaged in commerce . . . to discriminate in price between different purchasers of commodities of like grade and quality . . . where the effect of such discrimination may be substantially to lessen competition, or tend to create a monopoly." These terms generally have been interpreted in judicial review.

Commodities of Like Grade and Quality. The act does not apply to sales of services or intangibles such as electricity or advertising, since these are not commodities. Sellers do not violate the act unless they have sold similar commodities to two different purchasers. Products need not be interchangeable to be regarded as of like grade and quality. Moreover, general lines of merchandise—all of the same grade and quality—may be considered; it is not necessary that the products within any one line of merchandise be identical. Cans of different sizes have been held to be of like grade and quality when the cans were all of commercial grade and quality and gave substantially identical performance. In a landmark case discussed later, the Supreme Court indicated that the attachment of a brand name to a product does not add sufficient physical difference.

What Is Discrimination in Price? A successful complaint under this act must prove price discrimination, which has been interpreted by the Supreme Court to mean any price differential for products of the same quality sold to like customers. Generally, to discriminate in price means to sell a product to one customer at a different price from the one at which the product is sold to another customer.

Substantially Lessening Competition. The act does not make all price discrimination illegal per se. In most cases, for a practice to be considered illegal, it must be shown that the discrimination may tend to cause injury to competition. The interference with competition must be substantial, not trivial or sporadic. However, since the Robinson-Patman Act is supposed to be prophylactic, according to the Supreme Court, it does not require that the discriminations must in fact have harmed competition.

Defenses against Price Discrimination Claims

There are several situations in which charging different purchasers different prices can be justified or otherwise defended under the law. These are set forth in Sections 2(a) and 2(b) of the Robinson-Patman Act.

Cost Justification. If it is less costly to sell to one buyer than another, price differences may be permitted. According to Section 2(a), such differentials may be based on "differences in the cost of manufacture, sale, or delivery," which occur when different methods are used or different quantities of the products are sold or delivered. It is up to the seller to prove cost savings. Accounting and customer classification play a large role in determining the costs of selling. However, cost justification is a difficult defense, since it generally requires data concerning specific cost savings as well as a showing that the price differences matched the cost differentials.

Meeting Competition. Price differences are permitted (according to Section 2[b]) if a seller can show that the lower price was made "in good faith to meet an equally low price of a competitor." This defense relates to cases in which the seller is trying to meet the price a competitor is offering. The good-faith meeting of the lawful and equally low price of a competitor is a defense to the charge of price discrimination, even though it is shown that the price differential has an adverse effect on competition. However, the discriminating seller must meet, not beat, the competitor's price for this to be lawful. In such cases the seller must make an effort to verify the fact that the competing offer was made, and its amount. Such meeting of competition may be accomplished not only through reducing prices directly but by such indirect methods as furnishing free display cabinets or making deliveries on consignment to meet the competition put forward by competitors.

While the meet-but-not-beat rule has been relaxed somewhat in response to the realities of competitive bidding, a defense of meeting the competition may be unavailable if the seller knowingly beats the competition. In the private-sector bidding context, marketers should carefully review any requests from individual customers for special bid discounts, particularly when other customers purchase those products at a higher price and are likely to bid against the favored customer on an independent contract.[4]

The Changing Market Conditions. The law permits price changes in response to changing conditions in the marketability of goods. This includes conditions such as deterioration of perishable goods, obsolescence of seasonal goods, distress sales, and discontinuing the sale of certain goods. Local cutting of prices by a firm confronted with diminishing sales in an area or so as to meet a boycott has been held illegal.

Robinson-Patman defenses are not equally available for all cases under the act. Suits in this area are frequently designated as primary-line cases or secondary-line cases. These terms refer to the level of distribution at which the discrimination takes place. In a primary-line case, a discriminating seller may injure another seller. Price discrimination in a secondary-line case occurs among buyers.

INJURY TO PRIMARY-LINE COMPETITION

Injury to primary-line competition occurs when the discriminating seller inflicts injury against another seller. This situation has been characterized as predatory competition. Setting an unreasonably low price so as to inflict injury has been described as predatory pricing. A firm possessing large financial resources may reduce its prices, setting them below its costs at levels that make it impossible for its weaker rivals to survive. The resulting losses are accepted as an investment to be recovered after the rivals fail and the large firm can secure increased profits through monopoly. This practice was common in the heyday of the trusts, when reduction of prices under these circumstances was monopolistic in effect; it may now be held to violate the law. Cases against predatory pricing can be brought under both Section 2 of the Sherman Act and under restrictions on price discrimination in the Robinson-Patman Act.

Predatory Pricing

Predatory pricing can involve below-cost pricing, price discrimination, and price-warring.[5] Lowering prices in one particular trade area but not in others can provide an illustration of predatory pricing. Such geographic price discrimination can violate Section 2(a) of the Clayton Act. This is so even when all competing customers in the area are granted the reduction. However, to be a violation, the price-cutting must have the proscribed adverse effect on competition. Geographic price discrimination essentially relates to competition at the primary line—the seller's level; secondary-line injury is not often a consideration.

A historic case involving geographic price discrimination that was considered predatory pricing concerned companies selling frozen pies.[6]

Utah Pie Company, a small, local bakery in Salt Lake City, had been making and selling pies for over thirty years. The company entered the frozen pie market in the late 1950s in competition with several national firms. Utah Pie's location gave it a freight advantage, and it began selling frozen pies at prices substantially below the prices of the national companies' comparable pies. In one year, Utah Pie captured about two-thirds of the market, and its three competitors responded by sharply reducing their prices. Utah Pie's share of the market then declined to around 45%, but it continued to make a profit.

In the early 1960s, Utah Pie brought suit against its three competitors, charging them with predatory intent in price-cutting. The defendants had not met the lower prices of Utah Pie; they had simply cut their prices sharply below those prevailing in other national markets where they sold. The thrust of the case centered on the defendants' selling frozen pies in the Salt Lake City area at lower prices than in markets elsewhere. Although Utah Pie continued to earn a profit and, in fact, was a leader at times in moving prices down, the Supreme Court found that the three defendants were engaged in predatory pricing.

The Supreme Court sided with a jury award of treble damages to Utah Pie, under Section 2(a) of the Robinson Patman Act. Awards for charges of conspiracy in violation of Sections 1 and 2 of the Sherman Act were denied.

The Utah Pie decision seemed to indicate that a national firm will be inhibited from seeking to enter a market through price-cutting for fear that a competitor who is injured can recover treble damages. Some observers viewed this decision as having had an adverse impact on competition because it protected a competitor at the expense of competition. Moreover, such protection for a small firm does not ensure survival. Utah Pie went out of business in 1972 after experiencing management and product quality problems.

Legal Tests for Predatory Pricing

Although predatory pricing has long been condemned as offensive to businesspeople, there is little agreement for distinguishing legitimate from predatory pricing. Judicial assessment of predatory pricing complaints has focused mainly on rules that compare price and cost. Professors Areeda and Turner suggested a cost-based legal standard for deciding predatory price claims.[7] Initially they proposed that pricing below short-run marginal cost should be held as predatory. Since this marginal cost benchmark was difficult to compute, they proposed an alternative measure—average variable cost— which divides a firm's cost (less fixed charges) by the number of units produced and determines whether the prices were below cost.

This short-run cost standard may be summarized as follows:[8]

- Prices above average total cost are considered presumptively lawful and likely to withstand antitrust challenge.

- Prices above average variable cost and below average total cost are considered presumptively lawful and likely to withstand antitrust challenge.

- Prices below average variable cost are considered presumptively unlawful, and the burden is on the defendant to establish that such prices are justified and nonpredatory.

While the Areeda-Turner test is often discussed, the Supreme Court seems ambiguous about the role of cost-based standards in determining whether a price is predatory, and it has yet to issue an opinion in which those standards were utilized.[9]

In 1986, in one of its first predatory pricing cases since Utah Pie, the Supreme Court issued a decision concerning damages alleged to have resulted from the actions of a foreign-owned multinational corporation.[10] The court ruled that U.S. firms cannot recover antitrust damages for any conspiracy alleging pricing above competitive levels in the foreign nation. As to the issue of predatory pricing, however, the court suggested the use of economic plausibility to eliminate claims that lack common sense.[11] The court noted that a plaintiff who charges attempted monopolization by predatory pricing must prove the alleged monopolist did four illegal things:[12]

- The alleged monopolist intended specifically to control prices or destroy competition in some part of interstate or foreign commerce.

- The alleged monopolist directed predatory or anticompetitive conduct toward achieving monopoly.

- The alleged monopolist's conduct indicated a dangerous probability of success.

- The monopolist caused antitrust injury to the plaintiff because of actions that specifically violate the antitrust laws.

Despite the fact that the Supreme Court pronounced in 1986 that predatory pricing is rare, litigation about predatory pricing is still flourishing. The reluctance of many courts to adopt a per se price-cost rule is based on the belief that there may be instances in which prices above such cost measures are harmful to consumers in the long run.[13]

One suggestion for a practical approach to predation involves an inquiry consisting of three questions: one about the alleged predator, one about the nature of the market, and one about the pricing behavior at issue. The three questions are:[14]

1. Is the alleged predator a dominant firm (or does it have some other advantage that would enable it to become one)?

2. Do market structure and entry conditions make recoupment of a predatory investment possible?

3. Has the alleged predator invested in the destruction of its rival?

Despite a recent Supreme Court decision on this issue, a clear solution for judging whether prices are predatory has yet to be established.

Brooke Group, Ltd., formerly called Liggett Group Inc., sued Brown & Williamson Tobacco Corp. for using unfair price-cutting to try to drive it out of the market for so-called generic cigarettes. Brooke had introduced a line of low-price generic cigarettes sold in plain, black-and-white packages in an attempt to salvage its dwindling tobacco business. Brown & Williamson responded by introducing its own black-and-white generic brand and by offering wholesalers steeper, volume-based rebates than those available from Brooke. Brooke sued, alleging that Brown was trying to make generic cigarettes so unprofitable that either the market would disappear altogether or Brooke would suffer such losses it would be forced to limit its discounts.

In 1990, a federal court jury awarded Brooke nearly $50 million, which was automatically tripled to close to $150 million.[15] The verdict, however, was set aside by the trial judge, who noted that there was no economically plausible way for Brown & Williamson to recover from its losses on generic cigarette sales. A Court of Appeals affirmed, declaring that even though the competitor might have been harmed by the reduced prices there was no violation of the antitrust laws because other manufacturers could have responded competitively. Brown's sales below average variable cost would cause losses, and since there was no economically rational basis for the manufacturer to recover those losses and gain an additional profit (because of potential competition), it had not engaged in predatory pricing according to the appeals court. In 1993, the Supreme Court agreed to hear Brooke's appeal for reinstatement of its $150 million award.[16]

The Supreme Court declared that whether a claim alleges predatory pricing under Section 2 of the Sherman Act or primary-line price discrimination under the Robinson-Patman Act, two prerequisites to recovery remain the same: (1) A firm seeking to establish competitive injury resulting from a rival's low price must prove that the prices complained of are below an appropriate measure of its rival's costs. (2) A demonstration that the competitor had a reasonable prospect or, under Section 2 of the Sherman Act, a dangerous probability of recouping its investment in below-cost prices. Recoupment is the ultimate object of an unlawful predatory pricing scheme: it is the means by which a predator profits from predation.

The Supreme Court noted that these prerequisites to recovery are not easy to establish, and in fact predatory schemes are rarely tried and even more rarely successful. Moreover, the "mechanism by which a firm engages in predatory pricing—lowering prices—is the same mechanism by which a firm stimulates competition, because cutting prices in order to increase business often is the very essence of competition."

The cigarette industry as a whole faced declining demand and possessed substantial excess capacity—circumstances that would tend to break down patterns of oligopoly pricing and to produce competition. According to the court, the evidence indicates that "Brown & Williamson had no reasonable prospect of recouping its predatory losses and could not inflict the injury to competition the antitrust laws prohibit." Accordingly, the Supreme Court affirmed the judgment of the Court of Appeals.

Marketers' Response to Predatory Pricing

Marketers should adopt proactive strategies to combat and neutralize predation. Firms should develop environmental scanning methods and marketing strategies to identify and to protect themselves from such competition. Price changes and tactics of rival firms should be monitored in order to preempt predatory pricing strategies. Market channel relationships should also be watched for predatory agreements.

Despite the Supreme Court's decision, which apparently makes it more difficult to prove predatory pricing, the potential for such complaints still exists. In late 1993, a state court in Arkansas ruled that Wal-Mart Stores, the country's largest retailer, had illegally engaged in predatory pricing in one Arkansas county by selling pharmaceutical and beauty aids below cost.[17] According to the court, Wal-Mart's pricing policies, as carried out in its local discount store, had the intent of "injuring competitors and destroying competition" as defined in the Arkansas Unfair Trade Practices Act. Wal-Mart's stated pricing policy was "meet or beat the competition without regard to cost." The court declared that it was irrelevant that the chain sold its pharmaceutical and beauty aids line as a whole above cost.

The court awarded close to $300,000 in damages to the three independent pharmacies that sued, and it enjoined Wal-Mart's local store from selling items below cost. Under state laws, Wal-Mart's cost would include the invoice price plus the cost of doing business. Wal-Mart will appeal, but this decision may encourage the filing of more predatory pricing suits.

INJURY TO SECONDARY-LINE COMPETITION

Unlike primary-line competition, wherein a seller may inflict injury on another seller, secondary-line injury considers the effect of discriminatory prices on competitive buyers, for example, the effect of a price given by sellers to chain stores on their competitors—the small stores, which are unable to obtain the favorable price. For discrimination to exist there must be a competitive relationship between the two buyers. At the secondary level, the Robinson-Patman Act covers not only actual price reductions but also other marketing practices that are considered indirect forms of price discrimination, such as dummy brokerages and special promotional allowances.

Some of the pricing practices and systems that marketers utilize in their sales to competing customers may be defined as discriminatory and considered per se illegal under the Robinson-Patman Act. Other such practices that have the potential to be declared illegal are nevertheless defensible.

Standard Price Reduction Systems

Several standard price reduction systems are used by marketers in selling to competing customers. These are usually in the form of discounts offered for quantity purchases, they are payment for functions performed by the purchasers, or they result from favorable transportation terms.

Quantity Discounts

A traditional pricing practice is to offer quantity discounts. Such discounts can be based on the number of units, size of load, or number of dollars spent. Quantity is considered an element of pricing in the cost justification provisions. Thus, differentials based on quantities are protected if they represent the "due allowance for differences in the cost of manufacture, sale or delivery resulting from the differing . . . quantities in which products are sold or delivered."

The FTC has forbidden larger discounts on orders placed by chains and cooperative buying agencies where it found no savings in the cost of delivery and inadequate justification in the costs of production and sale. Even when quantity discounts can be justified, they can be forbidden when only relatively few customers can take advantage of such savings.[18] The Robinson-Patman Act authorizes the FTC to fix limits beyond which discounts for larger quantities may not be given, as when "available purchasers in greater quantities are so few as to render differentials on account thereof unjustly discriminatory or promotive of monopoly."

Functional Discounts

It is common practice for a seller to charge different prices to different types to distributors performing different functions. The traditional type of trade or functional discount is a simple one, granted to wholesalers but not to retailers. However, difficulties arise because of the dynamic business structure of the U.S. economy when functions become mixed or integrated. When retailers take on the functions traditionally provided by wholesalers, price discrimination problems may arise.

Up until recently, suppliers that sold at different levels had little to fear in a challenge to their functional discounts so long as the wholesale purchasers were bona fide wholesalers, doing little business in competition with the direct-buying retailers.[19] However, in 1990, the Supreme Court ruled that functional discounts not justified by the value of services rendered by wholesalers may be illegal.

The case concerned the different prices charged by an oil company to its wholesalers and retailers. Two wholesalers received a full discount on all their purchases even though most of their product was resold directly to consumers. Since the wholesalers competed in the retail market, this had an adverse effect on competition and constituted discrimination in price.[20] Thus discounts based merely on labels (e.g., wholesaler v. retailer) are not enough; consideration must be given to the different functions performed. Functional discount justification (as expressed in *Hasbrouck*) is a reasonable reimbursement for a wholesaler's service by comparison of the discount with value of the service to the seller and/or cost of the service to customers. This justification need not depend on a precise dollar-for-dollar relationship, but rather on what constitutes reasonable reimbursement of the wholesaler's cost. The fact that rigorous accounting is not required is the major point of distinction from the original cost justification defense under Section 2(a) of the act.

Guidelines for Using Functional Discounts. Sellers considering the use of functional discounts should develop procedures that incorporate the requirements in *Hasbrouck*.[21]

1. If the function is performed for a product eligible for a discount, then all competing wholesalers should have the opportunity to obtain that discount.

2. The allowance level should be at a uniform rate for all wholesalers based on the value of the service to the seller.

3. Although the term *value* is not defined in the *Hasbrouk* decision, a value calculation should be conservatively determined from objective sources. Value may mean what a seller would have paid for similar services from others; it may even require nationwide average cost.

4. When the seller is dealing with a single wholesaler who is not competing with other wholesalers, use of the customer cost standard would seem feasible. However, getting customers' costs is difficult.

5. Where the functional discount is based on the wholesaler's cost, wholesalers should be requested to provide cost data and to certify in advance (in the language of *Hasbrouck*) that the dis-

count constitutes no more than "a reasonable reimbursement for the purchaser's actual marketing functions."

6. Wholesaler's services that are promotional in nature should not be paid for—even if justified by wholesaler's costs—unless such payment is available on a proportional basis to all competing wholesalers. When such promotional payments are not available to all, it is considered per se illegal and does not require proof of substantial adverse competitive effect.

In summary, currently the cost justification defense offers marketers an opportunity to recognize and pass along to customers and consumers any legitimate savings created by customers in the total distribution program. If, however, such discounts cannot be cost justified and the competition or a competitor suffers direct or indirect injury, such discounts may be considered illegal.

Transportation Pricing Terms

Sellers may adopt any one of a variety of geographic pricing practices involving their cost of transportation to different markets. Some are considered lawful, but others may be attacked as discriminatory.

Uniform FOB Mill Price. Under this system, sellers quote prices for their merchandise to buyers from their plant or factory. To cover transportation costs, sellers then add the freight or delivery charges to each buyer's respective destinations. Thus buyers at different locations incur different costs in purchasing the seller's goods. Such sellers do not illegally discriminate, since the price is justified by the differences in shipping costs.

Delivered Pricing Systems. Under delivered pricing systems, sellers attempt to promote price uniformity so that buyers within a certain area pay the same price for the product regardless of the differences in shipping costs from the seller's plant to the customer's location. Such systems have been considered discriminatory, particularly when they involve the use of basing-points. Under a basing-point system, sellers quote prices to buyers not from their plants or factories but from some other geographic point, which has been selected as a basing point. A seller may use either a single basing-point system or a system that includes multiple basing points. Both of these systems have been condemned under law. They are attacked on the grounds that buyers who are located nearer to the seller's plant from where the shipments are made than to the basing point are required to pay phantom, or nonexistent, freight charges. Discrimination occurs, since competitors of those buyers who are situated near the basing point do not have the burden of phantom freight charges.

Basing-point pricing policies may result not only in price discrimination but also in collusion. Such pricing systems were popular in a variety of industries (e.g., steel and cement). Each firm in the industry agreed to use specified transportation rates in computing the delivered price of its customers. Thus the delivered prices quoted by all firms in an industry would be virtually identical.

Indirect Pricing Practices

Sections 2(c), 2(d), and 2(e) of the Robinson-Patman Act were designed to eliminate injury from the secondary line of competition. These sections cover specific marketing practices, other than actual price discounts, that are considered indirect forms of price discrimination: the creation of dummy brokerages, the payment of promotional allowances, and/or the furnishing of services or facilities to some customers and not to others.

Dummy Brokerages

Section 2(c) covers brokerage allowances and forbids the payment of a broker's commission to anyone but an independent broker. This is designed for situations in which sellers, who ordinarily give a fee to an independent broker for putting them in contact with a buyer, are requested by large buyers to sell directly to them. Such buyers may then request a brokerage allowance (essentially a price discount), since they saved the seller the cost of using a broker. This particular provision is interpreted to make such dummy brokerage payments illegal per se. Generally, proof of intent or knowledge is not required. There can be no justification on the basis of cost savings; nor is proof of injury to competition required.

Section 2(c) has also been applied to commercial bribery cases, involving the payment of a commission by a seller to the buyer's agent, who then retains the payment for personal use. In addition, the law has been applied to a variety of unethical or fraudulent transactions, including secret rebates.

The difficulty in finding an acceptable defense for dummy brokers should alert marketers to the hazards of violating this section. Marketers should therefore take note that inserting a broker into a distribution system, or withdrawing one, with concomitant direct selling or abstinence from direct dealing, may generate Section 2(c) problems. This may be true especially when the result is the differing treatment of buyers.

Promotional Allowances and Services

Sections 2(d) and 2(e) of the act require that promotional allowances to a firm's customers, whether in the form of payment, facilities, or services, must be made available on proportionately equal terms to those customers competing in the distribution of the firm's products.

The Supreme Court has held that the proscriptions in 2(d) and 2(e) are absolute and, unlike that in 2(a), do not require the showing of an injurious effect to competition. Nor can there be a defense of cost justification as is provided for discriminatory pricing under Section 2(a). However, it is possible to offer a defense that the furnishing of services or facilities to any purchaser was made in good faith to meet the services or facilities furnished by a competitor.

Sections 2(d) and 2(e) when enforced were done so primarily by the FTC rather than by private litigation or the Department of Justice. In an effort to encourage voluntary compliance with the law, the FTC issued guidelines for promotional allowances, commonly called the Fred Meyer Guides, after the Supreme Court case that first suggested they be prepared.[22] The guidelines were revised in 1990 to provide assistance to businesses seeking to comply with Sections 2(d) and 2(e) of the Robinson-Patman Act. Guides are what the name implies: guidelines for compliance with the law. They do not, however, have the force of law.

Guides for Advertising Allowances and Services

Competing Customers. Firms are not required to make such allowances or offer such services, but if they do, the allowances or services must be available and affirmatively offered to customers. Failure to notify competing customers of their availability may result in a violation of the law's requirements. Competing customers are all those businesses that compete in the resale of the seller's products of like grade and quality at the same functional level of distribution regardless of whether the businesses purchase directly from the seller or through the same intermediary.

Services and Facilities. The statute does not define *services and facilities*. A list providing examples of promotional services and facilities covered by the sections includes cooperative advertising, handbills, demonstrators and demonstrations, catalogs, cabinets, displays, prizes or merchandise for conducting promotional contests, and special packaging or package sizes.

Proportionally Equal Terms. No single way to make services and allowances available on proportionally equal terms is prescribed by law. The simplest method is to base the amount of allowances or services offered on the dollar volume or on the quantity of goods purchased by the customer. The new guides spell out in more detail how promotional allowances can legitimately be granted on the basis of either unit sales or dollar volume of sales. They also note that other methods may be acceptable and that mathematical precision is not required. However, if the seller offers an alternative plan and if the services rendered are of unequal value, problems can occur.

Direct dealing is not a requirement; retailers who buy a producer's goods through wholesalers can be customers of the producers and thus entitled to equitable treatment. The producer may use wholesalers to distribute payment and administer the promotional program, so long as the producer takes responsibility for seeing that benefits are available to competitors.

In keeping with the courts' current policy on resale price maintenance, the FTC's new Guides for Advertising Allowances, designed to aid business seeking to comply with the Robinson-Patman Act, deleted an example from its earlier guides, which stated that co-op allowances cannot be made conditional on the retailer's use of the suggested retail price in the ad. According to the FTC, this is more a subject for rule-of-reason analysis and a resale price maintenance issue than it is a Robinson-Patman Act issue.

Inducing or Receiving Discriminatory Prices

Although aggressive bargaining is not prohibited, the hard-bargaining buyer must be cautious. Section 2(f) of the Robinson-Patman Act is aimed at buyers and prohibits their knowing inducement or receipt of a price discrimination. Buyers must have knowledge that a price is illegal, or a duty to have known the fact. Such knowledge or the duty to have it can be demonstrated by trade experience. However, a buyer does not illegally induce a price difference if it is within one of the seller's defenses—that is, can be cost justified, is granted in good faith to meet competition, or is given in the course of changing market conditions.

Generally, if sellers are accused of illegal discrimination under the Robinson-Patman Act, they may present six arguments in their defense. They may:

1. Attempt to refute the government's contention that the discriminatory pricing is injurious to competition.
2. Show that the goods they sold at different prices are dissimilar.
3. Show that buyers to whom they sold at different prices are in noncompeting groups.
4. Show that the differences in price are justified by differences in cost.
5. Plead that they made the lower price in good faith to meet the price of a competitor.

6. Show that the discount was for special reasons, such as obsolescent or damaged merchandise.

Global Issues

Section 2(a) of the amended Clayton Act is limited to price discrimination that occurs in connection with commodities sold for use, consumption, or resale within the United States. It therefore does not prohibit price discrimination by exporters. However Sections 2(c), 2(d), and 2(e) and Section 3 of the Robinson-Patman Act contain no such limitation, but extend to any payment or acceptance of unearned brokerage, any discriminatory payment or furnishing of promotional services, and any covert or predatory geographic price discrimination or predatory price-cutting that occurs in commerce. Therefore U.S. law applies whenever such conduct affects U.S. commerce; that is, injures a domestic business.[23]

Price discrimination in import trade is of greater domestic concern than such discrimination in export trade. In this area, Section 2(a) prohibits an importer from discriminating among U.S. purchasers. A number of other federal statutes provide relief against a specific form of import price discrimination called dumping. Dumping occurs when a foreign manufacturer sells goods in the United States for less than fair value; that is, the foreign company charges less than it charges at home or in other markets.

The International Trade Administration (ITA) of the Commerce Department is responsible for making a determination as to whether a product is being dumped. If dumping is found, the International Trade Commission (ITC) must determine whether the dumping is causing or threatening a material injury or retarding establishment of a U.S. industry. If such injury is found, an assessment of a special duty is made in the amount of the difference between the home market price (or the price in other foreign markets) and the price at which the goods are sold in the United States. Judicial review of ITC's administrative proceedings is available before the Court of International Trade, and appeals of final decisions are available through the Court of Appeals for the Federal Circuit.[24]

Price discrimination in import trade may also occur indirectly when foreign governments subsidize certain exports. The Trade Agreements Act of 1979 and the Trade and Tariff Act of 1984 provide for imposition of countervailing duties in the amount of the government subsidy.

In September 1992, in an effort to "promote free and fair international competition," the Committee on the Judiciary of the Senate reported favorably on a bill to amend the 1916 AntiDumping Act.[25] The 1916 act was intended to combat the threat of unfair competition by putting foreign import traders in the same position as U.S. manufacturers with respect to the antitrust laws that proscribe price discrimination. It provides criminal penalties and treble damages for selling products in the United States at substantially less than their foreign market value, with the intent to restrain or monopolize trade or to destroy, injure, or prevent the establishment of a U.S. industry.

The proposed International Fair Competition Act of 1992 (S. 2610), like the statute it amends, proscribes unfair foreign competition that occurs in domestic markets. However, the bill alters key features of the 1916 act by deleting the act's criminal sanction and intent requirements. The intent requirement is to be removed because it is almost impossible to show intent on the part of the importer "to injure or destroy business in the United States."

However, the proposed act replaces the pricing standard with a two-part test. Under the new test, liability would be established if a foreign competitor's goods are sold at a price that is below average total cost and if the market from which the goods were exported is closed to effective international competition or otherwise lacks domestic price competition.

As noted in Chapter 1, the latest GATT round indicates that actions to resolve the antidumping disputes among foreign nations will be quicker and tougher.

SUMMARY

Federal antitrust and trade regulatory laws place prohibitions against sellers charging different prices to different customers (price discrimination). The Robinson-Patman Act declares, "It shall be unlawful . . . to discriminate in price between different purchasers of commodities of like grade and quality . . . where the effect of such discrimination may be substantially to lessen competition, or tend to create a monopoly."

There are several circumstances in which charging different prices can be defended under the law. They include cost justification (proof that it is less costly to sell to one buyer than another) and meeting the competition (whereby the seller can show that the lower price was made "in good faith to meet the equally low prices of a competitor). In addition, price variations are permitted in response to changing conditions in the marketability of goods. Such defenses are not equally available for all cases under the act. Suits in Robinson-Patman Act cases are designated as primary-line cases or secondary-line cases.

Injury to primary-line competition occurs when the discriminating seller inflicts injury against another seller. Setting an unreasonably low price so as to inflict injury is termed as predatory pricing. A firm possessing large financial resources may reduce its prices, setting them below its cost at levels that make it impossible for its weaker rivals to survive. The resulting losses are then accepted as an investment to be recovered after the rivals fail and the large firm can secure increased profits through monopoly.

According to a recent Supreme Court decision in this area, the precise definition of predatory pricing for application of the antitrust laws is unsettled. According to the court, there are two prerequisites to recovery under a predatory pricing action. First, the company that complains of competitive injury must prove that prices complained of are below an appropriate measure of its rival's cost. The second prerequisite to holding the competitor liable is a demonstration that the competitor had a reasonable prospect or a dangerous probability of recouping its investment in below-cost prices. The Supreme Court noted that these prerequisites to recovery are not easy to establish.

Injury to secondary-line competition occurs when the discriminatory price affects competitive buyers; for example, the effect of a seller's price to chain stores on the chain store's competitors—the small stores that are unable to obtain the favorable price. For discrimination to exist there must be a competitive relationship between the two buyers. Some pricing practices that marketers employ in their sales to competing customers may be defined as discriminatory and considered per se illegal. Other such practices that have the potential to be declared illegal are nevertheless defensible.

Price differences may occur through quantity discounts, may be payment for functions performed by the purchasers, or may result from favorable transportation terms. Injury to secondary-line competition may also occur through specific marketing practices—other than price discounts—that are considered indirect forms of price competition. These include the creation of dummy brokerages (generally considered per se illegal), the payment of excessive promotional allowances, and/or the furnishing of services or facilities to some customers and not to others.

CASES
Liggett Group Inc. *v.* Brown & Williamson Tobacco Corp. and Generic Products Corp., *CCH #69,817 (CA-4, May 11, 1992);* Brooke Group Ltd. *v.* Brown and Williamson Tobacco Corp., *CCH #70,277 (U.S. Sup. Ct., June 1993).*

FACTS

In recent years the cigarette market in the United States was composed primarily of six companies. Philip Morris and R. J. Reynolds held the two largest market shares, and Brown & Williamson the smallest. The other three are Liggett, Lorillard Inc., and American Tobacco Co. Prior to 1980, cigarettes were sold by these companies to distributors at the same price, and when one company increased the price, the others followed.

In 1980, when Liggett's share of the market declined to 2.3%, it introduced a line of generic cigarettes in black-and-white packages. The generic cigarettes were offered with volume rebates so that the price to distributors was about 30% lower than that charged for branded cigarettes. By 1984, Liggett's share of the cigarette market had increased to over 5%, and its generics became the fastest-growing segment of the market, in which overall sales of cigarettes were declining.

Other manufacturers introduced lower-priced cigarettes in 1983. Brown & Williamson began to observe that it was losing more sales to generic cigarettes proportionally than were other manufacturers. B&W decided to introduce its line of generic cigarettes in black-and-white packages and to reduce the price to distributors to below its average variable cost. After intensive competition in the total cigarette market, Liggett ended up with 3.5% of the market for cigarettes in the United States, and B&W with 11.36%.

Liggett instituted a lawsuit involving a Robinson-Patman Act claim that focused on B&W's pricing activity during 1984–1985, which it contended was predatory.

After a 115-day trial in a district court, the jury returned a verdict in favor of Liggett on its Robinson-Patman Act claim in the amount of $49.6 million, which was trebled to $148.8 million. The district court, however, noting that B&W had only 12% market share, reasoned that the company could not, as a matter of law, exercise market power unilaterally; the court vacated the award and entered judgment in favor of Brown & Williamson.

Liggett appealed and the Court of Appeals affirmed the district court's verdict, holding that the company's market share made it economically irrational to assume that it could recoup its losses and harvest additional gain.

Liggett appealed to the Supreme Court.

ISSUE

Did Brown & Williamson engage in predatory pricing in violation of the Robinson-Patman Act?

HOLDING

No. The Supreme Court affirmed the judgment of the appeals court and declared that predatory pricing without either actual or possible recoupment was not illegal.

REASONING

The Supreme Court examined the Court of Appeals reasoning, (referring to Brooke as Liggett, because of its former corporate name). The Supreme Court noted that *Utah Pie* was an early judicial inquiry in this area and did not purport to set forth explicit, general standards for establishing a violation of the Robinson-Patman Act. As the law has been explored since *Utah Pie*, it has become evident that primary-line competitive injury under the Robinson-Patman Act is of the same general character as the injury inflicted by predatory pricing schemes actionable under Section 2 of the Sherman Act. There are, however, differences between the two statutes. For example, Section 2 of the Sherman Act is interpreted to condemn predatory pricing when it poses "a dangerous possibility of monopolization." The Robinson-Patman Act requires only that there be "a reasonable possibility" of substantial injury to competition before its protections are triggered. However, the essence of the claim under either statute is the same: a business rival has priced its product in an unfair manner with an object to eliminate or retard competition and thereby gain and exercise control over prices in the relevant market.

Whether the claim alleges predatory pricing under Section 2 of the Sherman Act or primary-line price discrimination under the Robinson-Patman Act, two prerequisites to recovery remain the same: First, a plaintiff seeking to establish competitive injury resulting from a rival's low price must prove that the prices complained of are below an appropriate measure of its rival's costs. The second prerequisite to holding a competitor liable under the antitrust laws for charging low prices is a demonstration that the competitor had a reasonable prospect or, under Section 2 of the Sherman Act, a dangerous probability of recouping its investment in below-cost prices. Recoupment is the ultimate object of an unlawful predatory pricing scheme; it is the means by which a predator profits from predation.

For recoupment to occur, below-cost pricing must be capable of producing the intended effects on the firm's rivals, meaning, either driving them from the market or, as was alleged to be the goal here, causing them to raise their prices to supracompetitive levels within a disciplined oligopoly. Even if below-cost pricing could likely produce its intended effect on the target, there is still the further question of whether this would likely injure the competition.

According to the Supreme Court, these prerequisites to recovery are not easy to establish. As the court stated previously, "Predatory schemes are rarely tried and even more rarely successful. The mechanism by which a firm engages in predatory pricing—lowering prices—is the same mechanism by which a firm stimulates competition, because cutting prices in order to increase business often is the very essence of competition."

The court also rejected Liggett's theory that B&W's discriminatory volume rebates on its generic cigarettes are intended to preserve supracompetitive profits on branded cigarettes by pressuring the competitor to raise its generic cigarette prices through a process of tacit collusion with other cigarette companies. However, the court noted, the company and its oligopolistic competitors did not, and were not likely to, elevate prices above competitive levels.

Although list prices rose on both generic and branded cigarettes during the relevant period, the list prices were not the prices actually paid by consumers, since the cigarette companies had invested substantial sums in promotional schemes—including coupons, stickers, and giveaways—that reduced consumers' actual cost to less than list prices. In addition, during the relevant period, subgeneric cigarettes were introduced by the competitor, which widened the price difference between the highest-priced branded cigarette and the lowest-priced cigarette.

At the time the company entered the generic segment, the cigarette industry, as a whole, was facing declining demand and possessed substantial excess capacity—circumstances that would have tended to break down patterns of oligopoly pricing and to produce price competition. The larger number of product types and pricing variables also decreased the probability of effective parallel pricing.

The Supreme Court concluded that "the evidence cannot support a finding that Brown & Williamson's alleged scheme was likely to result in oligopolistic price coordination and sustained supracompetitive pricing in the generic segment of the national cigarette market. Without this, Brown & Williamson had no reasonable prospect of recouping its predatory losses and could not inflict the injury to competition the antitrust laws prohibit." The Supreme Court affirmed the judgment of the Court of Appeals.

DISCUSSION QUESTIONS

How is predatory pricing defined by the courts?
What type of issues may a business firm present in defense of a predatory pricing complaint?

CASE
Oreman Sales, Inc. v. Matsushita Electronic Corp. of America dba Panasonic Industrial Co., *CCH #69,709 (DC E LA, June 6, 1991) 768 F.Supp. 1174.*

FACTS

Oreman is a local wholesale distributor of electronic equipment, including computer printers. Panasonic, a U.S. affiliate distributor of a foreign manufacturer, manufactures electronic equipment, including computer printers. Beginning in 1985, Oreman and Panasonic made a series of agreements whereby Oreman would act as a distributor for some Panasonic products. Generally, the agreement made Oreman a nonexclusive wholesale distributor for certain Panasonic computer printers in a territory covering its state and six surrounding states.

A number of restrictions were placed in the agreements: for example, Panasonic specifically reserved the right to have itself and others compete directly with Oreman; Oreman was not to resell the products to customer locations outside its seven-state territory. Moreover, the agreement was an at-will agreement between the parties; that is, the agreement would renew automatically for successive one-year terms unless either party elected to terminate the agreement by written notice to the other no less than thirty days prior to the expiration date of the then current term.

Oreman alleges that in 1990, Panasonic "unilaterally terminated the agreement between the parties without cause."

In addition, Oreman alleges that Panasonic routinely discriminated in the prices of the major product lines purchased by Oreman, in violation of Section 2(a) of the Robinson-Patman Act. Discrimination was accomplished through discounts to meet competition to favored dealers. However, the purpose of these reductions was not, in fact, to meet competition, but rather to give lower prices to favored distributors. The effects of these price reductions were to substantially lessen competition among distributors of Panasonic products and to cause Oreman to lose sales and sustain injury.

ISSUES

1. Did Panasonic unilaterally terminate the agreement illegally?

2. Did Panasonic violate Section 2(a) of the Robinson-Patman Act by giving price discounts to some favored distributors?

HOLDING

1. No. The agreement was an at-will agreement, allowing either party to terminate. Moreover, the agreement between Oreman and Panasonic declared that neither party "shall be liable to the other . . . by virtue of the expiration or termination of this Agreement due to any reason whatsoever."

2. No. Panasonic did not violate the Robinson-Patman Act and engage in price discrimination even if it sold four models of printers to a distributor at higher prices than those at which it sold to competing distributors.

REASONING

The court focused on the price discrimination issue and noted that to survive a Robinson-Patman Act claim, a firm's complaint must allege at least the following facts: (1) the same seller made two or more contemporary sales (2) of commodities of similar grade and quality (3) at different prices; (4) at least one of the sales was in interstate commerce, and (5) the price discrimination injured the plaintiff and (6) tended to lessen competition of the commodity line (7) substantially.

Oreman's complaint failed on the last two points. Specifically, it failed to make factual allegations that any price discrimination by Panasonic lessened competition in any line of commerce, substantially or otherwise.

In respect to the line of commerce, the court declared that even if Panasonic sold four models of printers to a distributor at higher prices than those at which it sold to competing distributors, that alone would not constitute illegal price discrimination. The statutory focus of the Robinson-Patman Act was not on the sales of just those four models, but instead was on the entire line of commerce, that is, on the sales of comparable computer printer models made by the manufacturer's many competitors as well.

The court examined the issue of whether the Robinson-Patman Act protects individual competitors or competition and noted a shift toward the latter. In discussing injury to competitors versus injury to competition, the court declared that one competitor's mere inability to compete is not per se auctionable price discrimination under the Robinson-Patman Act.

In reference to substantial competitive injury, the court declared that Oreman made no factual allegations that favorable treatment by a single computer printer manufacturer for any other nonexclusive distributors had any noticeably adverse—much less substantial—effect on the competition in the sale of comparable computer printers in the United States. A simple perusal of any computer magazine or large newspaper from the past few years shows the myriads of manufacturers and models of computer printers.

In other words, Oreman's complaint does not allege facts that if proven "either show substantial injury to *competition* by market analysis, or show injury to a *competitor* accompanied by predatory intent."

DISCUSSION QUESTIONS

How do the issues involved differ between a claim of predatory pricing and a claim of price discrimination?

Explain the requirements necessary for a finding of price discrimination.

ENDNOTES

1. "Recent Efforts to Amend or Repeal the Robinson-Patman Act," House Report No. 94-1738, 94th Cong. 2nd Sess. (Washington, D.C.; U.S. Government Printing Office, 1976).
2. Terry Calvani and Gilde Breidenbach, "An Introduction to the Robinson-Patman Act and Its Enforcement by the Government," *Antitrust Law Journal* 59 (1991), 765–775.
3. Current Robinson-Patman Activities of the Commission," CCH #50,058, TRR (April 23, 1991).
4. Barbara O. Bruckmann, "Bidding in the Private Sector—Practical Advice for Avoiding Robinson-Patman Pitfalls," *Antitrust Law Journal* 59 (1991), 901–914.
5. Gregory T. Gunlach, "Predatory Practices in Competitive Interaction: Legal Limits and Antitrust Considerations," *Journal of Public Policy and Marketing* 9 (1990), 129–153.
6. *Utah Pie Co.* v. *Continental Baking Co.* 386 U.S. 685 (1967).
7. Phillip Areeda and Donald Turner, "Predatory Pricing and Related Practices Under Section 2 of the Sherman Act," *Harvard Law Review* 88 (1975), 697.
8. Gundlach, p. 139.
9. Page I. Austin, "Predatory Pricing Law since *Matsushita*," *Antitrust Law Journal* 58 (1990) 895–911.
10. *Mastsushita Electric Industrial Co.* v. *Zenith Radio Corp.*, 475 U.S. 574 (1986).
11. Susan S. DeSanti and William E. Kovacic, "*Matsushita*: Its Construction and Application by the Lower Courts," *Antitrust Law Journal* 59 (1991) 609–653.
12. Michael A. Kirkduggan, "Legal Developments in Marketing," *Journal of Marketing* 51 (January 1987), 110.
13. Austin, p. 907.
14. Richard T. Rapp, "Predatory Pricing Analysis: A Practical Synthesis," *Antitrust Law Journal* 59, (Summer 1990), 595–607.
15. *Liggett Group Inc.* v. *Brown & Williamson Tobacco Corp.* (1990) (M.D.N.C.; March 2, 1990).
16. *Brooke Group, Ltd.,* v. *Brown & Williamson Tobacco Corp.*, CCH #70,277 (U.S. Sup. Ct., June 1993).
17. *American Drugs, Inc.*, Ark Chanc. Ct., CCH #70,382 (October 1993).
18. *FTC* v. *Morton Salt Co.*, 334 U.S. 37, 1948.
19. David G. Hemminger, "Cost Justification—A Defense with New Applications," *Antitrust Law Journal* 59 (1991), 827–854.
20. *Texaco, Inc.,* v. *Hasbrouck* (U.S. Supr. Ct., 1990), Trade Cases #69,056.
21. Hemminger, pp. 846–848.
22. *FTC* v. *Fred Meyer, Inc.*, 88 S. Ct. 904 (1968).
23. Charles R. McManis, *Unfair Trade Practices*, 2d ed., (St. Paul, Minn.: West Publishing Co., 1988), pp. 424–426.
24. Ibid.
25. Senate Report 102–403 (September 16, 1992).

PART V

Legal Issues in Distribution Decisions

Legal Issues in Distribution Decisions

This chapter examines the legal restrictions in distribution decisions, particularly those that relate to vertical integration and exclusionary practices. Chapter 13 discusses the legal impact of restrictions on resale.

CHAPTER TWELVE

Vertical Integration and Exclusionary Practices

A channel of distribution is an organized network of agencies and institutions that, in combination, perform all the activities require to link producers with users to accomplish the marketing task.[1] These intermediaries—also called middlemen—generally perform marketing functions more efficiently than producers, since their operations have the benefit of low-cost volume capability.

A number of factors influence channel design, including the characteristics of the company, its competitors, the product, the target market, and the availability of middlemen. In selecting channel intermediaries, the producer must consider its ability to exercise channel control, avoid channel conflict, and secure channel goodwill. Thus appropriate channel design requires several interrelated decisions, many of which involve legal issues.

Distribution channels can range from direct (i.e., producers distribute their goods and services to consumers with no intervening levels of middlemen) to indirect (i.e., with many intervening intermediaries). There are no specific laws requiring or limiting the length of a distribution channel.

In the distribution of goods, close coordination between manufacturers and their channel members is frequently necessary to ensure that the proper levels of services, sales efforts, and other marketing efforts are provided for customers. However, the self-interests of manufacturers and their channel members often diverge. Generally, the fewer the intermediaries, the closer the control a manufacturer can exercise.

One solution to ensuring the mutuality of interests is vertical integration. This occurs when two or more separate stages in the channel are combined through ownership, including mergers and acquisitions. The extent to which a firm integrates vertically depends on relative operating costs or efficiencies.

Vertical integration is of two types: backward into the supplying market and forward into the channels of distribution. Growth and stability often require an ensured and continuing source of supply, so some firms make it a practice to own their own sources. Sears, Roebuck, for example, has a high degree of backward integration, and a large proportion of merchandise sold in Sears outlets is manufactured by the company's wholly (or partly) owned subsidiaries.

Forward integration provides a company with a competitive advantage through controlling the manner in which its merchandise is displayed, promoted, sold, repaired, and so on. Examples of forward integration are found in the automobile, oil, clothing, and food industries, where many manufacturers of these products have acquired retail outlets for their sales.

As discussed in detail in the chapter on merger decisions, the courts do not treat vertical integration as per se unlawful under the antitrust laws. Business organizations contemplating reorganization of their marketing structure by way of merger should utilize the advisory opinion procedure of the FTC and the business review letter procedure of the Department of Justice to obtain information in advance of making a decision to integrate. Although these methods of obtaining information are limited in scope and effectiveness, they do provide some input in a marketer's decision to integrate.

QUASI-INTEGRATION TECHNIQUES

Frequently, the costs to a manufacturer of monitoring, controlling, and offering the right incentives to employees in a far-flung distribution network may make vertical integration uneconomical.[2] When manufacturers feel it is more efficient or financially more desirable to use middlemen than to operate on only one level, some control over their marketing intermediaries can be exercised through several forms of quasi-integration. Such integration is secured through vertical restraints—that is, restrictions placed by the seller on the buyer. These vertical restraints are subject to the antitrust laws and can be classified into two categories:[3] those excluding or foreclosing competing firms from a market—referred to as exclusionary practices—and those restricting the distribution of the product—more specifically, restrictions on resale. Quasi-integration is often achieved by a multiple of these restraints.

This chapter examines exclusionary techniques. Chapter 13 discusses restrictions on resale.

Restraints through exclusionary practices relate to activities by sellers placing limits on the selection of customers with whom they will deal. This may occur through refusals to deal, exclusive dealing, tying arrangements, and reciprocal dealing.

Refusals to Deal

A general rule under the Sherman Act is that it does not restrict the right of a business to select customers; neither does it mandate selling to anyone. A business may choose how to disseminate products among distributors, wholesalers, jobbers, retailers, and industrial users. Section 2(a) of the Robinson-Patman Act reflects this right. And, as noted earlier, the Colgate Doctrine permits a trader or manufacturer engaged in an entirely private business to freely exercise independent discretion as to the parties with whom it chooses to deal. Generally, initial decisions to select channel members are at the discretion of the supplier and pose minimal danger of legal problems.

Manufacturers may decide to sell one line of their products to a particular dealer, but may refuse to sell another line to the same dealer. Such decisions are usually considered under the rule of reason; therefore they are unlikely to raise antitrust questions so long as legitimate business reasons are provided for the decisions.[4] The reasons include refusals to sell a high-priced line to mass merchandisers and refusals to sell industrial products to retailers who may have inadequate knowledge regarding the safe and proper use of such products. Refusals to deal may flow from a prospective customer's unwillingness to meet specified terms and conditions, such as territory or customer limitations. The legality of these terms and conditions can affect the antitrust propriety of the refusal.

Some channel managers may find it desirable to terminate a current dealer. This may result from the emergence of new and more efficient dealers, poor performance on the part of existing dealers, and changes in a manufacturer's marketing strategy. This situation, however, raises the most problematical questions of legality.[5] Moreover, if an illegal restraint is found, the injured distributor may recover three times the damages it is awarded by the jury.

The rule of reason generally is applied to business purposes—other than pricing—in determining whether a dealer termination was acceptable. Some reasons that have been considered valid include a dealer's poor performance in distribution and promotion, changing the distribution network to become more efficient, concern for product safety and service, the necessity to reduce exposure to product liability, and a customer's poor credit record.[6]

Reasons for termination, however, cannot be considered in a vacuum. Isolated, the refusal to deal may be lawful, but placed in its setting, it may be unlawful. Scammon and Sheffet recommend that manufacturers carefully document their marketing strategy including an outline of the roles and the expected performance of channel members. They should also conduct written performance reviews of their channel members on a regular basis.

This procedure is helpful in documenting the legitimate business purpose requiring dealer termination.

It should be clear that the right of refusal to deal is not absolute; it is limited by the extent to which the selection conflicts with the antitrust policies of the Sherman Act. Thus it is unlawful to exercise this right if the purpose is to monopolize trade or if it is accompanied by unlawful conduct.

Boycotts

Generally, concerted refusals to deal or group boycotts are illegal per se under the Sherman Act; occasionally, the rule of reason may be applied in considering this practice. Mostly, however, a boycott is considered illegal if two or more business concerns agree not to buy from or sell to a particular company. Forcing or inducing others to adhere to a boycott has also been condemned under the Sherman Act.

However, refusals to deal that involve no concerted action between horizontal competitors do not constitute per se unlawful group boycotts. Rather, such refusals tend to be treated as vertical restraints and subject to the rule-of-reason analysis.[7] Where there is no commercial purpose to an agreement not to deal with a company but rather an attempt at self-regulation within a group, a boycott charge will generally be subject to the rule-of-reason analysis. However, where the self-interest of the boycotting group and the proffered justifications merge, it is extremely difficult to satisfy the rule-of-reason standard. Where their rule's primary aims are to increase the group's power over nonmembers, they are suspect.

Essential Facility Doctrine

The essential facility doctrine[8] may be traced to theories underlying refusals to deal within antitrust law. The doctrine provides a basis for imposing antitrust liability for a firm's refusal to provide another firm access to something essential for competition in a particular market. A competitor's monopoly over facilities that are essential for serving denied customers has resulted in a number of successful challenges. These include challenges that permitted competitors access to airline computer reservation systems, local telephone lines, football stadiums, and multimountain ski-lift tickets.

The most recent explication of the requirements for establishing an essential facilities violation of the Sherman Act (under Sections 1 and 2) was outlined by a Court of Appeals, which allowed MCI access to AT&T's local telephone lines.[9] The critical elements, according to the court were:[10]

1. Control of the essential facility by a monopolist
2. A competitor's inability practically or reasonably to duplicate the essential facility

3. The denial of the use of the facility to a competitor

4. The feasibility of providing the facility

Recently Microsoft, the world's leading software manufacturer, has been under investigation by the Federal Tarde Commission (FTC) for alleged exclusionary practices involving its products. Competitors complain that Microsoft has an unfair advantage in the marketplace because it sells both operating systems and software applications. The competitors claim that since Microsoft's operating system is an essential facility for competition in the software industry, they should be allowed access to knowledge surrounding the system. The FTC's probe is still pending at this writing.

Gundlach and Bloom note that the increasing use of the essential facilities doctrine is at odds with accepted notions of competition and strategic advantage. They declare that marketers should be aware of the doctrine's implications, and they encourage researchers to examine issues such as the effects of denial of access of essential facilities as well as identifying strategies that may involve less overt methods of access denial than absolute refusal to deal.

Exclusive Dealing

Another exclusionary practice is exclusive dealing, wherein a supplier imposes restrictions on customers who agree not to deal with a supplier's competitors. Similar arrangements involve requirement contracts, whereby a purchaser agrees, for a specified time, to buy all or a specified percentage of its requirements of a product from a seller. Although such agreements are not per se illegal, a primary objection is the foreclosure of competition at the supplier level; another consideration is the restriction on customers' freedom to deal as they please.

Exclusive dealing should not be confused with an exclusive distributorship—a restriction on the distribution of a product and involving arrangements in which a supplier promises not to appoint more than one dealer in a territory. In fact, exclusive dealing restricts the dealer, whereas an exclusive distributorship places some restrictions on the supplier. Exclusive distributorships absent evidence of monopolization generally are considered legal. Exclusive dealing is more troublesome, and such arrangements are subject to challenge under the antitrust laws.

A number of a marketer's distribution problems may be resolved by exclusive dealing, which limits an intermediary's attention and efforts to one brand. It can help protect a manufacturer's brand-name reputation and product quality. It provides additional sales incentive for intermediaries and reduces transaction costs for manufacturers and their distributors.

Exclusive dealing may also contribute to the elimination of free riding. Manufacturers invest in product quality, image creation, and advertising; these activities provide an incentive for their dealers to compete aggressively in advertising the product and providing services. *Free riding* refers to efforts by other dealers who might seek to cash in on the benefits of this aggressive effort and therefore discourage the initial dealer efforts that advance the manufacturer's product. Price-cutters can attract business away from those dealers who provide the services and must charge higher prices to cover higher costs. Thus without exclusive dealing, while some dealers are investing to generate demand, price-cutters may take a free ride on those dealers' efforts. Moreover, other manufacturers may offer larger margins to aggressive dealers, who have attracted customers with their service, in order to induce these dealers to switch to the manufacturers' brands that have less customer pulling power.

Legality of Exclusive Dealing

Exclusive dealing agreements may violate Section 1 or 3 of the Sherman Act as an attempt to monopolize. Under Section 3 of the Clayton Antitrust Act, exclusive dealing is illegal if it substantially lessens competition or tends to create a monopoly. Under case law, however, exclusive dealing is judged under the rule of reason.

The chief concern in exclusive-dealing cases is exclusion of rivals through barriers to entry and expansion. Although lack of entry is not always anticompetitive, it is feared that exclusive dealing facilitates collusion or protects dominant-firm monopoly power. For collusion to occur, at least three conditions should exist:[11]

1. The industry should be highly concentrated and have other economic characteristics that facilitate collusion, such as homogeneous products, inelastic demand, and high fixed or uniform costs.

2. All leading firms must use exclusive dealing.

3. Potential dealers must be in short supply.

Substantiality Test for Exclusive Dealing

In an examination of the legality of exclusive dealing, consideration is given to whether or not the agreement lessens competition *substantially*.

To determine this, a court generally considers the type of goods involved, the geographic area where competition takes place, and, most important, the market share of the company involved. In fact, liability for exclusive dealing has traditionally been based on market share test. In *Tampa Electric*, the court stated that exclusive dealing was illegal if "the competition foreclosed by the contract is found to constitute a substantial share of the relevant market."[12] It appears that the greater the market share, the more likely that exclusive dealing will be considered illegal. However, the courts have followed no consistent pattern on market share illegality. Whereas in one case a 30% share was found to be legal, in another a 6.7% market share was declared illegal.[13]

The 1984 Department of Justice Merger Guidelines do not challenge exclusive dealing unless the market is highly concentrated and the foreclosure exceeds 25%. Since leading case histories in this area offer little evidence of exclusive-dealing collusion, dominant-firm monopolies, or entry blocked by exclusive dealing, it is likely that the law will reflect this approach in the future. Thus exclusive-dealing arrangements negotiated by sellers possessing a very small share of the relevant market are likely to be accepted by the courts. Similarly, exclusive arrangements of short duration are likely to survive regulatory scrutiny.

Tying Arrangements

Tying arrangements (tie-ins) provide another means whereby suppliers can place restrictions on purchasers. According to the Supreme Court, a tying arrangement is an agreement by a party to sell one product (the tying product) but only on the condition that the buyer also purchases a different (or tied) product. For example, a seller of a copying machine ties the sale of the copier (the tying product) to the buyer's purchase of the paper (the tied product). When a full line of products are tied, it is called full-line forcing.

Tying arrangements may provide a number of benefits for a supplier. There may be cost savings as well as greater efficiency in combining the sale of related goods. A demand can be created for a less popular product by tying it with a good for which there is a strong demand. In general, tying may facilitate the distribution of products and services.

Legality of Tying Arrangements

Tie-ins may constitute a violation of Sections 1 and 2 of the Sherman Act and Section 3 of the Clayton Act, and they may have legal consequences, such as the inability to enforce a patent or treble damages under antitrust laws.

Tying arrangements have been considered illegal per se provided certain threshold conditions are met: the purchase of one good must be conditioned on the purchase of a second good, the seller must enjoy sufficient market power in the typing good market, and the tying arrangement must involve a not insubstantial volume of commerce.[14]

Early use of tie-ins involved efforts by owners of a patented product to tie a second, usually unpatented, product to the tying product. Before the passage of the Clayton Act, companies with patents were permitted to use tying contracts. Thus the Supreme Court permitted the Dick Company to bind purchasers of its mimeograph machines to also buy from Dick their stencils, paper, and ink, holding that a patentee could impose whatever restrictions it might choose.[15] However, with passage of the Clayton Act, the court refused to permit patentees to extend the monopoly to cover other goods. Thus it struck down contracts requiring lessees of International Business Machines (IBM) to buy their tabulating cards from IBM. In the IBM case, the contracts were found to substantially lessen competition, because the patentee dominated the market for the process or product to which the unpatented commodity was tied.

In *IBM*, the court apparently followed the rule-of-reason approach.[16] First, it examined the extent of market power the seller had for the tying product. Next, it considered the quantitative effect of tie-in sales in the tied market. It also reviewed the defense that the tie-in was necessary because the cards were specially made for IBM machines and because other cards might injure the machines and the firm's reputation for efficient distribution of the tied product. However, the court held that this defense would apply only if no other reasonable and less harmful alternatives were available.

In 1947, the Supreme Court set a more rigorous standard in condemning a tying agreement under Section 3 of the Clayton Act in which International Salt required salt purchases to be tied to the purchase of International's patented salt dispenser. The court observed that International Salt sold approximately $500,000 worth of salt per year. Although it did not consider the total salt market, the court declared that the "volume of business affected by these contracts cannot be said to be insignificant or insubstantial."[17] Moreover, this was the first time the Supreme Court considered it a per se offense where the tying product did not have market dominance. The court declared, "It is unreasonable, per se, to foreclose competitors from any substantial market."

Since the Clayton Act's application is limited to the sale or lease of commodities, tie-ins have also been judged under Sherman Act standards. For a while it appeared that the Sherman Act standard (involving the rule of reason) was less likely to hold tie-ins illegal than the Clayton Act standards, which apparently applied a per se illegal approach. However, in subsequent cases involving the Sherman Act, the court applied the per se rule. Northern Pacific Railway's contracts for the sale of land adjoining its rail lines required purchasers to ship over Northern Pacific rails the commodities produced on such land. Since the tying product was land, not a commodity, the Supreme Court applied the Sherman Act, but nevertheless used a per se rule to condemn the tie-in. In Northern Pacific, (1) the test of per se illegality under the Sherman Act was extended and interpreted as not requiring an actual monopoly over the tying product but only "sufficient economic power . . . to appreciably restrain free competition in the market for the tied product," and (2) a "not insubstantial amount" is affected.

Moreover, in Northern Pacific the per se rule was applied for the first time outside the context of a patented or copyrighted tying article and essentially divorced from market share or other economic factors.[18]

However in *Jefferson Parish*,[19] the court endorsed a stricter approach to determination of market power and declared that a hospital's lack of dominant market position precluded a finding that a contract, under which the hospital required all users of its operating room to use the services of a single group of anesthesiologists, was per se illegal. Although the hospital had a 30% share of its local market, the court reasoned that the seller must also "restrain competition on the merits by forcing purchases that would not otherwise be made." Thus, under the *Jefferson Parish* decision, a condition of per se illegality is a finding that a defendant not only wields power in the tying product market but also uses that power to force purchasers into buying products that they otherwise would not have bought at all or would have bought on different terms.

Interpretations of Conditions for an Illegal Tie-In

Case law has provided a number of interpretations of conditions that must exist for a tying arrangement to be illegal. Currently, an unlawful tying arrangement prohibited by the Clayton Act and the Sherman Act is established by showing that (1) there are separate products; (2) the purchase of one (the tying product) is conditioned on the purchase of the other (the tied product); (3) the tying product's market power appreciably restrains free competition in the tied product's market; and (4) a not insubstantial amount of commerce in the tied product is affected.[20]

Separate and Distinct Products. No illegal tie-in can be proved when only one product is involved. For tying to occur there must be two distinct products. What constitutes two distinct products, however, is not always clear. A tie-in of condominium units to long-term leases to recreational facilities was found not to constitute an antitrust violation, since there was only one product involved.[21] However, a tie-in of the purchase of condominium units to the purchase of property-related services did satisfy the two-product rule. According to a court, condominium units and services were distinct items rather than parts of a leisure living package."[22]

In most of the recent tying cases, the courts have adopted a market-based rather than a functional approach to the determination of separate products. Generally a franchised trademarked product and its mark are now considered a single product.[23] Similarly a diet franchise and the diet tablets taken as part of a weight loss program constitute a single product. However, if a franchisor were to force the purchase of peripheral items (e.g., a requirement that Chicken Delight franchises purchase certain paper products), the franchise and the forced purchase would be separate products.

Market Power in the Tying Market. While actual market share dominance is not required under the *Jefferson Parish* decision, an essential characteristic of an invalid tying arrangement is the existence of coercion. When a seller exploits its control over the tying product to force the buyer into the purchase of a tied product that the buyer either did not want at all or might have preferred to purchase elsewhere, this is considered forcing and a violation of the Sherman Act. In the absence of forcing, courts have refused to find market power.[24]

The courts have tended to agree that no market power results from a trademark, since the mark only protects the name or symbol of the product to which it attaches, which creates no market power apart from that product. With these bases for finding market power eliminated, generally, franchisors have not be held to possess it.

In cases where the tying product is patented, the courts have found no market power and quoted Justice O'Connor's concurring *Jefferson Parish* opinion that a patent provides market power only if it precludes a competitor from offering a close substitute:

> A common misconception has been that a patent or copyright, a high market share, or a unique product that competitors are not able to offer suffices to demonstrate market power. While each of these three factors might help to give market power to a seller, it is also possible that a seller in these situations will have no market power; for example, a patent holder has no market power in any relevant sense if there are close substitutes for the patented product.

Not Insubstantial Amount of Commerce. The term *not insubstantial* has not been defined. However, the Supreme Court has noted that as little as $60,800 would not be considered insubstantial.[25]

Efficiency Analysis

Efficiency arguments have often been evaluated in nonprice vertical restraints. In holding that such restraints must be evaluated under the rule of reason, the court embraced the view that these restraints can promote interbrand competition by allowing a manufacturer to achieve certain efficiencies in the distribution of its products. In order to determine the extent of efficiency, some courts have utilized an efficiency screen, which relies heavily on economic theory. In some cases the courts have relied on economic theory rather than an examination of the factual record to predict that restraints are necessary in order to deter free riding and thereby encourage dealers to compete more aggressively against other brands.

This policy may change, however, as a result of the 1992 *Kodak* decision in which the Supreme Court declared that it "preferred to resolve antitrust claims on a case-by-case basis, 'focusing on the particular facts disclosed by the record,'" not theoretical arguments. The court said that "actual market realities" and the economic reality of the market at issue should be examined.[26]

Kodak, with a 12% share of the new equipment market for its copying and micrographic machines, also provides services and parts for its customers. Some services and parts are provided by independent service organizations (ISOs), which obtain parts with great difficulty. Kodak began to restrict sales of replacement parts only to buyers of Kodak equipment who use Kodak service to repair their own machines. The ISOs sued, claiming Kodak had unlawfully tied the sale of services for its machines to the sale of its parts.

Kodak sought summary judgment, citing three business justifications for its policy: first, that the policy was necessary to protect its reputation because servicing of Kodak equipment by ISOs might cause product malfunctions and customers might blame Kodak for these product failures; second, that the policy improved asset management by reducing inventory costs; and third, that allowing ISOs to service Kodak equipment would permit them to free ride on Kodak's product development and inventory investments.

In its decision, the Supreme Court held that factual questions existed regarding the efficiency and validity of each justification, making summary judgment inappropriate. The court noted that economic analysis is insufficient to determine market power and that "the proper market definition in this case can be determined only after a factual inquiry into the commercial realities faced by Kodak equipment owners." According to the court, "Kodak's contention that, as a matter of law, a single brand of a product or service can never be a relevant market contravenes cases of this court indicating that one brand of a product can constitute a separate market in some instances."

Kodak stands for the principle that antitrust cases should not be based solely on economic theory when that theory is inconsistent with the facts. In ruling against Kodak, the court refused to adopt as a matter of law the economic theory that a manufacturer lacking market power in the equipment market cannot restrict competition in the aftermarkets.

By holding that "difficult and costly" information gaps in markets for "complex durable goods" can confer "market power" on sellers in those markets, regardless of their market share, the Supreme Court appears to have altered the definition of *market power.* Since information gaps of the kind recognized in *Kodak* exist in almost every market, this change implies that, after *Kodak*, every company, no matter how small, may be subject to the heightened form of antitrust scrutiny previously reserved exclusively for firms with a high share of the relevant market.[27]

Defenses to Tying Arrangements

Some courts have articulated a requirement that the seller must have some form of economic interest in the tied product as another prong of the test for per se illegality. This interest may include indirect rebates on tied product sales as well as profits derived from sale of the tied product. In fact, some courts have treated a lack of economic benefits as a defense to a tying claim.

Based on Supreme Court decisions in *International Salt* and *IBM*, some lower courts have recognized that an otherwise per se unlawful tie-in does not violate the law if the defendant is able to prove that tie-in was implemented for a legitimate business purpose and no less restrictive alternative is available. Courts have listened to purported justifications for tie-ins, including goodwill, quality control, new-business necessity, customer convenience, safety, avoidance of products liability, and technological necessity.[28] These business justification defenses, however, are frequently unsuccessful. This is due to the strict application of the requirement that no alternative means are available to obtain the required business purposes. For example, courts have found that quality specifications and protection of goodwill can be achieved by quality specifications and testing outside suppliers' output.[29]

Efficiency Analysis as a Defense

According to Mary Lou Steptoe, Acting Director of the FTC Bureau of Competition, the Supreme Court's treatment of efficiencies in *Kodak* affects future vertical restraint cases in the following manner.[30] First, it appears to reverse any trend of acceptance of efficiency arguments based on mere assertions. Second, it underscores that proffered efficiencies must be legitimate, substantially sound, and supported by the evidence. It is less likely that courts will dismiss claims on the basis of theoretical efficiency arguments alone.

Beltone represents a case demonstrating the existence of credible efficiencies.[31] Beltone imposed certain restraints that resulted in de facto exclusive dealing for its hearing aid products. The evidence showed that identifying potential buyers of hearing aids is costly. Beltone had an extensive program of generating leads of potential buyers through the use of coupons in national advertisements. It distributed these leads to local Beltone dealers and argued that exclusive-dealing requirements were necessary to prevent dealers from selling competing products to customers whom Beltone was able to refer as a result of its investment in promoting its product. Without the obligation to sell Beltone products, the dealers could simply free ride on Beltone's lead-generating efforts. The commission concluded that the restraints had a "rational and efficient connection" in the protection of Beltone's investment in its lead-generating activities.

Reciprocal Dealing

Reciprocal dealing bears a resemblance to both tying arrangements and exclusive dealing, and it may be subject to attack under Sections 1 and 2 of the Sherman Act and Section 5 of the FTC Act. A reciprocal purchasing agreement occurs when supplier A agrees to buy products from B in return for B's agreement to buy products from A ("You buy from me, I buy from you"). As with tie-in sales there must be two separate products involved.

Reciprocity may restrain competition, since participants in the arrangement are foreclosed from the market. Price, quality, and service may cease to be the determinants of purchases, and the industry may become more concentrated. Such reciprocal agreements are considered per se unlawful if they affect a not insubstantial amount of commerce. However, findings of actual antitrust violations through reciprocity have been rare.[32]

SUMMARY

A channel of distribution is made up of intermediaries (also called middlemen) who in combination perform the marketing activities required to link producers with users. Distribution channels can range from direct (with no intervening levels of middlemen) to direct (with many intervening intermediaries). Companies that wish to exert significant control over their distribution network may engage in vertical integration with the channel members; such integration may be either backward into the supplying market or forward into the channels of distribution.

Other producers may use quasi-integration techniques to secure control over marketing intermediaries. Such integration is secured through two categories of vertical restraints: those excluding or foreclosing competing firms from a market and those restricting the distribution of the product. These vertical restraints may be subject to antitrust laws.

Restraints through exclusionary practices may occur through refusals to deal, exclusive dealing, tying arrangements, and reciprocal dealing. Tying arrangements are illegal per se providing certain threshold conditions are met; similarly, concerted boycotts in refusals to deal may be considered per se illegal. However, the other exclusionary practices are generally subject to rule-of-reason analysis in determining their legality.

CASE
Commodore Business Machines Inc., Plaintiff and Counterclaim-Defendant *v.* Montgomery Grant Inc., Defendant and Counterclaim-Plaintiff, and IDG Communications/Peterborough, Inc., Additional Defendant on Counterclaim, *CCH #70,120 (DC SD N.Y., January 13, 1993).*

FACTS

Commodore manufactures computers, and Montgomery Grant, a mail order retailer, was an authorized dealer of Commodore products. Commodore threatened to terminate Montgomery Grant as a dealer if it did not stop advertising discount prices of Commodore products. Commodore also removed prices from ads Montgomery Grant placed in a magazine Commodore owned. Montgomery Grant continued to advertise its discount prices in other publications. In 1988, Commodore terminated Montgomery Grant as an authorized dealer.

Montgomery Grant continued to sell Commodore products as it could get them and to advertise prices and other information. Commodore then filed suit against Montgomery Grant, claiming that the latter's advertising contained false, deceptive, and misleading representations.

Montgomery Grant filed counterclaims alleging that Commodore has entered into contracts, combinations, and conspiracies with its authorized dealers, with IDG/Peterborough, and with Montgomery Grant itself that are in violation of both federal and state antitrust statutes.

ISSUE

Is Commodore's termination of Montgomery Grant as an authorized dealer lawful?

HOLDING

Yes

REASONING

In examining the issues, the court noted that a manufacturer has "a right to deal or refuse to deal with whomever it likes, as long as it does so independently."[33] Under the Colgate Doctrine, formulated in *United States* v. *Colgate & Co.*,[34] a manufacturer can announce a policy regarding pricing or other restrictions and can refuse to deal with those distributors who fail to comply. If a manufacturer goes beyond this and employs other means, such as coerced agreements, to effect adherence to its resale prices, then it violates the Sherman Act.[35]

Montgomery Grant complained that Commodore's removal of the prices for its products from its authorized dealers' advertisements in a magazine which the manufacturer owned and published could have conspired to restrain trade. The court noted that such actions under certain circumstances could be considered restraint if the publisher were independent and Commodore had tried to coerce its dealers to maintain specific prices. However, in this case the court rejected this complaint, declaring the actions were unilateral and that the manufacturer's magazine was not the only vehicle in the industry in which the dealer could have advertised. The manufacturer could refuse to accept any advertisements in its sole discretion.

According to the court, a manufacturer that had announced a policy regarding pricing and did not go beyond this can terminate an authorized dealer and refuse to deal if the dealer continues to advertise discount prices on the manufacturer's product. However, if the manufacturer employs coerced agreements to effect dealer adherence to resale prices, such refusal to deal would be in violation of antitrust laws.

DISCUSSION QUESTIONS

What considerations are examined in determining whether a manufacturer can terminate an authorized dealer?

What specific actions would render such termination unlawful?

CASE
Eastman Kodak Co. *v.* Image Technical Services, Inc., *112 S. Ct. 2072 (1992).*

FACTS

Kodak had a 12% market share of the new equipment market for its copying and micrographic machines. Kodak provides service and parts for its customers but does so separately from selling the equipment. Kodak has a 100% monopoly on the sale of parts made either by itself or under exclusive contract with others. It also provides 80% to 95% of the service for its machines, and the remainder is handled either by large users who buy the parts from Kodak and do their own servicing or by independent service organizations (ISOs) that obtain the parts with great difficulty.

Kodak began to restrict its sales of replacement parts only to buyers of Kodak equipment who use Kodak service to repair their own machines. Kodak also required its original equipment manufacturers to agree not to sell parts to ISOs, and it pressured Kodak customers to use the same restrictions. As a result, some of the ISOs were driven out of business. The ISOs sued, claiming Kodak had unlawfully tied the sale of services for its machines to the sale of its parts and had unlawfully monopolized and attempted to monopolize the sale of service and parts for such machines.

A district court granted summary judgment for Kodak, but the Court of Appeals reversed. Kodak ultimately brought the case before the Supreme Court, requesting summary judgment based primarily on the fact that Kodak's lack of market power in the primary equipment market (12%) precluded—as a matter of law—the possibility of market power in the derivative aftermarkets of parts and service.

ISSUES

Has Kodak met the requirements for an award of summary judgment on the tying claim?

Have the ISOs presented genuine issues for trial as to whether Kodak has monopolized or attempted to monopolize the service and parts market in violation of Section 2 of the Sherman Act?

HOLDING

The Supreme Court held that Kodak has not met the requirement for an award of summary judgment on the tying claim.

The court declared that the ISOs' evidence that Kodak controls nearly 100% of the parts market and 80% to 95% of the service market, with no readily available substitutes, is sufficient to survive summary judgment on the possession of monopoly power.

REASONING

In this decision the Supreme Court departed from its economic theory approach to market power in reference to tying and indicated the need to examine "commercial realities."

The Supreme Court noted that parts and service constituted separate products and that the manufacturer had tied the sale of the two together. According to the court, Kodak's theory that its lack of market power in the primary equipment market precludes—as a matter of law—the possibility of market power in the derivative aftermarkets rests on the factual assumption that if it raised its parts or service prices above competitive levels, potential customers would simply stop buying its equipment. The court declared that Kodak's theory does not accurately describe actual market behavior, since there is neither evidence nor assertion that its equipment sales dropped after it raised its service prices.

In addition, Kodak's contention that as a matter of law, a single brand of a product or service can never be a relevant market contravenes cases of the court indicating that one brand of a product can constitute a separate market in some instances. The proper market definition in this case can be determined only after a factual inquiry into the commercial realities faced by Kodak equipment owners.

Evidence was presented that Kodak had taken exclusionary actions to maintain its parts monopoly and had used its control over parts to strengthen its monopoly share of the services market. Thus, liability turns on whether valid business reasons can explain Kodak's actions. However, none of its asserted business justifications—commitment to high-quality service, need to control inventory costs, and desire to prevent ISOs from free-riding on its capital investment—are sufficient to prove that it is entitled to a judgment as a matter of law.

The court noted that in the end, Kodak's arguments may prove to be correct. However, the court could not reach "these conclusions as a matter of law on a record this sparse." Accordingly the judgment by the Court of Appeals—denying summary judgment—was affirmed.

DISCUSSION QUESTIONS

What is a tying arrangement? What are the conditions for an illegal tie-in?

What kind of evidence is necessary to prove that such an arrangement violates the Sherman Act? What defenses may a firm offer for a tying arrangement?

ENDNOTES

1. Peter D. Bennett, ed., *Dictionary of Marketing Terms* (American Marketing Association, 1988).
2. Stanley I. Ornstein, "Exclusive Dealing and Antitrust," *Antitrust Bulletin* 34 (Spring 1989), 65–89.
3. Ernest Gellhorn, *Antitrust Law & Economics in a Nutshell* (St. Paul, Minn.: West Publishing Co., 1988), 278–281.
4. Debra L. Scammon and Mary Jane Sheffet, "Legal Issues in Channel Modification Decisions: The Question of Refusal to Deal," *Journal of Public Policy and Marketing* 5 (1986), 82–96.
5. Ibid., p. 88.
6. Ibid., p. 89.
7. *Lomar Wholesale Grocery, Inc.,* v. *Dieter's Gourmet Foods Inc.,* 824 F. 2d 582 (8th Cir. 1987).
8. Gregory T. Gundlach and Paul N. Bloom, "The Essential Facility Doctrine: Legal Limits and Antitrust Considerations," *Journal of Public Policy and Marketing* 12 (Fall 1993), 156–169.
9. Paul N. Bloom, George R. Milne, and Robert Adler, "Avoiding Misuse of New Information Technologies: Legal and Societal Considerations," *Journal of Marketing,* 58 (January 1994), p. 101.
10. *MCI Communications* v. *AT&T* 708 F. 2d 1081 (1983).
11. Ornstein, pp. 80–81.
12. *Tampa Electric Company* v. *Nashville Coal Co.,* 365 U.S. 320, 328 (1961).
13. *Standard Oil Co.* v. *United States,* 337 U.S. 293, 305–306 (1949); *Northern Pacific Railway Co.* v. *United States,* 356 U.S. 1 (1958).
14. Roger D. Blair and David L. Kaserman, "Vertical Integration, Tying and Alternative Vertical Control Mechanisms," *Connecticut Law Review* 20 (Spring 1988), 523–568.
15. *Henry* v. *A. B. Dick Co.* 224 U.S. 1 (1912).
16. *International Business Machines Corp.* v. *U.S.* 298 U.S. 131 (1938).
17. *International Salt Co.* v. *U.S.* 332 U.S. 392 (1947).
18. *Northern Pacific Railway Co.* v. *U.S.* 356 U.S. 1 (1958).
19. *Jefferson Parish Hospital District No. 2* v. *Hyde,* 466 U.S. 2 (1984).
20. Kenneth J. Burchfiel, "Patent Misuse and Antitrust Reform: Blessed Be the Tie." *Harvard Journal of Law and Technology* 4 (1991), 26–7.
21. Johnson & Nationwide Industries, Inc. (CA-7, 1983) 1983–82 Trade Cases #65,580, 715 F. 2d 1233.
22. Mission Hills Condominium Assn., M–I, v. Corley (ND Ill. 1983) 1983-2 Trade Cases #65,659, 570 F. Supp. 453.
23. Mark A. Hurwitz, "Bundling Patented Drugs and Medical Services: An Antitrust Analysis," *Columbia Law Review* 91 (June 1991), 1188–1220.
24. Lynn H. Pasahow, "Recent Developments in Tying Law," *Antitrust Law Journal* 57 (Summer 1988), 379–395.
25. *United States* v. *Loew's Inc.,* 371 U.S. 38, 49 (1962).
26. *Eastman Kodak Co.* v. *Image Technical Services, Inc.* et al., 112 S. Ct. 2072 (1992).
27. Michael S. Jacobs, "Market Power through Imperfect Information: The Staggering Implications of Eastman Kodak Co. v. Image Technical Services and a Modest Proposal for Limiting Them," *Maryland Law Review* 52 (1993), 336–373.
28. Beard v. Parkview Hosp., 1990-2 Trade Cases CCH #64,345 (6th Cir. 1990).

29. *Kentucky Fried Chicken* v. *Diversified Packaging Corp.* 549 F. 2d 368, 378 (5th Cir., 1977).
30. Vertical Restraints—FTC Enforcement, Bureau of Competition Acting Director's Views, TRR, CCH #50,130 (February 22, 1994).
31. Beltone Electronics Corp., 100 F.T.C. 68 (1982).
32. David C. Hjelmfelt, *Executive's Guide to Marketing, Sales and Advertising Law* (Englewood Cliffs, N.J.: Prentice-Hall, 1990) p. 77.
33. *Monsanto Co.* v. *Spray-Rite Service Corp.,* 465 U.S. 752, 761 (1984).
34. *United States* v. *Colgate & Co.*, 250 U.S. (1919).
35. *United States* v. *Parke, Davis & Co.*, 362 U.S. 29, 44 (1960).

CHAPTER THIRTEEN
Restrictions on Resale

The techniques for exercising control over distribution channels discussed in the previous chapter essentially relate to restrictions exercised by manufacturers concerning which distributors may sell their merchandise. These restraints are designed primarily to limit interbrand competition (i.e., competition from competing brands) through arrangements producers make with their distributors, for example, exclusive dealing, requirement contracts, and tie-ins.

Manufacturers frequently wish to limit competition between the sellers of their products. Here the competition occurs between sellers of the same brand of a product. Such intrabrand competition can be counterproductive in excess. Several arrangements are available whereby manufacturers may place restraints on the manner in which their goods are resold by their intermediaries. The kinds of arrangements include, for example, a manufacturer's requirement that a distributor or dealer sell, or not sell, to specified kinds of customers, in specified territories, at a designated location, under a specified business format, and the like. These restrictions on resale of a product are designed ostensibly to minimize intrabrand competition (i.e., competition among distributors of the same brand). Restraints imposed by a manufacturer on wholesalers and retailers who have purchased that manufacturer's products for resale have been the subject of much consideration under the antitrust laws.

LEGAL BACKGROUND

The law with respect to vertical and customer restraints has changed significantly since 1963. Prior to that time antitrust enforcers considered that effective competition involves both intrabrand and interbrand competition.

Since then several trends have emerged from relevant Supreme Court decisions.

White Motor Co. v. U.S. (1963)[1]

The Justice Department brought suit against White Motor Company, charging that its policy of limiting the area in which its dealers could sell or solicit customers constituted an agreement to restrain trade. The Supreme Court, however, refused to uphold a summary judgment of illegality as to vertical territorial and customer limitations. The court stated:

> We do not know enough of the economic and business stuff out of which these arrangements emerge. . . . They may be too dangerous to sanction . . . or the only practicable means a small company has for breaking into or starting in business. (372 U.S. at 263)

Other courts construed this statement as authorizing the application of the rule of reason to territorial and customer limitations.

U.S. v. Arnold Schwinn & Co. (1967)[2]

A landmark decision involving vertical territorial restraints occurred in the case of *Arnold Schwinn & Company*. Schwinn is a leading manufacturer of bicycles. In its distribution system, Schwinn relied on three sales methods: (1) wholesale sales to distributors who resold to retail dealers, (2) consignments to distributors who sold to retail dealers, and (3) direct sales and shipments to retail dealers upon orders taken by distributors. Schwinn's territorial allocation plan also called for wholesale selling only to franchised dealers within specified territories.

Schwinn defended its practice of vertical territorial restraints on the ground that intense interbrand competition its bicycles faced from competitors' bicycles sold through discount stores (which offered fewer services, but lower prices) required a decrease in intrabrand competition. Schwinn declared that it could not establish a valid and effective distribution network for its bicycles unless its outlets offered such services as bicycle assembly and adequate repair facilities. To motivate its outlets, Schwinn claimed that it had to ensure minimal intrabrand competition (by permitting its distributors to sell only to franchised dealers in specified territories).

The case went to the Supreme Court, which drew a distinction between outright sales and consignment selling. The court did not invalidate vertical territorial restraints in which the manufacturer retains title to the product, but it did invalidate as illegal per se vertical territorial restrictions that accompany a distribution arrangement for a product that the manufacturer *sells* to the reseller. In its majority opinion the court stated, "Once the manufacturer has parted with title and risk, he has parted with dominion over the product, and his effort thereafter to restrict territory or persons to whom the product may be transferred . . . is per se violation of . . . the Sherman Act."

Critics saw this "new dichotomy between the right to control distribution after the sale of a product and the right to control it before" as unrealistic.[3]

> Centuries ago it could perhaps be assumed that a manufacturer has no legitimate interest in what happened to his products once he has sold them to a middleman and they started their way down the channel of distribution. But this assumption no longer holds true in a day of sophisticated marketing policies.

Continental T.V., Inc., v. *GTE Sylvania, Inc. (1977)*[4]

The *Schwinn* doctrine concerning the establishment of vertical territorial restraints lasted for a decade, until it was modified by a Supreme Court decision in 1977.

The case involved Continental T.V., a dealer that held a Sylvania television set franchise. Sylvania, with a 5% market share, sold directly through franchised dealers under a contract that contained a location clause. Dealers were free to sell anywhere to any class of customers but agreed to operate only from locations approved by Sylvania. Continental contended that a provision of the franchise agreement with Sylvania that restricted locations where the company could sell Sylvania television sets was a violation of antitrust laws. Its argument was based on the fact that title to the television sets had passed from Sylvania to Continental.

The Supreme Court reversed *Schwinn*, indicating that *Schwinn* laid too much stress on "formalistic line-drawing" and that it was appropriate to "return to the rule of reason that governed vertical restrictions before *Schwinn.*" The Supreme Court's opinion did not rule specifically on the validity of the location clause but it was subsequently upheld.

In *Sylvania*, the court said that interbrand competition was the primary concern of antitrust laws[5] and that manufacturers could require dealers to perform presale and postsale informational services and thus, through reasonable nonprice restraints, control the course of their goods through commerce to the ultimate users.[6] In effect, the court said that some restrictions on intrabrand competition could actually enhance interbrand competition.[7]

The court noted that "demonstrable economic effect" might cause particular applications of vertical restrictions—that may have been prohibited per se—to be judged on the basis of whether or not they were "reasonable." However, vertical restrictions that have a "pernicious effect on competition" or lack "any redeeming virtue" are automatic violations of the antitrust laws (e.g., prohibiting the sale by retailers of franchised items to nonfranchised retailers). The court also specifically focused on price restraints, stating that "the per se illegality of price restrictions has been established firmly for many years and involves significantly different questions of analysis and policy."[8]

RESTRAINTS ON INTRABRAND COMPETITION

In order to limit intrabrand competition, manufacturers may offer territorial rights to appointed dealers so as to minimize competition with others also selling their product. Similarly, a manufacturer may impose customer restrictions when it has already developed sales contacts in a dealer's territory and thus may be unwilling to appoint a dealer, who might capture such sales. Exclusive distributorships may also be offered, whereby the supplier guarantees a single dealer that no other dealers will be appointed for the same territory. This latter arrangement frequently is in the form of a franchise and may require the distributor to operate according to a marketing plan specified by the manufacturer.

From the manufacturer's view, providing protection from intrabrand competition in a territorial area is necessary to motivate the dealer to devote intensive sales, service, and promotional efforts to the product. Such territorial restrictions serve to insulate appointed dealers from competition with others who may also sell the same product in their area. Dealers contend that with such protection they can extend their sales and promotional efforts, increase their scope of investment, and evade free riders. Free riders refers to invading dealers who provide none of these services outside their own areas, yet who take a free ride by making the sales the invaded dealer's efforts have generated. Free riders are able to offer a lower price largely because they do not have to pay for services outside their home territory.

Vertical Territorial and Customer Restraints

Vertical territorial and customer restraints can be of significant aid for the manufacturer wishing to control its distribution. These restrictions can take on different forms in an effort to limit intrabrand competition, from absolute confinement of reseller sales to lesser territorial allocations such as those discussed later.

Areas of Primary Responsibility

Under this arrangement, territories are assigned wherein distributors must represent the manufacturer to the latter's satisfaction and are subject to termination for failing to cover them adequately. However, distributors are not prohibited from sales elsewhere.

Location Clauses[9]

Location clauses restrict a distributor's resale operations to a specified physical site. Since customers can travel to any location they desire, and dealers may sell to them, this may reduce but not eliminate intrabrand competition. Location clauses could be included in franchise agreements and are widespread. GTE Sylvania utilized location clauses in the sale of its television sets, and the Supreme Court indicated that location restrictions should be judged by the rule of reason.

Profit Pass-Overs

Profit pass-overs were used fairly widely during the *Schwinn* era, when some territorial restraints were considered per se illegal. Such pass-overs require any distributor making a sale outside its designated territory to compensate the distributor in whose territory the sale is made. The amount may reflect the estimated cost of advertising or postsale service, which the compensated distributor is then responsible for. Depending on the amount, a pass-over could prove a disincentive to sales outside one's territory. Such pass-overs have been upheld in one case and denied in another. The latter decision may have been because the arrangement was categorized as horizontal rather than vertical.

Customer Restraints

Customer restraints may require a dealer to sell only to a particular class of customers or may prohibit a dealer from selling to certain classes of customers. For example, wholesale dealers of certain brands of bicycles are restricted to selling only to dealers who are authorized by the manufacturer to carry the line; wholesalers of heavy equipment may be prohibited from selling to government units or overseas.

Current Legal Status of Territorial and Customer Restraints

In recent years there has been very little government enforcement against territorial and customer restraints. There has been, however, private litigation in this area as an aftermath of dealer termination. Several circuit courts have upheld territorial or customer restrictions since *Sylvania*. The rationale is generally either that the restraint is needed to induce dealer investment or that the manufacturer lacks market power so that interbrand competition cannot be reduced and may be enhanced.[10]

It appears that location clauses and area-of-primary-responsibility clauses are likely to pass muster under the rule of reason. Profit pass-over clauses may also be less vulnerable under the rule of reason.

For the marketer, the *Sylvania* decision permits greater freedom in establishing vertical restrictions on retailers and distributors. These restrictions should be dictated by sound business reasons, which, as the court declared, could lead to potentially greater efficiencies. However, the *Sylvania* decision made it of critical importance for the courts to determine whether a particular restraint is acceptable under the rule of reason.

In a recent discussion of non-price vertical restraints, Mary Lou Steptoe, Acting Director of the FTC Bureau of Competition, stated the Federal Trade Commission has adopted a rule-of-reason approach that focuses on three potentially anticompetitive effects of such restraints. The FTC's decision in *Beltone* articulates that approach. Under a three-prong test, established in *Beltone*, the FTC considers actual collusion among competitors, the increased likelihood of anticompetitive interdependent behavior, and the enhancement or creation of market power by sellers.[11]

The first two prongs focus on the possibility that territorial or customer restraints may facilitate the exercise of market power through either tacit collusion or oligopolistic interdependence. The last prong examines whether the restraint will create or enhance market power. The concern is that exclusive-dealing arrangements "may increase the costs of entry and reduce opportunities for new entrants to distribute their products."[12] In *Beltone*, the exclusive dealing agreements affected only 16% of sales in the market, and the commission found the fact that recent entrants experienced little difficulty in establishing distribution networks to be decisive.

Since the decision in *Beltone*, the commission has modified consent orders to permit exclusive dealing arrangements when it found that markets were unconcentrated and that exclusive-dealing arrangements would not foreclose competition significantly. In addition, the commission has modified a number of consent orders involving territorial restraints.

However, the commission noted that the fact that its modification of these orders should not be taken as a lax attitude toward concerns about exclusionary conduct. Rather, where the potential for exclusive conduct arising out of vertical arrangements threatens to harm the competitive process, an antitrust remedy is appropriate.

FRANCHISING

There are no consistent or universally accepted definitions of what constitutes a franchise or what constitutes a distributorship.[13] Moreover, the legal definitions of franchises vary considerably from jurisdiction to jurisdiction.

Exclusive distribution is a form of market coverage in which a product is distributed through one particular wholesaler or retailer in a given market area. Franchising is defined as a contractual system of distributing goods and services whereby: one party (the franchisor) grants another party (the franchisee) the right to distribute or sell certain goods or services; the franchisee agrees to operate the business according to a marketing plan substantially prescribed by the franchisor; and the franchisee operates the business substantially under a trademark or trade name owned by the franchisor. Basic to all franchise operations is a licensing agreement under which franchisors grant franchisees the use of their trademarks.[14]

Kinds of Franchises

The term *franchise* has been applied to enough different business arrangements that one specific definition is difficult to find. In fact, there are various types of franchise agreements:

Manufacturing franchises involve agreements whereby a firm may manufacture and distribute a product under the franchisor's trademark (e.g., Sealy's and Coca-Cola).

Product distribution franchises permits the franchisee to distribute the merchandise produced by the trademark owner and use the trademark in the advertising and selling of these goods (e.g., Ford automobiles). This differs from a pure dealership arrangement, since it involves a detailed marketing plan. However, the franchisee's business format is not critical to the operation of the franchise.

Style of business or business-format franchises require the franchisee to operate retail outlets for the sale of goods and/or services in accordance with the franchisor's detailed instructions—including guidelines concerning the operation of the business and the appearance of the business location (e.g., Kentucky Fried Chicken restaurants).

While some of these arrangements relate to the resale of a manufacturer's product, they may also involve exclusionary practices, and thus exclusive dealing may take place within the framework of franchising.

Benefits and Disadvantages of Franchising

Franchises may provide benefits for both the franchisor and the franchisee. The franchisor is able to maintain a large number of outlets for its product or service without a significant capital investment. Franchisors can maintain strict control over their outlets' operations and supervise the service they provide for customers. Franchisors may obtain more desirable outlets for their products by offering exclusive agencies. They may develop motivated owner-operators, thus increasing their reputation and improving the image of their products on the part of their customers.

Disadvantages for the franchisor relate chiefly to the restricted number of outlets emerging from such an arrangement, as well as the relationship maintained between franchisors and their franchisees. Exclusive distribution not only places restraints on the manner in which merchandise is sold, but may also restrict the total sales volume of the manufacturer. There is the possibility of ill will being generated between the manufacturer and the franchisees, which may emanate from perceived (or actual) preferential treatment for some franchisors.

For the franchisee the franchise has been denoted as the "last frontier of the small businessperson." It represents a means by which an entrepreneur with limited capital and managerial or marketing expertise can start a business while minimizing risk. The franchisor provides many capabilities that the franchisee lacks, including experience, expertise, and advertising skills. Thus despite the publicized drawbacks of franchising—including deceptive advertising of opportunities and risk of termination of the franchise by the franchisor (now subject to regulatory control)—the government remains committed to franchising as a business opportunity.

Nonetheless, such relationships also involve a significant amount of control over franchisees' operations, a situation franchisees may ultimately resent. Additional support is derived from the passage of law attempting to eliminate some of the more obvious franchise abuses.

Trademark Rights

Basic to all franchise operations is a licensing agreement under which franchisors grant franchisees the use of their trademarks. The value of a trademark can be expanded significantly through licensing. This is an efficient and value-optimizing method that realizes a return on an investment in the trademark. Licensing under the Lanham Act created a defined set of legal rights known to the parties at the outset of any negotiations. Because the licensor and licensee know a mark is of no value without its associated goodwill, the self-interest of the parties effectively guarantees that both parties will try to preserve their investment.

Protecting the Franchisee

As a result of complaints about abuses in franchise relationships, laws have been enacted on the federal and state levels to protect franchisees against unfair treatment by franchisors.[15] Since franchise relations frequently are marked by a vast inequality of bargaining power, a franchisor's decision to terminate the relationship will generally destroy a franchisee's business. The Federal Automobile Dealers' Franchise Act (15 U.S.C.A. Sec. 1221) permits an auto dealer to bring an action in federal court to prevent a franchisor who is not acting "in good faith and without coercion" from terminating the franchise relationship. The Federal Petroleum Marketing Practices Act (15 U.S.C.A. Sec. 2801-2842) limits the permissible reasons for terminating the franchise of a motor fuel distributor or dealer and specifies certain procedures for terminating a franchise.

A number of state statutes also provide protection from franchise termination. Fifteen states, Puerto Rico, and the Virgin Islands have statutes that provide franchisees some protection against termination of their franchises. The protection afforded by these so-called relationship statutes ranges from Wisconsin's requirement that termination or nonrenewal be for good cause to Mississippi's requirement of ninety days' prior written notice of termination or nonrenewal.

Federal Trade Commission Rule

In 1979, in response to perceived franchising abuses, the FTC promulgated several Trade Regulation Rules designed to protect a prospective franchisee prior to the purchase of the franchise. The FTC rule mandates disclosure of specific information in commercial relationships in which:

1. the franchisor offers, sells, or distributes goods, commodities, or services which meet the franchisor's quality standards or which are identified by the franchisor's mark;

2. the franchisor exercises significant control over or gives the franchisee significant assistance in the franchisor's method of operation; and

3. the franchisee is required to make a payment of $500 or more to the franchisor or persons affiliated with the franchisor at any time before or within six months after the business opens.[16]

Therefore, to create a distribution relationship that falls outside the FTC rule, a supplier can prohibit the use of its trademarks or service marks, refrain from providing any marketing assistance or exerting any control over its dealers, or choose not to collect a franchise fee within six months of the time the business relationship is established.[17]

To minimize misunderstandings between the franchisor and franchisee, the FTC rule requires extensive advance disclosure of the full facts about the franchisor and the various restrictions under which the franchisee must operate. In addition, important terms contained within the franchise agreement must be disclosed prior to execution of the agreement. The FTC has issued a set of guides to facilitate interpretation of this rule.

Current Legality of Franchising

Franchising is a form of vertical territorial restriction presumably designed to limit intrabrand competition. Thus it is subject to the same rule-of-reason interpretations as other vertical restraints.

In the *Sylvania* decision, the Supreme Court favored interbrand competition even if intrabrand competition was foreclosed. According to this decision, territorial restraints will not be found to be per se illegal if they do not have a "pernicious effect on competition without redeeming value.[18] Increased interbrand competition appears to be acceptable "redeeming value."

As noted earlier, many franchise cases had been litigated on the tying issue. Franchisees argued that the franchisor is selling two or more distinctive products: a franchise, the trademark, and the lease. The courts, however, have declared that a trademark may not be separate from the product and that a franchise agreement is little more than a trademark license. In the case of tie-ins, franchisors may require franchisees to buy certain items from them if the specifications for these products are a trade secret or are too complex to be entrusted to others. Carvel has successfully required its franchisees to purchase its soft ice cream mix, since the specifications for the mix are a closely guarded trade secret. If the trademark is identified with a specific product, franchisors may require franchisees to purchase that product only from them. Examples include Baskin-Robbins ice cream and Shell gasoline. Moreover, if sound business reasons exist, franchisors may require franchisees to purchase certain items from other, unrelated companies, so long as those companies do not pay anything to the franchisors.[19]

Termination and Nonrenewal of Franchises

A number of situations exist whereby a franchisor can lawfully terminate a franchisee. Thus distributors may be terminated as poor credit risks, for poor sales performance, for ineffective performance, and for failure to properly stock and advertise the franchisor's product. A manufacturer that has relied on independent distributors may terminate these independents and assume the distribution function itself.

Most states permit termination or nonrenewal of franchises pursuant to the terms of the franchise agreement. In some states, nonrenewal is treated the same as termination. A common approach provides that the franchisor must give a lengthy period of notice of nonrenewal of the franchise—for example, 180 days.

Preventive techniques for avoiding disputes over termination include communication with franchisees; clear contractual provisions and standards; good documentation of relationships; and fair procedures, including appeal procedures. A franchisor's field representatives can be used to check on the facilities, operations, and personnel of the franchisee. The field representative not only monitors performance but can serve as a channel of communication between the franchisor and franchisee.

Clear contractual provisions should be in the agreement, and the franchisor should carefully follow these provisions in termination decisions.[20] Complete records should be kept concerning agreements, evaluation forms, internal memoranda, correspondence, and the like. Franchisors should make certain that termination is carried out in an evenhanded manner, so as to avoid complaints of discriminatory termination.

Maintaining a Franchise Compliance Program

Franchisors should develop and maintain programs to ensure they are in compliance with laws that affect their operations. Such a program should include compliance with registration and disclosure laws. An express policy should be described in a written statement and circulated to all employees. The compliance program should also include a discussion of decisions to terminate or to refuse to renew a franchise. Efforts should be made to avoid termination and nonrenewal by recognizing and correcting a franchisee's shortcomings at their inception. Guidelines should be issued for performance evaluations that track the requirements of state or federal law in this area. Evaluations should be done periodically on the basis of several performance criteria.

It may be desirable for some franchisors to provide for arbitration on some major issues, so as to avoid protracted litigation.

DUAL DISTRIBUTION

Manufacturers may distribute their goods directly or indirectly. For the former, vertical interaction provides a means for direct distribution to consumers; the latter—indirect distribution—is generally conducted through independent intermediaries. A third choice involves a combination of the two whereby a manufacturer distributes both directly and through independent distributors—this combination is called dual distribution.

Several advantages accrue to a manufacturer who adopts a dual distribution system: It may be more efficient to sell to some customers, for example, those who place large orders and require direct services. Manufacturers may be able to police their combined distribution system more effectively. In some areas, manufacturers may not be able to find desirable distributors who can perform their service requirements adequately. Dual distribution may also provide a competitive stimulus for independent distributors.

Such an arrangement also has the potential for problems, particularly when a franchise system is involved. Thus when a franchisor sells products or services to its own outlets as well as through independent franchisees, it may be in direct competition with its franchisee. In such dual distribution networks, the franchisor acts as both a supplier to and a competitor with its independent franchisees. Typically there is resentment on the part of independent distributors, who feel manufacturers may be offering special benefits to their own distributors.

There are also legal considerations: dual distribution may be considered to facilitate price squeezes on independent dealers and to implement price discrimination. The franchisor's relationship with its franchisees is vertical; however, when the franchisor reserves certain customers or territories for its own direct sales, it simultaneously has a horizontal relationship with its franchisees. In antitrust issues, horizontal and vertical distribution arrangements have been accorded different legal standards.[21]

Legality of Dual Distribution

When considered by itself, the courts have generally found the dual distribution system to be legal.[22] Independent automobile dealers have brought numerous actions against domestic automobile manufacturers for operating or financing factory dealerships in competition with them. However, the manufacturers' right to do so has withstood these challenges. Problems occur when the issue of predation arises. Thus even if dual distribution is legal, when combined with a predatory purpose it would constitute an illegal restraint of trade. Although a manufacturer is free to contractually end its business relationship with independent dealers, it apparently cannot do so indirectly through price competition. Moreover, a dual distribution may be questioned when it is accompanied by restrictions on competing intrabrand distributors. It appears as though such restrictions are motivated by anticompetitive purposes.

Nonprice restraints imposed by dual distributors may be considered as vertical and subject to the rule of reason. A primary concern in evaluating such restrictions is whether they lessen interbrand competition. Moreover, restraints imposed by dual distributors present greater competitive concerns than do restraints imposed by manufacturers who do not compete with their distributors.

Scammon and Sheffet offer several guidelines to franchisors to help avoid legal problems in dual distribution:

- Franchisors should be solely responsible for imposing restrictions even if franchisees may benefit from them.
- Franchisors should be sure their actions cannot be construed as an attempt to monopolize business or to minimize competition for franchisor-owned outlets.
- Restraints on intrabrand competition should be imposed only in an effort to enhance the ability of the franchise system to compete on an interbrand basis.

CHECKLIST FOR A VERTICAL DISTRIBUTION PLAN[23]

The rule of reason is not carefully defined and therefore leaves open areas for interpretation. Sands and Posch offer a checklist of questions that should be addressed in developing a distribution plan with greater confidence that it will satisfy the law. Distribution plans that are less likely to withstand attack by a private or regulatory body include those that (1) substantially lessen interbrand competition, and/or (2) have tended to create a monopoly, and/or (3) lead to artificially high prices as a result of the decline in interbrand competition. To make such a determination, the plan should be examined for the inclusion of relationships with unreasonable restraints of trade (e.g., price-fixing, group boycotts, allocation of business by improper bidding, and tying arrangements).

Less likely to be subject to adverse interpretations are distribution plans that prevent vertical integration of the industry and promote interbrand competition and those that involve a new entrant in the market, an established seller struggling to survive, and a firm with a declining market share. Similarly, plans that are likely to survive a challenge are those involving products that are inherently dangerous, are provided with properly controlled built-in safeguards, are highly perishable, or are protected by a patent or a trademark.

GLOBAL CONSIDERATIONS[24]

Manufacturers can expand their channels of distribution through the licensing and franchising of their trademarks. A primary purpose of the Trademark Law Revision Act was to remove the current preference for foreign companies applying to register trademarks in the United States. The

United States was the only developed country that required use of a mark before application for registration. Foreign companies, however, could register their marks in the United States under Section 44 of the Lanham Act, which allowed the foreign organization to base its registration on an application in a foreign country within the previous six months. Earlier, it had been thought necessary for such foreign-based applicants to at least allege use of the mark somewhere, though not necessarily in the United States. However, in the 1984 *Crocker* decision of the Trademark Trial and Appeal Board, it was held that a Section 44 applicant was not required to allege prior use of the trademark anywhere in order to obtain the priority registration.

Prior to the revision of the Lanham Act, token use was considered an opportunity for U.S. firms to be placed on an equal footing with foreign companies in securing trademark registration. Under token use, a single (or very limited) sale of the product bearing the mark was sufficient to satisfy the use in commerce requirement. However, token use was criticized as delaying the filing of trademark applications, perpetuating clogging of the trademark register, placing significant risks on introducing new products and services, and giving preference to certain industries over others (Senate Report 1988). Token use often can be accomplished cheaply by a large consumer products company considering a new trademark for a current product; however, this may not be the case for small companies that are financially insecure. In the service industry it is difficult to take advantage of token use; for example, how does one make limited use of a hotel or restaurant under a new service mark in order to be considered to be using the mark? Furthermore, trademark owners have not been completely comfortable with the sometimes contrived nature of token first sales and the legal uncertainties they may create.

The new definition of a trademark eliminates token use and presents intent to use as an attempt to remove the disparity between foreign company and U.S. company registration rights. The revision does not provide complete parity because U.S. registration can still be secured by a foreign firm without an actual use in commerce, whereas intent to sue by a U.S. firm still requires proof of actual use prior to registration. However, foreign applicants as well as Americans must now be prepared to show a bona fide intent to use the mark in the United States.

Gray Market Activities

The value of a trademark to a manufacturer can be expanded significantly through franchising and licensing. Though the Revision Act did not focus on these activities, a recent U.S. Supreme Court decision upholding the legality of gray market imports may affect such relationships. This decision is of particular concern to multinational companies and their dealer networks.

According to the Supreme Court, a gray market good is a foreign-manufactured good, bearing a valid U.S. trademark, that is imported without the consent of the U.S. trademark owner.[25] These markets are gray and not black because the goods imported through such markets are not counterfeit or stolen. Gray marketing involves the selling of trademarked products through channels of distribution that are not authorized by the trademark holder. When it occurs in an international setting, it is considered parallel importing.[26] Parallel imports have ranged from mineral water to Caterpillar excavators. The size of the U.S. gray market has been estimated at greater than $6 billion a year.[27]

Multinational companies are concerned about gray market activities for several reasons.[28] Those firms face the risk of tarnishing their brand image when customers realize that the product is sold at a lower price through alternative channels. Gray market activities may strain manufacturer-dealer relationships. In some instances the gray market may expand the total market for the trademark owner, providing greater sales, but accurate forecasting, pricing strategies, and other marketing efforts can be disrupted by an unexpected expansion of gray market imports. The Coalition to Preserve the Integrity of American Trademarks, formed in 1983, is now made up of more than forty companies that have suffered the erosion of product image and marketing investment.

For consumers, the principal benefit of gray marketing activities is lower prices. Nonetheless, such goods may not meet quality standards imposed on goods made for sale in the United States. The result can be a hazardous situation when the goods are, for example, foods, pharmaceuticals, or cosmetics (*Congressional Record*, 1988). Gray market goods may lack a manufacturer's warranty because their sale is not authorized by the manufacturer. A thriving gray market also contributes to the trade deficit.

There are some legal bars to gray market importation. The Lanham Act has a provision that excludes the importation of a copied or simulated mark (or counterfeit trademarked goods) but does not cover genuine marks. Section 526 of the Tariff Act prohibits importation of goods "of foreign manufacture" that bear a U.S. trademark without the U.S. owner's consent. Though this section as originally enacted in 1922 remains unchanged today, the Customs Service regulation promulgating Section 526 allowed some exceptions to the trademark owner's ability to exclude gray market imports. These exceptions are known as the authorized-use situation and the common control situation. The authorized-use exception allows importation of gray market goods when the domestic trademark holder has authorized the use of its mark by a foreign manufacturer on foreign-produced goods. The common control exception allows importation of gray market goods if the foreign manufacturer and the domestic trademark holder "are owned by the same person or business entity or the foreign and domestic trademark owners are parent and subsidiary companies or are subject to common ownership or control."[29]

In recent years courts have struggled with the Customs Service interpretation, creating uncertainty as to the legality of gray market imports. In 1988, a Supreme Court decision attempted to settle the conflict among federal courts over this issue. In *K Mart Corp.* v. *Cartier, Inc.*, the court declared that the Customs Service may not allow entry of gray market goods under the authorized-use exception of Section 526. The exception had been interpreted to permit importation of foreign-manufactured goods bearing a valid U.S. trademark if the U.S. trademark owner had licensed the use of the trademark to an independent foreign manufacturer. In *K Mart* the court prohibits the importation of gray market goods in cases where the trademark is applied to the foreign goods merely with the authorization of the U.S. trademark owner.

The court, however, agreed to continue to allow entry into the United States of gray market imports where the foreign manufacturer and the trademark owner are subject to common control. Common control of the trademark at issue (which represents the greatest proportion of gray market imports) involves three types of domestic-foreign affiliations.[30]

1. Foreign firm and domestic subsidiary situation: a foreign firm's domestic subsidiary owns the U.S. trademark for the foreign-produced goods bearing the trademark.

2. Domestic firm and foreign subsidiary situation: a U.S.-based firm owns a foreign subsidiary that produces the goods bearing a U.S. trademark owned by the U.S. firm.

3. Domestic firm and foreign division situation: a U.S. firm maintains a division located in a foreign country that produces goods bearing a U.S. trademark owned by the U.S. firm.

Marketers' Responses to Gray Market Activities

The *K Mart* decision may be seen as a boon to consumers in the form of lower prices, and to the discount retail industry—the primary source of gray market goods for consumers. However, according to Maskulka and Gulas, manufacturers being hurt by gray marketing have basically lost control and must reassert control if they want to end gray marketing of their products.[31] Unfortunately, some managements will only have the opportunity to react to gray markets. Others can implement strategies to prevent and minimize the effects of gray market activity.

Cavusgil and Sikora offer a comprehensive list of reactive and proactive responses to the problem.[32] Recommended reactive strategies include dealer support, which can be in the form of dealer education and promotion of dealer strengths while building doubt in customers' minds about gray market warranties and guaranties. Manufacturers can offer options to customers to accent intangible product differences; such options include short-term rentals, special financing, and guaranteed service, maintenance, and buy-backs.

More aggressive confrontation can be employed in the form of temporary price-cutting, as well as interference with the supplies of channel members participating in gray market activities. Manufacturers such as IBM that have found their products involved in gray markets have instituted a product-tracking system. This system enables the manufacturer to identify diverters and subsequently eliminate them.[33] Other firms have used tracking systems and have employed detectives to identify diverters.

Though dealer-termination activities may raise restraint-of-trade complaints, a recent court decision provides support for such efforts by authorized importers to discourage gray market imports. To prevent the importation and sale of gray market products, an exclusive authorized importer of Japanese electronic products and its U.S. distributors placed a ban on transshipping between authorized and unauthorized dealers and threatened not to do business with any authorized dealer doing business with the parallel importer. The court evaluated this ban in the light of possible antitrust violations. Despite allegations that such efforts would cause other Japanese manufacturers to do the same, thereby resulting in the elimination of parallel importation of Japanese electronic musical instruments and the destruction of alternative suppliers of such products in the United States, the court found that the procompetitive justifications for such efforts negate the anticompetitive effect of such conduct.[34]

According to the court, the warranty, advertising, and quality assurance programs of the manufacturer and its exclusive distributor were designed to encourage dealer participation in advertising, investing in, and promoting the manufacturer's products in order to increase competition within the market as a whole. The ban on transshipment, as well as efforts to discourage parallel import, were legitimately designed to protect the production goals and distribution strategies of the manufacturer and its exclusive distributor.

Recent court decisions also indicate that trademark owners may still retain private remedies against importers of gray market goods under the Lanham Act. Importation of goods that are genuine and that are covered by the common control exception to Section 526 of the Tariff Act may, by virtue of foreign language packaging and instructions used as well as disparities in warranty protection and possible disparities in quality, have a likelihood of confusing customers in violation of the Lanham Act.[35]

Multinational companies will find it beneficial to include proactive strategies in developing marketing plans (Cavusgil and Sikora, 1988). Such proactive strategies can include product/service differentiation to appeal in specific markets, thus preventing the development of large price differentials that trigger gray market activities. A strong dealer development program may ward off a gray market attack, and a marketing information system tracking gray market activities is necessary to identify distribution system leakages and take the necessary corrective action. Marketing managers are cautioned to examine each of the proposed strategies carefully and evaluate trade-offs among the strategies in terms of implementation costs, long-term effectiveness, and legal risks.

SUMMARY

In the design of a channel of distribution, several arrangements are available whereby manufacturers may place restrictions on resale of their products. These restraints are ostensibly designed to minimize intrabrand competition (i.e., competition among distributors of the same brand). Such arrangements include territorial allocations, customer restrictions, and exclusive distributorships.

Territorial allocations may be in the form of areas of primary responsibility, location clauses, and profit pass-overs. Customer restraints may require a dealer to sell only to a particular class of customers or may prohibit the dealer from selling to certain classes of customers. In recent years there has been little government enforcement over territorial and customer restraints. There has been, however, private litigation in this area as an aftermath of dealer termination.

Exclusive distributorships are generally offered in the form of a franchise, which may require the distributor to operate according to a marketing plan specified by the manufacturer. As a result of complaints of abuses in franchise relationships, laws have been enacted on the federal and state levels to protect franchisees against unfair treatment by franchisors. On the federal level, the FTC has promulgated a Trade Regulation Rule designed to protect the prospective franchisee prior to the purchase of a franchise. The rule mandates advance disclosure of the full facts about the franchisor and the various restrictions under which the franchise must operate. Important terms contained within the franchise agreement must be disclosed prior to execution of the agreement.

Manufacturers may use dual distribution—distributing both directly and through independent dealers. When considered by themselves, the courts have generally found dual distributions systems legal. However, this system cannot be combined with a predatory purpose, and it may be challenged when it is accompanied by restrictions on competing intrabrand distributors.

Gray marketing involves selling trademarked products through channels of distribution that are not authorized by the trademark owner. Gray market goods are foreign-manufactured goods bearing a valid trademark that are imported without the consent of the U.S. trademark owner. United States companies may suffer erosion of product image and marketing investment when gray market goods are permitted to be imported into the United States.

Although the Customs Service can restrict the importation of gray market goods under Section 526 of the Tariff Act, it has allowed some entries under the authorized use exception of Section 526. In a 1988 decision, the Supreme Court declared that the Customs Service may not allow entry of gray market goods under the authorized use exception of Section 526. The court, however, agreed to continue to allow entry into the United States of gray market imports when the foreign manufacturer and the trademark owner are subject to common control.

CASE
Matrix Essentials, Inc. *v.* Emporium Drug Mart, Inc., *CCH #70,196 (CA 5, No. 91-4457, April 19, 1993).*

FACTS

Matrix is a manufacturer of specialty haircare products, which are usually sold only in haircutting salons. These products bear Matrix's registered trademark and often (but not always) have a label stating that they are intended to be sold only in professional salons. Matrix's products are distributed to wholesale distributors who are bound by contract to resell Matrix products only to licensed cosmetologists.

Matrix wishes its products either to be used by licensed cosmetologists on their customers in a salon or to be sold by a cosmetologist to a consumer.

Such consumer sales are to be accompanied by a consultation so that consumers may be offered the particular Matrix product appropriate for their hair and scalp condition. Matrix spends several millions of dollars each year to train cosmetologists in the use and sale of Matrix products. It does not, however, attempt to ensure that consumer sales of its products are made only after consultation.

Emporium is a high-volume, low-markup drugstore chain. In 1988, Emporium procured and stocked a large quantity of Matrix products. A group of local salons and Matrix's local wholesale distributor complained to Matrix. Matrix authorized its local distributor to buy out Emporium's stock of Matrix products at Matrix's expense. However, Emporium was able to restock its shelves with Matrix products, and Matrix demanded that Emporium cease its unauthorized sale of Matrix products.

When Emporium refused, Matrix filed a suit alleging unfair competition. Emporium filed a counterclaim alleging that Matrix and its distributors and salon retailers had engaged in an unlawful conspiracy to restrain trade in violation of Section 1 of the Sherman Act.

ISSUE

Did Matrix's enforcement of its contract provision that required wholesale distributors to resell the products only to licensed cosmetologists violate the antitrust laws?

HOLDING

No. This vertical restraint did not violate antitrust laws.

REASONING

The court declared that vertical restraints that do not deal with price-fixing are not per se illegal and instead are subject to a rule-of-reason analysis. There is no evidence of Matrix's price-fixing, and therefore the court conducted a rule-of-reason review.

Under the rule of reason, in order to support Emporium's antitrust claim, the evidence must tend to exclude the possibility that Matrix acted independently in restricting distribution of its products. According to the court, there is evidence that Matrix acted independently. Matrix had a policy of selling its products only through salons (because this ensured the concurrent availability of cosmetologist consultation) long before it received complaints from salons and distributors about sale by a retailer. This reinforced the finding that Matrix had acted independently.

Emporium's antitrust claim was also based on the fact that a group of salons and distributors first noticed that Emporium was stocking Matrix products and that the salons and distributors notified and requested action from Matrix. The court declared, however, that distributor complaints are to be expected in a situation such as this one and are not by themselves indicative of an illegal horizontal conspiracy.

DISCUSSION QUESTIONS

What kinds of vertical restrictions on resale are typically imposed in channel design?

What are the criteria the courts use to determine whether a vertical restraint is illegal? How does this differ from the criteria imposed to examine horizontal restraints?

CASE
FTC *v.* Minuteman Press International, Inc., *DC ENY, CV No. 93 2496, BNA ATTR, June 7, 1993.*

FACTS

Minuteman Press and its wholly owned subsidiary Speedy Sign-A-Rama USA, Inc., had sold retail sign franchises nationwide since 1975 and 1987, respectively. In their presentations to potential buyers, the firms made specific gross sales projections and claimed that profits could be as high as one-third of the franchisee's gross sales. However, few, if any, franchisees realized such gross sales or profits.

In addition, the firms failed to disclose to prospective buyers that the defendants would impose a transfer fee—ranging from $9,500 to $11,500—on franchisees who sold or assigned their franchises. Moreover, the firms made earnings claims without providing prospective buyers with earnings documents.

ISSUE

Are the firms subject to a complaint of violation of FTC's Franchise Rule?

HOLDING

Yes. The FTC filed a complaint alleging that the firms had violated the FTC's Franchise Rule.

REASONING

The FTC's Franchise Rule, in effect since 1979, requires anyone selling a franchise to provide prospective buyers with a complete and accurate disclosure document containing twenty-one categories of information, including: the history and management experience of the franchisor, the identities and business experience of its directors, and the names and addresses of operating franchises in the geographic area of the prospective franchisees. If a franchisor makes earnings claims, the rule requires it to provide prospective investors with a document substantiating the claims.

According to the FTC's complaint, the firms violated the Franchise Rule by failing to disclose transfer fees and by making earnings claims without providing the required documents.

DISCUSSION QUESTIONS

Why did the FTC adopt a Franchise Rule?
What concerns should marketers address in creating and maintaining franchises?

ENDNOTES

1. *White Motor Co.* v. *U.S.*, 372 U.S. 253 (1963).
2. *U.S.* v. *Arnold Schwinn & Co.*, 388 U.S. 365 (1967).
3. Betty Bock, "Antitrust Issues in Restricting Sales Territories and Outlets," in *Studies in Business Economics*, No. 98 (New York: National Industrial Conference Board, 1976), p. 31.
4. *Continental T.V., Inc.*, v. *GTE Sylvania, Inc.*, 433 U.S. 36 (1977).
5. 433 U.S. at 52 n. 19.
6. Id. at 57–59.
7. William B. Slowey, "The Effect of *GTE Sylvania* on Antitrust Jurisprudence," *Antitrust Law Journal*, 60 (1991), 12–15.
8. 433 U.S. at 51 n. 18.
9. John F. Cady, "Reasonable Rules and Rules of Reason: Vertical Restrictions on Distributors," *Journal of Marketing* 46 (Summer 1982), 27–37.
10. Vertical Restraints—FTC Enforcement Bureau of Competition Acting Director's Views, TRR CCH #50,130 (February 1994).
11. *Beltone Electronics Corp.*, 100 F.T.C. 68 (1982).
12. 100 F.T.C. at 207.
13. W. M. Garner, *Franchise and Distribution Law and Practice*, Vol. 1 (Deerfield, Ill.: Callaghan & Company, 1990).
14. Peter D. Bennett, ed., *Dictionary of Marketing Terms*, American Marketing Association, 1988.
15. Brian E. Butler and Lynn Bodi, "Protection of Multiline Sellers by State Relationship Statutes," *Franchise Law Journal* (Spring 1991), 3–12.
16. 16 C.F.R. Sec. #436.2.
17. Kim A. Lambert and Charles G. Miller, "The Definition of a Franchise: A Survey of Existing State Legislative and Judicial Guidance," *Franchise Law Journal* (Fall 1989), 3–30.

18. *Continental TV, Inc.*, v. *GTE Sylvania, Inc.*, 433 U.S. 36 (1977).

19. Richard M. Steuer, *A Guide to Marketing Law: What Every Seller Should Know* (New York: Law & Business Harcourt, Brace, Jovanovich, 1986), p. 63.

20. Garner, 1007.

21. Debra L. Scammon and Mary Jane Sheffet, "Legal Issues in Franchising: Problems of Dual Distribution," *1989 AMA Educator's Proceedings*, eds. Paul Bloom et al. (Chicago: American Marketing Association, 1989), p. 292.

22. Robert Zwirb, "Dual Distribution and Antitrust Law," *Loyola University of LA Law Review* 21 (June 1988), 1273–1342.

23. Saul Sands and Robert J. Posch Jr. "A Checklist of Questions for Firms Considering a Vertical Distribution Plan," *Journal of Marketing* 46 (Summer 1982), 38–43.

24. Dorothy Cohen, "Trademark Strategy Revisited," *Journal of Marketing* 55 (July 1991), 53–55.

25. *K Mart Corp.* v. *Cartier, Inc.*, 108 S. Ct. 1811 (1988).

26. Dale F. Duhan and Mary Jane Sheffet, "Gray Markets and the Legal Status of Parallel Importation," *Journal of Marketing* 52 (July 1988), 75–83.

27. Paul I. J. Fleischut, "The Current State of the United States Gray Market: The Common-Control Exception Survives for Now," *Missouri Law Review* 54 (Spring 1989), 414–423.

28. Tamer S. Cavusgil and Ed Sikora, "How Multinationals Can Counter Gray Market Imports," *Columbia Journal of World Business* 23 (Winter 1988), 75–85.

29. Raymond R. Mandra, "*K Mart Corp.* v. *Cartier, Inc.*: Is Continued Gray Market Importation a Result of Gray Statutory Language or Judicial Legislation?" *Pace Law Review* 10 (Winter 1990), 245–272.

30. Ibid.

31. James M. Maskulka and Charles S. Gulas, "Long Term Damages of Gray Market Sales," *Business* 37 (January–February–March 1987), 25–31.

32. Cavusgil and Sikora, p. 75–85.

33. Larry S. Lowe and Kevin F. McCrohan, "MInimize the Impact of the Gray Market," *Journal of Business Strategy* 11 (November/December 1989), 47–50.

34. *Yamaha International Corp. and Yamaha Electronics Corp.* v. *ABC International Traders, Inc., et al.*, TRR, CCH #68,874 (DC CD Cal., December 1989).

35. *Duracell Inc.* v. *Global Imports, Inc.*, 12 USPQ2d 1651 (1989).

PART VI

Legal Issues in Merger and Joint Venture Decisions

Legal Issues in Merger and Joint Venture Decisions

This chapter examines the rules and regulations that affect the growth and diversification of organizations through mergers and joint ventures.

CHAPTER FOURTEEN
Growth and Diversification through Mergers and Joint Ventures

Business growth and diversification are accepted dynamics of the economy. Such growth may occur through the expansion of product lines and/or the development of new products. Early in U.S. business history, many firms achieved growth internally, through the development of patents, control over resources, increases in productivity, and so on. E. I. Du Pont de Nemour, General Motors, and the large steel companies grew this way. More recently, much of the growth in business has been external—by acquisition of or merger or other relationship, including joint ventures, with other businesses.

Classification of Mergers

Mergers occur when two formerly independent entities are united in a new independent entity. Acquisitions, amalgamations, and consolidations all represent mergers. The different types of mergers are generally classified in three broad categories: horizontal, vertical, and conglomerate.

Horizontal Mergers. Companies can expand horizontally by acquiring firms directly competing in the sale of similar goods or services and in the same geographic market.

Vertical Mergers. Vertical mergers occur when a firm acquires either a customer—called forward vertical integration—or a supplier—called backward vertical integration.

Conglomerate Merger. A conglomerate merger is one in which one company acquires another company that is not in a competitive relationship and does not have a customer-supplier relationship with the acquiring firm.

Reasons for Mergers

There are many reasons why firms may merge. For some firms, internal growth may be too costly, too time-consuming, and/or too risky. These organizations may turn to external means such as acquisition of other firms for expansion. Companies may wish to merge so as to acquire another firm's existing resources such as its patents, sources of raw materials, distribution network and existing reputation. There may be tax savings from the combination, or stock market advantages may result from the ability of the merged firm to show a significant profit.

By joining two separate business entities into one, the proponents of the merger hope to create a synergistic effect; that is, the resulting firm will be greater than the sum of its parts. Such synergism might stem from the acquired product's ability to strengthen the firm's present line by either satisfying customer demands or broadening the customer base. The acquisition might increase utilization of existing resources, such as physical facilities not currently operating at capacity levels.

Marketers should be aware, in reference to mergers, that two premises must be established.[1] Aside from such unusual situations as an immediate need for cash or estate planning, owners usually will sell their business only when they believe that the business will be worth less to them in the future. Conversely, prospective purchasers will be interested in acquiring a business only if they believe that the acquired firm will be worth more to them in the future.

In recent years there has been an increase in big-company merger activity, primarily involving the technological field. In the past, mergers generally brought together companies with existing products such as food and cigarettes, and the mergers were evaluated on whether the increased market shares could limit competition and raise prices.

Large mergers are being proposed in the technological fields such as cable/television/and computers. Evaluations of such mergers require consideration of the rapid changes in technology and of the need to be competitive both nationally and globally. At this writing a proposed merger of Bell Atlantic Corp. and Telecommunications Inc. is being evaluated by the Clinton Administration.

Antitrust Laws that Impact on Mergers

Public policy toward growth indicates that not all bigness is necessarily bad. Nonetheless, large firms can exert some influence over prices and product supply to the detriment of small firms. Such potential evils have given rise to the government's antitrust policy expressed primarily in attempts to decelerate the movement toward mergers and acquisitions, limit barriers to entry, and curtail the tendency toward concentration.

Mergers may have no impact on the market in which they operate when the merged firms may be too small or entry into their markets may be easily accomplished. In fact, mergers by small firms may tend to increase competition. The task of antitrust merger law is to weed out those mergers that "tend substantially to lessen competition."

Under the federal antitrust laws, mergers are subject to Sections 1 and 2 of the Sherman Act. Section 1 prohibits mergers that constitute an unreasonable restraint of trade. Section 2 prohibits mergers that create a monopoly or constitute an attempt, combination, or conspiracy to monopolize. Mergers are also subject to Section 7 of the Clayton Act, which prohibits mergers if their effect "may be substantially to lessen competition, or to tend to create a monopoly."

Initially the Sherman Act was applied to mergers. The Supreme Court took the position that all mergers between directly competing firms constituted a combination in restraint of trade and therefore violated Section 1. Subsequently the Supreme Court began to substitute a rule-of-reason approach by which mergers leading to monopoly were to be tested. In applying a less than rigid rule-of-reason standard, the court held that a consolidation of most of the steel industry into one firm possessing 80% to 90% of capacity in some basic lines did not violate either Section 1 or 2 of the Sherman Act.[2]

Since the rule-of-reason standard did not forbid mergers unless they were designed to create a monopoly, few mergers failed under this standard.[3] In partial response to that situation, Section 7 of the Clayton Act was adopted in order to limit stock acquisitions. However, the provision banned only purchases of stock and seemed to provide loopholes in the form of asset acquisitions. Thus in 1950, in the Celler-Kefauver Amendment, Congress rewrote Section 7 of the Clayton Act to close the asset acquisitions loophole. Section 7 now reads, "No person engaged in commerce . . . shall acquire . . . the whole or any part of the stock . . . or assets of another person engaged also in commerce . . . where . . . the effect of such acquisition may be substantially to lessen competition, or to tend to create a monopoly."

The Federal Trade Commission (FTC) and the Department of Justice have jurisdiction over mergers. Each of these agencies can file complaints under Section 7 of the amended Clayton Act. The Department of Justice can also utilize the Sherman Act, and the FTC can use Section 5 of the FTC Act ("unfair methods of competition in commerce are declared unlawful") to prosecute merger cases.

Section 5 is much more general than the Clayton and Sherman antitrust acts that outlaw certain types of mergers—such as those that result in price increases and agreements that restrain trade. A 1972 Supreme Court decision declared that Section 5 empowers the FTC "to define and proscribe unfair competitive practices even though the practice does not infringe either on the letter or the spirit of the law."[4] Recently the FTC indicated it plans to use Section 5 to challenge practices that are not specifically covered by the antitrust laws, but that may cause consumer harm.

States also have antitrust statutes. Enforcement is conducted by state and territorial attorneys general. The National Association of Attorneys General recently proposed horizontal merger guidelines to coordinate the various state statutes and to harmonize with the Department of Justice Merger Guidelines (discussed later) "to the maximum extent feasible."[5]

Premerger Notification Requirements

The Hart-Scott-Rodino Antitrust Improvements Act of 1976 established a premerger notification program. The primary objective of the program is to avoid some of the difficulties that antitrust enforcement agencies encounter when they challenge anticompetitive conditions after they occur. However, the act has provided firms with the opportunity to learn in advance of making merger decisions whether the FTC is likely to institute an antimerger case.

The FTC has prepared a series of Guides to assist firms in determining (1) which proposed business transactions are subject to the premerger notification requirements and (2) how to comply with the requirements.[6] Guide I presents a basic introduction to the premerger notification program. Guide II explains how to determine which transactions are subject to premerger notification and waiting requirements. Other Guides are forthcoming.

Under Guide I, as a general matter, the rules require both parties to file notification if all of the following conditions have been met:[7]

1. One person has sales or assets of at least $100 million;

2. The other person has sales or assets of at least $10 million; and

3. As a result of the transaction, the acquiring person will hold a total amount of stock or assets of the acquired person valued at more than $15 million, or, in some stock transactions, even if the stock held is valued at $15 million or less, if it represents more than 50% of the outstanding stock of the issuer being acquired and the issuer is of a certain size (a determination of size is complicated and requires reference to the Rules of the Act).

There are a number of transactions that are exempt from reporting requirements. For example, acquisition of the voting securities of a foreign issuer may be exempt if the foreign company did no business in the United States and holds no assets in the United States.[8]

In 1989, the FTC began collecting a filing fee of $20,000 from each person who is required to file a premerger notification and report fee. As of 1993, the filing fee was increased to $25,000. Recently, a motion picture exhibitor was required by a consent decree to pay a civil penalty of $950,000 to settle charges that it had failed to comply with the premerger reporting provisions of Section 7A of the Clayton Act in connection with its acquisition of more than $15 million of the stock of a carbonated beverage company.[9]

After filing, the parties must then observe a waiting period, which is fifteen days in the case of a cash tender offer and thirty days for all other types of transactions. These may be extended by issuance of a request for additional information and documentary material.

The FTC recommends that firms use the Guides to assist them in determining which proposed business transactions are subject to the premerger requirements and how to comply with them. The Commission also notes that if a firm still has questions, the Premerger Notification Office of the Federal Trade Commission (telephone 202-326-3100) will be happy to assist.[10]

HORIZONTAL MERGERS

Various changes have occurred over time in the manner in which horizontal mergers have been tested to determine their legality. Over the years the following factors have been found relevant in testing horizontal mergers.[11]

- The extent of concentration in the relevant market
- The shares of the company in this market
- Changes in barriers to entry
- The elimination of a major independent company from a market with relatively few firms

The courts have generally supported enforcement agencies in their attacks on horizontal mergers. Nonetheless, the standards by which mergers have been measured seem to vary over time. In an effort to establish some uniformity, the Department of Justice issued a new set of rules in 1982 outlining when it would prosecute mergers as a violation of Section 7, and it revised them two years later. In 1992, the Department of Justice and the Federal Trade Commission jointly issued Horizontal Merger Guidelines, revising the department's 1984 guidelines and the FTC's 1982 Statement Concerning Horizontal Merger Guidelines.[12] This marks the first time that the two federal agencies that share antitrust enforcement jurisdiction have issued joint guidelines.

1992 Horizontal Merger Guidelines

These guidelines articulate the analytical framework applied in determining whether a merger is likely substantially to lessen competition. They set forth a methodology for such analysis once the necessary facts are available. These facts may be derived from the documents and statements of both the merging firms and other sources.

The basic theme of the 1992 Guidelines is that mergers should not be permitted to create or enhance market power; this is designed to clarify the 1984 Guidelines, which express as their primary concern the risk that a merger will facilitate collusion. Market power, in economic terms, is the ability to act in a less than perfectly competitive manner with respect to raising prices and restricting output. According to the guidelines, market power to a seller is the ability to profitably maintain prices above competitive levels for a significant period of time. Market power also emerges from the ability of a single buyer (a monopsonist) or a coordinating group of buyers to depress the price paid for a product to a level that is below the competitive price and thereby depress output. A merger is unlikely to create or enhance market power unless it significantly increases concentration and results in a concentrated market, properly defined and measured.

Defining the Market

A relevant market is described by a product or group of products and the geographic area where it is produced or sold.

Product Market. This is considered a product or group of products such that a hypothetical profit-maximizing firm that was the only present and future seller of those products likely would impose at least a "small but significant nontransitory" (generally set at 5%) increase in price.

Geographic Market. For each product market in which both merging firms participate, a determination is made of the geographic market or markets in which the firm's products sell. Identification of firms that participate in the relevant market begins with all firms that currently produce or sell in that market; this may include vertically integrated firms.

Measuring the Market

Market shares are calculated for all firms identified as market participants. Market shares can be expressed either in dollar terms through measurement of sales, shipments, or production or in physical terms through measurement of sales, shipments, production, capacity, or reserves.

Market shares are assigned to foreign competitors in the same way as they are assigned to domestic competitors. However, if the exchange rates fluctuate significantly, market shares may be measured over a period longer than one year.

Concentration and Market Shares

Market concentration is a function of the number of firms in a market and their respective market shares. The Herfindahl-Hirschman Index (HHI) is used as an aid to interpretation of market data. The HHI is calculated by summing the squares of the individual market shares of all the participants. For example, a market consisting of four firms with market shares of 30%, 30%, 20%, and 20% has an HHI of 2600 ($30^2 + 30^2 + 20^2 + 20^2 = 2600$).

The HHI ranges from 10,000—in the case of pure monopoly (one firm at 100% share squared)—to a number approaching zero in a market with firms that have insignificant shares.

The increase in concentration as measured by the HHI can be calculated independently of the overall market concentration by doubling (twice) the product of the market shares of the merging firms. For example, a merger of two firms with 5% and 10% of the market would increase the HHI by 100 ($5 \times 10 \times 2 = 100$).

The spectrum of market concentration as measured by HHI is divided into three regions that can be broadly characterized as follows.

- *Unconcentrated (HHI below 1000):* A postmerger HHI below 1000 is considered unlikely to have adverse competitive effects and ordinarily requires no further analysis.

- *Moderately concentrated (HHI between 1000 and 1800):* At this level a postmerger HHI increase of less than 100 points is unlikely to have adverse competitive consequences. However, a merger producing an HHI increase of more than 100 points in a moderately concentrated market potentially raises significant competitive concerns.

- *Highly concentrated (HHI above 1800):* A merger producing an HHI increase of less than 50 points, even in highly concentrated markets postmerger, is likely to have competitive consequences and ordinarily requires no further analysis. However, a merger producing an HHI increase of more than 50 points in highly concentrated markets postmerger potentially raises significant competitive concerns. When the postmerger HHI exceeds 1800, it will be presumed that a merger producing an HHI increase of more than 100 points is likely to create or enhance market power.

Mergers are analyzed in terms of various potential adverse competitive effects, including the lessening of competition through coordinated interaction by reaching terms of coordination that are profitable to the firms involved. Competition may be lessened through unilateral effects such as elevating price or suppressing output.

Potential Defenses

Some mergers are not likely to enhance market power. The conditions relevant to this situation include entry, efficiency, and failing firm.

Entry. A merger is not likely to create market power if entry into the market is so easy that market participants, after the merger, either collectively or unilaterally could not profitably maintain a price increase above merger levels. Entry is easy if entry would be timely (within two years), likely (if it would be profitable at premerger prices and such prices could be secured by the entrant), and sufficient in its magnitude, character, and scope to deter or counteract the competitive effects of concerns. When entry is likely it is generally sufficient; however, it may not be sufficient if, as a result of control, the tangible and intangible assets required for entry are not adequately available for entrants to respond fully to their sales opportunities. However, in markets where entry is that easy (i.e., where entry passes the tests of timeliness, likelihood, and sufficiency), the merger raises no antitrust concerns and ordinarily requires no further analysis.

Efficiency. Some mergers that otherwise might be challenged may reasonably be necessary to achieve significant net efficiencies. Such efficiencies include, but are not limited to, achieving economies of scale, better integration of production facilities, plant specialization, lower transportation costs, and similar efficiencies relating to the specific manufacturing, servicing, or distribution operations of the merging firms. Claimed efficiencies resulting from reductions in general selling, administrative, and overhead expenses may also be considered. However, the latter efficiencies may be difficult to demonstrate.

Failing Firm. The failing firm doctrine, which has been recognized by the U.S. Supreme Court, is a defense to an otherwise unlawful merger.[13] Thus a merger is unlikely to create or enhance market power if the following circumstances are met: (1) the allegedly failing firm would be unable to meet its financial obligations in the near future; (2) it would not be able to reorganize successfully under Chapter 11 of the Bankruptcy Act; (3) it has made unsuccessful good-faith efforts of acquisition of assets of the failing firm that would both keep its tangible and intangible assets in the relevant market and pose a less severe danger to competition than does the proposed merger; and (4) absent the acquisition, the assets of the failing firm would exit the relevant market.

VERTICAL MERGERS

Vertical mergers involve control within a single enterprise of multiple stages in the production and distribution of an end product. A firm is said to be vertically integrated when it operates at more than one stage in the production or distribution process. Such integration may be forward or backward and there are varying degrees to the extent of integration.

Forward Vertical Integration

Forward vertical integration is said to occur when the producer of an intermediate good absorbs the next stage in the production or marketing process as a commodity moves toward the final consumer. Some firms are fully vertically integrated. In the petroleum industry, for example, major oil companies not only produce and refine crude oil but also distribute to consumers through their own or franchised service stations. Other oil firms may be only partially integrated, performing, say, the refining and wholesaling functions.

Backward Vertical Integration

Backward vertical integration occurs when a retailer or wholesaler acquires a manufacturer. Sears, a retail establishment, acquired the manufacturers of many of the products sold in its outlets; this was backward integration.

Reasons for Vertical Mergers

A major reason for a firm to become fully vertically integrated is to maintain control. The firm controls the manner in which a product is produced, where and how it is sold, and the price at which it is sold, and it has the ability to gather information pertinent to its decision making at all levels of production and distribution.

Complete vertical integration is costly, however, and therefore some firms use partial integration, relying on independents to perform some of the required functions.

Control of Vertical Mergers

Vertical integration was once routinely challenged by the Justice Department and the Federal Trade Commission. In 1962, the Supreme Court expressed concern over vertical market foreclosure when the Brown Shoe Company, the fourth-largest shoe manufacturer in the country, which also controlled 1,230 retail outlets, sought to acquire G. R. Kinney Company, Inc.[14] Kinney was a retailer of shoes that operated the largest family-style shoe store chain in the United States. This case involved both horizontal *and* vertical integration, in that both Brown and Kinney manufactured shoes and distributed them through their respective retail outlets. The primary impact of their vertical merger, however, was the possible foreclosure of Kinney's retail outlets to other shoe manufacturers.

Despite the fact that likely foreclosure from this merger was minimal (less than 2% of shoe sales in a deconcentrated market), the Supreme Court condemned the merger. Employing an analysis that focused on economic and historical factors, the court considered the following issues.[15]

1. Whether the merger was to take place in an industry not yet concentrated.
2. Whether the industry had a recent trend toward domination by few market leaders or had been fairly consistent in its distribution of market shares among companies.
3. Whether suppliers had easy access to markets and buyers to suppliers, or whether substantial business was foreclosed to competition. And
4. Whether new entry in the industry was possible without undue difficulty.

The court argued that in the face of the evidence there was a trend toward vertical integration in the shoe industry and that Brown would use its ownership of Kinney to force Brown shoes into Kinney stores. Accordingly, the Supreme Court ruled the merger should be proscribed.

In the most recent Supreme Court decision on vertical integration, involving Ford's acquisition of Autolite, manufacturer of spark plugs, the court ruled against Ford also on foreclosure grounds.[16] There are two markets for spark plugs: the original equipment market and the replacement market, which is usually referred to as the aftermarket. Ford had purchased its spark plugs from Champion, which was the largest independent spark plug manufacturer. However, Ford wished to participate in the aftermarket and decided it would be cheaper to acquire Autolite than to enter the field as a newcomer. The Justice Department challenged the merger on the grounds that it might reduce competition; the Supreme Court agreed.[17] According to the court, Ford's acquisition of Autolite (1) resulted in "the foreclosure of Ford as a purchaser of about ten percent of the total industry output" and (2) eliminated one of the two major independent spark plug manufacturers, thereby aggravating an already oligopolistic market.

Currently, vertical mergers are likely to be challenged under Section 7 of the Clayton Act, when "the effect of such acquisition may be substantially to lessen competition, or to tend to create a monopoly." Essentially the Supreme Court endorsed a rule-of-reason approach for vertical merger cases brought under Section 7. Under this approach the parties involved must argue many elements, attempting to show that anticompetitive effects are not unreasonable. Thus such mergers may be found illegal if a supplier has such a large market share that the arrangement unreasonably restrains competition.

In 1982, the Justice Department issued a revised set of guidelines, indicating that vertical mergers would generally not be challenged unless they were likely to increase barriers to entry in a concentrated market or facilitate collusion in the market of the acquired firm. The government has not challenged any vertical mergers since the early 1980s. Recent decisions have made it more difficult for private firms to challenge vertical mergers in court.[18]

CONGLOMERATE MERGERS

Because of earlier government restrictions and guidelines for both horizontal and vertical integration, many firms turned to diversification—the acquisition of companies in apparently unrelated industrial groups. This is also known as conglomeration.

Types of Conglomerate Mergers

Conglomerate mergers can take a variety of forms; moreover they can range from short-term to permanent mergers. There are generally three types:

1. *Product line extension*—in which the acquiring firm adds related items to its existing products (e.g., adding laundry bleach to a detergent producer);

2. *Geographic market extension*—in which the merging firms previously sold the same product but in different geographic areas

(e.g., a supplier of natural gas to California acquires the assets of a supplier of natural gas to other states); and

3. *Pure conglomerate*—in which the merging firms have no obvious business link and are functionally and economically unrelated (e.g., a soap company acquiring an electronics company).

Reasons for Diversification

Diversification enables firms to take advantage of tax incentives, credit, advances in technology and management.[19] These reasons are, of course, in addition to the desire to increase overall profit, reduce risk, and generally enhance long-term growth. Further, there is a degree of marketing strategy implicit in the desire to combine interests in ostensibly unrelated fields of endeavor.[20] Diversification may result in significant efficiencies, such as: in the use of outlets, in the use of a sales force, and in promotional efforts.

Since the transactions that form conglomerates generally involve firms in separate markets, the merger has no direct effect on the competition; nor is there any immediate change in the market structure. However, conglomerate acquisitions may lessen future competition by eliminating a potential entrant into the market. Furthermore, a large conglomerate may create anticompetitive effects by using its economic power to raise barriers to entry. The diversified company may also affect competition through a shift in its marketing techniques, such as channeling all its advertising in one product or lowering its prices to customers in one area (to the detriment of small firms located there) while increasing prices elsewhere.

Control of Conglomerate Mergers

Several tests have been used in determining the legality of conglomerate mergers; they emerge from the potential competition theory and the deep pocket theory.

Potential Competition

Since a conglomerate merger consists of mergers between companies that are not actual competitors, the courts have considered the elimination of potential competition in determining the legality of such mergers. According to this concept, potential competition—consisting of companies waiting in the wings to enter the market if the present competitors step out of the line—serves to keep competition at an acceptable level.

In a major market extension case, the Supreme Court used the term *potential competition* for the first time.[21] El Paso, the sole supplier of natural gas to California, acquired the stock of Pacific Northwest Pipeline Corp., a supplier of the trans-Rocky Mountain states, who had never been in the California market. Prior to the merger, Pacific had tried to obtain a license to serve the California market. Although the Federal Power Commission had rejected Pacific's application, the company still had large gas reserves in the surrounding states. The Supreme Court ruled that this acquisition violated Section 7, because the strong potential for competition was eliminated—the likelihood that Pacific Northwest would enter the California market.

The FTC used the potential competition theory in the Procter & Gamble case when it coined the term *product-extension merger.*[22] Procter & Gamble had acquired Clorox Chemical Co., the nation's largest producer of household liquid bleach, controlling almost 49% of the bleach market. Procter & Gamble, a manufacturer of soaps, detergents, and cleansers, accounted for 54% of the sales in that market, but it neither made nor sold bleach.

In considering the legality of this merger, the Supreme Court, noting that all liquid bleach was chemically identical, concentrated on the power of advertising and sale promotion that was available through the resources of Procter & Gamble. The court declared that such acquisition by a powerful firm of a smaller, but already dominant, firm may substantially reduce competition in the industry by raising entry barriers and dissuading smaller firms from competing. In addition, the court believed there was a strong possibility that if Procter & Gamble had not acquired Clorox, it would have itself entered the bleach market, and thus, perhaps the only potential candidate for entry into the bleach market was eliminated. The court concluded that the acquisition violated Section 7 of the Clayton Act.

In reference to the actual-potential-competition theory, the courts established two preconditions: (1) the evidence must show that the potential entrant had some way to enter the market other than by buying the target firm and (2) such market entry had the substantial likelihood of deconcentrating the target market or of producing other procompetitive effects.[23]

Deep Pocket

According to the deep pocket or (rich parent) theory, a company that has been acquired by a large, well-funded company will be able to make use of the parent's reserve capital in order to wage a price war or compete aggressively in other marketing areas. The court accepted this theory in the Procter & Gamble case, for Procter & Gamble had the resources to command advertising and other marketing advantages (e.g., cross-couponing, free samples) and it would usurp the legitimate shares of the smaller rivals.

Current Activities

To some extent conglomerate mergers are not a high-priority issue under current enforcement activities. Conglomerate mergers received intense scrutiny for a time, but less so in the 1980s. The Merger Guidelines issued by the Department of Justice and the FTC clearly focus on control of horizontal mergers, but declare that these guides do not relate to nonhorizontal mergers except where such mergers have horizontal effects.

JOINT VENTURES

The term *joint venture* involves the organizing and conducting of a separate business by two or more persons or firms who pool their assets and skills. For example, corporation A and corporation B form corporation C, each parent owning 50% of C's stock. The joint venture need not be a large organization; indeed it may have a limited objective and be short-lived. Both domestic and foreign corporations may join in a venture.

Reasons for Joint Ventures

Joint ventures were not widely used prior to the 1950s, but their creation and use have increased significantly in recent years. A number of reasons encourage the development of joint ventures.[24] A firm may not have sufficient cash to engage in a project, and a joint venture may increase economies of scale and spread the risk. A joint venture may be the only way a U.S. company can break into certain foreign markets, because some nations insist that their own national companies have at least a 50% interest in a foreign company that wishes to do business within their boundaries.

Control of Joint Ventures

Joint ventures do not easily fit into the usual merger concepts. Joint venture is a distinctive form of amalgamation, since it does not culminate in a single business entity by means of the disappearance of a previously existing firm. Nevertheless, the concentration of power, policy, and industrial resources has magnified with the increase in joint ventures, and their operation may be suspected of restraining competition.

The potential competition doctrine—the mainstay of the attack on conglomerate mergers under Section 7 of the Clayton Act—was first applied in connection with a joint venture between two chemical companies.[25] Olin Mathieson Chemical Corporation and Pennsalt Chemicals Corporation, both large companies, formed a jointly owned (50-50) corporation called Penn-

Olin Chemical Company, to produce sodium chlorate in a plant in Kentucky. Pennsalt, in Oregon, the third-largest producer of sodium chlorate (a bleaching agent used primarily in the pulp and paper industry), sold it in the West. Olin Mathieson, an industrial chemical firm, did not produce sodium chlorate but used it extensively in its chemical applications and sold it in the Southeast for Pennsalt. For Pennsalt the venture represented market extension: it could now sell its products in the southeastern part of the country and acquire a sales force with established contacts. For Olin, the venture represented product extension: it could produce a product it had always purchased for resale.

Prior to the joint venture, both Olin and Pennsalt had undertaken studies of the feasibility of entering the southeastern market, but they formed a joint venture and built the plant jointly. The district court considered this and found that both firms had the resources and expertise to enter the market individually. However, the court did not have evidence that convinced it that each company would build its own plant, and it believed also that since a joint venture may make for a stronger competitor, competition was therefore enhanced, not lessened, so it dismissed the charges.

The Supreme Court disagreed, however, and applied the principle of potential competition. Even if only one of the two firms were to enter this market, at least the other firm might still be at the edge of the market as a potential competitor who might enter at any time. The Supreme Court remanded the case to the district court to determine the probability that one of the companies would have entered the market. The court delineated a number of criteria that might be considered in determining whether a particular joint venture was in violation of Section 7:[26]

> the number and power of the competitors in the relevant market; the background of their growth; the power of the joint ventures; the relationship of their lines of commerce; the competition existing between them and the power of each in dealing with the competitors of the other; the setting in which the joint venture was created; the reasons and necessities for its existence; the joint venture's line of commerce and the relationship thereof to that of its parents; the adaptability of its line of commerce to noncompetitive practices; the potential power of the joint venture in the relevant market; an appraisal of what the competition in the relevant market would have been if one of the joint venturers had entered it alone instead of through Penn-Olin; the effect, in the event of this occurrence, of the other joint venturer's potential competition; and such other factors as might indicate potential risk to competition in the relevant market.

Research and Development Joint Ventures

Research and development (R&D) is considered critical to aid in the creation of new technology. In order to promote R&D, the National Cooperative Research Act of 1984 (NCRA) was passed.[27] The act prohibits courts from condemning a joint R&D venture on antitrust grounds unless the joint venture is proven to have anticompetitive effects that outweigh the joint venture's procompetitive benefits. The act also establishes a procedure whereby firms may notify the Department of Justice and the FTC of their cooperative ventures and thus qualify for a single-damage limitation on civil antitrust liability. According to a Senate subcommittee report, the NCRA has been highly successful in encouraging joint R&D ventures that involve everything from chipmaking and steelmaking processes to superconductors. Moreover, the fears that NCRA would foster anticompetitive activities have not been realized.[28]

National Cooperative Production Amendments of 1993[29]

In June 1993, President Clinton signed the National Cooperative Production Amendments (NCPA) into law. These amendments to the National Cooperative Research Act grant the antitrust protections provided under NCRA to joint ventures for production, as well as those established for R&D.

The NCPA clarifies the application of the antitrust rule-of-reason to research, development, and production joint ventures and provides for special attorney's fees for relevant cases. The amendments also limit the possible monetary damages resulting from antitrust actions to the actual—as opposed to treble—damages. The rule-of-reason and attorney's-fee provisions automatically apply to all joint ventures covered by the amendments.

In order to obtain damage protection, however, any party to a joint venture may (not later than ninety days after entering a written agreement to form the venture) file with the attorney general and the FTC simultaneously a written notification disclosing the identities of all parties to the venture and the nature and objectives of the venture.

Under new Section 7 of the act, the damage limitation provision does not apply to a joint venture's production of a product, process, or service unless (1) the principal facilities for such production are located in the United States or its territories, and (2) each person who controls any party to such venture (including such party itself) is a U.S. person or a foreign person from a country whose law accords antitrust treatment no less favorable to U.S. persons than to such country's domestic persons with respect to participation in joint venture production.

Health Care Joint Ventures

Although efforts to curb joint ventures that provide research and technology have declined, recent concerns have been expressed about increases in the formation of joint ventures in the health care market. The Department of Justice has indicated willingness to proceed against price-fixing and other plainly anticompetitive agreements even when those agreements operate under the guise of a preferred provider organization (PPO) or independent practice association (IPA) and the department will proceed criminally in cases where the conduct is illegal per se and there are no mitigating factors.[30] Even legitimate joint ventures will have to pass muster under a rigorous rule-of-reason analysis.

The FTC has noted the antitrust implications of a joint venture by physicians that may not integrate their core practices but that comprises ancillary fields. Typically, this type of joint venture involves a group of physicians who form a partnership to set up, say, a clinical laboratory, a physical therapy center, or a diagnostic imaging facility.[31] There are concerns that such physician-owners may be yielding to the temptation to then (1) prescribe goods and services offered by the venture for which the need is marginal or nonexistent and (2) refer patients to their venture when an evaluation of price and quality would dictate the choice of a competitor.

The principal antitrust concern with physician-owned joint ventures is the creation or enhancement of market power in the market for the ancillary goods or services offered by the joint venture. When such market power has been attained, the antitrust laws may have been violated because the entity was created by an aggregation of competitors into a single dominant venture or by other exclusionary conduct.

In 1993, the Department of Justice and the FTC issued statements of their antitrust enforcement policies regarding mergers and other joint activities undertaken by health care providers.[32] The statements were designed to provide guidance for health care providers in the form of antitrust safety zones or safe harbors that describe the circumstances under which the Agencies will not challenge conduct under the antitrust laws:

> The Agencies will not challenge, absent extraordinary circumstances, a merger in which one of the merging hospitals has less than 100 licensed beds and an average daily inpatient census of less than 40 patients.

> They will not challenge joint ventures involving high-technology or other expensive equipment that must be shared in order to allow the hospitals to recover the costs involved, and does not include a hospital that could have offered a competing service to the joint venture.

The collective provision of nonprice information by physicians to purchasers of health care services will not be challenged.

Hospital participation in written surveys of prices for hospital services or wages, salaries or benefits of hospital personnel will not be challenged where (1) the survey is managed by a third party, (2) the information collected for the survey is more than three months old, and (3) the price or cost data reported are based on data from at least five hospitals and aggregated so that compensation paid by particular hospitals cannot be identified.

Joint purchasing arrangements will not be challenged if the group's purchases account for less than 35% of the total purchases of the relevant product or service and the cost accounts for less than 20% of the total revenues from all products or services sold by each participant in the agreement.

Physician joint ventures that are controlled by physicians and that jointly market the services of their member physicians will not be challenged if the physician network is composed of 20% or less of the physicians in each physician specialty in the relevant geographic market, when the members share substantial financial risk.

Consolidation in the Telecommunications Industry

The movement toward a national information infrastructure has raised antitrust questions. The assistant attorney general in charge of the U.S. Department of Justice Antitrust Division; the FTC chairperson; and Senator Howard M. Metzenbaum, chair of the Senate Committee on the Judiciary, Subcommittee on Antitrust, Monopolies and Business Rights, have recommended that the Antitrust Division and the FTC create special units of experienced antitrust lawyers to oversee the communications industry.[33]

Some observers are claiming that mergers and joint ventures between telephone, cable, and other types of communications companies will speed the development of the information superhighway. Senator Metzenbaum has doubts whether the kind of rapid and unfocused consolidation that has been proposed will speed or retard such future developments in the telecommunications industry.

Oversight is considered necessary to prevent the industry from restructuring itself in a manner that could impede head-to-head competition or concentrate emerging markets. It is suggested that every proposed telecommunications deal, whether a merger, an acquisition, or a joint venture, be closely scrutinized. The federal antitrust agencies should challenge any telecommunications deal that eliminates the most likely source of potential competition.

Noting that the telecommunications industry is crucial to preserving the free flow of ideas, Senator Metzenbaum quoted Professor Robert Pitofsky, a noted antitrust expert, who wrote:

> Th[e] concern about concentrated economic power should be given added weight where the merger (or wave of mergers) concerns companies involved in the communication of ideas. . . . In those industries there is more at stake than high prices and low quality to consumers— there is a fundamental issue of avoiding centralized control over access to the marketplace of ideas.

INTERNATIONAL OPERATIONS

It is beyond the scope of this book to provide an in-depth discussion of mergers in international markets. Nonetheless, it may be useful to offer some information concerning the U.S. approach to antitrust enforcement in international operations.

There are a number of antitrust laws that are likely to have significance in international business transactions. The Sherman Act prohibits "contracts . . . in restraint of trade or commerce among the several states, or with foreign nations." Similarly, the Clayton Act and the FTC Act define commerce to include foreign nations. Several other acts also impact on international business operations.

Webb-Pomerene Act

The Webb-Pomerene Act of 1918 provides a limited antitrust exemption for the formation of competing businesses to engage in collective export sales. The exemption applies only to the export of "goods, wares, or merchandise."[34] It does not apply to conduct that has an anticompetitive effect or that injures domestic competitors of the members of an export association. Associations seeking an exemption under this act must file their articles of agreement and annual report with the FTC, but preformation approval from the FTC is not required.

Export Trading Company Act of 1982

This act is designed to increase U.S. exports of goods and services by encouraging more efficient export trade services for U.S. producers and suppliers, by reducing restrictions on trade financing, and by reducing uncertainty concerning application of the U.S. antitrust laws to U.S. export trade.[35]

The act establishes a procedure by which persons engaged in U.S. export trade can obtain an export trade certificate of review. The certificate provides significant protection from the antitrust laws; it does have its limitations, however. Conduct that falls outside the scope of the certificate is fully subject to enforcement actions. If the certificate is obtained by fraud, it is void from the outset. Moreover, the certificate provides no protection from foreign laws.

Department of Justice Guidelines for International Operations Antitrust Enforcement Policy

According to the Department of Justice, in enforcing its antitrust laws it focuses on protecting U.S. consumers from anticompetitive conduct. To protect U.S. consumer welfare, the department's enforcement efforts must sometimes reach outside the territorial limits of the United States.

General Approach

Like most domestic transactions, the vast majority of international business transactions do not raise antitrust concerns. The Guidelines are designed to ensure that uncertainty about the department's enforcement policy does not cause businesses to limit unobjectionable transactions or to avoid efficient and productive arrangements that benefit consumers. Nevertheless, the Guidelines make plain the department's commitment to prosecute naked restraints of trade, such as horizontal price-fixing, bid rigging, and market allocation, which have no connection with achieving the significant integrative efficiencies that benefit U.S. consumers and that almost certainly reduce output and/or raise prices to the detriment of U.S. consumers.[36]

However, one major distinction between domestic and foreign antitrust enforcement is that regard for international comity (respect for the other countries' laws) may require that the department, in determining whether to challenge a conduct, consider the interests of other nations that also may have jurisdiction over international business conduct.[37]

The Department of Justice provides a number of hypothetical case discussions to illustrate how it would analyze various situations.[38] Although the outcome depends on the specific facts and circumstances of each case, the case discussions indicate when the department is likely to take antitrust enforcement action in several possible merger situations. Some of these are discussed briefly here.

Merger of a U.S. Firm and a Foreign Firm. When a U.S. firm and a foreign firm propose a merger, if both firms are engaged in commerce in the United States, the proposed acquisition is clearly subject to Section 7 of the Clayton Act, and the merger would be treated accordingly.

Acquisition of a Foreign Potential Competitor. Where a U.S. firm that manufactures and sells product X in the United States plans to merge with a foreign firm that sells product X in its own country and not in the United States, the Department of Justice would consider whether the foreign firm was about to enter the market independently in the near future if it did not merge with the U.S. firm. The department would also consider the extent of concentration in the current market. However, even if the relevant market were highly concentrated, eliminating the foreign firm through a merger would not have any significant anticompetitive effect if there were several other potential entrants in addition to this firm.

Merger of Two Foreign Firms. Two foreign firms that are the most significant producers of product X outside the United States supply 60% of the total amount of this product consumed in the United States. Each company has assets in the United States, but both companies' facilities for producing the product are located in the respective foreign country. The two companies have announced that they intend to merge.

Since both companies sell product X in the United States, this merger would be subject to Section 7 of the Clayton Act. However, it is unlikely that the Department of Justice would challenge the merger, notwithstanding any possible anticompetitive effects it might have on U.S. commerce. Since both of the merging firms are foreign and all of their assets involved in producing and distributing X are located outside the United States, it would be difficult, if not impossible, to obtain effective relief that would preserve competition in the United States.

This does not mean, however, that the department would never challenge a merger between foreign firms that would have a substantial anticompetitive effect in the United States. For example, if either of the foreign firms had production facilities or substantial distribution assets that were used to produce or distribute X and located in the United States, the department would probably request additional information concerning the likely competitive effects of the merger. The department would use procedures under the Hart-Scott-Rodino Act, Civil Investigative Demands, or informal requests as appropriate. The department would then likely challenge the merger if it concluded, after reviewing such information, that the merger would likely result in reduced output and higher prices to U.S. consumers without any offsetting efficiency experts.

Direct Consumer Injury

The 1988 International Operations Guidelines had a footnote that generally had been interpreted as foreclosing enforcement actions against anticompetitive conduct in foreign markets unless the conduct resulted in direct harm to U.S. consumers. In April 1992, the Department of Justice announced a change in its antitrust enforcement policy that would permit it to challenge foreign business conduct that harms U.S. exports when the conduct would have violated antitrust laws if it had occurred in the United States.[39]

The department declared that antitrust enforcement action will be taken against overseas conduct that restrains U.S. exports, whether or not there is direct harm to consumers, when it is clear that:

1. The conduct has a direct, substantial, and reasonably foreseeable effect on exports of goods and services from the United States.

2. The conduct involves anticompetitive activities that violate the U.S. antitrust laws, being, in most cases, group boycotts, collusive pricing, and other exclusionary activities. And

3. U.S. courts have jurisdiction over foreign persons or corporations engaged in such conduct.

The department will notify and consult with foreign governments when appropriate. If the conduct is also unlawful under the importing country's antitrust laws and that country is prepared to take action against such conduct, the department is prepared to work with that country.

SUMMARY

Mergers are formed when two independent entities are united in a new independent entity in order to grow and diversify. Mergers may have no impact on the market in which they operate, since the merged firms may be too small. However, there is the potential for large firms to exert some influences over prices and product supply to the detriment of small firms.

Federal antitrust law embodied in the Sherman, Clayton, and FTC acts is designed to weed out those mergers that "tend substantially to lessen competition." The Federal Trade Commission and the Department of Justice have jurisdiction over mergers. Under certain conditions, firms that wish to merge are required to present premerger notification to the FTC.

Mergers may be classified as horizontal, vertical, or conglomerate. Horizontal mergers are most likely to be subject to close scrutiny. The Department of Justice and the Federal Trade Commission have recently issued Horizontal Merger Guidelines, which articulate the analytical framework applied in determining whether a merger is likely to substantially lessen competition. The basic theme of the 1992 Guidelines is that mergers should not be permitted to create or enhance market power.

Vertical mergers are likely to be challenged under Section 7 of the Clayton Act when "the effect of such acquisition may be substantially to lessen competition, or to create a monopoly." Essentially the Supreme Court endorsed a rule-of-reason approach for vertical merger cases brought under Section 7. In 1982, the Justice Department issued revised guidelines indicating that vertical mergers would generally not be challenged unless they were likely to increase barriers to entry in a concentrated market or facilitate collusion in the market of the acquired firm. As of this writing, the government has not challenged any vertical mergers since the early 1980s.

Conglomerate mergers, wherein the acquisition of companies occurs between unrelated industrial groups, may be one of two types: product-line extensions and geographic extensions. The courts have used the elimination-of-potential-competition doctrine in determining the legality of such mergers. To some extent conglomerate mergers are not a high-priority issue under current enforcement activities.

A joint venture involves the organizing and conducting of a separate business by two or more persons or firms who pool their assets and skills. It represents a distinctive form of amalgamation, since it does not culminate in a single business entity through the disappearance of a previously existing firm.

The potential-competition doctrine has been applied to determining the legality of joint ventures. According to this concept—companies waiting in the wings to enter the market if the present competitors step out of line— serve to keep competition at an acceptable level. The Supreme Court has delineated a number of criteria that might be considered in determining whether a particular joint venture was in violation of Section 7 of the Clayton Act.

Several acts have been passed that limit antitrust activities and specify liability against specific types of joint ventures such as research and development and production joint ventures.

In its international operations enforcement policy, the Department of Justice has established a number of guidelines relevant to mergers with foreign firms.

CASE
United States *v.* The Gillette Co. et al., *CCH #70,210 (DC DC #93-0573, May 5, 1993).*

FACTS

The Gillette Company posted a tender offer on March 23, 1993, to purchase all outstanding stock and options of Parker Pen Holdings, Ltd., a British premium fountain pen manufacturer. The two companies were in communication with the Antitrust Division of the Department of Justice concerning a potential violation of Section 7 of the Clayton Act.

Based on 1991 sales, Gillette, through its Waterman brand, controls approximately 21% of the U.S. premium fountain pen market; Parker has a 19% share; and the third major firm in the market and current top seller, Richemont, maker of Montblanc pens, possess almost 40% of the premium fountain pen trade.

The U.S. Justice Department, concerned that the effect of the combination of Gillette and Parker "may be substantially to lessen competition" in the premium fountain pen market, brought suit, seeking a temporary restraining order on the proposed acquisition, a preliminary injunction, and a permanent injunction, barring any combination of the two defendants.

ISSUE

Should the court grant a preliminary injunction as to the proposed acquisition?

HOLDING

No. The proposed acquisition of a British premium fountain pen manufacturer by a U.S. competitor is not likely to substantially lessen competition in the market for premium writing instruments. The Department of Justice failed to demonstrate likelihood of success on the merits in an action to enjoin the proposed acquisition should the case go to trial.

REASONING

The test for a preliminary injunction in this circuit requires that the court balance:

1. the likelihood of the plaintiff's success on the merits;
2. the threat of irreparable injury to the plaintiff in the absence of an injunction;

3. the possibility of substantial harm to other interested parties from a grant of injunctive relief; and

4. the interest of the public.

Likelihood of Success

To demonstrate likelihood of success in a Section 7 case, the plaintiff must meet two criteria: (1) it must demonstrate that the proposed combination will affect a line of commerce—this includes demonstration of a relevant product market and a relevant geographic market, and (2) it must demonstrate that the combination "may be substantially to lessen competition."

Line of Commerce: The Justice Department alleges that the relevant line of commerce is premium fountain pens, defined as "high-quality refillable fountain pens that have established a premium image among consumers" or, as the court suggested, "refillable fountain pens with a suggested retail price (SRP) of between $50 and $400." The relevant geographic market is the United States.

Gillette and Parker assert that the market for fountain pens cannot exclude pens with SRPs of less than $50 or more than $400. They declared the delineation should be expanded to include other high-line writing instruments (with an SRP in excess of $10). They assert that the relevant geographic market is Planet Earth.

Determining a price range: The court declared that the Justice Department has demonstrated that a separate market for fountain pens in the $50 to $400 range exists. The relevant product market hinges on a determination of those products to which consumers will turn given reasonable variations in price. The definition must exclude items to which a limited number of buyers will turn or, in technical terms, products whose cross-elasticities of demand are small.

The court found the Justice Department provided ample evidence that should the price of a fountain pen costing, for example, $60 be increased in a nontrivial fashion, consumers will nonetheless purchase the now-costlier pen rather than substitute a less expensive, less prestigious model.

Similarly, fountain pens priced above $400 are not interchangeable with pens costing less than $400. There is a threshold beyond which pens become mere collector's items or jewelry pieces. The department has demonstrated that the fountain pen makers may be divided into three submarkets: base fountain pens (less than $50), premium fountain pens ($50 to $400), and jewelry fountain pens ($401 and up).

However, according to the court, this premium subset of fountain pen devotees does not encompass the entire universe of consumers. There is a larger market, which includes a much larger subset of fountain pen consumers who will substitute other writing instruments for fountain pens. For these consumers, fountain pens are in direct competition with ballpoint pens, rollerball pens, and pencils.

The court therefore defined the market as all premium writing instruments, which includes mechanical pencils, refillable ballpoint, rollerball, and fountain pens with a suggested retail price from $40 to $400. The court used the lower boundary, since several of the fountain pen models that retail in the $50 to $55 range are members of product families in which the ballpoint pen retails for approximately $40.

Since the Justice Department has not alleged that this market, including other modes of writing, is highly concentrated either before or after the merger and has not demonstrated that the merger will have anticompetitive effects on this market, the court found that the department is not likely to succeed on the merits at trial and could not have obtained a preliminary injunction against the proposed acquisition.

"Substantially to lessen competition": Although the court rested its decision on the department's failure to meet its case as to the broader relevant market, in "an abundance of caution" it examined whether the proposed merger is likely substantially to lessen competition. The court noted there is ample evidence that the merged company will not be able to increase prices on premium fountain pens unilaterally and that the merger will not create a decrease in new products or innovations; in addition, there is no evidence that there will be any collusion in the market between Gillette and Montblanc, the current top seller of premium fountain pens. Accordingly, the court concluded there was no likelihood of anticompetitive effects from the merger.

Irreparable Injury

The court accepted the department's representation that, should the court fail to enter a preliminary injunction, the court probably will be left powerless to fashion relief if it were to find a Clayton Act violation after a full trial. The department alleges that under the United Kingdom's Protection of Trading Interests Act of 1980, the government of the United Kingdom could preclude any divestiture of Parker by Gillette.

Substantial Harm to Other Parties

Parker and Gillette claimed that a decision adverse to them will create irreparable injury, since both parties have asserted that the agreement for Gillette to acquire Parker must be consummated by May 6, 1993; otherwise, the agreement is void, and negotiations may cease. The court noted that this decision whether to negotiate further is within control of the company. However, the court cannot ignore that a transaction valued in excess of $440 million may have potential overall benefits to the company and the public.

The Interest of the Public

Since any merger likely will not be reversible, the court assumes that the interest of the public weighs in favor of an injunction.

In a balance of the four factors for a preliminary injunction, even if the court gives the department full credit for the other two criteria-irreparable injury and the interest of the public—and has afforded Gillette no weight on the criterion of injury to other parties, the fact that the department has failed to demonstrate that it is likely to succeed on the merits should this case go to trial, indicates the court may not enter a preliminary injunction on this record.

Global Issues[40]

The Monopolies and Mergers Commission (MMC) of the United Kingdom provided clearance for U.S.-based Gillette's bid to acquire Parker Pen.

Parker Pen has around half the British market, by value, for refillable pens. Gillette already owns two significant brands—Waterman and Paper Mate—which represent a further 7% of the market for refillables.

Clearance for the merger was offered based on MMC's view that any attempt by Gillette to exploit its added market strength would be constrained by the large retailers' bargaining strength and the actual or potential competitors to whom they could turn. The MMC noted that, "Although more expensive pens have better quality nibs, finishes and mechanisms, there is no great technical difference between pens and production processes are comparatively simple. There have been a number of recent entrants and some multiple retailers who have successfully introduced own-brand pens."

DISCUSSION QUESTIONS

Discuss the standards used by this circuit court to define the relevant market in considering this merger between a U.S. firm and a foreign firm.

Assume the court accepted the Department of Justice's definition of the relevant product market as "refillable fountain pens with a suggested retail price of between $50 and $400" and the relevant geographic area as the United States. How would the Department of Justice measure the extent of concentration in the relevant market, with specific reference to the Herfindahl-Hirschman Index?

CASE
SCFC ILC, Inc., dba MountainWest Financial *v.* Visa U.S.A. Inc., *CCH #70,021 (DC D of U, Case No. 91-C-47B, November 5, 1992).*

FACTS

For purposes of this case, Visa is known as a joint venture. A joint venture is simply a combination of separate companies that join for the purpose of cooperating in a particular business venture. Joint ventures are permitted because they may lead to the creation of new products in an efficient manner. The members of the joint venture may cooperate in carrying out its purpose. A joint venture is permitted to adopt rules and practices that are reasonable and that further the economic self-interest of its members; however, it may not unreasonably restrain trade.

Mountainwest is a wholly owned subsidiary of Sears Consumer Financial Corporation and Dean Witter Financial Services Group, which are themselves wholly owned subsidiaries of Sears, Roebuck and Co. Visa U.S.A. Inc. is a nonstock corporation that is owned by approximately 6,000 of its member banks located throughout the United States.

Sears had purchased a Utah thrift in 1990 and attempted to expand its membership in the Visa card issuing company, but its request for the printing of 1.5 million new cards was denied. Sears claims that Visa unreasonably restrained its ability to compete against other financial institutions in the issuing of general-purpose charge cards in Utah and throughout the United States. Sears does not challenge Visa's right to enact rules that do not unreasonably restrain trade. However, it challenges one specific rule, Bylaw 2.06, which excludes Sears and its affiliates from membership in Visa. According to Sears this bylaw is an unreasonable restraint of trade because its purpose and effect are to prevent increased price competition in the issuing of general-purpose charge cards.

Visa denied Sears' allegations and claimed that its rule excluding competitors such as Discover and American Express from being owner/members of Visa USA was not accompanied by attempts to fix or control the price, volume, or terms upon which charge cards are issued by its members. Therefore any effect of Bylaw 2.06 on competition among issuers necessarily must be insubstantial.

ISSUE

Has Visa's joint venture rule that prohibited Sears from joining the joint venture had a substantially harmful effect on competition in the market for issuance of general-purpose charge cards in the United States?

HOLDINGS

The jury answered the questions submitted to them in the special verdict as follows:

Question No. 1: Has Sears proved, by a preponderance of evidence, that Visa's Bylaw 2.06 has a substantially harmful effect on competition in the relevant market? Answer: Yes.

Question No. 2: Has Sears proved, by a preponderance of the evidence, that the harmful effects substantially outweigh any beneficial effect on competition in the relevant market? Answer: Yes.

Question No. 3: Has Sears proved, by a preponderance of the evidence, that it was injured by Visa's Bylaw 2.06? Answer: Yes.

The jury found that the charge card joint venture ban of a competitor restrained trade.

REASONING

The jury was given a number of instructions for arriving at a verdict. In general, the law permits businesses to retain the fruits of their investment and to refuse to share their property with competitors. However, if a joint venture's refusal has a substantial adverse effect on competition, then it may be found unlawful.

Sears must prove that Visa's activities substantially harmed competition in a relevant market. The relevant market is the market for the issuance of general-purpose charge cards in the United States as a whole. General-purpose charge cards are those that can be used in a wide variety of retail establishments; examples are Visa cards and Discover cards. These are distinguished from special-purpose charge cards such as gasoline company charge cards and individual department store charge cards.

To show an unreasonable restraint of trade, Sears must prove the following by a preponderance of the evidence:

- First, that Visa's restraint had a substantially harmful effect on competition in the relevant market; and

- Second, that any harmful effect on competition substantially outweighs any beneficial effect on competition.

In a determination of the impact on competition, Visa's market power as well as how much the market was affected by Visa's restraint must be considered. Market power is the power to profitably raise or maintain prices above competitive levels or to reduce output by excluding competition in the relevant market. In a consideration of market power, Visa's market share may be considered, but market share may not always by itself show Visa's market power. In a determination of whether the restraint influenced or affected the price, output or product quality in the relevant market should also be considered.

If it is determined that Visa has unreasonably restrained trade in the relevant market, then it next must be determined whether Sears was injured by Visa's actions. Proving injury does not require Sears to prove a dollar amount, but only that Sears was in fact injured by Visa's alleged restraint of trade. It is important to understand that injury and the amount of damages are different concepts. The jury was to determine only the antitrust liability issue. Damages would be determined at later hearings.

DISCUSSION QUESTIONS

Explain the concept of a joint venture and the reasons for government support of such organizational arrangements.

Discuss the factors to be considered in determining whether a joint venture is in restraint of trade.

ENDNOTES

1. Earl W. Kinter, *Primer on the Law of Mergers* (New York: Macmillan, 1973).
2. *United States* v. *United States Steel Corp.*, 251 U.S. 417 (1920).
3. Kintner, pp. 157–158.
4. *FTC* v. *Sperry & Hutchison Co.*, 405 U.S. 233 (1972).
5. National Association of Attorneys General, "Horizontal Merger Guidelines, Proposed Revisions," Trade Reg. Repo. No. 226 (September 3, 1992).
6. FTC Guides: Premerger Notification Procedures, CCH, TRR, No. 145 (February 12, 1991).
7. Ibid., p. 3.
8. Rule 802.50 (b), 16 C.F.R. #802.50(b).
9. *United States* v. *General Cinema Corp.*, CCH #69,681 (U.S. D.C., D.C., January 8, 1992).
10. FTC Guides, p. 27.
11. Louis W. Stern and Thomas L. Eovaldi, *Legal Aspects of Marketing Strategy: Antitrust and Consumer Protection Issues* (Englewood Cliffs, N.J.: Prentice-Hall, 1984), p. 159.
12. Horizontal Merger Guidelines–1992, TRR, CCH #13,103 (April 7, 1992).
13. *U.S.* v. *General Dynamics Corp.*, 415 U.S. 486, 507 (1974); *U.S.* v. *Greater Buffalo Press, Inc.*, 402 U.S. 549, 555 (1971).
14. *Brown Shoe Co.* v. *United States*, 370 U.S. 294 (1962).
15. A. D. Neale and D. G. Goyder, *The Antitrust Laws of the U.S.A.* (New York: Cambridge University Press, 1980), p. 187.
16. *Ford Motor Co.* v. *U.S.*, 405 U.S. 562 (1972).
17. Roger D. Blair and David L. Kaserman, "Vertical Integration, Tying, and Alternative Vertical Control Mechanisms," *Connecticut Law Review* 20 (Spring 1988), 523–568.
18. Susan A. Samuelson and Thomas A. Balmer, "Antitrust Revisited—Implications for Competitive Strategy," *Sloan Management Review* (Fall 1988), 79–87.
19. Joel Dean, "Causes and Consequences of Growth by Conglomerate Merger: An Introduction," *St. John's Law Review* 44 (Spring 1970), 15–19.

20. Louis W. Stern, "Acquisitions: Another Viewpoint," *Journal of Marketing* 31 (July 1967), 39-46.
21. *U.S.* v. *El Paso Natural Gas Co.*, 376 U.S. 651 (1964).
22. *FTC* v. *Procter & Gamble, Co.*, 386 U.S. 568 (1967).
23. *United States* v. *Falstaff Brewing Corp.*, 410 U.S. 602, 625, 639 (1974).
24. Marshall C. Howard, *Antitrust and Trade Regulations* (Englewood Cliffs, N.J.: Prentice Hall, 1983), p. 242.
25. *U.S.* v. *Penn-Olin Chemical Co.*, 378 U.S. 158 (1964).
26. 378 U.S. 177.
27. 15 U.S.C. 4301–4305.
28. Senate Committee Report, The National Cooperative Research Act Extension of 1991, 102d Cong., 1st Sess., 102–146 (September 10, 1991).
29. P.L. No. 103–42.
30. DOJ Merger Guidelines Revision Update, TRR, CCH #50,072 (February 11, 1992).
31. Health Care Antitrust Enforcement—FTC Director Views, TRR, CCH #50,703 (February 11, 1992).
32. "Joint Federal Enforcement Policies, Health Care Antitrust," TRR Report No. 280 (September 17, 1993).
33. "Consolidation in Telecommunications Industry—Senator Metzenbaum's Views," TRR, CCH #50,126 (December 21, 1993).
34. 15 U.S.C. 4461–65 (1982).
35. 15 U.S.C. 4001–4053 (1982).
36. Department of Justice Guidelines, International Operations and Enforcement Policy, CCH, TRR, No. 24 (November 10, 1988).
37. Ibid., p. 1.
38. Ibid., pp. 106–130.
39. Foreign Restraints on U.S. Exports—Consumer Injury, TRR, CCH #13,108 (April 3, 1992).
40. "UK Commission Clears Bid by Gillette to Buy Parker Pen," *BNA, ATTR* 46 (1993), p. 179.

Index

345